Best Writings of John Calvin:
The Essential Works of a Reformation Giant

John Calvin; Caleb Sinclair

GRAPEVINE INDIA

Published by

GRAPEVINE INDIA PUBLISHERS PVT LTD

www.grapevineindia.com
Delhi | Mumbai
email: grapevineindiapublishers@gmail.com

Ordering Information:
Quantity sales: Special discounts are available on quantity
purchases by corporations, associations, and others.
For details, reach out to the publisher.

First published by Grapevine India 2023

Welcome to our Christian book collection!

For access to more Christian audiobooks,

send a blank email to

thegoodchristian10@gmail.com.

Contents

1.

The Human Mind Naturally
Endued with the Knowledge of God.

We lay it down as a position not to be controverted, that the human mind, even by natural instinct, possesses some sense of a Deity. For that no man might shelter himself under the pretext of ignorance, God hath given to all some apprehension of his existence, the memory of which he frequently and insensibly renews; so that, as men universally know that there is a God, and that he is their Maker, they must be condemned by their own testimony, for not having worshipped him and consecrated their lives to his service. If we seek for ignorance of a Deity, it is nowhere more likely to be found, than among tribes the most stupid and furthest from civilization. But, as the celebrated Cicero observes, there is no nation so barbarous, no race so savage, as not to be firmly persuaded of the being of a God.[7] Even those who in other respects appear to differ but little from brutes, always retain some sense of religion; so fully are the minds of men possessed with this common principle, which is closely interwoven with their original composition. Now, since there has never been a country or family, from the beginning of the world, totally destitute of religion, it is a tacit confession, that some sense of the Divinity is inscribed on every heart. Of this opinion, idolatry itself furnishes ample proof. For we know how reluctantly man would degrade himself to exalt other creatures above him. His preference of worshipping a piece of wood or stone, to being thought to have no god, evinces the impression of a Deity on the human mind to be very strong, the obliteration of which is more difficult than a total change of the natural disposition; and this is certainly changed, whenever man leaves his natural pride, and voluntarily descends to such meannesses under the notion of worshipping God.

II. It is most absurd, then, to pretend, as is asserted by some, that religion was the contrivance of a few subtle and designing men, a political machine to confine the simple multitude to their duty, while those who inculcated the worship of God on others, were themselves far from believing that any god existed. I confess, indeed, that artful men have introduced many inventions into religion, to fill the vulgar with reverence, and strike them with terror, in order to obtain the greater command over their minds. But this they never could have accomplished, if the minds of men had not previously been possessed of a firm persuasion of the existence of God, from which the propensity to religion proceeds. And that they who cunningly imposed on the illiterate, under the pretext of religion, were themselves wholly destitute of any knowledge of God, is quite incredible. For though there were some in ancient times, and many arise in the present age, who deny the existence of God, yet, in spite of their reluctance, they are continually receiving proofs of what they desire to disbelieve. We read of no one guilty of more audacious or unbridled contempt of the Deity than Caligula; yet no man ever trembled with greater distress at any instance of Divine wrath, so that he was constrained to dread the Divinity whom he professed to despise. This you may always see exemplified in persons of similar character. For the most audacious contemners of God are most alarmed, even at the noise of a falling leaf. Whence arises this, but from the vengeance of the Divine Majesty, smiting their consciences the more powerfully in proportion to their efforts to fly from it? They try every refuge to hide themselves from the Lord's presence, and to efface it from their minds; but their attempts to elude it are all in vain. Though it may seem to disappear for a moment, it presently returns with increased violence; so that, if they have any remission of the anguish of conscience, it resembles the sleep of persons intoxicated, or subject to frenzy, who enjoy no placid rest while sleeping, being continually harassed with horrible and tremendous dreams. The impious themselves, therefore, exemplify the observation, that the idea of a God is never lost in the human mind.

III. It will always be evident to persons of correct judgment, that the idea of a Deity impressed on the mind of man is indelible. That all have by nature an innate persuasion of the Divine existence, a persuasion inseparable from their very constitution, we have abundant evidence in the contumacy of the wicked, whose furious struggles to extricate themselves from the fear of God are unavailing. Though Diagoras, and others like him, turn to ridicule what all ages have believed of religion;[68] though Dionysius scoff at the judgment of Heaven,—it is but a forced laughter, for the worm of a guilty conscience torments them within, worse than if they were seared with hot irons. I agree not with Cicero, that errors in process of time become obsolete, and that religion is increased and ameliorated daily. For the world, as will shortly be observed, uses its utmost endeavours to banish all knowledge of God, and tries every method of corrupting his worship. I only maintain, that while the stupid insensibility which the wicked wish to acquire, to promote their contempt of God, preys upon their minds, yet the sense of a Deity, which they ardently desire to extinguish, is still strong, and frequently discovers itself. Whence we infer, that this is a doctrine, not first to be learned in the schools, but which every man from his birth is self-taught, and which, though many strain every nerve to banish it from them, yet nature itself permits none to forget. Now, if the end for which all men are born and live, be to know God,—and unless the knowledge of God have reached this point, it is uncertain and vain,—it is evident, that all who direct not every thought and action of life to this end, are degenerated from the law of their creation. Of this the heathen philosophers themselves were not ignorant. This was Plato's meaning, when he taught that the chief good of the soul consists in similitude to God, when the soul, having a clear knowledge of him, is wholly transformed into his likeness.[69] The reasoning also of Gryllus, in Plutarch, is very accurate, when he affirms, that men entirely destitute of religion, not only do not excel the brutes, but are in many respects far more wretched, being obnoxious to evil under so many forms, and always dragging on a tumultuous and restless life. The worship of God is therefore the only thing which renders men superior to brutes, and makes them aspire to immortality.

2.

The Knowledge of God Conspicuous in the Formation and Continual Government of the World.

As the perfection of a happy life consists in the knowledge of God, that no man might be precluded from attaining felicity, God hath not only sown in the minds of men the seed of religion, already mentioned, but hath manifested himself in the formation of every part of the world, and daily presents himself to public view, in such a manner, that they cannot open their eyes without being constrained to behold him. His essence indeed is incomprehensible, so that his Majesty is not to be perceived by the human senses; but on all his works he hath inscribed his glory in characters so clear, unequivocal, and striking, that the most illiterate and stupid cannot exculpate themselves by the plea of ignorance. The Psalmist therefore, with great propriety, exclaims, "He covereth himself with light as with a garment;"[79] as if he had said, that his first appearance in visible apparel was at the creation of the world, when he displayed those glories which are still conspicuous on every side. In the same place, the Psalmist compares the expanded heavens to a royal pavilion;—he says that "he layeth the beams of his chambers in the waters; maketh the clouds his chariot; walketh upon the wings of the wind;" and maketh the winds and the lightnings his swift messengers. And because the glory of his power and wisdom is more refulgently displayed above, heaven is generally called his palace. And, in the first place, whithersoever you turn your eyes, there is not an atom of the world in which you cannot behold some brilliant sparks at least of his glory. But you cannot at one view take a survey of this most ample and beautiful machine in all its vast extent, without being completely overwhelmed with its infinite splendour. Wherefore the author of the Epistle to the Hebrews elegantly represents the worlds as the manifestations of invisible things;[80] for the exact symmetry of the universe is a mirror, in which we may contemplate the otherwise invisible God. For which reason the Psalmist[81] attributes to the celestial bodies a language universally known; for they afford a testimony of the Deity too evident to escape the observation even of the most ignorant people in the world. But the Apostle more distinctly asserts this manifestation to men of what was useful to be known concerning God; "for the invisible things of him from the creation of the world are clearly seen, being understood by the things that are made, even his eternal power and godhead."[82]

II. Of his wonderful wisdom, both heaven and earth contain innumerable proofs; not only those more abstruse things, which are the subjects of astronomy, medicine, and the whole science of physics, but those things which force themselves on the view of the most illiterate of mankind, so that they cannot open their eyes without being constrained to witness them. Adepts, indeed, in those liberal arts, or persons just initiated into them, are thereby enabled to proceed much further in investigating the secrets of Divine Wisdom. Yet ignorance of those sciences prevents no man from such a survey of the workmanship of God, as is more than sufficient to excite his admiration of the Divine Architect. In disquisitions concerning the motions of the stars, in fixing their situations, measuring their distances, and distinguishing their peculiar properties, there is need of skill, exactness, and industry; and the providence of God being more clearly revealed by these discoveries, the mind ought to rise to a sublimer elevation for the contemplation of his glory. But since the meanest and most illiterate of mankind, who are furnished with no other assistance than their own eyes, cannot be ignorant of the excellence of the Divine skill, exhibiting itself in that endless, yet regular variety of the innumerable celestial host,—it is evident, that the Lord abundantly manifests his wisdom to every individual on earth. Thus it belongs to a man of preëminent ingenuity to examine, with the critical exactness of Galen, the connection, the symmetry, the beauty, and the use of the various parts of the human body. But the composition of the human body is universally acknowledged to be so ingenious, as to render its Maker the object of deserved admiration.

III. And therefore some of the philosophers[83] of antiquity have justly called man a microcosm, or world in miniature; because he is an eminent specimen of the power, goodness, and wisdom of God, and contains in him wonders enough to occupy the attention of our minds, if we are not indisposed to such a study. For this reason, Paul, having remarked that the blind "might feel after God and find him," immediately adds, that "he is not far from every one of us;"[84] because every man has undoubtedly an inward perception of the celestial goodness, by which he is quickened. But if, to attain some ideas of God, it be not necessary for us to go beyond ourselves, what an unpardonable indolence is it in those who will not descend into themselves that they may find him! For the same reason, David, having briefly celebrated the wonderful name and honour of God, which are universally conspicuous, immediately exclaims, "What is man, that thou art mindful of him?"[85] Again, "Out of the mouths of babes and sucklings thou hast ordained strength." Thus declaring not only that the human race is a clear mirror of the works of God, but that even infants at the breast have tongues so eloquent for the publication of his glory, that there is no necessity for other orators; whence he hesitates not to produce them as fully capable of confuting the madness of those whose diabolical pride would wish to extinguish the name of God. Hence also what Paul quotes from Aratus, that "we are the offspring of God;"[86] since his adorning us with such great excellence has proved him to be our Father. So, from the dictates of common sense and experience, the heathen poets called him the Father of men. Nor will any man freely devote himself to the service of God, unless he have been allured to love and reverence him, by first experiencing his paternal love.

IV. But herein appears the vile ingratitude of men—that, while they ought to be proclaiming the praises of God for the wonderful skill displayed in their formation, and the inestimable bounties he bestows on them, they are only inflated with the greater pride. They perceive how wonderfully God works within them, and experience teaches them what a variety of blessings they receive from his liberality. They are constrained to know, whether willingly or not, that these are proofs of his divinity: yet they suppress this knowledge in their hearts. Indeed, they need not go out of themselves, provided they do not, by arrogating to themselves what is given from heaven, smother the light which illuminates their minds to a clearer discovery of God. Even in the present day, there are many men of monstrous dispositions, who hesitate not to pervert all the seeds of divinity sown in the nature of man, in order to bury in oblivion the name of God. How detestable is this frenzy, that man, discovering in his body and soul a hundred vestiges of God, should make this very excellence a pretext for the denial of his being! They will not say that they are distinguished from the brutes by chance; but they ascribe it to nature, which they consider as the author of all things, and remove God out of sight. They perceive most exquisite workmanship in all their members, from the head to the feet. Here also they substitute nature in the place of God. But above all, the rapid motions of the soul, its noble faculties, and excellent talents, discover a Divinity not easily concealed; unless the Epicureans, like the Cyclops, from this eminence should audaciously wage war against God. Do all the treasures of heavenly wisdom concur in the government of a worm five feet in length? and shall the universe be destitute of this privilege? To state that there is in the soul a certain machinery corresponding to every part of the body, is so far from obscuring the divine glory, that it is rather an illustration of it. Let Epicurus answer; what concourse of atoms in the concoction of food and drink distributes part into excrements and part into blood, and causes the several members to perform their different offices with as much diligence as if so many souls by common consent governed one body?

V. But my present concern is not with that sty of swines: I rather address those who, influenced by preposterous subtilties, would indirectly employ that frigid dogma of Aristotle to destroy the immortality of the soul, and deprive God of his rights. For, because the organs of the body are directed by the faculties of the soul, they pretend the soul to be so united to the body as to be incapable of subsisting without it; and by their eulogies of nature do all they can to suppress the name of God. But the powers of the soul are far from being limited to functions subservient to the body. For what concern has the body in measuring the heavens, counting the number of the stars, computing their several magnitudes, and acquiring a knowledge of their respective distances, of the celerity or tardiness of their courses, and of the degrees of their various declinations? I grant, indeed, the usefulness of astronomy, but only remark that, in these profound researches relating to the celestial orbs, there is no corporeal coöperation, but that the soul has its functions distinct from the body. I have proposed one example, whence inferences may readily be drawn by the readers. The manifold agility of the soul, which enables it to take a survey of heaven and earth; to join the past and the present; to retain the memory of things heard long ago; to conceive of whatever it chooses by the help of imagination; its ingenuity also in the invention of such admirable arts,—are certain proofs of the divinity in man. Besides, in sleep, it not only turns and moves itself round, but conceives many useful ideas, reasons on various subjects, and even divines future events. What shall we say, but that the vestiges of immortality impressed upon man are absolutely indelible? Now, what reason can be given, why man, who is of divine original, should not acknowledge his Creator? Shall we indeed, by the judgment with which we are endued, discern right from wrong, and shall there be no judge in heaven? Shall we, even in our sleep, have some remains of intelligence, and shall there be no God to govern the world? Shall we be esteemed the inventers of so many useful arts, that God may be defrauded of his praise? Whereas experience abundantly teaches, that all we have is variously distributed to us by some superior Being. The clamour of some, about a secret inspiration animating the whole world, is not only weak, but altogether profane. They are pleased with the celebrated passage of Virgil—

"Know, first, a spirit, with an active flame,

Fills, feeds, and animates this mighty frame;

Runs through the watery worlds, the fields of air,

The ponderous earth, the depths of heaven; and there

Glows in the sun and moon, and burns in every star.

Thus, mingling with the mass, the general soul

Lives in the parts, and agitates the whole.

From that celestial energy began

The low-browed brute, th' imperial race of man,

The painted birds who wing th' aërial plain,

And all the mighty monsters of the main;

Their souls at first from high Olympus came," &c.

Just as if the world, which is a theatre erected for displaying the glory of God, were its own creator! For thus writes the same poet in another place, following the common opinion of the Greeks and Latins—

"Led by such wonders, sages have opined,

That bees have portions of a heavenly mind;

That God pervades, and, like one common soul,

Fills, feeds, and animates the world's great whole;

That flocks, herds, beasts, and men, from him receive

Their vital breath; in him all move and live;

That souls discerpt from him shall never die,

But back resolved to God and heaven shall fly,

And live for ever in the starry sky."

See the efficacy of that jejune speculation concerning a universal mind animating and actuating the world, in the production and encouragement of piety in the human heart. This more fully appears also from the profane expressions of the filthy Lucretius, which are deductions from the same principle.[80] Its true tendency is to set up a shadowy deity, and to banish all ideas of the true God, the proper object of fear and worship. I confess, indeed, that the expression, that nature is God, may be used in a pious sense by a pious mind; but, as it is harsh and inconsistent with strict propriety of speech, nature being rather an order prescribed by God, it is dangerous in matters so momentous, and demanding peculiar caution, to confound the Deity with the inferior course of his works.

VI. Let us remember, then, in every consideration of our own nature, that there is one God, who governs all natures, and who expects us to regard him, to direct our faith to him, to worship and invoke him. For nothing is more preposterous than to enjoy such splendid advantages, which proclaim within us their divine origin, and to neglect the Author who bountifully bestows them. Now, what illustrious specimens of his power have we to arrest our attention! unless it be possible for us not to know what strength is required to sustain with his word this immense fabric of heaven and earth; now by his mere nod to shake the heaven with roaring peals of thunder, to consume whatever he choose with lightnings, and set the atmosphere on fire with the flame; now to disturb it with tempests in various forms, and immediately, if he please, to compose all to instantaneous serenity; to restrain, suspended as it were in air, the sea, which, by its elevation, seems to threaten the earth with continual devastation; now raising it in a tremendous manner, by the tumultuous violence of the winds, and now appeasing the waves to render it calm. To this purpose are the numerous praises of the power of God, drawn from the testimonies of nature, particularly in the book of Job, and in the prophecies of Isaiah; which I now purposely omit, as they will be more suitably introduced, when I discuss the scriptural account of the creation of the world. Only I wished at present to hint, that this way of seeking God, by tracing the lineaments which, both above and below us, exhibit such a lively adumbration of him, is common to aliens, and to those who belong to his family. His power leads us to the consideration of his eternity; because he, from whom all things derive their origin, must necessarily be eternal and self-existent. But if we inquire the reason that induced him first to create all things, and now to preserve them, we shall find the sole cause to be his own goodness. But though this be the only cause, it should be more than sufficient to attract us to love him; since, according to the Psalmist,[90] there is no creature that does not participate in the effusions of his mercy.

VII. In the second species of his works, such as happen out of the ordinary course of nature, the proofs of his perfections are equally clear. For he so regulates his providence in the government of human society, that, while he exhibits, in innumerable ways, his benignity and beneficence to all, he likewise declares, by evident and daily indications, his clemency to the pious, and his severity to the wicked and ungodly. For no doubt can be entertained respecting his punishment of flagitious crimes; inasmuch as he clearly demonstrates himself to be the guardian and avenger of innocence, in prospering with his blessing the life of good men, in assisting their necessities, assuaging and comforting their sorrows, alleviating their calamities, and providing in all things for their safety. Nor should it perplex or eclipse his perpetual rule of righteousness, that he frequently permits the wicked and guilty for a time to exult in impunity; but suffers good men to be undeservedly harassed with much adversity, and even to be oppressed by the iniquitous malice of the ungodly. We ought rather to make a very different reflection; that, when he clearly manifests his wrath in the punishment of one sin, he hates all sins; and that, since he now passes by many sins unpunished, there will be a judgment hereafter, till which the punishment is deferred. So, also, what ample occasion he supplies us for the consideration of his mercy, while, with unwearied benignity, he pursues the miserable, calling them back to himself with more than paternal indulgence, till his beneficence overcomes their depravity!

VIII. To this end the Psalmist,[91] mentioning that God, in desperate cases, suddenly and wonderfully succors, beyond all expectation, those who are miserable and ready to perish, either protecting from beasts of prey such as are wandering in deserts, and, at length, reconducting them into the right way, or supplying with food the needy and hungry, or delivering captives from dreary dungeons and iron chains, or bringing the shipwrecked safe into port, or healing the diseases of some who are almost dead, or scorching the earth with excessive heat and drought, or fertilizing it with the secret showers of his mercy, or elevating the meanest of the vulgar, or degrading nobles from their dignified stations,—the Psalmist, I say, having proposed such examples as these, infers from them that what are accounted fortuitous accidents, are so many proofs of his heavenly providence, especially of his paternal clemency; and that hence the pious have cause to rejoice, while the mouths of the impious and reprobate are stopped. But, since the majority of men, immersed in their errors, are blind amidst the greatest opportunities of seeing, he accounts it a rare instance of singular wisdom discreetly to consider these works of God;[92] from the sight of which, some, who, in other instances, discover the greatest acuteness, receive no benefit. And, notwithstanding all the displays of the glory of God, scarcely one man in a hundred, is really a spectator of it. His power and wisdom are equally conspicuous. His power is illustriously manifested, when the ferocity of the impious, universally deemed insuperable, is quelled in an instant, their arrogance subdued, their strongest fortresses demolished, their weapons and armour broken in pieces, their strength diminished, their machinations confounded, and they fall by their own exertions; when the audacity, which exalted itself above the heavens, is thrown down to the centre of the earth; when, on the contrary, "the poor are raised out of the dust, and the needy out of the dunghill;"[93] the oppressed and afflicted extricated from distressing extremities, and the desperate restored to a good hope; when the unarmed are victorious over those who are armed, the few over the many, the weak over the strong. But his wisdom is eminently displayed in ordering every dispensation at the best possible time, confounding the greatest worldly sagacity, "taking the wise in their own craftiness,"[94] and finally disposing all things according to the dictates of the highest reason.

IX. We see that there is no need of any long or laborious argumentation, to obtain and produce testimonies for illustrating and asserting the Divine Majesty; since, from the few which we have selected and cursorily mentioned, it appears that they are every where so evident and obvious, as easily to be distinguished by the eyes, and pointed out with the fingers. And here it must again be observed, that we are invited to a knowledge of God; not such as, content with empty speculation, merely floats in the brain, but such as will be solid and fruitful, if rightly received and rooted in our hearts. For the Lord is manifested by his perfections: perceiving the influence and enjoying the benefits of which, we must necessarily be more acutely impressed with such a knowledge, than if we imagined a Deity of whose influence we had no perception. Whence we conclude this to be the right way, and the best method of seeking God; not with presumptuous curiosity to attempt an examination of his essence, which is rather to be adored than too curiously investigated; but to contemplate him in his works, in which he approaches and familiarizes, and, in some measure, communicates himself to us. To this the Apostle referred, when he said, that he is not to be sought far off, since, by his attribute of omnipresence, he dwells in every one of us.[95] Therefore David, having before confessed his greatness ineffable, after he descends to the mention of his works, adds, that he will "declare this greatness."[96] Wherefore it becomes us also to apply ourselves to such an investigation of God, as may fill our understanding with admiration, and powerfully interest our feelings. And, as Augustine somewhere teaches, being incapable of comprehending him, and fainting, as it were, under his immensity, we must take a view of his works, that we may be refreshed with his goodness.[97]

X. Now, such a knowledge ought not only to excite us to the worship of God, but likewise to awaken and arouse us to the hope of a future life. For when we consider, that the specimens given by the Lord, both of his clemency and of his severity, are only begun, and not completed, we certainly should esteem these as preludes to greater things, of which the manifestation and full exhibition are deferred to another life. When we see that pious men are loaded with afflictions by the impious, harassed with injuries, oppressed with calumnies, and vexed with contumelious and opprobrious treatment; that the wicked, on the contrary, flourish, prosper, obtain ease and dignity, and all with impunity,—we should immediately conclude, that there is another life, to which is reserved the vengeance due to iniquity, and the reward of righteousness. Moreover, when we observe the faithful frequently chastised by the Lord's rod, we may conclude, with great certainty, that the impious shall not always escape his vengeance. For that is a wise observation of Augustine—"If open punishment were now inflicted for every sin, it would be supposed that nothing would be reserved till the last judgment. Again, if God now did not openly punish any sin, it would be presumed that there was no divine providence."[98] It must therefore be confessed, that in each of the works of God, but more especially in the whole considered together, there is a bright exhibition of the divine perfections; by which the whole human race is invited and allured to the knowledge of God, and thence to true and complete felicity. But, though those perfections are most luminously portrayed around us, we only discover their principal tendency, their use, and the end of our contemplation of them, when we descend into our own selves, and consider by what means God displays in us his life, wisdom, and power, and exercises towards us his righteousness, goodness, and mercy. For, though David justly complains that unbelievers are fools, because they consider not the profound designs of God in the government of mankind,[99] yet there is much truth in what he says in another place—that the wonders of Divine Wisdom in this respect exceed in number the hairs of our head. But as this argument must be treated more at large in due course, I at present omit it.

XI. But, notwithstanding the clear representations given by God in the mirror of his works, both of himself and of his everlasting dominion, such is our stupidity, that, always inattentive to these obvious testimonies, we derive no advantage from them. For, with regard to the structure and very beautiful organization of the world, how few of us are there, who, when lifting up their eyes to heaven, or looking round on the various regions of the earth, direct their minds to the remembrance of the Creator, and do not rather content themselves with a view of his works, to the total neglect of their Author! And with respect to those things that daily happen out of the ordinary course of nature, is it not the general opinion, that men are rolled and whirled about by the blind temerity of fortune, rather than governed by the providence of God? Or if, by the guidance and direction of these things, we are ever driven (as all men must sometimes be) to the consideration of a God, yet, when we have rashly conceived an idea of some deity, we soon slide into our own carnal dreams, or depraved inventions, corrupting by our vanity the purity of divine truth. We differ from one another, in that each individual imbibes some peculiarity of error; but we perfectly agree in a universal departure from the one true God, to preposterous trifles. This disease affects, not only the vulgar and ignorant, but the most eminent, and those who, in other things, discover peculiar sagacity. How abundantly have all the philosophers, in this respect, betrayed their stupidity and folly! For, to spare others, chargeable with greater absurdities, Plato himself, the most religious and judicious of them all, loses himself in his round globe. And what would not befall others, when their principal men, whose place it was to enlighten the rest, stumble upon such gross errors! So also, while the government of human actions proves a providence too plainly to admit of a denial, men derive no more advantage from it, than if they believed all things to be agitated forwards and backwards by the uncertain caprice of fortune; so great is our propensity to vanity and error! I speak exclusively of the excellent of mankind, not of the vulgar, whose madness in the profanation of divine truth has known no bounds.

XII. Hence that immense flood of errors, which has deluged the whole world. For every man's understanding is like a labyrinth to him; so that it is not to be wondered at, that the different nations were drawn aside into various inventions, and even that almost every individual had his own particular deity. For, amidst the union of temerity and wantonness with ignorance and darkness, scarcely a man could be found who did not frame to himself some idol or phantasm instead of God. Indeed, the immense multitude of gods proceeding from the mind of man, resembles the ebullition of waters from a vast and ample spring, while every one, with an extreme licentiousness of error, invents one thing or another concerning God himself. It is not necessary here to compose a catalogue of the superstitions which have perplexed the world; for it would be an endless task; and, without a word more being said, the horrible blindness of the human mind sufficiently appears from such a multiplicity of corruptions. I pass over the rude and unlearned vulgar. But among the philosophers, who attempted with reason and learning to penetrate heaven, how shameful is the diversity! In proportion to the vigour of his natural genius, and the polish acquired by art and science, each of them seemed to give the more specious colouring to his own opinion; but, on a close inspection, you will find them all fading colours. The Stoics said, in their own opinion very shrewdly, that from all the parts of nature may be collected various names of God, but yet that the one God is not therefore divided; as if we were not already too much inclined to vanity, without being further and more violently seduced into error, by the notion of such a various abundance of gods. The mystical theology of the Egyptians also shows that they all sedulously endeavoured to preserve the appearance of reason in the midst of their folly. And any thing apparently probable might at first sight, perhaps, deceive the simple and incautious; but there never was any human invention by which religion was not basely corrupted. And this confused diversity imboldened the Epicureans, and other gross despisers of piety, to reject all idea of God. For, seeing the wisest of men contending with each other for contrary opinions, they hesitated not, from their dissensions, and from the frivolous and absurd doctrines maintained by the different parties, to infer, that it was vain and foolish for men to torment themselves with investigations concerning God, who does not exist. And this they thought they might do with impunity, supposing that a compendious denial of any God at all would be better than feigning uncertain gods, and thereby occasioning endless controversies.

They reason very ignorantly, or rather endeavour to conceal their own impiety behind the ignorance of men, which not at all justifies any encroachment on God. But from the general confession, that there is no subject productive of so many dissensions among the learned as well as the unlearned, it is inferred, that the minds of men, which err so much in investigations concerning God, are extremely blind and stupid in celestial mysteries. Others commend the answer of Simonides, who, being asked by Hiero the Tyrant what God was, requested a day to consider it. When the tyrant, the next day, repeated the inquiry, he begged to be allowed two days longer; and, having often doubled the number of days, at length answered, "The longer I consider the subject, the more obscure it appears to me." He prudently suspended his opinion on a subject so obscure to him; yet this shows that men, who are taught only by nature, have no certain, sound, or distinct knowledge, but are confined to confused principles; so that they worship an unknown God.

XIII. Now, it must also be maintained, that whoever adulterates the pure religion, (which must necessarily be the case of all who are influenced by their own imagination,) he is guilty of a departure from the one God. They will profess, indeed, a different intention; but what they intend, or what they persuade themselves, is of little importance; since the Holy Spirit pronounces all to be apostates, who, in the darkness of their minds, substitute demons in the place of God. For this reason Paul declares the Ephesians to have been "without God"—till they had learned from the gospel the worship of the true God. Nor should this be restricted to one nation only, since, in another place, he asserts of men in general, that they "became vain in their imaginations," after the majesty of the Creator had been discovered to them in the structure of the world. And therefore the Scripture, to make room for the only true God, condemns, as false and lying, whatever was formerly worshipped as divine among the Gentiles, and leaves no Deity but in Mount Sion, where flourished the peculiar knowledge of God. Indeed, among the Gentiles, the Samaritans, in the days of Christ, seemed to approach very nearly to true piety; yet we hear, from the mouth of Christ, that they "worshipped they knew not what;" whence it follows, that they were under a vain and erroneous delusion. In fine, though they were not all the subjects of gross vices, or open idolaters, there was no pure and approved religion, their notions being founded only in common sense. For, though there were a few uninfected with the madness of the vulgar, this assertion of Paul remains unshaken, that "none of the princes of this world knew the wisdom of God." But if the most exalted have been involved in the darkness of error, what must be said of the dregs of the people! Wherefore it is not surprising if the Holy Spirit reject, as spurious, every form of worship which is of human contrivance; because, in the mysteries of heaven, an opinion acquired by human means, though it may not always produce an immense mass of errors, yet always produces some. And though no worse consequence follow, it is no trivial fault to worship, at an uncertainty, an unknown god; of which, however, Christ pronounces all to be guilty who have not been taught by the law what god they ought to worship. And indeed the best legislators have proceeded no further than to declare religion to be founded upon common consent. And even Socrates, in Xenophon, praises the answer of Apollo, which directed that every man should worship the gods according to the rites of his country, and the custom of his own city. But whence had mortals this right of determining, by their own authority, what far exceeds all the world? or who could so acquiesce in the decrees of the rulers or the ordinances of the people, as without hesitation to receive a god delivered to him by the authority of man? Every man will rather abide by his own judgment, than be subject to the will of another. Since, then, the following of the custom of a city, or the consent of antiquity, in divine worship, is too weak and frail a bond of piety, it remains for God himself to give a revelation concerning himself from heaven.

XIV. Vain, therefore, is the light afforded us in the formation of the world to illustrate the glory of its Author; which, though its rays be diffused all around us, is insufficient to conduct us into the right way. Some sparks, indeed, are kindled, but smothered before they have emitted any great degree of light. Wherefore the Apostle, in the place before cited, says, "By faith we understand that the worlds were framed by the word of God;" thus intimating, that the invisible Deity was represented by such visible objects, yet that we have no eyes to discern him, unless they be illuminated through faith by an internal revelation of God. Nor does Paul, where he observes, that "that which may be known of God is manifest" in the creation of the world, design such a manifestation as human sagacity may comprehend; but rather shows, that its utmost extent is to render men inexcusable. The same writer also, though in one place he denies that God is to be traced far off, seeing he dwells within us, yet teaches, in another place, the consequences of such a proximity. God, says he, "in times past suffered all nations to walk in their own ways. Nevertheless he left not himself without witness, in that he did good, and gave us rain from heaven, and fruitful seasons, filling our hearts with food and gladness." Though the Lord, then, is not destitute of a testimony concerning himself, while with various and most abundant benignity he sweetly allures mankind to a knowledge of him, yet they persist in following their own ways, their pernicious and fatal errors.

XV. But whatever deficiency of natural ability prevents us from attaining the pure and clear knowledge of God, yet, since that deficiency arises from our own fault, we are left without any excuse. Nor indeed can we set up any pretence of ignorance, that will prevent our own consciences from perpetually accusing us of indolence and ingratitude. Truly it would be a defence worthy to be admitted, if a man should plead that he wanted ears to hear the truth, for the publication of which even the mute creatures are supplied with most melodious voices; if he should allege that his eyes are not capable of seeing what is demonstrated by the creatures without the help of the eyes; if he should plead mental imbecility, while all the irrational creatures instruct us. Wherefore we are justly excluded from all excuse for our uncertain and extravagant deviations, since all things conspire to show us the right way. But, however men are chargeable with sinfully corrupting the seeds of divine knowledge, which, by the wonderful operation of nature, are sown in their hearts, so that they produce no good and fair crop, yet it is beyond a doubt, that the simple testimony magnificently borne by the creatures to the glory of God, is very insufficient for our instruction. For as soon as a survey of the world has just shown us a deity, neglecting the true God, we set up in his stead the dreams and phantasms of our own brains; and confer on them the praise of righteousness, wisdom, goodness, and power, due to him. We either obscure his daily acts, or pervert them by an erroneous estimate; thereby depriving the acts themselves of their glory, and their Author of his deserved praise.

3.

One Divine Essence, Containing Three Persons; Taught in the Scriptures from the Beginning.

What is taught in the Scriptures concerning the immensity and spirituality of the essence of God, should serve not only to overthrow the foolish notions of the vulgar, but also to refute the subtleties of profane philosophy. One of the ancients, in his own conception very shrewdly, said, that whatever we see, and whatever we do not see, is God. But he imagined that the Deity was diffused through every part of the world. But, although God, to keep us within the bounds of sobriety, speaks but rarely of his essence, yet, by those two attributes, which I have mentioned, he supersedes all gross imaginations, and represses the presumption of the human mind. For, surely, his immensity ought to inspire us with awe, that we may not attempt to measure him with our senses; and the spirituality of his nature prohibits us from entertaining any earthly or carnal speculations concerning him. For the same reason, he represents his residence to be "in heaven;" for though, as he is incomprehensible, he fills the earth also; yet, seeing that our minds, from their dulness, are continually dwelling on the earth, in order to shake off our sloth and inactivity, he properly raises us above the world. And here is demolished the error of the Manichees, who, by maintaining the existence of two original principles, made the devil, as it were, equal to God. This certainly was both dividing the unity of God, and limiting his immensity. For their daring to abuse certain testimonies of Scripture betrayed a shameful ignorance; as the error itself evidenced an execrable madness. The Anthropomorphites also, who imagined God to be corporeal, because the Scripture frequently ascribes to him a mouth, ears, eyes, hands, and feet, are easily refuted. For who, even of the meanest capacity, understands not, that God lisps, as it were, with us, just as nurses are accustomed to speak to infants? Wherefore, such forms of expression do not clearly explain the nature of God, but accommodate the knowledge of him to our narrow capacity; to accomplish which, the Scripture must necessarily descend far below the height of his majesty.

II. But he also designates himself by another peculiar character, by which he may be yet more clearly distinguished; for, while he declares himself to be but One, he proposes himself to be distinctly considered in Three Persons, without apprehending which, we have only a bare and empty name of God floating in our brains, without any idea of the true God. Now, that no one may vainly dream of three gods, or suppose that the simple essence of God is divided among the three Persons, we must seek for a short and easy definition, which will preserve us from all error. But since some violently object to the word Person, as of human invention, we must first examine the reasonableness of this objection. When the Apostle denominates the Son the express image of the hypostasis of the Father, he undoubtedly ascribes to the Father some subsistence, in which he differs from the Son. For to understand this word as synonymous with Essence, (as some interpreters have done, as though Christ, like wax impressed with a seal, represented in himself the substance of the Father,) were not only harsh, but also absurd. For the essence of God being simple and indivisible, he who contains all in himself, not in part, or by derivation, but in complete perfection, could not, without impropriety, and even absurdity, be called the express image of it. But since the Father, although distinguished by his own peculiar property, hath expressed himself entirely in his Son, it is with the greatest reason asserted that he hath made his hypostasis conspicuous in him; with which the other appellation, given him in the same passage, of "the brightness of his glory," exactly corresponds. From the words of the Apostle, we certainly conclude, that there is in the Father a proper hypostasis, which is conspicuous in the Son. And thence also we easily infer the hypostasis of the Son, which distinguishes him from the Father. The same reasoning is applicable to the Holy Spirit; for we shall soon prove him also to be God; and yet he must, of necessity, be considered as distinct from the Father. But this is not a distinction of the essence, which it is unlawful to represent as any other than simple and undivided. It follows, therefore, if the testimony of the Apostle be credited, that there are in God three *hypostases*. And, as the Latins have expressed the same thing by the word *person*, it is too fastidious and obstinate to contend about so clear a matter. If we wish to translate word for word, we may call it *subsistence*. Many, in the same sense, have called it *substance*. Nor has the word *person* been used by the Latins only; but the Greeks also, for the sake of testifying their consent to this doctrine, taught the existence of three προσωπα (persons) in God. But both Greeks and Latins, notwithstanding any verbal difference, are in perfect harmony respecting the doctrine itself.

III. Now, though heretics rail at the word *person*, or some morose and obstinate men clamorously refuse to admit a name of human invention; since they cannot make us assert that there are three, each of whom is entirely God, nor yet that there are more gods than one, how very unreasonable is it to reprobate words which express nothing but what is testified and recorded in the Scriptures! It were better, say they, to restrain not only our thoughts, but our expressions also, within the limits of the Scripture, than to introduce exotic words, which may generate future dissensions and disputes; for thus we weary ourselves with verbal controversies; thus the truth is lost in altercation; thus charity expires in odious contention. If they call every word exotic, which cannot be found in the Scriptures in so many syllables, they impose on us a law which is very unreasonable, and which condemns all interpretation, but what is composed of detached texts of Scripture connected together. But if by exotic they mean that which is curiously contrived, and superstitiously defended, which tends to contention more than to edification, the use of which is either unseasonable or unprofitable, which offends pious ears with its harshness, and seduces persons from the simplicity of the Divine word, I most cordially embrace their modest opinion. For I think that we ought to speak of God with the same religious caution, which should govern our thoughts of him; since all the thoughts that we entertain concerning him merely from ourselves, are foolish, and all our expressions absurd. But there is a proper medium to be observed: we should seek in the Scriptures a certain rule, both for thinking and for speaking; by which we may regulate all the thoughts of our minds, and all the words of our mouths. But what forbids our expressing, in plainer words, those things which, in the Scriptures, are, to our understanding, intricate and obscure, provided our expressions religiously and faithfully convey the true sense of the Scripture, and are used with modest caution, and not without sufficient occasion? Of this, examples sufficiently numerous are not wanting. But, when it shall have been proved, that the Church was absolutely necessitated to use the terms Trinity and Persons, if any one then censures the novelty of the words, may he not be justly considered as offended at the light of the truth? as having no other cause of censure, but that the truth is explained and elucidated?

IV. But such verbal novelty (if it must have this appellation) is principally used, when the truth is to be asserted in opposition to malicious cavillers, who elude it by crafty evasions; of which we have too much experience in the present day, who find great difficulty in refuting the enemies of pure and sound doctrine: possessed of serpentine lubricity, they escape by the most artful expedients, unless they are vigorously pursued, and held fast when once caught. Thus the ancients, pestered with various controversies against erroneous dogmas, were constrained to express their sentiments with the utmost perspicuity, that they might leave no subterfuges to the impious, who availed themselves of obscure expressions, for the concealment of their errors. Unable to resist the clear testimonies of the Scriptures, Arius confessed Christ to be God, and the Son of God; and, as though this were all that was necessary, he pretended to agree with the Church at large. But, at the same time, he continued to maintain that Christ was created, and had a beginning like other creatures. To draw the versatile subtlety of this man from its concealment, the ancient Fathers proceeded further, and declared Christ to be the eternal Son of the Father, and consubstantial with the Father. Here impiety openly discovered itself, when the Arians began inveterately to hate and execrate the name ὁμοούσιος, (consubstantial.) But if, in the first instance, they had sincerely and cordially confessed Christ to be God, they would not have denied him to be consubstantial with the Father. Who can dare to censure those good men, as quarrelsome and contentious, for having kindled such a flame of controversy, and disturbed the peace of the Church on account of one little word? That little word distinguished Christians, who held the pure faith, from sacrilegious Arians. Afterwards arose Sabellius, who considered the names of Father, Son, and Holy Spirit, as little more than empty sounds; arguing, that they were not used on account of any real distinction, but were different attributes of God, whose attributes of this kind are numerous. If the point came to be controverted, he confessed, that he believed the Father to be God, the Son God, and the Holy Spirit God; but he would readily evade all the force of this confession, by adding, that he had said no other than if he had called God potent, and just, and wise. And thus he came to another conclusion, that the Father is the Son, and that the Holy Spirit is the Father, without any order or distinction. The good doctors of that age, who had the interest of religion at heart, in order to counteract the wickedness of this man, maintained, on the contrary, that they ought really to acknowledge three peculiar properties in one God. And, to defend themselves against his intricate subtleties, by the plain and simple truth, they affirmed, that they truly subsisted in the one God; or, what is the same, that in the unity of God there subsisted a trinity of Persons.

V. If, then, the words have not been rashly invented, we should beware lest we be convicted of fastidious temerity in rejecting them. I could wish them, indeed, to be buried in oblivion, provided this faith were universally received, that the Father, Son, and Holy Spirit, are the one God; and that nevertheless the Son is not the Father, nor the Spirit the Son, but that they are distinguished from each other by some peculiar property. I am not so rigidly precise as to be fond of contending for mere words. For I observe that the ancients, who otherwise speak on these subjects with great piety, are not consistent with each other, nor, in all cases, with themselves. For what forms of expression, adopted by councils, does Hilary excuse! To what extremes does

Augustine sometimes proceed! How different are the Greeks from the Latins! But of this variation, let one example suffice: when the Latins would translate the word ὁμοούσιος, they called it *consubstantial*, signifying the *substance* of the Father and the Son to be one, and thus using *substance* for *essence*. Whence also Jerome, writing to Damasus, pronounces it to be sacrilege to say that there are three *substances* in God. Yet, that there are three *substances* in God, you will find asserted in Hilary more than a hundred times. But how perplexed is Jerome on the word *hypostasis*! For he suspects some latent poison in the assertion, that there are three *hypostases* in God. And if any one uses this word in a pious sense, he refrains not from calling it an improper expression; if, indeed, he was sincere in this declaration, and did not rather knowingly and wilfully endeavour to asperse, with a groundless calumny, the bishops of the East, whom he hated. He certainly discovers not much ingenuousness in affirming that, in all the profane schools, οὐσία (essence) is the same as ὑπόστασις, (hypostasis,) which the trite and common use of the words universally contradicts. More modesty and liberality are discovered by Augustine, who, though he asserts that the word *hypostasis*, in this sense, is new to Latin ears, yet leaves the Greeks their usual phraseology, and even peaceably tolerates the Latins, who had imitated their language; and the account of Socrates, in the sixth book of his Tripartite History, seems to imply, that it was by ignorant men that it had first been improperly applied to this subject. The same Hilary accuses the heretics of a great crime, in constraining him, by their wickedness, to expose to the danger of human language those things which ought to be confined within the religion of the mind; plainly avowing that this is to do things unlawful, to express things inexpressible, to assume things not conceded. A little after, he largely excuses himself for his boldness in bringing forward new terms; for, when he has used the names of nature, Father, Son, and Spirit, he immediately adds, that whatever is sought further, is beyond the signification of language, beyond the reach of our senses, beyond the conception of our understanding. And, in another place, he pronounces that happy were the bishops of Gaul, who had neither composed, nor received, nor even known, any other confession but that ancient and very simple one, which had been received in all the churches from the days of the Apostles. Very similar is the excuse of Augustine, that this word was extorted by necessity, on account of the poverty of human language on so great a subject, not for the sake of expressing what God is, but to avoid passing it over in total silence, that the Father, Son, and Spirit are three. This moderation of those holy men should teach us, not to pass such severe censures on those who are unwilling to subscribe to expressions adopted by us, provided they are not actuated by pride, perverseness, or disingenuous subtlety. But let them also, on the other hand, consider the great necessity which constrains us to use such language, that, by degrees, they may at length be accustomed to a useful phraseology. Let them also learn to beware, since we have to oppose the Arians on one side, and the Sabellians on the other, lest, while they take offence at both these parties being deprived of all opportunity of evasion, they cause some suspicion that they are themselves the disciples either of Arius or of Sabellius. Arius confesses, "that Christ is God;" but maintains also, "that he was created, and had a beginning." He acknowledges that Christ is "one with the Father;" but secretly whispers in the ears of his disciples, that he is "united to him," like the rest of the faithful, though by a singular privilege. Say that he is *consubstantial*, you tear off the mask from the hypocrite, and yet you add nothing to the Scriptures. Sabellius asserts, "that the names Father, Son, and Spirit, are expressive of no distinction in the Godhead." Say that they are three, and he will exclaim, that you are talking of "three gods." Say, "that in the one essence of God there is a trinity of Persons," and you will at once express what the Scriptures declare, and will restrain such frivolous loquacity. Now, if any persons are prevented, by such excessive scrupulousness, from admitting these terms, yet not one of them can deny, that, when the Scripture speaks of one God, it should be understood of a unity of substance; and that, when it speaks of three in one essence, it denotes the Persons in this trinity. When this is honestly confessed, we have no further concern about words. But I have found, by long and frequent experience, that those who pertinaciously contend about words, cherish some latent poison; so that it were better designedly to provoke their resentment, than to use obscure language for the sake of obtaining their favour.

VI. But, leaving the dispute about terms, I shall now enter on the discussion of the subject itself. What I denominate a Person, is a subsistence in the Divine essence, which is related to the others, and yet distinguished from them by an incommunicable property. By the word *subsistence* we mean something different from the word *essence*. For, if the *Word* were simply God, and had no peculiar property, John had been guilty of impropriety in saying that he was always *with God.* When he immediately adds, that *the Word* also *was God,* he reminds us of the unity of the essence. But because he could not be *with God,* without subsisting in the Father, hence arises that subsistence, which, although inseparably connected with the essence, has a peculiar mark, by which it is distinguished from it. Now, I say that each of the three subsistences has a relation to the others, but is distinguished from them by a peculiar property. We particularly use the word *relation,* (or *comparison,*) here, because, when mention is made simply and indefinitely of God, this name pertains no less to the Son and Spirit, than to the Father. But whenever the Father is compared with the Son, the property peculiar to each distinguishes him from the other. Thirdly, whatever is proper to each of them, I assert to be incommunicable, because whatever is ascribed to the Father as a character of distinction, cannot be applied or transferred to the Son. Nor, indeed, do I disapprove of the definition of Tertullian, if rightly understood: "That there is in God a certain distribution or economy, which makes no change in the unity of the essence."

VII. But before I proceed any further, I must prove the Deity of the Son and of the Holy Spirit; after which we shall see how they differ from each other. When the Scripture speaks of *the Word of God,* it certainly were very absurd to imagine it to be only a transient and momentary sound, emitted into the air, and coming forth from God himself; of which nature were the oracles, given to the fathers, and all the prophecies. It is rather to be understood of the eternal wisdom residing in God, whence the oracles, and all the prophecies, proceeded. For, according to the testimony of Peter, the ancient Prophets spake by the Spirit of Christ no less than the Apostles and all the succeeding ministers of the heavenly doctrine. But, as Christ had not yet been manifested, we must necessarily understand that the Word was begotten of the Father before the world began. And if the Spirit that inspired the Prophets was the Spirit of the Word, we conclude, beyond all doubt, that the Word was truly God. And this is taught by Moses, with sufficient perspicuity, in the creation of the world, in which he represents the Word as acting such a conspicuous part. For why does he relate that God, in the creation of each of his works, said, Let this or that be done, but that the unsearchable glory of God may resplendently appear in his image? Captious and loquacious men would readily evade this argument, by saying, that the *Word* imports an order or command; but the

Apostles are better interpreters, who declare, that the worlds were created by the Son, and that he "upholds all things by the word of his power." For here we see that the *Word* intends the nod or mandate of the Son, who is himself the eternal and essential Son of the Father. Nor, to the wise and sober, is there any obscurity in that passage of Solomon, where he introduces Wisdom as begotten of the Father before time began, and presiding at the creation of the world, and over all the works of God. For, to pretend that this denotes some temporary expression of the will of God, were foolish and frivolous; whereas God then intended to discover his fixed and eternal counsel, and even something more secret. To the same purpose also is that assertion of Christ, "My Father worketh hitherto, and I work." For, by affirming that, from the beginning of the world, he had continually cooperated with the Father, he makes a more explicit declaration of what had been briefly glanced at by Moses. We conclude, therefore, that God spake thus at the creation, that the Word might have his part in the work, and so that operation be common to both. But John speaks more clearly than all others, when he represents *the Word*, who from the beginning *was God with God*, as in union with the Father, the original cause of all things. For to the Word he both attributes a real and permanent essence, and assigns some peculiar property; and plainly shows how God, by speaking, created the world. Therefore, as all Divine revelations are justly entitled *the word of God*, so we ought chiefly to esteem that substantial Word the source of all revelations, who is liable to no variation, who remains with God perpetually one and the same, and who is God himself.

VIII. Here we are interrupted by some clamorous objectors, who, since they cannot openly rob him of his divinity, secretly steal from him his eternity. For they say, that the Word only began to exist, when God opened his sacred mouth in the creation of the world. But they are too inconsiderate in imagining something new in the substance of God. For, as those names of God, which relate to his external works, began to be ascribed to him after the existence of those works, as when he is called the Creator of heaven and earth, so piety neither acknowledges nor admits any name, signifying that God has found any thing new to happen to himself. For, could any thing, from any quarter, effect a change in him, it would contradict the assertion of James, that "every good gift and every perfect gift is from above, and cometh down from the Father of lights, with whom is no variableness or shadow of turning." Nothing, then, is more intolerable, than to suppose a beginning of that Word, which was always God, and afterwards the Creator of the world. But they argue, in their own apprehension most acutely, that Moses, by representing God as having then spoken for the first time, implies also, that there was no Word in him before; than which nothing is more absurd. For it is not to be concluded, because any thing begins to be manifested at a certain time, that it had no prior existence. I form a very different conclusion; that, since, in the very instant when God said, "Let there be light," the power of the Word was clearly manifested, the Word must have existed long before. But if any one inquires, how long, he will find no beginning. For he limits no certain period of time, when he himself says, "O Father, glorify thou me with thine own self, with the glory which I had with thee before the world was." Nor is this omitted by John; for, before he descends to the creation of the world, he declares that the Word "was in the beginning with God." We therefore conclude again, that the Word, conceived of God before time began, perpetually remained with him, which proves his eternity, his true essence, and his divinity.

IX. Though I advert not yet to the person of the Mediator, but defer it to that part of the work which will relate to redemption, yet, since it ought, without controversy, to be believed by all, that Christ is the very same Word clothed in flesh, any testimonies which assert the Deity of Christ, will be very properly introduced here. When it is said, in the forty-fifth Psalm, "Thy throne, O God, is for ever and ever," the Jews endeavour to evade its force, by pleading that the name Elohim is applicable also to angels, and to men of dignity and power. But there cannot be found in the Scripture a similar passage, which erects an eternal throne for a creature; for he is not merely called God, but is also declared to possess an eternal dominion. Besides, this title is never given to a creature, without some addition, as when it is said that Moses should be "a god to Pharaoh." Some read it in the genitive case, "Thy throne is of God," which is extremely insipid. I confess, indeed, that what is eminently and singularly excellent, is frequently called Divine; but it sufficiently appears from the context, that such a meaning would be uncouth and forced, and totally inapplicable here. But, if their perverseness refuse to yield this point, there certainly is no obscurity in Isaiah, where he introduces Christ as God, and as crowned with supreme power, which is the prerogative of God alone. "His name," says he, "shall be called the Mighty God, the Father of eternity," &c. Here also the Jews object, and invert the reading of the passage in this manner: "This is the name by which the mighty God, the Father of eternity, shall call him," &c.; so that they would leave the Son only the title of Prince of peace. But to what purpose would so many epithets be accumulated in this passage on God the Father, when the design of the prophet is to distinguish Christ by such eminent characters as may establish our faith in him? Wherefore, there can be no doubt that he is there denominated the Mighty God, just as, a little before, he is called Immanuel. But nothing can be required plainer than a passage in Jeremiah, that this should be the name whereby the Branch of David shall be called "Jehovah our righteousness." For since the Jews themselves teach, that all other names of God are mere epithets, but that this alone, which they call ineffable, is a proper name expressive of his Essence, we conclude, that the Son is the one eternal God, who declares, in another place, that he "will not give his glory to another." This also they endeavour to evade, because Moses imposed this name on an altar which he built, and Ezekiel on the city of the new Jerusalem. But who does not perceive, that the altar was erected as a monument of Moses having been exalted by God, and that Jerusalem is honoured with the name of God, only as a testimony of the Divine presence? For thus speaks the prophet: "The name of the city shall be, Jehovah is there." But Moses expresses himself thus: He "built an altar, and called the name of it Jehovah-nissi," (my exaltation.) But there is more contention about another passage of Jeremiah, where the same title is given to Jerusalem in these words: "This is the name wherewith she shall be called, Jehovah our righteousness." But this testimony is so far from opposing the truth which we are defending, that it rather confirms it. For, having before testified that Christ is the true Jehovah, from whom righteousness proceeds, he now pronounces that the church will have such a clear apprehension of it, as to be able to glory in the same name. In the former place, then, is shown the original cause of righteousness, in the latter the effect.

X. Now, if these things do not satisfy the Jews, I see not by what cavils they can evade the accounts of Jehovah having so frequently appeared in the character of an angel. An angel is said to have appeared to the holy fathers. He claims for himself the name of the eternal God. If it be objected, that this is spoken with regard to the character which he sustains, this by no means removes the difficulty. For a servant would never rob God of his honour, by permitting sacrifice to be offered to himself. But the angel, refusing to eat bread, commands a sacrifice to be offered to Jehovah. He afterwards demonstrates that he is really Jehovah himself. Therefore Manoah and his wife conclude, from this evidence, that they have seen, not a mere angel, but God himself. Hence he says, "We shall surely die, because we have seen God." When his wife replies, "If the Lord were pleased to kill us, he would not have received" a sacrifice "at our hands," she clearly acknowledges him to be God, who before is called an angel. Moreover, the reply of the angel himself removes every doubt: "Why askest thou after my name, seeing it is wonderful?" So much the more detestable is the impiety of Servetus, in asserting that God never appeared to Abraham and the other patriarchs, but that they worshipped an angel in his stead. But the orthodox doctors of the church have truly and wisely understood and taught, that the same chief angel was the Word of God, who even then began to perform some services introductory to his execution of the office of Mediator. For though he was not yet incarnate, he descended, as it were, in a mediatorial capacity, that he might approach the faithful with greater familiarity. His familiar intercourse with men gave him the name of an angel; yet he still retained what properly belonged to him, and continued the ineffably glorious God. The same truth is attested by Hosea, who, after relating the wrestling of Jacob with an angel, says, "The Lord (Jehovah) God of hosts; Jehovah is his memorial." Servetus again cavils, that God employed the person of an angel; as though the prophet did not confirm what had been delivered by Moses,—"Wherefore is it that thou dost ask after my name?" And the confession of the holy patriarch, when he says, "I have seen God face to face," sufficiently declares, that he was not a created angel, but one in whom resided the fulness of Deity. Hence, also, the representation of Paul, that Christ was the conductor of the people in the wilderness; because, though the time of his humiliation was not yet arrived, the eternal Word then exhibited a type of the office to which he was appointed. Now, if the second chapter of Zechariah be strictly and coolly examined, the angel who sends another angel is immediately pronounced the God of hosts, and supreme power is ascribed to him. I omit testimonies innumerable on which our faith safely rests, although they have little influence on the Jews. For when it is said in Isaiah, "Lo, this is our God; we have waited for him, and he will save us; this is Jehovah;" all who have eyes may perceive that this is God, who arises for the salvation of his people. And the emphatical repetition of these pointed expressions forbids an application of this passage to any other than to Christ. But still more plain and decisive is a passage of Malachi, where he prophesies, that "the Lord, who was then sought, should come into his temple." The temple was exclusively consecrated to the one Most High God; yet the prophet claims it as belonging to Christ. Whence it follows, that he is the same God that was always worshipped among the Jews.

XI. The New Testament abounds with innumerable testimonies. We must, therefore, endeavour briefly to select a few, rather than to collect them all. Though the Apostles spake of him after he had appeared in flesh as the Mediator, yet all that I shall adduce will be adapted to prove his eternal Deity. In the first place, it is worthy of particular observation, that the apostle represents those things which were predicted concerning the eternal God, as either already exhibited in Christ, or to be accomplished in him at some future period. The prediction of Isaiah, that the Lord of Hosts would be "for a stone of stumbling, and for a rock of offence to both the houses of Israel," Paul asserts to have been fulfilled in Christ. Therefore he declares, that Christ is the Lord of Hosts. There is a similar instance in another place: "We shall all stand," says he, "before the judgment-seat of Christ. For it is written, As I live, saith the Lord, every knee shall bow to me, and every tongue shall confess to God." Since God, in Isaiah, declares this concerning himself, and Christ actually exhibits it in his own person, it follows, that he is that very God, whose glory cannot be transferred to another. The apostle's quotation from the Psalms also, in his Epistle to the Ephesians, is evidently applicable to none but God: "When he ascended up on high, he led captivity captive:" understanding that ascension to have been prefigured by the exertions of the Divine power in the signal victories of David over the heathen nations, he signifies, that the text was more fully accomplished in Christ. Thus John attests that it was the glory of the Son which was revealed in a vision to Isaiah; whereas the prophet himself records that he saw the majesty of God. And those praises which the Apostle, in the Epistle to the Hebrews, ascribes to the Son, beyond all doubt most evidently belong to God: "Thou, Lord, in the beginning, hast laid the foundation of the earth; and the heavens are the works of thine hands," &c. Again, "Let all the angels of God worship him." Nor is it any misapplication of them, when he refers them to Christ; since all that is predicted in those Psalms has been accomplished only by him. For it was He who arose and had mercy upon Zion; it was He who claimed as his own the dominion over all nations and islands. And why should John, after having affirmed, at the commencement of his Gospel, that the Word was always God, have hesitated to attribute to Christ the majesty of God? And why should Paul have been afraid to place Christ on the tribunal of God, after having so publicly preached his Divinity, when he called him "God blessed for ever?" And, to show how consistent he is with himself on this subject, he says, also, that "God was manifest in the flesh." If he is "God blessed for ever," he is the same to whom this apostle, in another place, affirms all glory and honour to be due. And he conceals not, but openly proclaims, that, "being in the form of God," he "thought it not robbery to be equal with God, but made himself of no reputation." And, lest the impious might object, that he is a sort of artificial God, John goes further, and affirms, that "This is the true God, and eternal life;" although we ought to be fully satisfied by his being called God, especially by a witness who expressly avers that there are no more gods than one; I mean Paul, who says, "though there be that are called gods, whether in heaven or in earth; to us there is but one God, of whom are all things." When we hear, from the same mouth, that "God was manifested in the flesh," that "God hath purchased the Church with his own blood,"—why do we imagine a second God, whom he by no means acknowledges? And there is no doubt that all the pious were of the same opinion. Thomas, likewise, by publicly confessing him to be "his Lord and God," declares him to be the same true God whom he had always worshipped.

XII. If we judge of his Divinity from the works which the Scriptures attribute to him, it will thence appear with increasing evidence. For when he said, that he had, from the beginning, continually coöperated with the Father, the Jews, stupid as they were about his other declarations, yet perceived, that he assumed to himself Divine power; and, therefore, as John informs us, they "sought the more to kill him; because he not only had broken the sabbath, but said also that God was his Father, making himself equal with God." How great, then, must be our stupidity, if we perceive not this passage to be a plain assertion of his Divinity! To preside over the world by his almighty providence, and to govern all things by the rod of his own power, (which the Apostle attributes to him,) belongs exclusively to the Creator. And he participates with the Father, not only in the government of the world, but also in all other offices, which cannot be communicated to creatures. The Lord proclaims, by the prophet, "I, even I, am he that blotteth out thy transgressions, for mine own sake." According to this declaration, when the Jews thought that Christ committed an injury against God, by undertaking to forgive sins, he not only asserted in express terms, that this power belonged to him, but proved it by a miracle. We see, therefore, that he hath not the ministry, but the power of remission of sins, which the Lord declares shall never be transferred from himself to another. Is it not the prerogative of God alone to examine and penetrate the secret thoughts of the heart? Yet Christ possessed that power; which is a proof of his Divinity.

XIII. But with what perspicuity of evidence does it appear in his miracles! Though I grant that the Prophets and Apostles performed miracles similar and equal to his, yet there is a considerable difference in this respect, that they, in their ministry, dispensed the favours of God, whereas his miracles were performed by his exertions of his own power. He sometimes, indeed, used prayer, that he might glorify the Father; but, in most instances, we perceive the manifest displays of his own power. And how should not he be the true author of miracles, who, by his own authority, committed the dispensation of them to others? For the Evangelists relate, that he gave his Apostles power to raise the dead, to heal the leprous, to cast out devils, &c. And they performed that ministry in such a manner, as plainly to discover, that the power proceeded solely from Christ. "In the name of Jesus Christ," says Peter, "arise and walk." It is no wonder, therefore, that Christ should bring forward his miracles, to convince the incredulity of the Jews, since, being performed by his own power, they afforded most ample evidence of his Divinity. Besides, if out of God there be no salvation, no righteousness, no life, but Christ contains all these things in himself, it certainly demonstrates him to be God. Let it not be objected, that life and salvation are infused into him by God; for he is not said to have received salvation, but to be himself salvation. And if no one be good but God alone, how can he be a mere man who is, I will not say good and righteous, but goodness and righteousness itself? Even from the beginning of the creation, according to the testimony of an Evangelist, "in him was life; and the life" then existed as "the light of men." Supported by such proofs, therefore, we venture to repose our faith and hope on him; whereas we know that it is impious and sacrilegious for any man to place his confidence in creatures. He says, "Ye believe in God, believe also in me." And in this sense Paul interprets two passages of Isaiah—"Whosoever believeth on him shall not be ashamed." Again, "There shall be a root of Jesse, that shall rise to reign over the Gentiles; in him shall the Gentiles trust." And why should we search for more testimonies from Scripture, when this declaration occurs so frequently, "He that believeth on me hath everlasting life"? The invocation, arising from faith, is also directed to him; which, nevertheless, peculiarly belongs, if any thing peculiarly belongs, to the Divine majesty. For a prophet says, "Whosoever shall call on the name of the Lord (Jehovah) shall be delivered." And Solomon, "The name of the Lord is a strong tower: the righteous runneth into it, and is safe." But the name of Christ is invoked for salvation: it follows, therefore, that he is Jehovah. Moreover, we have an example of such invocation in Stephen, when he says, "Lord Jesus, receive my spirit." And afterwards in the whole Church, as Ananias testifies in the same book: "Lord,

I have heard by many of this man, how much evil he hath done to thy saints—that call on thy name." And to make it more clearly understood, that "all the fulness of the Godhead dwelleth bodily in Christ," the Apostle confesses that he had introduced among the Corinthians no other doctrine than the knowledge of him, and that this had been the only subject of his preaching. What a remarkable and important consideration is it, that the name of the Son only is preached to us, whereas God commands us to glory in the knowledge of himself alone! Who can dare to assert that he is a mere creature, the knowledge of whom is our only glory? It must also be remarked, that the salutations prefixed to the epistles of Paul implore the same blessings from the Son as from the Father; whence we learn, not only that those things, which our heavenly Father bestows, are obtained for us by his intercession, but that the Son, by a communion of power, is himself the author of them. This practical knowledge is unquestionably more certain and solid than any idle speculation. For then the pious mind has the nearest view of the Divine presence, and almost touches it, when it experiences itself to be quickened, illuminated, saved, justified, and sanctified.

XIV. Wherefore the proof of the Deity of the Spirit must be derived principally from the same sources. There is no obscurity in the testimony of Moses, in the history of the creation, that the Spirit of God was expanded on the abyss or chaos; for it signifies, not only that the beautiful state of the world which we now behold owes its preservation to the power of the Spirit, but that, previously to its being thus adorned, the Spirit was engaged in brooding over the confused mass. The declaration of Isaiah bids defiance to all cavils: "And now the Lord God, and his Spirit, hath sent me." For the Holy Spirit is united in the exercise of supreme power in the mission of Prophets, which is a proof of his Divine majesty. But the best confirmation, as I have remarked, we shall derive from familiar experience. For what the Scriptures ascribe to him, and what we ourselves learn by the certain experience of piety, is not at all applicable to any creature. For it is he who, being universally diffused, sustains and animates all things in heaven and in earth. And this very thing excludes him from the number of creatures, that he is circumscribed by no limits, but transfuses through all his own vigorous influence, to inspire them with being, life, and motion: this is clearly a work of Deity. Again, if regeneration to an incorruptible life be more important and excellent than any present life, what must we think of him from whose power it proceeds? But the Scripture teaches, in various places, that he is the author of regeneration by a power not derived, but properly his own; and not of regeneration only, but likewise of the future immortality. Finally, to him, as well as to the Son, are applied all those offices which are peculiar to Deity. For he "searcheth even the deep things of God," who admits no creature to a share in his councils. He bestows wisdom and the faculty of speech; whereas the Lord declares to Moses, that this can only be done by himself. So through him we attain to a participation of God, to feel his vivifying energy upon us. Our justification is his work. From him proceed power, sanctification, truth, grace, and every other blessing we can conceive; since there is but one Spirit, from whom every kind of gifts descends. For this passage of Paul is worthy of particular attention: "There are diversities of gifts, and there are differences of administrations, but the same Spirit;" because it represents him, not only as the principle and source of them, but also as the author; which is yet more clearly expressed a little after in these words: "All these worketh that only and the self-same Spirit, dividing to every man severally as he will." For if he were not a subsistence in the Deity, judgment and voluntary determination would never be ascribed to him. Paul, therefore, very clearly attributes to the Spirit Divine power, and thereby demonstrates him to be an hypostasis or subsistence in God.

XV. Nor does the Scripture, when it speaks of him, refrain from giving him the appellation of God. For Paul concludes that we are the temple of God, because his Spirit dwelleth in us. This must not be passed over without particular notice; for the frequent promises of God, that he will choose us for a temple for himself, receive no other accomplishment, than by the inhabitation of his Spirit in us. Certainly, as Augustine excellently observes, "If we were commanded to erect to the Spirit a temple of wood and stone, forasmuch as God is the sole object of worship, it would be a clear proof of his Divinity; how much clearer, then, is the proof, now that we are commanded, not to erect one, but to be ourselves his temples!" And the Apostle calls us sometimes the temple of God, and sometimes the temple of the Holy Spirit, both in the same signification. Peter, reprehending Ananias for having "lied to the Holy Ghost," told him that he had "not lied unto men, but unto God." And where Isaiah introduces the Lord of hosts as the speaker, Paul informs us that it is the Holy Spirit who speaks. Indeed, while the Prophets invariably declare, that the words which they utter are those of the Lord of hosts, Christ and the Apostles refer them to the Holy Spirit; whence it follows, that he is the true Jehovah, who is the primary author of the prophecies. Again, God complains that his anger was provoked by the perverseness of the people; Isaiah, in reference to the same conduct, says, that "they vexed his Holy Spirit." Lastly, if blasphemy against the Spirit be not forgiven, either in this world or in that which is to come, whilst a man may obtain pardon who has been guilty of blasphemy against the Son, this is an open declaration of his Divine majesty, to defame or degrade which is an inexpiable crime. I intentionally pass over many testimonies which were used by the fathers. To them there appeared much plausibility in citing this passage from David, "By the word of the Lord were the heavens made, and all the host of them by the breath of his mouth;" to prove that the creation of the world was the work of the Holy Spirit, as well as of the Son. But since a repetition of the same thing twice is common in the Psalms, and in Isaiah "the spirit of his mouth" means the same as "his word," this is but a weak argument. Therefore I have determined to confine myself to a sober statement of those evidences on which pious minds may satisfactorily rest.

XVI. As God afforded a clearer manifestation of himself at the advent of Christ, the three Persons also then became better known. Among many testimonies, let us be satisfied with this one: Paul connects together these three, Lord, Faith, and Baptism, in such a manner as to reason from one to another. Since there is but one faith, hence he proves that there is but one Lord; since there is but one baptism, he shows that there is also but one faith. Therefore, if we are initiated by baptism into the faith and religion of one God, we must necessarily suppose him to be the true God, into whose name we are baptized. Nor can it be doubted but that in this solemn commission, "Baptize them in the name of the Father, and of the Son, and of the Holy Ghost," Christ intended to testify, that the perfect light of faith was now exhibited. For this is equivalent to being baptized into the name of the one God, who hath clearly manifested himself in the Father, Son, and Spirit; whence it evidently appears, that in the Divine Essence there exist three Persons, in whom is known the one God. And truly, since faith ought not to be looking about hither and thither, or to be wandering through the varieties of inconstancy, but to direct its views towards the one God, to be fixed on him, and to adhere to him,—it may easily be proved from these premises, that, if there be various kinds of faith, there must also be a plurality of gods. Baptism, being a sacrament of faith, confirms to us the unity of God, because it is but one. Hence, also, we conclude, that it is not lawful to be baptized, except into the name of the one God; because we embrace the faith of him, into whose name we are baptized. What, then, was intended by Christ, when he commanded baptism to be administered in the name of the Father, and of the Son, and of the Holy Spirit, but that one faith ought to be exercised in the Father, Son, and Spirit? and what is that but a clear testimony, that the Father, the Son, and the Holy Spirit, are the one God? Therefore, since it is an undeniable truth, that there is one God, and only one, we conclude the Word and Spirit to be no other than the very Essence of the Deity. The greatest degree of folly was betrayed by the Arians, who confessed the Divinity of the Son, but denied him to possess the substance of God. Nor were the Macedonians free from a similar delusion, who would explain the term "Spirit" to mean only the gifts of grace conferred upon man. For as wisdom, understanding, prudence, fortitude, and the fear of the Lord, proceed from him, so he alone is the Spirit of wisdom, prudence, fortitude, and piety. Nor is he himself divided according to the distribution of his graces; but, as the Apostle declares, how variously soever they are divided, he always remains one and the same.

XVII. On the other hand, also, we find in the Scriptures a distinction between the Father and the Word, between the Word and the Spirit; in the discussion of which the magnitude of the mystery reminds us that we ought to proceed with the utmost reverence and sobriety. I am exceedingly pleased with this observation of Gregory Nazianzen: "I cannot think of the *one*, but I am immediately surrounded with the splendour of the *three*; nor can I clearly discover the *three*, but I am suddenly carried back to the *one*." Wherefore let us not imagine such a trinity of Persons, as includes an idea of separation, or does not immediately recall us to the unity. The names of Father, Son, and Spirit, certainly imply a real distinction; let no one suppose them to be mere epithets, by which God is variously designated from his works; but it is a distinction, not a division. The passages already cited show, that the Son has a property, by which he is distinguished from the Father; because the Word had not been with God, or had his glory with the Father, unless he had been distinct from him. He likewise distinguishes the Father from himself, when he says, "that there is another that beareth witness of him." And to the same effect is what is declared in another place, that the Father created all things by the Word; which he could not have done, unless he had been in some sense distinct from him. Besides, the Father descended not to the earth, but he who came forth from the Father. The Father neither died nor rose again, but he who was sent by the Father. Nor did this distinction commence at the incarnation, but it is evident, that, before that period, he was the only begotten in the bosom of the Father. For who can undertake to assert, that the Son first entered into the bosom of the Father, when he descended from heaven to assume a human nature? He, therefore, was in the bosom of the Father before, and possessed his glory with the Father. The distinction between the Holy Spirit and the Father is announced by Christ, when he says, that he "proceedeth from the Father." But how often does he represent him as another, distinct from himself! as when he promises that "another Comforter" should be sent, and in many other places.

XVIII. I doubt the propriety of borrowing similitudes from human things, to express the force of this distinction. The fathers sometimes practise this method; but they likewise confess the great disproportion of all the similitudes which they introduce. Wherefore I greatly dread, in this instance, every degree of presumption; lest the introduction of any thing unseasonable should afford an occasion of calumny to the malicious, or of error to the ignorant. Yet it is not right to be silent on the distinction which we find expressed in the Scriptures; which is this—that to the Father is attributed the principle of action, the fountain and source of all things; to the Son, wisdom, counsel, and the arrangement of all operations; and the power and efficacy of the action is assigned to the Spirit. Moreover, though eternity belongs to the Father, and to the Son and Spirit also, since God can never have been destitute of his wisdom or his power, and in eternity we must not inquire after any thing prior or posterior,—yet the observation of order is not vain or superfluous, while the Father is mentioned as first; in the next place the Son, as from him; and then the Spirit, as from both. For the mind of every man naturally inclines to the consideration, first, of God; secondly, of the wisdom emanating from him; and lastly, of the power by which he executes the decrees of his wisdom. For this reason the Son is said to be from the Father, and the Spirit from both the Father and the Son; and that in various places, but nowhere more clearly than in the eighth chapter of the Epistle to the Romans, where the same Spirit is indifferently denominated "the Spirit of Christ," and "the Spirit of him that raised up Christ from the dead," and that without any impropriety. For Peter also testifies that it was the Spirit of Christ by whom the prophets prophesied; whereas the Scripture so frequently declares that it was the Spirit of God the Father.

XIX. This distinction is so far from opposing the most absolute simplicity and unity of the Divine Being, that it affords a proof that the Son is one God with the Father, because he has the same Spirit with him; and that the Spirit is not a different substance from the Father and the Son, because he is the Spirit of the Father and of the Son. For the whole nature is in each hypostasis, and each has something peculiar to himself. The Father is entirely in the Son, and the Son entirely in the Father, according to his own declaration, "I am in the Father, and the Father in me;" nor do ecclesiastical writers allow that one is divided from the other by any difference of essence. "These distinctive appellations," says Augustine, "denote their reciprocal relations to each other, and not the substance itself, which is but one." This explanation may serve to reconcile the opinions of the fathers, which would otherwise appear totally repugnant to each other. For sometimes they state that the Son originates from the Father, and at other times assert that he has essential Divinity from himself, and so is, together with the Father, the one first cause of all. Augustine, in another place, admirably and perspicuously explains the cause of this diversity, in the following manner: "Christ, considered in himself, is called God; but with relation to the Father, he is called the Son." And again, "The Father, considered in himself, is called God; but with relation to the Son, he is called the Father. He who, with relation to the Son, is called the Father, is not the Son; he who, with relation to the Father, is called the Son, is not the Father; they who are severally called the Father and the Son, are the same God." Therefore, when we speak simply of the Son, without reference to the Father, we truly and properly assert him to be self-existent, and therefore call him the sole first cause; but, when we distinctly treat of the relation between him and the Father, we justly represent him as originating from the Father. The first book of Augustine on the Trinity is entirely occupied with the explication of this subject; and it is far more safe to rest satisfied with that relation which he states, than by curiously penetrating into the sublime mystery, to wander through a multitude of vain speculations.

XX. Therefore, let such as love sobriety, and will be contented with the measure of faith, briefly attend to what is useful to be known; which is, that, when we profess to believe in one God, the word *God* denotes a single and simple essence, in which we comprehend three Persons, or hypostases; and that, therefore, whenever the word *God* is used indefinitely, the Son and Spirit are intended as much as the Father; but when the Son is associated with the Father, that introduces the reciprocal relation of one to the other; and thus we distinguish between the Persons. But, since the peculiar properties of the Persons produce a certain order, so that the original cause is in the Father, whenever the Father and the Son or Spirit are mentioned together, the name of God is peculiarly ascribed to the Father: by this method the unity of the essence is preserved, and the order is retained; which, however, derogates nothing from the Deity of the Son and Spirit. And indeed, as we have already seen that the Apostles assert him to be the Son of God, whom Moses and the Prophets have represented as Jehovah, it is always necessary to recur to the unity of the essence. Wherefore it would be a detestable sacrilege for us to call the Son another God different from the Father; because the simple name of God admits of no relation; nor can God, with respect to himself, be denominated either the one or the other. Now, that the name "Jehovah," in an indefinite sense, is applicable to Christ, appears even from the words of Paul: "for this thing I besought the Lord thrice;" because, after relating the answer of Christ, "My grace is sufficient for thee," he immediately subjoins, "That the power of Christ may rest upon me." For it is certain that the word "Lord" is there used for "Jehovah;" and to restrict it to the person of the Mediator, would be frivolous and puerile, since it is an absolute declaration, containing no comparison between the Son and the Father. And we know that the Apostles, following the custom of the Greek translators, invariably use the word Κυριος, (Lord,) instead of Jehovah. And, not to seek far for an example of this, Paul prayed to the Lord in no other sense than is intended in a passage of Joel, cited by Peter: "Whosoever shall call on the name of the Lord shall be saved." But for the peculiar ascription of this name to the Son, another reason will be given in its proper place; suffice it at present to observe that, when Paul had prayed to God absolutely, he immediately subjoins the name of Christ. Thus also the whole Deity is by Christ himself denominated "a Spirit." For nothing opposes the spirituality of the whole Divine essence, in which are comprehended the Father, the Son, and the Spirit; which is plain from the Scripture. For as we there find God denominated a Spirit, so we find also the Holy Spirit, forasmuch as he is an hypostasis of the whole essence, represented both as the Spirit of God, and as proceeding from God.

XXI. But since Satan, in order to subvert the very foundations of our faith, has always been exciting great contentions concerning the Divine essence of the Son and Spirit, and the distinction of the Persons; and in almost all ages has instigated impious spirits to vex the orthodox teachers on this account; and is also endeavouring, in the present day, with the old embers, to kindle a new flame; it becomes necessary here to refute the perverse and fanciful notions which some persons have imbibed. Hitherto it has been our principal design to instruct the docile, and not to combat the obstinate and contentious: but now, having calmly explained and proved the truth, we must vindicate it from all the cavils of the wicked; although I shall make it my principal study, that those who readily and implicitly attend to the Divine word, may have stable ground on which they may confidently rest. On this, indeed, if on any of the secret mysteries of the Scripture, we ought to philosophize with great sobriety and moderation; and also with extreme caution, lest either our ideas or our language should proceed beyond the limits of the Divine word. For how can the infinite essence of God be defined by the narrow capacity of the human mind, which could never yet certainly determine the nature of the body of the sun, though the object of our daily contemplation? How can the human mind, by its own efforts, penetrate into an examination of the essence of God, when it is totally ignorant of its own? Wherefore let us freely leave to God the knowledge of himself. For "he alone," as Hilary says, "is a competent witness for himself, being only known by himself." And we shall certainly leave it to him, if our conceptions of him correspond to the manifestations which he has given us of himself, and our inquiries concerning him are confined to his word. There are extant on this argument five homilies of Chrysostom against the Anomœi; which, however, were not sufficient to restrain the presumptuous garrulity of those sophists. For they discovered no greater modesty in this instance than in every other. The very unhappy consequences of this temerity should warn us to study this question with more docility than subtlety, and not allow ourselves to investigate God any where but in his sacred word, or to form any ideas of him but such as are agreeable to his word, or to speak any thing concerning him but what is derived from the same word. But if the distinction of Father, Son, and Spirit, in the one Deity, as it is not easy to be comprehended, occasions some understandings more labour and trouble than is desirable, let them remember that the mind of man, when it indulges its curiosity, enters into a labyrinth; and let them submit to be guided by the heavenly oracles, however they may not comprehend the height of this mystery.

XXII. To compose a catalogue of the errors, by which the purity of the faith has been attacked on this point of doctrine, would be too prolix and tedious, without being profitable; and most of the heretics so strenuously exerted themselves to effect the total extinction of the Divine glory by their gross reveries, that they thought it sufficient to unsettle and disturb the inexperienced. From a few men there soon arose numerous sects, of whom some would divide the Divine essence, and others would confound the distinction which subsists between the Persons. But if we maintain, what has already been sufficiently demonstrated from the Scripture, that the essence of the one God, which pertains to the Father, to the Son, and to the Spirit, is simple and undivided, and, on the other hand, that the Father is, by some property, distinguished from the Son, and likewise the Son from the Spirit, the gate will be shut, not only against Arius and Sabellius, but also against all the other ancient heresiarchs. But since our own times have witnessed some madmen, as Servetus and his followers, who have involved every thing in new subtleties, a brief exposure of their fallacies will not be unuseful. The word *Trinity* was so odious and even detestable to Servetus, that he asserted all Trinitarians, as he called them, to be Atheists. I omit his impertinent and scurrilous language, but this was the substance of his speculations: That it is representing God as consisting of three parts, when three Persons are said to subsist in his essence, and that this triad is merely imaginary, being repugnant to the Divine unity. At the same time, he maintained the Persons to be certain external ideas, which have no real subsistence in the Divine essence, but give us a figurative representation of God, under this or the other form; and that in the beginning there was no distinction in God, because the Word was once the same as the Spirit; but that, after Christ appeared God of God, there emanated from him another God, even the Spirit. Though he sometimes glosses over his impertinencies with allegories, as when he says, that the eternal Word of God was the Spirit of Christ with God, and the reflection of his image, and that the Spirit was a shadow of the Deity, yet he afterwards destroys the Deity of both, asserting that, according to the mode of dispensation, there is a part of God in both the Son and the Spirit; just as the same Spirit, substantially diffused in us, and even in wood and stones, is a portion of the Deity. What he broached concerning the Person of the Mediator, we shall examine in the proper place. But this monstrous fiction, that a Divine Person is nothing but a visible appearance of the glory of God, will not need a prolix refutation. For when John pronounces that the Word (Λογος) was God before the creation of the world, he sufficiently discriminates him from an ideal form. But if then also, and from the remotest eternity, that Word (Λογος) who was God, was with the Father, and possessed his own glory with the Father, he certainly could not be an external or figurative splendour; but it necessarily follows, that he was a real hypostasis, subsisting in God himself. But although no mention is made of the Spirit, but in the history of the creation of the world, yet he is there introduced, not as a shadow, but as the essential power of God, since Moses relates that the chaotic mass was supported by him. It then appeared, therefore, that the eternal Spirit had always existed in the Deity, since he cherished and sustained the confused matter of the heaven and earth, till it attained a state of beauty and order. He certainly could not then be an image or representation of God, according to the dreams of Servetus. But in other places he is constrained to make a fuller disclosure of his impiety, saying that God, in his eternal reason, decreeing for himself a visible Son, has visibly exhibited himself in this manner; for if this be true, there is no other Divinity left to Christ, than as he has been appointed a Son by an eternal decree of God. Besides, he so transforms those phantasms, which he substitutes instead of the hypostases, that he hesitates not to imagine new accidents or properties in God. But the most execrable blasphemy of all is, his promiscuous confusion of the Son of God and the Spirit with all the creatures. For he asserts that in the Divine essence there are parts and divisions, every portion of which is God; and especially that the souls of the faithful are coëternal and consubstantial with God; though in another place he assigns substantial Deity, not only to the human soul, but to all created things.

XXIII. From the same corrupt source has proceeded another heresy, equally monstrous. For some worthless men, to escape the odium and disgrace which attended the impious tenets of Servetus, have confessed, indeed, that there are three Persons, but with this explanation, that the Father, who alone is truly and properly God, hath created the Son and Spirit, and transfused his Deity into them. Nor do they refrain from this dreadful manner of expressing themselves, that the Father is distinguished from the Son and Spirit, as being the sole possessor of the Divine essence. Their first plea in support of this notion is, that Christ is commonly called the Son of God; whence they conclude that no other is properly God but the Father. But they observe not, that although the name of God is common also to the Son, yet that it is sometimes ascribed to the Father (κατ' ἐξοχην) by way of eminence, because he is the fountain and original of the Deity; and this in order to denote the simple unity of the essence. They object, that if he is truly the Son of God, it is absurd to account him the Son of a Person. I reply, that both are true; that he is the Son of God, because he is the Word begotten of the Father before time began, for we are not yet speaking of the Person of the Mediator; and to be explicit, we must notice the Person, that the name of God may not be understood absolutely, but for the Father; for if we acknowledge no other to be God than the Father, it will be a manifest degradation of the dignity of the Son. Whenever mention is made of the Deity, therefore, there must no opposition be admitted between the Father and the Son, as though the name of the true God belonged exclusively to the Father. For surely the God who appeared to Isaiah, was the only true God; whom, nevertheless, John affirms to have been Christ. He likewise, who by the mouth of Isaiah declared that he was to be a rock of offence to the Jews, was the only true God; whom Paul pronounces to have been Christ. He who proclaims by Isaiah, "As I live, every knee shall bow to me," is the only true God; but Paul applies the same to Christ. To the same purpose are the testimonies recited by the Apostle—"Thou, Lord, hast laid the foundation of the earth and the heavens;" and "Let all the angels of God worship him." These ascriptions belong only to the one true God; whereas he contends that they are properly applied to Christ. Nor is there any force in that cavil, that what is proper to God is transferred to Christ, because he is the brightness of his glory. For, since the name Jehovah is used in each of these passages, it follows that in respect of his Deity he is self-existent. For, if he is Jehovah, he cannot be denied to be the same God, who in another place proclaims by Isaiah, "I am the first and I am the last; and beside me there is no God." That passage in Jeremiah also deserves our attention—"The gods that have not made the heavens and the earth, even they shall perish from the earth, and from under these heavens;" whilst, on the contrary, it must be acknowledged, that the Deity of the Son of God is frequently proved by Isaiah from the creation of the world. But how shall the Creator, who gives existence to all, not be self-existent, but derive his essence from another? For whoever asserts that the Son owes his essence to the Father, denies him to be self-existent. But this is contradicted by the Holy Spirit, who gives him the name of Jehovah. Now, if we admit the whole essence to be solely in the Father, either it will be divisible, or it will be taken away from the Son; and so, being despoiled of his essence, he will be only a titular god. The Divine essence, according to these triflers, belongs solely to the Father, inasmuch as he alone possesses it, and is the author of the essence of the Son. Thus the Divinity of the Son will be a kind of emanation from the essence of God, or a derivation of a part from the whole. Now, they must of necessity concede, from their own premises, that the Spirit is the Spirit of the Father only; because if he be a derivation from the original essence, which belongs exclusively to the Father, he cannot be accounted the Spirit of the Son; which is refuted by the testimony of Paul, where he makes him common to Christ and the Father. Besides, if the Person of the Father be expunged from the Trinity, wherein will he differ from the Son and Spirit, but in being himself the sole Deity? They confess that Christ is God, and yet differs from the Father. Some distinctive character is necessary, also, to discriminate the Father from the Son. They who place this in the essence, manifestly destroy the true Deity of Christ, which cannot exist independently of the essence, that is, of the entire essence. The Father certainly cannot differ from the Son, unless he have something peculiar to himself, which is not common to the Son. What will they find, by which to distinguish him? If the difference be in the essence, let them tell us whether he has communicated the same to the Son. But this could not be done partially; for it would be an abomination to fabricate a demigod. Besides, this would miserably dismember the Divine essence. The necessary conclusion then is, that it is entirely and perfectly common to the Father and the Son. And if this be true, there cannot, in respect of the essence, be any difference between them. If it be objected that the Father, notwithstanding this communication of his essence, remains the only God with whom the essence continues, then Christ must be a figurative god, a god in appearance and name only, not in reality; because nothing is more proper to God than to be, according to that declaration, "I AM hath sent me unto you."

XXIV. We might readily prove from many passages the falsehood of their assumption, that, whenever the name of God is mentioned absolutely in the Scripture, it means only the Father. And in those places which they cite in their own defence, they shamefully betray their ignorance, since the Son is there added; from which it appears, that the name of God is used in a relative sense, and therefore is particularly restricted to the Person of the Father. Their objection, that, unless the Father alone were the true God, he would himself be his own Father, is answered in a word. For there is no absurdity in the name of God, for the sake of dignity and order, being peculiarly given to him, who not only hath begotten of himself his own wisdom, but is also the God of the Mediator, of which I shall treat more at large in its proper place. For since Christ was manifested in the flesh, he is called the Son of God, not only as he was the eternal Word begotten of the Father before time began, but because he assumed the person and office of a Mediator, to unite us to God. And since they so presumptuously exclude the Son from Divine honours, I would wish to be informed, when he declares that there is none good but the one God, whether he deprives himself of all goodness. I speak not of his human nature, lest they should object, that, whatever goodness it had, it was gratuitously conferred on it. I demand whether the eternal Word of God be good or not. If they answer in the negative, they are sufficiently convicted of impiety; and if in the affirmative, they cut the throat of their own system. But though, at the first glance, Christ seems to deny himself the appellation of good, he furnishes, notwithstanding, a further confirmation of our opinion. For, as that is a title which peculiarly belongs to the one God, forasmuch as he had been saluted as good, merely according to a common custom, by his rejection of false honour, he suggested that the goodness which he possessed was Divine. I demand, also, when Paul affirms that God alone is immortal, wise, and true, whether he thereby degrades Christ to the rank of those who are mortal, unwise, and false. Shall not he then be immortal who from the beginning was life itself, and the giver of immortality to angels? Shall not he be wise who is the eternal Wisdom of God? Shall not he be true who is truth itself? I demand further, whether they think that Christ ought to be worshipped. For, if he justly claims this as his right, that every knee should bow before him, it follows that he is that God, who, in the law, prohibited the worship of any one but himself. If they will have this passage in Isaiah, "I am, and there is no God besides me," to be understood solely of the Father, I retort this testimony on themselves; since we see that whatever belongs to God is attributed to Christ. Nor is there any room for their cavil, that Christ was exalted in the humanity in which he had been abased; and that, with regard to his humanity, all power was given to him in heaven and in earth; because, although the regal and judicial majesty extends to the whole Person of the Mediator, yet, had he not been God manifested in the flesh, he could not have been exalted to such an eminence, without God being in opposition to himself. And Paul excellently determines this controversy, by informing us that he was equal with God, before he abased himself under the form of a servant. Now, how could this equality subsist, unless he had been that God whose name is JAH and JEHOVAH, who rides on the cherubim, whose kingdom is universal and everlasting? No clamour of theirs can deprive Christ of another declaration of Isaiah: "Lo, this is our God, we have waited for him;" since in these words he describes the advent of God the Redeemer, not only for the deliverance of the people from exile in Babylon, but also for the complete restoration of the church. Nor do they gain any thing by another cavil, that Christ was God in his Father. For although we confess, in point of order and degree, that the Father is the fountain of the Deity, yet we pronounce it a detestable figment, that the essence belongs exclusively to the Father, as though he were the author of the Deity of the Son; because, on this supposition, either the essence would be divided, or Christ would be only a titular and imaginary god. If they admit that the Son is God, but inferior to the Father, then in him the essence must be begotten and created, which in the Father is unbegotten and uncreated. I know that some scorners ridicule our concluding a distinction of Persons from the words of Moses, where he introduces God thus speaking: "Let us make man in our image." Yet pious readers perceive how frigidly and foolishly Moses would have introduced this conference, if in one God there had not subsisted a plurality of Persons. Now, it is certain that they whom the Father addressed, were uncreated; but there is nothing uncreated, except the one God himself. Now, therefore, unless they grant that the power to create, and the authority to command, were common to the Father, the Son, and the Spirit, it will follow, that God did not speak thus within himself, but directed his conversation to some exterior agents. Lastly, one place will easily remove their two objections at once. For when Christ himself declares, that God is a Spirit, it would be unreasonable to restrict this solely to the Father, as though the Word were not also of a spiritual nature. But if the name of Spirit is equally as applicable to the Son as to the Father, I conclude that the Son is comprehended under the indefinite name of God. Yet he immediately subjoins, that none are approved worshippers of the Father, but those who worship him in spirit and in truth. Whence follows another consequence, that, because Christ performs the office of a Teacher, in a station of inferiority, he ascribes the name of God to the Father, not to destroy his own Deity, but by degrees to raise us to the knowledge of it.

XXV. But they deceive themselves in dreaming of three separate individuals, each of them possessing a part of the Divine essence. We teach, according to the Scriptures, that there is essentially but one God; and, therefore, that the essence of both the Son and the Spirit is unbegotten. But since the Father is first in order, and hath of himself begotten his wisdom, therefore, as has before been observed, he is justly esteemed the original and fountain of the whole Divinity. Thus God, indefinitely, is unbegotten; and the Father also is unbegotten with regard to his Person. They even foolishly suppose, that our opinion implies a quaternity; whereas they are guilty of falsehood and calumny, in ascribing to us a figment of their own; as though we pretended that the three Persons are as so many streams proceeding from one essence, when it is evident, from our writings, that we separate not the Persons from the essence, but, though they subsist in it, make a distinction between them. If the persons were separated from the essence, there would perhaps be some probability in their argument; but then there would be a trinity of Gods, not a trinity of persons contained in one God. This solves their frivolous question, whether the essence concurs to the formation of the Trinity; as though we imagined three Gods to descend from it. Their objection, that then the Trinity would be without God, is equally impertinent. Because, though it concurs not to the distinction as a part or member, yet the Persons are not independent of it, nor separate from it; for the Father, unless he were God, could not be the Father; and the Son is the Son only as he is God. Therefore we say, that the Deity is absolutely self-existent; whence we confess, also, that the Son, as God, independently of the consideration of Person, is self-existent; but as the Son, we say, that he is of the Father. Thus his essence is unoriginated; but the origin of his Person is God himself. And, indeed, the orthodox writers, who have written on the Trinity, have referred this name only to the Persons; since to comprehend the essence in that distinction, were not only an absurd error, but a most gross impiety. For it is evident that those who maintain that the Trinity consists in a union of the Essence, the Son, and the Spirit, annihilate the essence of the Son and of the Spirit; otherwise the parts would be destroyed by being confounded together; which is a fault in every distinction. Finally, if the words *Father* and *God* were synonymous—if the Father were the author of the Deity—nothing would be left in the Son but a mere shadow; nor would the Trinity be any other than a conjunction of the one God with two created things.

XXVI. Their objection, that Christ, if he be properly God, is not rightly called the Son of God, has already been answered; for when a comparison is made between one Person and another, the word *God* is not used indefinitely, but is restricted to the Father, as being the fountain of the Deity, not with regard to the essence, as fanatics falsely pretend, but in respect of order. This is the sense in which we ought to understand that declaration of Christ to his Father: "This is life eternal, that they might know thee, the only true God, and Jesus Christ, whom thou hast sent." For, speaking in the capacity of Mediator, he holds an intermediate station between God and men; yet without any diminution of his majesty. For, although he abased himself, yet he lost not his glory with the Father, which was hidden from the world. Thus the Apostle to the Hebrews, though he acknowledges that Christ was made for a short time inferior to the angels, yet, nevertheless, hesitates not to assert, that he is the eternal God, who laid the foundation of the earth. We must remember, therefore, that whenever Christ, in the capacity of Mediator, addresses the Father, he comprehends, under the name of God, the Divinity which belongs also to himself. Thus, when he said to his Apostles, "I go unto the Father, for my Father is greater than I," he attributes not to himself a secondary Divinity, as if he were inferior to the Father with respect to the eternal essence, but because, having obtained the glory of heaven, he gathers together the faithful to a participation of it with him; he represents the Father to be in a station superior to himself, just as the illustrious perfection of the splendour which appears in heaven excels that degree of glory which was visible in him during his incarnate state. For the same reason, Paul says, in another place, that Christ "shall deliver up the kingdom to God, even the Father, that God may be all in all." Nothing would be more absurd than to deny perpetual duration to the Deity of Christ. Now, if he will never cease to be the Son of God, but will remain for ever the same as he has been from the beginning, it follows, that by the name *Father* is intended the one sole Divine essence, which is common to them both. And it is certain that Christ descended to us, in order that, exalting us to the Father, he might at the same time exalt us to himself also, as being one with the Father. It is therefore neither lawful nor right to restrict the name of God exclusively to the Father, and to deny it to the Son. For even on this very account John asserts him to be the true God, that no one might suppose, that he possessed only a secondary degree of Deity, inferior to the Father. And I wonder what can be the meaning of these fabricators of new gods, when, after confessing that Christ is the true

God, they immediately exclude him from the Deity of the Father; as though there could be any true God but one alone, or as though a transfused Divinity were any thing but a novel fiction.

XXVII. Their accumulation of numerous passages from Irenæus, where he asserts the Father of Christ to be the only and eternal God of Israel, is a proof either of shameful ignorance, or of consummate wickedness. For they ought to have considered, that that holy man was then engaged in a controversy with some madmen, who denied that the Father of Christ was the same God that has spoken by Moses and the Prophets, but maintained that he was I know not what sort of phantasm, produced from the corruption of the world. His only object, therefore, is to show that no other God is revealed in the Scripture than the Father of Christ, and that it is impious to imagine any other; and therefore we need not wonder at his frequently concluding, that there never was any other God of Israel than he who was preached by Christ and his Apostles. So, now, on the other hand, when a different error is to be opposed, we shall truly assert, that the God who appeared formerly to the patriarchs, was no other than Christ. If it be objected that it was the Father, we are prepared to reply, that, while we contend for the Divinity of the Son, we by no means reject that of the Father. If the reader attends to this design of Irenæus, all contention will cease. Moreover, the whole controversy is easily decided by the sixth chapter of the third book, where the good man insists on this one point: That he who is absolutely and indefinitely called God in the Scripture, is the only true God; but that the name of God is given absolutely to Christ. Let us remember that the point at issue, as appears from the whole treatise, and particularly from the forty-sixth chapter of the second book, was this: That the appellation of Father is not given in an enigmatical and parabolical sense to one who is not truly God. Besides, in another place he contends, that the Son is called God, as well as the Father, by the Prophets and Apostles. He afterwards states how Christ, who is Lord, and King, and God, and Judge of all, received power from him who is God of all; and that is with relation to the subjection in which he was humbled even to the death of the cross. And a little after he affirms, that the Son is the Creator of heaven and earth, who gave the law by the hand of Moses, and appeared to the patriarchs. Now, if any one pretends that Irenæus acknowledges the Father alone as the God of Israel, I shall reply, as is clearly maintained by the same writer, that Christ is one and the same; as also he applies to him the prophecy of Habakkuk: "God shall come from the south." To the same purpose is what we find in the ninth chapter of the fourth book: "Therefore Christ himself is, with the Father, the God of the living." And in the twelfth chapter of the same book he states, that Abraham believed in God, inasmuch as Christ is the Creator of heaven and earth, and the only God.

XXVIII. Their pretensions to the sanction of Tertullian are equally unfounded, for, notwithstanding the occasional harshness and obscurity of his mode of expression, yet he unequivocally teaches the substance of the doctrine which we are defending; that is, that whereas there is one God, yet by dispensation or economy there is his Word; that there is but one God in the unity of the substance, but that the unity, by a mysterious dispensation, is disposed into a trinity; that there are three, not in condition, but in degree; not in substance, but in form; not in power, but in order. He says, indeed, that he maintains the Son to be second to the Father; but he applies this only to the distinction of the Persons. He says somewhere, that the Son is visible; but after having stated arguments on both sides, he concludes that, as the Word, he is invisible. Lastly, his assertion that the Father is designated by his Person, proves him to be at the greatest distance from the notion which we are refuting. And though he acknowledges no other God than the Father, yet the explanations which he gives in the immediate context show that he speaks not to the exclusion of the Son, when he denies the existence of any other God than the Father; and that therefore the unity of Divine government is not violated by the distinction of persons. And from the nature and design of his argument it is easy to gather the meaning of his words. For he contends, in opposition to Praxeas, that although God is distinguished into three Persons, yet neither is there a plurality of gods, nor is the unity divided. And because, according to the erroneous notion of Praxeas, Christ could not be God, without being the Father, therefore Tertullian bestows so much labour upon the distinction. His calling the Word and Spirit a portion of the whole, though a harsh expression, yet is excusable; since it has no reference to the substance, but only denotes the disposition and economy, which belongs solely to the Persons, according to the testimony of Tertullian himself. Hence also that question, "How many Persons suppose you that there are, O most perverse Praxeas, but as many as there are names?" So, a little after, "that they may believe the Father and the Son, both in their names and Persons." These arguments, I conceive, will suffice to refute the impudence of those who make use of the authority of Tertullian in order to deceive the minds of the simple.

XXIX. And certainly, whoever will diligently compare the writings of the fathers, will find in Irenæus nothing different from what was advanced by others who succeeded him. Justin Martyr is one of the most ancient; and he agrees with us in every point. They may object that the Father of Christ is denominated the one God by him as well as by the rest. The same is asserted also by Hilary, and even in harsher terms: he says, that eternity is in the Father; but does this imply a denial of the Divine essence to the Son? On the contrary, he had no other design than to maintain the same faith which we hold. Nevertheless, they are not ashamed to cull out mutilated passages, in order to induce a belief that he patronized their error. If they wish any authority to be attached to their quotation of Ignatius, let them prove that the Apostles delivered any law concerning Lent, and similar corruptions; for nothing can be more absurd than the impertinencies which have been published under the name of Ignatius. Wherefore their impudence is more intolerable, who disguise themselves under such false colours for the purpose of deception. Moreover, the consent of antiquity manifestly appears from this circumstance, that in the Nicene Council, Arius never dared to defend himself by the authority of any approved writer; and not one of the Greek or Latin fathers, who were there united against him, excused himself as at all dissenting from his predecessors. With regard to Augustine, who experienced great hostility from these disturbers, his diligent examination of all the writings of the earlier fathers, and his respectful attention to them, need not be mentioned. If he differs from them in the smallest particulars, he assigns the reasons which oblige him to dissent from them. On this argument also, if he finds any thing ambiguous or obscure in others, he never conceals it. Yet he takes it for granted, that the doctrine which those men oppose has been received without controversy from the remotest antiquity; and yet that he was not uninformed of what others had taught before him, appears even from one word in the first book of his Treatise on the Christian Doctrine, where he says, that unity is in the Father. Will they pretend that he had then forgotten himself? But he elsewhere vindicates himself from this calumny, where he calls the Father the fountain of the whole Deity, because he is from no other; wisely considering that the name of God is especially ascribed to the Father, because, unless the original be from him, it is impossible to conceive of the simple unity of the Deity. These observations, I hope, will be approved by the pious reader, as sufficient to refute all the calumnies, with which Satan has hitherto laboured to pervert or obscure the purity of this doctrine. Finally, I trust that the whole substance of this doctrine has been faithfully stated and explained, provided my readers set bounds to their curiosity, and are not unreasonably fond of tedious and intricate controversies. For I have not the least expectation of giving satisfaction to those who are pleased with an intemperance of speculation. I am sure I have used no artifice in the omission of any thing, from a supposition that it would make against me. But, studying the edification of the Church, I have thought it better not to touch upon many things, which would be unnecessarily burdensome to the reader, without yielding him any profit. For to what purpose is it to dispute, whether the Father be always begetting? For it is foolish to imagine a continual act of generation, since it is evident that three Persons have subsisted in God from all eternity.

4.

Man, In His Present State, Despoiled of Freedom of Will, and Subjected to a Miserable Slavery.

Since we have seen that the domination of sin, from the time of its subjugation of the first man, not only extends over the whole race, but also exclusively possesses every soul, it now remains to be more closely investigated, whether we are despoiled of all freedom, and, if any particle of it yet remain, how far its power extends. But, that we may the more easily discover the truth of this question, I will first set up by the way a mark, by which our whole course must be regulated. The best method of guarding against error is to consider the dangers which threaten us on every side. For when man is declared to be destitute of all rectitude, he immediately makes it an occasion of slothfulness; and because he is said to have no power of himself for the pursuit of righteousness, he totally neglects it, as though it did not at all concern him. On the other hand, he cannot arrogate any thing to himself, be it ever so little, without God being robbed of his honour, and himself being endangered by presumptuous temerity. Therefore, to avoid striking on either of these rocks, this will be the course to be pursued—that man, being taught that he has nothing good left in his possession, and being surrounded on every side with the most miserable necessity, should, nevertheless, be instructed to aspire to the good of which he is destitute, and to the liberty of which he is deprived; and should be roused from indolence with more earnestness, than if he were supposed to be possessed of the greatest strength. The necessity of the latter is obvious to every one. The former, I perceive, is doubted by more than it ought to be. For this being placed beyond all controversy, that man must not be deprived of any thing that properly belongs to him, it ought also to be manifest how important it is that he should be prevented from false boasting. For if he was not even then permitted to glory in himself, when by the Divine beneficence he was decorated with the noblest ornaments, how much ought he now to be humbled, when, on account of his ingratitude, he has been hurled from the summit of glory to the abyss of ignominy! At that time, I say, when he was exalted to the most honourable eminence, the Scripture attributes nothing to him, but that he was created after the image of God; which certainly implies that his happiness consisted not in any goodness of his own, but in a participation of God. What, then, remains for him now, deprived of all glory, but that he acknowledge God, to whose beneficence he could not be thankful, when he abounded in the riches of his favour? and that he now, at least, by a confession of his poverty, glorify him, whom he glorified not by an acknowledgment of his blessings? It is also no less conducive to our interests than to the Divine glory, that all the praise of wisdom and strength be taken away from us; so that they join sacrilege to our fall, who ascribe to us any thing more than truly belongs to us. For what else is the consequence, when we are taught to contend in our own strength, but that we are lifted into the air on a reed, which being soon broken, we fall to the ground. Though our strength is placed in too favourable a point of view, when it is compared to a reed. For it is nothing but smoke, whatever vain men have imagined and pretend concerning it. Wherefore it is not without reason, that that remarkable sentence is so frequently repeated by Augustine, that free will is rather overthrown than established even by its own advocates. It was necessary to premise these things for the sake of some, who, when they hear that human power is completely subverted in order that the power of God may be established in man, inveterately hate this whole argument, as dangerous and unprofitable; which yet appears to be highly useful to us, and essential to true religion.

II. As we have just before said that the faculties of the soul consist in the mind and the heart, let us now consider the ability of each. The philosophers, indeed, with general consent, pretend, that in the mind presides Reason, which like a lamp illuminates with its counsels, and like a queen governs the will; for that it is so irradiated with Divine light as to be able to give the best counsels, and endued with such vigour as to be qualified to govern in the most excellent manner; that Sense, on the contrary, is torpid and afflicted with weakness of sight, so that it always creeps on the ground, and is absorbed in the grossest objects, nor ever elevates itself to a view of the truth; that Appetite, if it can submit to the obedience of reason, and resist the attractions of sense, is inclined to the practice of virtues, travels the path of rectitude, and is formed into will; but that, if it be devoted to the servitude of sense, it is thereby so corrupted and depraved as to degenerate into lust. And as, according to their opinion, there reside in the soul those faculties which I have before mentioned, understanding, sense, and appetite, or will,—which appellation is now more commonly used,—they assert that the understanding is endued with reason, that most excellent guide to a good and a happy life, provided it only maintains itself in its own excellence, and exerts its innate power; but that the inferior affection of the soul, which is called *sense*, and by which it is seduced into error, is of such a nature that it may be tamed and gradually conquered by the rod of reason. They place the will in the middle station between reason and sense, as perfectly at liberty, whether it chooses to obey reason, or to submit to the violence of sense.

III. Sometimes, indeed, being convinced by the testimony of experience, they admit how extremely difficult it is for a man to establish within him the kingdom of reason; while he is exposed at one time to the solicitations of alluring pleasures, at another to the delusions of pretended blessings, and at others to the violent agitations of immoderate passions, compared by Plato to so many cords dragging him in various directions. For which reason Cicero says that the sparks kindled by nature are soon extinguished by corrupt opinions and evil manners. But when such maladies have once taken possession of the human mind, they acknowledge their progress to be too violent to be easily restrained; nor do they hesitate to compare them to fierce horses, who, having rejected reason, like horses that have thrown off the charioteer, indulge themselves in every extravagance, without the least restraint. But they consider it as beyond all controversy, that virtue and vice are in our own power; for if it be at our election, they say, to do this or that, therefore it must also be, to abstain from doing it. And, on the other hand, if we are free to abstain from it, we must also be free to do it. But we appear freely and voluntarily to do those things which we do, and to abstain from those things from which we abstain; therefore, if we do any good action, when we please we may omit it; if we perpetrate any evil, that also we may avoid. Moreover, some of them have advanced to such a degree of presumption, as to boast, that we are indebted to the gods for our life, but for a virtuous and religious one to ourselves; whence also that assertion of Cicero, in the person of Cotta, that, since every man acquires virtue for himself, none of the wise men have ever thanked God for it.

"For," says he, "we are praised for virtue, and in virtue we glory; which would not be the case, if it were a gift of God, and did not originate from ourselves." And a little after: "This is the judgment of all men, that fortune must be asked of God, but that wisdom must be derived from ourselves." This, then, is the substance of the opinion of all the philosophers, that the reason of the human understanding is sufficient for its proper government; that the will, being subject to it, is indeed solicited by sense to evil objects, but, as it has a free choice, there can be no impediment to its following reason as its guide in all things.

IV. Among the ecclesiastical writers, though there has not been one who would not acknowledge both that human reason is grievously wounded by sin, and that the will is very much embarrassed by corrupt affections, yet many of them have followed the philosophers far beyond what is right. The early fathers appear to me to have thus extolled human power from a fear lest, if they openly confessed its impotence, they might, in the first place, incur the derision of the philosophers, with whom they were then contending; and, in the next place, might administer to the flesh, of itself naturally too torpid to all that is good, a fresh occasion of slothfulness. To avoid delivering any principle deemed absurd in the common opinion of mankind, they made it their study, therefore, to compromise between the doctrine of the Scripture and the dogmas of the philosophers. Yet it appears from their language, that they principally regarded the latter consideration, that they might leave no room for slothfulness. Chrysostom says, "Since God has placed good and evil things in our power, he has given us freedom of choice; and he constrains not the unwilling, but embraces the willing." Again: "Oftentimes a bad man, if he will, is changed into a good one; and a good one falls into inactivity, and becomes bad; because God has given us naturally a free will, and imposes no necessity upon us, but, having provided suitable remedies, permits the event to depend entirely on the mind of the patient." Again: "As without the assistance of Divine grace we can never do any thing aright, so unless we bring what is our own, we shall never be able to gain the favour of heaven." He had before said, "That it may not be entirely of the Divine assistance, it behoves us also to bring something." And this is an expression very familiar with him: "Let us bring what is ours; God will supply the rest." Agreeably to which Jerome says, "That it belongs to us to begin, and to God to complete; that it is ours to offer what we can, but his to supply our deficiencies." In these sentences you see they certainly attributed to man more than could justly be attributed to him towards the pursuit of virtue; because they supposed it impossible to awaken our innate torpor, otherwise than by arguing that this alone constitutes our guilt; but with what great dexterity they did it, we shall see in the course of our work. That the passages which we have recited are exceedingly erroneous, will be shortly proved. Although the Greeks, beyond all others, and among them particularly Chrysostom, have exceeded all bounds in extolling the ability of the human will, yet such are the variations, fluctuations, or obscurities of all the fathers, except Augustine, on this subject, that scarcely any thing certain can be concluded from their writings. Therefore we shall not scrupulously enumerate the particular opinions of them all, but shall at times select from one and another so much as the explication of the argument shall appear to require. Succeeding writers, being every one for himself ambitious of the praise of subtlety in the defence of human nature, gradually and successively fell into opinions more and more erroneous; till at length man was commonly supposed to be corrupted only in his sensual part, but to have his will in a great measure, and his reason entirely, unimpaired. In the mean time, it was proclaimed by every tongue, that the natural talents in men were corrupted, but the supernatural taken away—an expression of Augustine, of the import of which scarcely one man in a hundred had the slightest idea. For myself, if I meant clearly to state wherein the corruption of nature consists, I could easily content myself with this language. But it is of great importance to examine with attention what ability is retained by man in his present state, corrupted in all the parts of his nature, and deprived of supernatural gifts. This subject, therefore, has been treated in too philosophical a manner by those who gloried in being the disciples of Christ. For the Latins have always retained the term *free will*, as though man still remained in his primitive integrity. And the Greeks have not been ashamed to use an expression much more arrogant; for they called it αυτεξουσιον, denoting that man possesses sovereign power over himself. Since all men, therefore, even the vulgar, are tinctured with this principle, that man is endued with free will, and some of those who would be thought intelligent know not how far this freedom extends,—let us first examine the meaning of the term, and then let us describe, according to the simplicity of the Scripture, the power which man naturally possesses to do either good or evil. What *free will* is, though the expression frequently occurs in all writers, few have defined. Yet Origen appears to have advanced a position to which they all assented, when he calls it a power of *reason* to discern good and evil, of *will* to choose either. Nor does Augustine differ from him, when he teaches that it is a power of reason and will, by which good is chosen when grace assists; and evil, when grace is wanting. Bernard, while he affects greater subtlety, has expressed himself with more obscurity: he says, it is a consent on account of the liberty of will, which cannot be lost, and the judgment of reason, which cannot be avoided. The definition of Anselm is not sufficiently plain, who states it to be a power of preserving rectitude for its own sake. Therefore Peter Lombard and the schoolmen have rather adopted the definition of Augustine, because it was more explicit, and did not exclude the grace of God, without which they perceived that the will had no power of itself. But they also make such additions of their own, as they conceived to be either better, or conducive to further explication. First, they agree that the word *arbitrium, will* or *choice*, should rather be referred to reason, whose office it is to discern between good and evil; and that the epithet *free* belongs properly to the faculty of the will, which is capable of being inclined to either. Wherefore, since liberty belongs properly to the will, Thomas Aquinas says, that it would be a very good definition, if free will were called *an elective power*, which, being composed of understanding and appetite, inclines rather to appetite. We see where they represent the power of free will to be placed; that is, in the reason and will. It now remains briefly to inquire how much they attribute respectively to each.

V. Common and external things, which do not pertain to the kingdom of God, they generally consider as subject to the free determination of man; but true righteousness they refer to the special grace of God and spiritual regeneration. With a view to support this notion, the author of the treatise "On the Vocation of the Gentiles" enumerates three kinds of will—the first a sensitive, the second an animal, and the third a spiritual one; the two former of which he states to be freely exercised by us, and the last to be the work of the Holy Spirit in us. The truth or falsehood of this shall be discussed in the proper place; for my design at present is briefly to recite the opinions of others, not to refute them. Hence, when writers treat of free will, their first inquiry respects not its ability in civil or external actions, but its power to obey the Divine law. Though

I confess the latter to be the principal question, yet I think the other ought not to be wholly neglected; and for this opinion I hope to give a very good reason. But a distinction has prevailed in the schools, which enumerates three kinds of liberty—the first, freedom from necessity, the second, freedom from sin, the third, freedom from misery; of which the first is naturally inherent in man, so that nothing can ever deprive him of it: the other two are lost by sin. This distinction I readily admit, except that it improperly confounds necessity with coaction. And the wide difference between these things, with the necessity of its being considered, will appear in another place.

VI. This being admitted will place it beyond all doubt, that man is not possessed of free will for good works, unless he be assisted by grace, and that special grace which is bestowed on the elect alone in regeneration. For I stop not to notice those fanatics, who pretend that grace is offered equally and promiscuously to all. But it does not yet appear, whether he is altogether deprived of power to do good, or whether he yet possesses some power, though small and feeble; which of itself can do nothing, but by the assistance of grace does also perform its part. Lombard, in order to establish this notion, informs us that two sorts of grace are necessary to qualify us for the performance of good works. One he calls operative, by which we efficaciously will what is good; the other coöperative, which attends as auxiliary to a good will. This division I dislike, because, while he attributes an efficacious desire of what is good to the grace of God, he insinuates that man has of his own nature antecedent, though ineffectual, desires after what is good; as Bernard asserts that a good will is the work of God, but yet allows that man is self-impelled to desire such a good will. But this is very remote from the meaning of Augustine, from whom, however, Lombard would be thought to have borrowed this division. The second part of it offends me by its ambiguity, which has produced a very erroneous interpretation. For they have supposed that we coöperate with the second sort of Divine grace, because we have it in our power either to frustrate the first sort by rejecting it, or to confirm it by our obedience to it. The author of the treatise "On the Vocation of the Gentiles" expresses it thus—that those who have the use of reason and judgment are at liberty to depart from grace, that they may be rewarded for not having departed, and that what is impossible without the coöperation of the Spirit, may be imputed to their merits, by whose will it might have been prevented. These two things I have thought proper to notice as I proceed, that the reader may perceive how much I dissent from the sounder schoolmen. For I differ considerably more from the later sophists, as they have departed much further from the judgment of antiquity. However, we understand from this division, in what sense they have ascribed free will to man. For Lombard at length pronounces, that we are not therefore possessed of free will, because we have an equal power to do or to think either good or evil, but only because we are free from constraint. And this liberty is not diminished, although we are corrupt, and the slaves of sin, and capable of doing nothing but sin.

VII. Then man will be said to possess free will in this sense, not that he has an equally free election of good and evil, but because he does evil voluntarily, and not by constraint. That, indeed, is very true; but what end could it answer to decorate a thing so diminutive with a title so superb? Egregious liberty indeed, if man be not compelled to serve sin, but yet is such a willing slave, that his will is held in bondage by the fetters of sin. I really abominate contentions about words, which disturb the

Church without producing any good effect; but I think that we ought religiously to avoid words which signify any absurdity, particularly when they lead to a pernicious error. How few are there, pray, who, when they hear free will attributed to man, do not immediately conceive, that he has the sovereignty over his own mind and will, and is able by his innate power to incline himself to whatever he pleases? But it will be said, all danger from these expressions will be removed, if the people are carefully apprized of their signification. But, on the contrary, the human mind is naturally so prone to falsehood, that it will sooner imbibe error from one single expression, than truth from a prolix oration; of which we have a more certain experiment than could be wished in this very word. For neglecting that explanation of the fathers, almost all their successors have been drawn into a fatal self-confidence, by adhering to the original and proper signification of the word.

VIII. But if we regard the authority of the fathers—though they have the term continually in their mouths, they at the same time declare with what extent of signification they use it. First of all, Augustine, who hesitates not to call the will a slave. He expresses his displeasure in one place against those who deny free will; but he declares the principal reason for it, when he says, "Only let no man dare so to deny the freedom of the will, as to desire to excuse sin." Elsewhere he plainly confesses, that the human will is not free without the Spirit, since it is subject to its lusts, by which it is conquered and bound. Again: that when the will was overcome by the sin into which it fell, nature began to be destitute of liberty. Again: that man, having made a wrong use of his free will, lost both it and himself. Again: that free will is in a state of captivity, so that it can do nothing towards righteousness. Again: that the will cannot be free, which has not been liberated by Divine grace. Again: that the Divine justice is not fulfilled, while the law commands, and man acts from his own strength; but when the Spirit assists, and the human will obeys, not as being free, but as liberated by God. And he briefly assigns the cause of all this, when, in another place, he tells us, that man at his creation received great strength of free will, but lost it by sin. Therefore, having shown that free will is the result of grace, he sharply inveighs against those who arrogate it to themselves without grace. "How, then," says he, "do miserable men dare to be proud of free will, before they are liberated, or of their own strength, if they have been liberated?" Nor do they consider that the term *free will* signifies liberty. But "where the Spirit of the Lord is, there is liberty." If, therefore, they are the slaves of sin, why do they boast of free will? "For of whom a man is overcome, of the same is he brought in bondage." But if they have been liberated, why do they boast as of their own work? Are they so much at liberty as to refuse to be the servants of him who says, "Without me ye can do nothing"? Besides, in another place, also, he seems to discountenance the use of that expression, when he says that the will is free, but not liberated; free from righteousness, enslaved to sin. This sentiment he also repeats and applies in another place, where he maintains that man is not free from righteousness, but by the choice of his will, and that he is not made free from sin, but by the grace of the Saviour. He who declares that human liberty is nothing but an emancipation or manumission from righteousness, evidently exposes it to ridicule as an unmeaning term. Therefore, if any man allows himself the use of this term without any erroneous signification, he will not be troubled by me on that account: but because I think that it cannot be retained without great danger, and that, on the contrary, its abolition would be very beneficial to the Church, I would neither use it myself, nor wish it to be used by others who may consult my opinion.

IX. Perhaps I may be thought to have raised a great prejudice against myself, by confessing that all the ecclesiastical writers, except Augustine, have treated this subject with such ambiguities or variations, that nothing certain can be learned from their writings. For some will interpret this, as though I intended to deprive them of the right of giving their suffrages, because their opinions are all adverse to mine. But I have had no other object in view than simply and faithfully to consult the benefit of pious minds, who, if they wait to discover the sentiments of the fathers on this subject, will fluctuate in perpetual uncertainty. At one time they teach man, despoiled of all strength of free will, to have recourse to grace alone; at another, they either furnish, or appear to furnish, him with armour naturally his own. Yet that, amidst all this ambiguity of expression, esteeming the strength of man as little or nothing, they have ascribed the praise of every thing that is good entirely to the Holy Spirit, is not difficult to prove, if I introduce some passages from them, in which this sentiment is clearly maintained. For what is the meaning of that assertion of Cyprian, so frequently celebrated by Augustine, "That we ought to glory in nothing, because we have nothing of our own;" but that man, completely impoverished in himself, should learn to depend entirely on God? What is the meaning of that observation of Augustine and Eucherius, when they represent Christ as the tree of life, to whom whosoever shall have stretched forth his hand shall live; and free will as the tree of knowledge of good and evil, and say that whosoever forsakes the grace of God and tastes of it shall die? What is the meaning of that assertion of Chrysostom, that every man by nature is not only a sinner, but altogether sin? If we have not one good quality, if from his head to his feet man be entirely sin, if it be wrong even to try how far the power of the will extends,—how, then, can it be right to divide the praise of a good work between God and man? I could introduce many such passages from other fathers; but lest any one should cavil, that I select only those things which favour my own cause, but artfully omit those which oppose it, I refrain from such a recital. I venture to affirm, however, that though they sometimes too highly extol free will, yet their design was to teach man to discard all reliance on his own power, and to consider all his strength as residing in God alone. I now proceed to a simple explication of the truth in considering the nature of man.

X. But I am obliged to repeat here, what I premised in the beginning of this chapter—that he who feels the most consternation, from a consciousness of his own calamity, poverty, nakedness, and ignominy, has made the greatest proficiency in the knowledge of himself. For there is no danger that man will divest himself of too much, provided he learns that what is wanting in him may be recovered in God. But he cannot assume to himself even the least particle beyond his just right, without ruining himself with vain confidence, and incurring the guilt of enormous sacrilege, by transferring to himself the honour which belongs to God. And whenever our minds are pestered with this cupidity, to desire to have something of our own, which may reside in ourselves rather than in God, we may know that this idea is suggested by the same counsellor, who excited in our first parents the desire of resembling "gods, knowing good and evil." If that term be diabolical, which exalts man in his own opinion, let us not admit it, unless we wish to take the counsel of an enemy. It is pleasant, indeed, to have so much innate strength as to confide in and be satisfied with ourselves. But from being allured into this vain confidence, let us be deterred by the many awful sentences which severely humble us to the dust; such as "Cursed be the man that trusteth in man, and maketh flesh his arm." Again: "God delighteth not in the strength of the horse; he taketh not pleasure in the legs of a man. The Lord taketh pleasure in them that fear him, in those that hope in his mercy." Again: "He giveth power to the faint; and to them that have no might he increaseth strength. Even the youths shall faint and be weary, and the young men shall utterly fall; but they that wait upon the Lord shall renew their strength." The tendency of all which is to prevent us from depending, in the smallest degree, on our own strength, if we wish God to be propitious to us, who "resisteth the proud, but giveth grace unto the humble." Then let us remember these promises; "I will pour water upon him that is thirsty, and floods upon the dry ground:" again; "Ho! every one that thirsteth, come ye to the waters:" which declare, that none are admitted to a participation of the blessings of God, but those who are pining away with a sense of their own poverty. Nor should such promises as this of Isaiah be overlooked: "The sun shall be no more thy light by day; neither for brightness shall the moon give light unto thee; but the Lord shall be unto thee an everlasting light." The Lord certainly does not deprive his servants of the splendour of the sun or of the moon; but because he will appear exclusively glorious in them, he calls off their confidence to a great distance, even from those things which in their opinion are the most excellent.

XI. I have always, indeed, been exceedingly pleased with this observation of Chrysostom, that humility is the foundation of our philosophy; but still more with this of Augustine: "As a rhetorician," says he, "on being interrogated what was the first thing in the rules of eloquence, replied, 'Pronunciation;' and on being separately interrogated what was the second, and what was the third, gave the same reply; so, should any one interrogate me concerning the rules of the Christian religion, the first, second, and third, I would always reply, Humility." Now, he does not consider it as humility, when a man, conscious to himself of some little power, abstains from pride and haughtiness; but when he truly feels his condition to be such that he has no refuge but in humility, as he elsewhere declares. "Let no man," says he, "flatter himself: of himself he is a devil: every blessing he enjoys is only from God. For what have you that is your own, but sin? Take to yourself sin, which is your own; for righteousness belongs to God." Again: "Why do men so presume on the ability of nature? It is wounded, maimed, distressed, and ruined. It needs a true confession, not a false defence." Again: "When every one knows, that in himself he is nothing, and that he cannot assist himself, the arms are broken within him, and the contentions are subsided." But it is necessary that all the weapons of impiety should be broken in pieces and consumed, that you may remain unarmed, and have no help in yourself. The greater your weakness is in yourself, so much the more the Lord assists you. So in the seventieth Psalm he forbids us to remember our own righteousness, that we may know the righteousness of God; and shows that God so recommends his grace to us, that we may know that we are nothing, and are solely dependent on the Divine mercy, being of ourselves altogether evil. Here, then, let us not contend with God concerning our right, as though what is attributed to him were deducted from our welfare. For as our humility is his exaltation, so the confession of our humility has an immediate remedy in his commiseration. Now, I do not expect that a man unconvinced should voluntarily submit, and, if he has any strength, withdraw his attention from it to be reduced to true humility; but I require, that, discarding the malady of self-love and love of strife, which blinds him, and leads him to entertain too high an opinion of himself, he should seriously contemplate himself in the faithful mirror of the Scripture.

XII. And, indeed, I much approve of that common observation which has been borrowed from Augustine, that the natural talents in man have been corrupted by sin, but that of the supernatural ones he has been wholly deprived. For by the latter are intended, both the light of faith and righteousness, which would be sufficient for the attainment of a heavenly life and eternal felicity. Therefore, when he revolted from the Divine government, he was at the same time deprived of those supernatural endowments, which had been given him for the hope of eternal salvation. Hence it follows, that he is exiled from the kingdom of God, in such a manner, that all the affections relating to the happy life of the soul, are also extinguished in him, till he recovers them by the grace of regeneration. Such are faith, love to God, charity towards our neighbours, and an attachment to holiness and righteousness. All these things, being restored by Christ, are esteemed adventitious and preternatural; and therefore we conclude that they had been lost. Again, soundness of mind and rectitude of heart were also destroyed; and this is the corruption of the natural talents. For although we retain some portion of understanding and judgment together with the will, yet we cannot say that our mind is perfect and sound, which is oppressed with debility and immersed in profound darkness; and the depravity of our will is sufficiently known. Reason, therefore, by which man distinguishes between good and evil, by which he understands and judges, being a natural talent, could not be totally destroyed, but is partly debilitated, partly vitiated, so that it exhibits nothing but deformity and ruin. In this sense John says, that "the light" still "shineth in darkness," but that "the darkness comprehendeth it not." In this passage both these ideas are clearly expressed—that some sparks continue to shine in the nature of man, even in its corrupt and degenerate state, which prove him to be a rational creature, and different from the brutes, because he is endued with understanding; and yet that this light is smothered by so much ignorance, that it cannot act with any degree of efficacy. So the will, being inseparable from the nature of man, is not annihilated; but it is fettered by depraved and inordinate desires, so that it cannot aspire after any thing that is good. This, indeed, is a complete definition, but requires more diffuse explication. Therefore, that the order of our discourse may proceed according to the distinction we have stated, in which we divided the soul into understanding and will, let us first examine the power of the understanding. To condemn it to perpetual blindness, so as to leave it no intelligence in any thing, is repugnant, not only to the Divine word, but also to the experience of common sense. For we perceive in the mind of man some desire of investigating truth, towards which he would have no inclination, but from some relish of it previously possessed. It therefore indicates some perspicuity in the human understanding, that it is attracted with a love of truth; the neglect of which in the brutes argues gross sense without reason; although this desire, small as it is, faints even before its entrance on its course, because it immediately terminates in vanity. For the dulness of the human mind renders it incapable of pursuing the right way of investigating the truth; it wanders through a variety of errors, and groping, as it were, in the shades of darkness, often stumbles, till at length it is lost in its wanderings; thus, in its search after truth, it betrays its incapacity to seek and find it. It also labours under another grievous malady, frequently not discerning what those things are, the true knowledge of which it would be proper to attain, and therefore torments itself with a ridiculous curiosity in fruitless and unimportant inquiries. To things most necessary to be known it either never adverts, or contemptuously and rarely digresses; but scarcely ever studies them with serious application. This depravity being a common subject of complaint with heathen writers, all men are clearly proved to have been implicated in it. Wherefore Solomon, in his Ecclesiastes, after having enumerated those pursuits in which men consider themselves as displaying superior wisdom, concludes with pronouncing them to be vain and frivolous.

XIII. Yet its attempts are not always so fruitless, but that it makes some discoveries, particularly when it applies itself to inferior things. Nor is it so stupid, as to be without some slender notion also of superior ones, however negligently it attends to the investigation of them; but it possesses not an equal ability for both. For it is when it goes beyond the limits of the present life, that it is chiefly convinced of its own imbecility. Wherefore, that we may better perceive how far it proceeds in every case according to the degrees of its ability, it will be useful for us to propose the following distinction; that there is one understanding for terrestrial things, and another for celestial ones. I call those things terrestrial which do not pertain to God and his kingdom, to true righteousness, or to the blessedness of a future life; but which relate entirely to the present life, and are in some sense confined within the limits of it. Celestial things are the pure knowledge of God, the method of true righteousness, and the mysteries of the heavenly kingdom. In the first class are included civil polity, domestic economy, all the mechanical arts and liberal sciences; in the second, the knowledge of God and of the Divine will, and the rule for conformity to it in our lives. Now, in regard to the first class, it must be confessed, that as man is naturally a creature inclined to society, he has also by nature an instinctive propensity to cherish and preserve that society; and therefore we perceive in the minds of all men general impressions of civil probity and order. Hence it is that not a person can be found who does not understand, that all associations of men ought to be governed by laws, or who does not conceive in his mind the principles of those laws. Hence that perpetual consent of all nations, as well as all individuals, to the laws, because the seeds of them are innate in all mankind, without any instructor or legislator. I regard not the dissensions and contests which afterwards arise, while some desire to invert all justice and propriety, to break down the barriers of the laws, and to substitute mere cupidity in the room of justice, as is the case with thieves and robbers. Others—which is a fault more common—think that unjust which legislators have sanctioned as just; and, on the contrary, pronounce that to be laudable which they have forbidden. For the former of these hate not the laws from an ignorance that they are good and sacred; but, inflamed with the violence of their passions, manifestly contend against reason, and under the influence of their lawless desires, execrate that which their judgments approve. The controversy of the latter of these is by no means repugnant to that original idea of equity which we have mentioned; for when men dispute with each other on the comparative merits of different laws, it implies their consent to some general rule of equity. This clearly argues the debility of the human mind, which halts and staggers even when it appears to follow the right way. Yet it is certainly true, that some seeds of political order are sown in the minds of all. And this is a powerful argument, that in the constitution of this life no man is destitute of the light of reason.

XIV. Next follow the arts, both liberal and manual; for learning which, as there is in all of us a certain aptitude, they also discover the strength of human ingenuity. But though all men are not capable of learning every art, yet it is a very sufficient proof of the common energy, that scarcely an individual can be found, whose sagacity does not exert itself in some particular art. Nor have they an energy and facility only in learning, but also in inventing something new in every art, or in amplifying and improving what they have learned from their predecessors. Though this excited Plato erroneously to assert that such an apprehension is only a recollection of what the soul knew in its preëxistent state, before it came into the body, it constrains us, by the most cogent reasons, to acknowledge that the principle of it is innate in the human mind. These instances, therefore, plainly prove, that men are endued with a general apprehension of reason and understanding. Yet it is such a universal blessing, that every one for himself ought to acknowledge it as the peculiar favour of God. To this gratitude the Author of nature himself abundantly excites us, by his creation of idiots, in whom he represents the state of the human soul without his illumination, which, though natural to all, is nevertheless a gratuitous gift of his beneficence towards every individual. But the invention and methodical teaching of these arts, and the more intimate and excellent knowledge of them, which is peculiar to a few, are no solid argument of general perspicacity; yet, belonging to both the pious and the impious, they are justly numbered among the natural talents.

XV. Whenever, therefore, we meet with heathen writers, let us learn from that light of truth which is admirably displayed in their works, that the human mind, fallen as it is, and corrupted from its integrity, is yet invested and adorned by God with excellent talents. If we believe that the Spirit of God is the only fountain of truth, we shall neither reject nor despise the truth itself, wherever it shall appear, unless we wish to insult the Spirit of God; for the gifts of the Spirit cannot be undervalued without offering contempt and reproach to the Spirit himself. Now, shall we deny the light of truth to the ancient lawyers, who have delivered such just principles of civil order and polity? Shall we say that the philosophers were blind in their exquisite contemplation and in their scientific description of nature? Shall we say that those, who by the art of logic have taught us to speak in a manner consistent with reason, were destitute of understanding themselves? Shall we accuse those of insanity, who by the study of medicine have been exercising their industry for our advantage? What shall we say of all the mathematics? Shall we esteem them the delirious ravings of madmen? On the contrary, we shall not be able even to read the writings of the ancients on these subjects without great admiration; we shall admire them, because we shall be constrained to acknowledge them to be truly excellent. And shall we esteem any thing laudable or excellent, which we do not recognize as proceeding from God? Let us, then, be ashamed of such great ingratitude, which was not to be charged on the heathen poets, who confessed that philosophy, and legislation, and useful arts, were the inventions of their gods. Therefore, since it appears that those whom the Scripture styles "natural men," ψυχικους, have discovered such acuteness and perspicacity in the investigation of sublunary things, let us learn from such examples, how many good qualities the Lord has left to the nature of man, since it has been despoiled of what is truly good.

XVI. Yet let us not forget that these are most excellent gifts of the Divine Spirit, which for the common benefit of mankind he dispenses to whomsoever he pleases. For if it was necessary that the Spirit of God should infuse into Bezaleel and Aholiab the understanding and skill requisite for the construction of the tabernacle, we need not wonder if the knowledge of those things, which are most excellent in human life, is said to be communicated to us by the Spirit of God. Nor is there any reason for inquiring, what intercourse with the Spirit is enjoyed by the impious who are entirely alienated from God. For when the Spirit of God is said to dwell only in the faithful, that is to be understood of the Spirit of sanctification, by whom we are consecrated as temples to God himself. Yet it is equally by the energy of the same Spirit, that God replenishes, actuates, and quickens all creatures, and that, according to the property of each species which he has given it by the law of creation. Now, if it has pleased the Lord that we should be assisted in physics, logic, mathematics, and other arts and sciences, by the labour and ministry of the impious, let us make use of them; lest, if we neglect to use the blessings therein freely offered to us by God, we suffer the just punishment of our negligence. But, lest any one should suppose a man to be truly happy, when he is admitted to possess such powerful energies for the discovery of truth relating to the elements of this world, it must likewise be added, that all that faculty of understanding, and the understanding which is the consequence of it, is, in the sight of God, a fleeting and transitory thing, where there is not a solid foundation of truth. For the sentiment of Augustine, with whom, as we have observed, the Master of the Sentences and the Schoolmen have been constrained to coincide, is strictly true—that as the gratuitous or supernatural gifts were taken away from man after the fall, so these natural ones which remained have been corrupted; not that they can be defiled in themselves as proceeding from God, but because they have ceased to be pure to polluted man, so that he can obtain no praise from them.

XVII. Let us conclude, therefore, that it is evident in all mankind, that reason is a peculiar property of our nature, which distinguishes us from the brute animals, as sense constitutes the difference between them and things inanimate. For whereas some are born fools and idiots, that defect obscures not the general goodness of God. Such a spectacle should rather teach us that what we retain ought justly to be ascribed to his indulgence; because, had it not been for his mercy to us, our defection would have been followed by the total destruction of our nature. But whereas some excel in penetration, others possess superior judgment, and others have a greater aptitude to learn this or that art, in this variety God displays his goodness to us, that no one may arrogate to himself as his own what proceeds merely from the Divine liberality. For whence is it that one is more excellent than another, unless it be to exalt in our common nature the special goodness of God, which in the preterition of many, proclaims that it is under an obligation to none? Moreover, God inspires particular motions according to the vocation of each individual; of which many examples occur in the book of the Judges, where the Spirit of the Lord is said to "come upon" those whom he called to govern the people. Finally, in all important actions there is a special instinct; for which reason it is said that Saul was followed by valiant men, "whose hearts God had touched." And Samuel, when he predicts his inauguration into the kingdom, thus expresses himself: "The Spirit of the Lord will come upon thee, and thou shalt be turned into another man." And this is extended to the whole course of his government; as it is afterwards narrated concerning David, that "the Spirit of the Lord came upon him from that day forward." But the same expression is used in other places in reference to particular impulses. Even in Homer, men are said to excel in abilities, not only as Jupiter has distributed to every one, but according as he guides him from day to day. And experience clearly shows, since the most ingenious and sagacious of mankind frequently stand still in profound astonishment, that the minds of men are subject to the power and will of

God to govern them every moment; for which reason it is said, that "he taketh away the heart of the chief people of the earth, and causeth them to wander in a wilderness where there is no way." Yet in this diversity we perceive some remaining marks of the Divine image, which distinguish the human race in general from all the other creatures.

XVIII. We now proceed to show what human reason can discover, when it comes to the kingdom of God, and to that spiritual wisdom, which consists chiefly in three things—to know God, his paternal favour towards us, on which depends our salvation, and the method of regulating our lives according to the rule of the law. In the two first points, but especially in the second, the most sagacious of mankind are blinder than moles. I do not deny that some judicious and apposite observations concerning God may be found scattered in the writings of the philosophers; but they always betray a confused imagination. The Lord afforded them, as we have before observed, some slight sense of his Divinity, that they might not be able to plead ignorance as an excuse for impiety, and sometimes impelled them to utter things, by the confession of which they might themselves be convinced. But they saw the objects presented to their view in such a manner, that by the sight they were not even directed to the truth, much less did they arrive at it; just as a man, who is travelling by night across a field, sees the coruscations of lightning extending for a moment far and wide, but with such an evanescent view, that so far from being assisted by them in proceeding on his journey, he is re-absorbed in the darkness of the night before he can advance a single step. Besides, those few truths, with which they, as it were, fortuitously besprinkle their books, with what numerous and monstrous falsehoods are they defiled! Lastly, they never had the smallest idea of that certainty of the Divine benevolence towards us, without which the human understanding must necessarily be full of immense confusion. Human reason, then, neither approaches, nor tends, nor directs its views towards this truth, to understand who is the true God, or in what character he will manifest himself to us.

XIX. But because, from our being intoxicated with a false opinion of our own perspicacity, we do not without great difficulty suffer ourselves to be persuaded, that in Divine things our reason is totally blind and stupid, it will be better, I think, to confirm it by testimonies of Scripture, than to support it by arguments. This is beautifully taught by John, in that passage which I lately cited, where he says that, from the beginning, "in God was life, and the life was the light of men. And the light shineth in darkness; and the darkness comprehended it not." He indicates, indeed, that the soul of man is irradiated with a beam of Divine light, so that it is never wholly destitute either of some little flame, or at least of a spark of it; but he likewise suggests that it cannot comprehend God by that illumination. And this because all his sagacity, as far as respects the knowledge of God, is mere blindness. For when the Spirit calls men "darkness," he at once totally despoils them of the faculty of spiritual understanding. Wherefore he asserts that believers, who receive Christ, are "born not of blood, nor of the will of the flesh, nor of the will of man, but of God;" as though he had said that the flesh is not capable of such sublime wisdom as to conceive of God and Divine things, without being illuminated by the Spirit of God; as Christ testified that his being known by Peter was owing to a special revelation of the Father.

XX. If we were firmly persuaded of what, indeed, ought not to be questioned, that our nature is destitute of all those things which our heavenly Father confers on his elect through the Spirit of regeneration, here would be no cause of hesitation. For this is the language of the faithful by the mouth of the Prophet: "With thee is the fountain of life; in thy light we shall see light." The Apostle confirms the same, when he says that "no man can say that Jesus is Lord, but by the Holy Ghost." And John the Baptist, perceiving the stupidity of his disciples, exclaims, that "a man can receive nothing except it be given him from above." That by "gift" he intends a special illumination, not a common faculty of nature, is evident from the complaint which he makes of the inefficacy of the many discourses in which he had recommended Christ to his disciples. "I see that words are unavailing to instruct the minds of men in Divine things, unless God give them understanding by his Spirit." And Moses also, when he reproaches the people for their forgetfulness, yet at the same time remarks, that they cannot be wise in the mysteries of God but by the Divine favour. He says, "Thine eyes have seen the signs and those great miracles; yet the Lord hath not given you a heart to perceive, and eyes to see, and ears to hear." What more would he express, if he had called them blockheads, destitute of all understanding in the consideration of the works of God? Whence the Lord, by the Prophet, promises, as an instance of peculiar grace, that he will give the Israelites "a heart to know" him; plainly suggesting that the mind of man has no spiritual wisdom any further than as it is enlightened by him. Christ also has clearly confirmed this by his own declaration, that no man can come to him, except the Father draw him. What! is he not himself the lively image of the Father, representing to us all "the brightness of his glory"? Therefore, he could not better manifest the extent of our capacity for the knowledge of God, than when he affirms that we have no eyes to behold his image where it is so plainly exhibited. What! did he not descend to the earth in order to discover to men the will of the Father? And did he not faithfully fulfil the object of his mission? He certainly did; but his preaching is not at all efficacious, unless the way to the heart be laid open by the internal teaching of the Spirit. Therefore, none come to him but they who have heard and learned of the Father. What is the nature of this hearing and learning? It is when the Spirit, by a wonderful and peculiar power, forms the ears to hear and the mind to understand. And lest this should appear strange, he cites the prophecy of Isaiah, where, predicting the restoration of the Church, he says, that all those who shall be saved "shall be taught of the Lord." If God there predicts something peculiar concerning his elect, it is evident that he speaks not of that kind of instruction which is common also to the impious and profane. It must be concluded, therefore, that there is no admission into the kingdom of God, but for him whose mind has been renewed by the illumination of the Holy Spirit. But Paul expresses himself more clearly than all the others. Having professedly entered upon this argument, after he has condemned all human wisdom as folly and vanity, and even reduced it to nothing, he comes to this conclusion: "The natural man receiveth not the things of the Spirit of God; for they are foolishness unto him; neither can he know them, because they are spiritually discerned." Whom does he call the natural man? him who depends on the light of nature. He, I say, has no apprehension of the mysteries of God. Why so? because through slothfulness he neglects them? Nay, even his utmost endeavours can avail nothing, "because they are spiritually discerned." This implies, that being entirely concealed from human perspicacity, they are discovered only by the revelation of the Spirit; so that where the illumination of the Spirit is not enjoyed, they are deemed foolishness itself. He had before extolled "the things which God hath prepared for them that love him" above the capacity of our eyes, our ears, and our minds; he had even asserted that human wisdom was a kind of veil, by which the mind is prevented from a discovery of God. What do we want more? The Apostle pronounces that "God hath made foolish the wisdom of this world;" and shall we ascribe to it such a degree of sagacity, as would enable it to penetrate to God, and to the most secret recesses of the heavenly kingdom? Far be from us such extreme stupidity.

XXI. That which he here detracts from men, he in another place ascribes exclusively to God. Praying for the Ephesians, he says, "May God, the Father of glory, give unto you the Spirit of wisdom and revelation." You hear now that all wisdom and revelation is the gift of God. What follows? "The eyes of your understanding being enlightened." If they need a new revelation, they are certainly blind of themselves. It follows, "that ye may know what is the hope of your calling," &c. He confesses, then, that the minds of men are not naturally capable of so great knowledge, as to know their own calling. Nor let any Pelagian here object, that God assists this stupidity or ignorance, when, by the teaching of his word, he directs the human understanding to that which, without a guide, it never could have attained. For David had the law, in which all desirable wisdom was comprised: yet, not content with this, he requested that his eyes might be opened to consider the mysteries of that law. By this expression he clearly signifies, that the sun arises on the earth, where the word of God shines on mankind; but that they derive little advantage from it, till he himself either gives them eyes or opens them, who is therefore called "the Father of lights;" because wherever he shines not by his Spirit, every thing is covered with darkness. Thus also the Apostles were rightly and abundantly taught by the best of all teachers: yet, if they had not needed the Spirit of truth to instruct their minds in that very doctrine which they had previously heard, they would not have been commanded to expect him. If, in imploring any favour of God, we confess our need, and if his promising it argues our poverty, let no man hesitate to acknowledge, that he is incapable of understanding the mysteries of God, any further than he has been illuminated by Divine grace. He who attributes to himself more understanding, is so much the blinder, because he does not perceive and acknowledge his blindness.

XXII. It remains for us to notice the third branch of knowledge, relating to the rule for the proper regulation of our life, which we truly denominate the knowledge of works of righteousness; in which the human mind discovers somewhat more acuteness than in the two former particulars. For the Apostle declares, that "when the Gentiles, which have not the law, do by nature the things contained in the law, these, having not the law, are a law unto themselves; which show the work of the law written in their hearts, their conscience also bearing witness, and their thoughts the mean while accusing or else excusing one another." If the Gentiles have naturally the righteousness of the law engraven on their minds, we certainly cannot say that they are altogether ignorant how they ought to live. And no sentiment is more commonly admitted, than that man is sufficiently instructed in a right rule of life by that natural law of which the Apostle there speaks. But let us examine for what purpose this knowledge of the law was given to men; and then it will appear how far it can conduct them towards the mark of reason and truth. This is evident also from the words of Paul, if we observe the connection of the passage. He had just before said, "As many as have sinned without law, shall also perish without law; and as many as have sinned in the law, shall be judged by the law." Because it might appear absurd that the Gentiles should perish without any previous knowledge, he immediately subjoins that their conscience supplies the place of a law to them, and is therefore sufficient for their just condemnation. The end of the law of nature, therefore, is, that man may be rendered inexcusable. Nor will it be improperly defined in this manner—That it is a sentiment of the conscience sufficiently discerning between good and evil, to deprive men of the pretext of ignorance, while they are convicted even by their own testimony. Such is the indulgence of man to himself, that in the perpetration of evil actions he always gladly diverts his mind as much as he possibly can from all sense of sin; which seems to have induced Plato to suppose, that no sin is committed but through ignorance. This remark of his would be correct, if the hypocrisy of men could go so far in the concealment of their vices, as that the mind would have no consciousness of its guilt before God. But since the sinner, though he endeavours to evade the knowledge of good and evil imprinted on his mind, is frequently brought back to it, and so is not permitted to shut his eyes, but compelled, whether he will or not, sometimes to open them, there is no truth in the assertion, that he sins only through ignorance.

XXIII. Themistius, another philosopher, with more truth, teaches that the human understanding is very rarely deceived in the universal definition, or in the essence of a thing; but that it falls into error, when it proceeds further, and descends to the consideration of particular cases. There is no man, who, if he be interrogated in a general way, will not affirm homicide to be criminal; but he who conspires the death of his enemy, deliberates on it as a good action. The adulterer will condemn adultery in general; but will privately flatter himself in his own. Here lies the ignorance—when a man, proceeding to a particular case, forgets the rule which he had just fixed as a general position. This subject is very excellently treated by Augustine, in his exposition of the first verse of the fifty-seventh Psalm. The observation of Themistius, however, is not applicable to all cases; for sometimes the turpitude of the crime so oppresses the conscience of the sinner, that, no longer imposing on himself under the false image of virtue, he rushes into evil with the knowledge of his mind and the consent of his will. This state of mind produced these expressions, which we find in a heathen poet: "I see the better path, and approve it; I pursue the worse." Wherefore the distinction of Aristotle between incontinence and intemperance appears to me to be highly judicious. Where incontinence predominates, he says, that by the perturbation of the affections or passions, the mind is deprived of particular knowledge, so that in its own evil actions it observes not that criminality which it generally discovers in similar actions committed by other persons; and that when the perturbation has subsided, penitence immediately succeeds; that intemperance is not extinguished or broken by a sense of sin, but, on the contrary, obstinately persists in the choice of evil which it has made.

XXIV. Now, when you hear of a universal judgment in man to discriminate between good and evil, you must not imagine that it is every where sound and perfect. For if the hearts of men be furnished with a capacity of discriminating what is just and unjust, only that they may not excuse themselves with the plea of ignorance, it is not at all necessary for them to discover the truth in every point; it is quite sufficient if they understand so much that they can avail themselves of no subterfuge, but being convicted by the testimony of their own conscience, even now begin to tremble at the tribunal of God. And if we will examine our reason by the Divine law, which is the rule of perfect righteousness, we shall find in how many respects it is blind. It certainly is far from reaching the principal points in the first table; such as relate to trust in God, ascribing to him the praise of goodness and righteousness, the invocation of his name, and the true observation of the Sabbath. What mind, relying on its natural powers, ever imagined that the legitimate worship of God consisted in these and similar things? For when profane men intend to worship God, though they are recalled a hundred times from their vain and nugatory fancies, yet they are always relapsing into them again. They deny that sacrifices are pleasing to God, unaccompanied with sincerity of heart; thereby testifying that they have some ideas concerning the spiritual worship of God, which, nevertheless, they immediately corrupt by their false inventions. For it is impossible ever to persuade them that every thing is true which the law prescribes concerning it. Shall I say that the mind of man excels in discernment, which can neither understand of itself, nor hearken to good instructions? Of the precepts of the second table it has a little clearer understanding, since they are more intimately connected with the preservation of civil society among men. Though even here it is sometimes found to be deficient; for to every noble mind it appears very absurd to submit to an unjust and imperious despotism, if it be possible by any means to resist it. A uniform decision of human reason is, that it is the mark of a servile and abject disposition patiently to bear it, and of an honest and ingenuous mind to shake it off. Nor is the revenging of injuries esteemed a vice among the philosophers. But the Lord, condemning such excessive haughtiness of mind, prescribes to his people that patience which is deemed dishonourable among men. But in the universal observation of the law, the censure of concupiscence wholly escapes our notice. For the natural man cannot be brought to acknowledge the disorders of his inward affections. The light of nature is smothered, before it approaches the first entrance of this abyss. For when the philosophers represent the inordinate affections of the mind as vices, they intend those which appear and manifest themselves in the grosser external actions; but those corrupt desires which more secretly stimulate the mind, they consider as nothing.

XXV. Wherefore, as Plato has before been deservedly censured for imputing all sins to ignorance, so also we must reject the opinion of those who maintain that all sins proceed from deliberate malice and pravity. For we too much experience how frequently we fall into error even when our intention is good. Our reason is overwhelmed with deceptions in so many forms, is obnoxious to so many errors, stumbles at so many impediments, and is embarrassed in so many difficulties, that it is very far from being a certain guide. Paul shows its deficiency in the sight of the Lord in every part of our life, when he denies "that we are sufficient of ourselves to think any thing as of ourselves." He does not speak of the will or of the affections, but he also divests us of every good thought, that we may not suppose it possible for our minds to conceive how any action may be rightly performed. Are all our industry, perspicacity, understanding, and care so depraved, that we cannot conceive or meditate any thing that is right in the sight of God? To us, who do not contentedly submit to be stripped of the acuteness of our reason, which we esteem our most valuable endowment, this appears too harsh; but in the estimation of the Holy Spirit, who knows that all the thoughts of the wisest of men are vain, and who plainly pronounces every imagination of the human heart to be only evil, such a representation is consistent with the strictest truth. If whatever our mind conceives, agitates, undertakes, and performs, be invariably evil, how can we entertain a thought of undertaking any thing acceptable to God, by whom nothing is accepted but holiness and righteousness? Thus it is evident that the reason of our mind, whithersoever it turns, is unhappily obnoxious to vanity. David was conscious to himself of this imbecility, when he prayed that understanding might be given him, to enable him rightly to learn the commandments of the Lord. For his desire to obtain a new understanding implies the total insufficiency of his own. And this he does not once, but almost ten times in one Psalm he repeats the same petition—a repetition indicating the greatness of the necessity which urges him thus to pray. What David requests for himself alone, Paul frequently supplicates for the churches at large. "We do not cease to pray for you," says he, "and to desire, that ye might be filled with the knowledge of his will in all wisdom and spiritual understanding; that ye might walk worthy of the Lord unto all pleasing." Whenever he represents that as a blessing of God, we should remember that he thereby testifies it to be placed beyond the ability of man. Augustine so far acknowledges this defect of reason in understanding the things of God, that he thinks the grace of illumination no less necessary to our minds than the light of the sun to our eyes. And not content with this, he subjoins the following correction—that we ourselves open our eyes to behold the light, but that the eyes of our minds remain shut, unless they are opened by the Lord. Nor does the Scripture teach us that our minds are illuminated only on one day, so as to enable them to see afterwards without further assistance; for the passage just quoted from Paul relates to continual advances and improvements. And this is clearly expressed by David in these words: "With my whole heart have I sought thee; O let me not wander from thy commandments." For after having been regenerated, and made a more than common progress in true piety, he still confesses his need of perpetual direction every moment, lest he should decline from that knowledge which he possessed. Therefore, in another place, he prays for the renewal of a right spirit, which he had lost by his sin; because it belongs to the same God to restore that which he originally bestowed, but of which we have been for a time deprived.

XXVI. We must now proceed to the examination of the will, to which principally belongs the liberty of choice; for we have before seen that election belongs rather to the will than to the understanding. In the first place, that the opinion advanced by philosophers, and received by general consent, that all things, by a natural instinct, desire what is good, may not be supposed to prove the rectitude of the human will, let us observe, that the power of free choice is not to be contemplated in that kind of appetite, which proceeds rather from the inclination of the nature than from the deliberation of the mind. For even the schoolmen confess that there is no action of free choice, but when reason sees and considers the rival objects presented to it; meaning that the object of appetite must be such as is the subject of choice, and that deliberation precedes and introduces choice. And in fact, if you examine the desire of good which is natural to man, you will find that he has it in common with the brutes. For they also desire to be happy, and pursue every agreeable appearance which attracts their senses. But man neither rationally chooses as the object of his pursuit that which is truly good for him, according to the excellency of his immortal nature, nor takes the advice of reason, nor duly exerts his understanding; but without reason, without reflection, follows his natural inclination, like the herds of the field. It is therefore no argument for the liberty of the will, that man is led by natural instinct to desire that which is good; but it is necessary that he discern what is good according to right reason; that as soon as he knows it, he choose it; and as soon as he has chosen it, he pursue it. To remove every difficulty, we must advert to two instances of false argumentation. For the desire here intended is not a proper motion of the will, but a natural inclination; and the good in question relates not to virtue or righteousness, but to condition; as when we say a man is well or in good health. Lastly, though man has the strongest desire after what is good, yet he does not pursue it. There is no man to whom eternal felicity is unwelcome, yet no man aspires to it without the influence of the Spirit. Since, therefore, the desire of happiness natural to man furnishes no argument for the liberty of the will, any more than a tendency in metals and stones towards the perfection of their nature argues liberty in them, let us consider, in some other particulars, whether the will be in every part so entirely vitiated and depraved that it can produce nothing but what is evil; or whether it retain any small part uninjured which may be the source of good desires.

XXVII. Those who attribute it to the first grace of God, that we are able to will effectually, seem, on the contrary, to imply that the soul has a faculty of spontaneously aspiring to what is good, but that it is too weak to rise into a solid affection, or to excite any endeavour. And there is no doubt that the schoolmen have in general embraced this opinion, which was borrowed from Origen and some of the fathers, since they frequently consider man in things purely natural, as they express themselves, according to the description given by the Apostle in these words: "The good that I would, I do not; but the evil which I would not, that I do. To will is present with me; but how to perform that which is good, I find not." But this is a miserable and complete perversion of the argument which Paul is pursuing in that passage. For he is treating of the Christian conflict, which he more briefly hints at to the Galatians; the conflict which the faithful perpetually experience within themselves in the contention between the flesh and the spirit. Now, the spirit is not from nature, but from regeneration. But that the Apostle speaks concerning the regenerate, is evident from his assertion, that in himself dwelt nothing good, being immediately followed by an explanation that he meant it of his flesh. And therefore he affirms that it is not he that does evil, but sin that dwells in him. What is the meaning of this correction, "in me, that is, in my flesh?" It is as if he had expressed himself in the following manner: No good resides in me originating from myself, for in my flesh can be found nothing that is good. Hence follows that form of exculpation: "I do no evil, but sin that dwelleth in me;" which is inapplicable to any but the regenerate, who, with the prevailing bias of their souls, aim at what is good. Now, the conclusion which is subjoined places all this in a clear point of view: "I delight," says he, "in the law of God after the inward man; but I see another law in my members, warring against the law of my mind." Who has such a dissension in himself, but he who, being regenerated by the Divine Spirit, carries about with him the relics of his flesh? Therefore Augustine, though he had at one time supposed that discourse to relate to the natural state of man, retracted his interpretation, as false and inconsistent. And, indeed, if we allow that men destitute of grace have some motions towards true goodness, though ever so feeble, what answer shall we give to the Apostle, who denies that we are sufficient of ourselves to entertain even a good thought? What reply shall we make to the Lord, who pronounces, by the mouth of Moses, that every imagination of the human heart is only evil? Since they have stumbled on a false interpretation of one passage, therefore, there is no reason why we should dwell on their opinion. Rather let us receive this declaration of Christ, "Whosoever committeth sin is the servant of sin." We are all sinners by nature; therefore we are all held under the yoke of sin. Now, if the whole man be subject to the dominion of sin, the will, which is the principal seat of it, must necessarily be bound with the firmest bonds. Nor would there otherwise be any consistency in the assertion of Paul, "that it is God that worketh in us to will," if any will preceded the grace of the Spirit. Farewell, then, all the idle observations of many writers concerning preparation; for although the faithful sometimes petition that their hearts may be conformed to the Divine law, as David does in many places, yet it should be remarked that even this desire of praying originates from God. This we may gather from the language of David; for when he wishes a clean heart to be created within him, he certainly does not arrogate to himself the beginning of such a creation. Let us rather, therefore, attend to this advice of Augustine: "God will prevent you in all things: do you also sometimes prevent his wrath." How? "Confess that you have all those things from God; that whatever good you have, it is from him; but whatever evil, from yourself." And a little after, "Nothing is ours, but sin."

5.

Redemption For Lost Man to Be Sought in Christ.

The whole human race having perished in the person of Adam, our original excellence and dignity, which we have noticed, so far from being advantageous to us, only involves us in greater ignominy, till God, who does not acknowledge the pollution and corruption of man by sin to be his work, appears as a Redeemer in the person of his only begotten Son. Therefore, since we are fallen from life into death, all that knowledge of God as a Creator, of which we have been treating, would be useless, unless it were succeeded by faith exhibiting God to us as a Father in Christ. This, indeed, was the genuine order of nature, that the fabric of the world should be a school in which we might learn piety, and thence be conducted to eternal life and perfect felicity. But since the fall, whithersoever we turn our eyes, the curse of God meets us on every side, which, whilst it seizes innocent creatures and involves them in our guilt, must necessarily overwhelm our souls with despair. For though God is pleased still to manifest his paternal kindness to us in various ways, yet we cannot, from a contemplation of the world, conclude that he is our Father, when our conscience disturbs us within, and convinces us that our sins afford a just reason why God should abandon us, and no longer esteem us as his children. We are also chargeable with stupidity and ingratitude; for our minds, being blinded, do not perceive the truth; and all our senses being corrupted, we wickedly defraud God of his glory. We must therefore subscribe to the declaration of Paul: "For after that in the wisdom of God, the world by wisdom knew not God, it pleased God by the foolishness of preaching to save them that believe." What he denominates the wisdom of God, is this magnificent theatre of heaven and earth, which is replete with innumerable miracles, and from the contemplation of which we ought wisely to acquire the knowledge of God. But because we have made so little improvement in this way, he recalls us to the faith of Christ, which is despised by unbelievers on account of its apparent folly. Wherefore, though the preaching of the cross is not agreeable to human reason, we ought, nevertheless, to embrace it with all humility, if we desire to return to God our Creator, from whom we have been alienated, and to have him reassume the character of our Father. Since the fall of the first man, no knowledge of God, without the Mediator, has been available to salvation. For Christ speaks not of his own time only, but comprehends all ages, when he says that "this is life eternal, to know thee, the only true God, and Jesus Christ, whom thou hast sent." And this aggravates the stupidity of those who set open the gate of heaven to all unbelievers and profane persons, without the grace of Christ, whom the Scripture universally represents as the only door of entrance into salvation. But if any man would restrict this declaration of Christ to the period of the first promulgation of the gospel, we are prepared with a refutation. For it has been a common opinion, in all ages and nations, that those who are alienated from God, and pronounced accursed, and children of wrath, cannot please him without a reconciliation. Here add the answer of Christ to the woman of Samaria: "Ye worship ye know not what: we know what we worship; for salvation is of the Jews." In these words he at once condemns all the religions of the Gentiles as false, and assigns a reason for it; because under the law the Redeemer was promised only to the chosen people; whence it follows that no worship has ever been acceptable to God, unless it had respect to Christ. Hence also Paul affirms that all the Gentiles were without God, and destitute of the hope of life. Now, as John teaches us that life was from the beginning in Christ, and that the whole world are fallen from it, it is necessary to return to that fountain; and therefore Christ asserts himself to be the life, as he is the author of the propitiation. And, indeed, the celestial inheritance belongs exclusively to the children of God. But it is very unreasonable that they should be considered in the place and order of his children, who have not been engrafted into the body of his only begotten Son. And John plainly declares that "they who believe in his name become the sons of God." But as it is not my design in this place to treat professedly of faith in Christ, these cursory hints shall at present suffice.

II. Therefore God never showed himself propitious to his ancient people, nor afforded them any hope of his favour, without a Mediator. I forbear to speak of the legal sacrifices, by which the faithful were plainly and publicly instructed that salvation was to be sought solely in that expiation, which has been accomplished by Christ alone. I only assert, that the happiness of the Church has always been founded on the person of Christ. For though God comprehended in his covenant all the posterity of Abraham, yet Paul judiciously reasons, that Christ is in reality that Seed in whom all the nations were to be blessed; since we know that the natural descendants of that patriarch were not reckoned as his seed. For, to say nothing of Ishmael and others, what was the cause, that of the two sons of Isaac, the twin-brothers Esau and Jacob, even when they were yet unborn, one should be chosen and the other rejected? How came it to pass that the first-born was rejected, and that the younger obtained his birthright? How came the majority of the people to be disinherited? It is evident, therefore, that the seed of Abraham is reckoned principally in one person, and that the promised salvation was not manifested till the coming of Christ, whose office it is to collect what had been scattered abroad. The first adoption, therefore, of the chosen people, depended on the grace of the Mediator; which, though it is not so plainly expressed by Moses, yet appears to have been generally well known to all the pious. For before the appointment of any king in the nation, Hannah, the mother of Samuel, speaking of the felicity of the faithful, thus expressed herself in her song: "The Lord shall give strength unto his king, and exalt the horn of his anointed." Her meaning in these words is, that God will bless his Church. And to this agrees the oracle, which is soon after introduced: "I will raise me up a faithful priest, and he shall walk before mine anointed." And there is no doubt that it was the design of the heavenly Father to exhibit in David and his posterity a lively image of Christ. With a design to exhort the pious, therefore, to the fear of God, he enjoins them to "kiss the Son;" which agrees with this declaration of the gospel: "He that honoureth not the Son honoureth not the Father." Therefore, though the kingdom was weakened by the revolt of the ten tribes, yet the covenant, which God had made with David and his successors, could not but stand, as he also declared by the Prophets: "I will not rend away all the kingdom, but will give one tribe to thy son, for David my servant's sake, and for Jerusalem's sake which I have chosen." This is repeated again and again. It is also expressly added, "I will for this afflict the seed of David, but not for ever." At a little distance of time it is said, "For David's sake did the Lord his God give him a lamp in Jerusalem, to set up his son after him, and to establish Jerusalem." Even when the state was come to the verge of ruin, it was again said, "The Lord would not destroy Judah, for David his servant's sake, as he promised him to give him alway a light, and to his children." The sum of the whole is this—that David alone was chosen, to the rejection of all others, as the perpetual object of the

Divine favour; as it is said, in another place, "He forsook the tabernacle of Shiloh; he refused the tabernacle of Joseph, and chose not the tribe of Ephraim; but chose the tribe of Judah, the mount Zion, which he loved. He chose David also his servant, to feed Jacob his people, and Israel his inheritance." Finally, it pleased God to preserve his Church in such a way, that its security and salvation should depend on that head. David therefore exclaims, "The Lord is their strength, and he is the saving strength of his anointed;" and immediately adds this petition: "Save thy people, and bless thine inheritance;" signifying that the state of the Church is inseparably connected with the government of Christ. In the same sense he elsewhere says, "Save, Lord; let the king hear us when we call." In these words he clearly teaches us that the faithful resort to God for assistance, with no other confidence than because they are sheltered under the protection of the king. This is to be inferred from another psalm: "Save, O Lord! Blessed be he that cometh in the name of the Lord;" where it is sufficiently evident that the faithful are invited to Christ, that they may hope to be saved by the power of God. The same thing is alluded to in another prayer, where the whole Church implores the mercy of God: "Let thy hand be upon the man of thy right hand, upon the Son of man whom thou madest strong for thyself." For though the author of the psalm deplores the dissipation of all the people, yet he ardently prays for their restoration in their head alone. But when Jeremiah, after the people were driven into exile, the land laid waste, and all things apparently ruined, bewails the miseries of the Church, he principally laments that by the subversion of the kingdom, the hope of the faithful was cut off. "The breath of our nostrils, the anointed of the Lord, was taken in their pits, of whom we said, Under his shadow we shall live among the heathen." Hence it is sufficiently evident, that since God cannot be propitious to mankind but through the Mediator, Christ was always exhibited to the holy fathers under the law, as the object to which they should direct their faith.

III. Now, when consolation is promised in affliction, but especially when the deliverance of the Church is described, the standard of confidence and hope is erected in Christ alone. "Thou wentest forth for the salvation of thy people, even for salvation with thine anointed," says Habakkuk. And whenever the Prophets mention the restoration of the Church, they recall the people to the promise given to David concerning the perpetuity of his kingdom. Nor is this to be wondered at; for otherwise there would be no stability in the covenant. To this refers the memorable answer of Isaiah. For when he saw that his declaration concerning the raising of the siege, and the present deliverance of Jerusalem, was rejected by that unbelieving king, Ahaz, he makes rather an abrupt transition to the Messiah: "Behold, a virgin shall conceive, and bear a son;" indirectly suggesting, that although the king and the people, in their perverseness, rejected the promise which had been given them, as though they would purposely labour to invalidate the truth of God, yet that his covenant would not be frustrated, but that the Redeemer should come at his appointed time. Finally, all the Prophets, in order to display the Divine mercy, were constantly careful to exhibit to view that kingdom of David, from which redemption and eternal salvation were to proceed. Thus Isaiah: "I will make an everlasting covenant with you, even the sure mercies of David. Behold, I have given him for a witness to the people;" because in desperate circumstances the faithful could have no hope, any otherwise than by his interposition as a witness, that God would be merciful to them. Thus also Jeremiah, to comfort them who were in despair, says, "Behold, the days come, saith the Lord, that I will raise unto David a righteous Branch. In his days Judah shall be saved, and Israel shall dwell safely." And Ezekiel: "I will set up one Shepherd over them, and he shall feed them, even my servant David. And I the Lord will be their God, and my servant David a prince among them; and I will make with them a covenant of peace." Again, in another place, having treated of their incredible renovation, he says, "David my servant shall be king over them; and they all shall have one Shepherd. Moreover I will make a covenant of peace with them; it shall be an everlasting covenant with them." I select a few passages out of many, because I only wish to apprize the reader, that the hope of the pious has never been placed any where but in Christ. All the other Prophets also uniformly speak the same language. As Hosea: "Then shall the children of Judah and the children of Israel be gathered together, and appoint themselves one head." And in a subsequent chapter he is still more explicit: "The children of Israel shall return, and seek the Lord their God, and David their king." Micah also, discoursing on the return of the people, expressly declares, "their king shall pass before them, and the Lord on the head of them." Thus Amos, intending to predict the restoration of the people, says, "In that day I will raise up the tabernacle of David that is fallen, and close up the breaches thereof; and I will raise up his ruins." This implies that the only standard of salvation was the restoration of the regal dignity in the family of David, which was accomplished in Christ. Zechariah, therefore, living nearer to the time of the manifestation of Christ, more openly exclaims, "Rejoice greatly, O daughter of Zion; shout, O daughter of Jerusalem: behold, thy King cometh unto thee: he is just, and having salvation." This corresponds with a passage from a psalm, already cited: "The Lord is the saving strength of his anointed. Save thy people;" where salvation is extended from the head to the whole body.

IV. It was the will of God that the Jews should be instructed by these prophecies, so that they might direct their eyes to Christ whenever they wanted deliverance. Nor, indeed, notwithstanding their shameful degeneracy, could the memory of this general principle ever be obliterated—that God would be the deliverer of the Church by the hand of Christ, according to his promise to David; and that in this manner the covenant of grace, in which God had adopted his elect, would at length be confirmed. Hence it came to pass, that when Christ, a little before his death, entered into Jerusalem, that song was heard from the mouths of children, "Hosanna to the Son of David." For the subject of their song appears to have been derived from a sentiment generally received and avowed by the people, that there remained to them no other pledge of the mercy of God, but in the advent of the Redeemer. For this reason Christ commands his disciples to believe in him, that they may distinctly and perfectly believe in God: "Ye believe in God, believe also in me." For though, strictly speaking, faith ascends from Christ to the Father, yet he suggests, that though it were even fixed on God, yet it would gradually decline, unless he interposed, to preserve its stability. The majesty of God is otherwise far above the reach of mortals, who are like worms crawling upon the earth. Wherefore, though I do not reject that common observation that God is the object of faith, yet I consider it as requiring some correction. For it is not without reason that Christ is called "the image of the invisible God;" but by this appellation we are reminded, that unless God reveal himself to us in Christ, we cannot have that knowledge of him which is necessary to salvation. For although among the Jews the scribes had by false glosses obscured the declarations of the Prophets concerning the Redeemer, yet Christ assumed it for granted, as if allowed by common consent, that there was no other remedy for the confusion into which the Jews had fallen, nor any other mode of deliverance for the Church, but the exhibition of the Mediator. There was not, indeed, such a general knowledge as there ought to have been, of the principle taught by Paul, that "Christ is the end of the law;" but the truth and certainty of this evidently appears both from the law itself and from the Prophets. I am not yet treating of faith; there will be a more suitable place for that subject in another part of the work. Only let this be well fixed in the mind of the reader; that the first step to piety is to know that God is our Father, to protect, govern, and support us till he gathers us into the eternal inheritance of his kingdom; that hence it is plain, as we have before asserted, that there can be no saving knowledge of God without Christ; and consequently that from the beginning of the world he has always been manifested to all the elect, that they might look to him, and repose all their confidence in him. In this sense Irenæus says that the Father, who is infinite in himself, becomes finite in the Son; because he has accommodated himself to our capacity, that he may not overwhelm our minds with the infinity of his glory. And fanatics, not considering this, pervert a useful observation into an impious reverie, as though there were in Christ merely a portion of Deity, an emanation from the infinite perfection; whereas the sole meaning of that writer is, that God is apprehended in Christ, and in him alone. The assertion of John has been verified in all ages, "Whosoever denieth the Son, the same hath not the Father." For though many in ancient times gloried in being worshippers of the Supreme Deity, the Creator of heaven and earth, yet, because they had no Mediator, it was impossible for them to have any real acquaintance with the mercy of God, or persuasion that he was their Father. Therefore, as they did not hold the head, that is, Christ, all their knowledge of God was obscure and unsettled; whence it came to pass, that degenerating at length into gross and vile superstitions, they betrayed their ignorance, like the Turks in modern times; who, though they boast of having the Creator of heaven and earth for their God, yet only substitute an idol instead of the true God as long as they remain enemies to Christ.

6.

Faith Defined, and Its Properties Described.

All these things will be easily understood when we have given a clearer definition of faith, that the reader may perceive its nature and importance. But it will be proper to recall to his remembrance, what has been already stated; that God has given us his law as the rule of our conduct, and that, if we are guilty of even the smallest breach of it, we are exposed to the dreadful punishment of eternal death, which he denounces. Again, that since it is not only difficult, but entirely above our strength, and beyond the utmost extent of our ability, to fulfil the law as he requires,—if we only view ourselves, and consider what we have demerited, we have not the least hope left, but, as persons rejected by God, are on the verge of eternal perdition. In the third place, it has been explained, that there is but one method of deliverance, by which we can be extricated from such a direful calamity; that is, the appearance of Christ the Redeemer, by whose means our heavenly Father, commiserating us in his infinite goodness and mercy, has been pleased to relieve us, if we embrace this mercy with a sincere faith, and rely on it with a constant hope. But we must now examine the nature of this faith, by which all who are the adopted sons of God enter on the possession of the heavenly kingdom; since it is certain, that not every opinion, nor even every persuasion, is equal to the accomplishment of so great a work. And we ought to be the more cautious and diligent in our meditations and inquiries on the genuine property of faith, in proportion to the pernicious tendency of the mistakes of multitudes in the present age on this subject. For a great part of the world, when they hear the word *faith*, conceive it to be nothing more than a common assent to the evangelical history. And even the disputes of the schools concerning faith, by simply styling God the object of it, (as I have elsewhere observed,) rather mislead miserable souls by a vain speculation, than direct them to the proper mark. For, since God "dwelleth in the light, which no man can approach unto," there is a necessity for the interposition of Christ, as the medium of access to him. Whence he calls himself "the light of the world," and in another place, "the way, and the truth, and the life;" because "no man cometh unto the Father," who is the fountain of life, "but by him;" because he alone knows the Father, and reveals him to believers.

For this reason Paul asserts, that he esteemed nothing worthy of being known but Jesus Christ; and in the twentieth Chapter of the Acts declares, that he had preached faith in Christ; and in another place, he introduces Christ speaking in the following manner: "I send thee unto the Gentiles, that they may receive forgiveness of sins, and inheritance among them which are sanctified by faith, that is in me." This apostle tells us, that the glory of God is visible to us in his person, or (which conveys the same idea) that "the light of the knowledge of the glory of God" shines "in his face." It is true, that faith relates to the one God; but there must also be added a knowledge of Jesus Christ, whom he has sent. For God himself would be altogether concealed from us, if we were not illuminated by the brightness of Christ. For this purpose the Father has deposited all his treasures with his only begotten Son, that he might reveal himself in him; and that, by such a communication of blessings, he might express a true image of his glory. For as it has been observed, that we require to be drawn by the Spirit, that we may be excited to seek Christ, so we should also be apprized, that the invisible

Father is to be sought only in this image. On which subject, Augustine, treating of the object of faith, beautifully remarks, "that we ought to know whither we should go, and in what way;" and immediately after he concludes, "that he who unites Deity and humanity in one person, is the way most secure from all errors; for that it is God towards whom we tend, and man by whom we go; but that both together can be found only in Christ." Nor does Paul, when he speaks of faith in God, intend to subvert what he so frequently inculcates concerning faith, whose stability is wholly in Christ. And Peter most suitably connects them together, when he says, that "by him we believe in God."

II. This evil, then, as well as innumerable others, must be imputed to the schoolmen, who have, as it were, concealed Christ, by drawing a veil over him; whereas, unless our views be immediately and steadily directed to him, we shall always be wandering through labyrinths without end. They not only, by their obscure definition, diminish, and almost annihilate, all the importance of faith, but have fabricated the notion of implicit faith, a term with which they have honoured the grossest ignorance, and most perniciously deluded the miserable multitude. Indeed, to express the fact more truly and plainly, this notion has not only buried the true faith in oblivion, but has entirely destroyed it. Is this faith—to understand nothing, but obediently to submit our understanding to the Church? Faith consists not in ignorance, but in knowledge; and that not only of God, but also of the Divine will. For we do not obtain salvation by our promptitude to embrace as truth whatever the Church may have prescribed, or by our transferring to her the province of inquiry and of knowledge. But when we know God to be a propitious Father to us, through the reconciliation effected by Christ, and that Christ is given to us for righteousness, sanctification, and life,—by this knowledge, I say, not by renouncing our understanding, we obtain an entrance into the kingdom of heaven. For, when the apostle says, that "with the heart man believeth unto righteousness, and with the mouth confession is made unto salvation," he indicates, that it is not sufficient for a man implicitly to credit what he neither understands, nor even examines; but he requires an explicit knowledge of the Divine goodness, in which our righteousness consists.

III. I do not deny (such is the ignorance with which we are enveloped) that many things are very obscure to us at present, and will continue to be so, till we shall have cast off the burden of the flesh, and arrived nearer to the presence of God. On such subjects, nothing would be more proper than a suspension of judgment, and a firm resolution to maintain unity with the Church. But that ignorance combined with humility should, under this pretext, be dignified with the appellation of Faith, is extremely absurd. For faith consists in a knowledge of God and of Christ, not in reverence for the Church. And we see what a labyrinth they have fabricated by this notion of theirs, so that the ignorant and inexperienced, without any discrimination, eagerly embrace as oracular every thing obtruded upon them under the name of the Church; sometimes even the most monstrous errors. This inconsiderate credulity, though it be the certain precipice of ruin, is, nevertheless, excused by them on the plea that it credits nothing definitively, but with this condition annexed, if such be the faith of the Church. Thus they pretend that truth is held in error, light in darkness, and true knowledge in ignorance. But, not to occupy any more time in refuting them, we only admonish the reader to compare their doctrine with ours; for the perspicuity of the truth will of itself furnish a sufficient refutation. For the question with them is not, whether faith be yet involved in many relics of ignorance, but they positively assert, that persons are possessed of true faith, who are charmed with their ignorance, and even indulge it, provided they assent to the authority and judgment of the Church concerning things unknown; as if the Scripture did not universally inculcate that knowledge is united with faith.

IV. We grant, that during our pilgrimage in the world, our faith is implicit, not only because many things are yet hidden from our view, but because our knowledge of every thing is very imperfect, in consequence of the clouds of error by which we are surrounded. For the greatest wisdom of those who are most perfect, is to improve, and to press forward with patient docility. Therefore Paul exhorts the faithful, if they differ from each other on any subject, to wait for further revelation. And experience teaches us, that till we are divested of the flesh, our knowledge falls far short of what might be wished; in reading also, many obscure passages daily occur, which convince us of our ignorance. With this barrier God restrains us within the bounds of modesty, assigning to every one a measure of faith, that even the most learned teacher may be ready to learn. We may observe eminent examples of this implicit faith in the disciples of Christ, before they were fully enlightened. We see with what difficulty they imbibed the first rudiments; how they hesitated even at the most minute particulars; what inconsiderable advances they made even while hanging on the lips of their Master; and when they ran to the grave at the intelligence of the women, his resurrection was like a dream to them. The testimony already borne by Christ to their possession of faith, forbids us to say that they were entirely destitute of it; indeed, if they had not been persuaded that Christ would rise from the dead, they would have felt no further concern about him. The women were not induced by superstition to embalm with spices the body of a deceased man, of whose life there was no hope; but though they credited his declarations, whose veracity they well knew, yet the ignorance, which still occupied their minds, involved their faith in darkness, so that they were almost lost in astonishment. Whence also they are said at length to have believed, when they saw the words of Christ verified by facts; not that their faith then commenced, but the seed of faith, which had been latent, and as it were dead in their hearts, then shot forth with additional vigour. They had therefore a true but an implicit faith, because they received Christ with reverence as their only teacher: being taught by him, they were persuaded that he was the author of their salvation; and they believed that he came from heaven, that through the grace of the Father he might assemble all his disciples there. But we need not seek a more familiar proof of this point, than that some portion of unbelief is always mixed with faith in every Christian.

V. We may also style that an implicit faith, which in strict propriety is nothing but a preparation for faith. The evangelists relate that many believed, who, only being filled with admiration at the miracles of Christ, proceeded no further than a persuasion that he was the promised Messiah, although they had little or no knowledge of evangelical doctrine. Such reverence, which induced them cheerfully to submit themselves to Christ, is dignified with the title of faith, of which, however, it was merely the commencement. Thus the nobleman, or courtier, who believed the promise of Christ concerning the healing of his son, when he returned to his house, according to the testimony of the evangelist, believed again; that is, first he esteemed as an oracle what he had heard from the lips of Christ; but afterwards he devoted himself to his authority to receive his doctrine. It must be understood, however, that he was docile and ready to learn; that the word *believe*, in the first place, denotes a particular faith; but in the second place, it numbers him among the disciples who had given their names to Christ. John gives us a similar example in the Samaritans, who believed the report of the woman, so as to run with eagerness to Christ; but who, after having heard him, said to the woman, "Now we believe, not because of thy saying; for we have heard him ourselves, and know, that this is indeed the Christ, the Saviour of the world." Hence it appears, that persons not yet initiated into the first elements, but only inclined to obedience, are called believers; not, indeed, with strict propriety, but because God, in his goodness, distinguishes that pious disposition with such a great honour. But this docility, connected with a desire of improvement, is very remote from that gross ignorance which stupefies those who are content with such an implicit faith as the Papists have invented. For if Paul severely condemns those who are "ever learning, yet never come to the knowledge of the truth," how much greater ignominy do they deserve who make it their study to know nothing!

VI. This, then, is the true knowledge of Christ—to receive him as he is offered by the Father, that is, invested with his gospel; for, as he is appointed to be the object of our faith, so we cannot advance in the right way to him, without the guidance of the gospel. The gospel certainly opens to us those treasures of grace, without which Christ would profit us little. Thus Paul connects faith as an inseparable concomitant with doctrine, where he says, "Ye have not so learned Christ; if so be ye have been taught by him, as the truth is in Jesus." Yet I do not so far restrict faith to the gospel, but that I admit Moses and the prophets to have delivered what was sufficient for its establishment; but because the gospel exhibits a fuller manifestation of Christ, it is justly styled by Paul, "the words of faith and of good doctrine." For the same reason, in another place, he represents the law as abolished by the coming of faith; comprehending under this term the new kind of teaching, by which Christ, since his appearance as our Master, has given a brighter display of the mercy of the Father, and a more explicit testimony concerning our salvation. The more easy and convenient method for us will be, to descend regularly from the genus to the species. In the first place, we must be apprized, that faith has a perpetual relation to the word, and can no more be separated from it, than the rays from the sun, whence they proceed. Therefore God proclaims by Isaiah, "Hear, and your souls shall live." And that the word is the fountain of faith, is evident from this language of John: "These are written, that ye might believe." The Psalmist also, intending to exhort the people to faith, says, "To-day, if ye will hear his voice;" and to hear, generally means to believe. Lastly, it is not without reason that in Isaiah, God distinguishes the children of the Church from strangers, by this character, that they shall all be his disciples, and be taught by him; for, if this were a benefit common to all, why should he address himself to a few? Correspondent with this is the general use of the words "believers," and "disciples," as synonymous, by the evangelists, on all occasions, and by Luke in particular, very frequently in the Acts of the Apostles; in the ninth Chapter of which, he extends the latter epithet even to a woman. Wherefore, if faith decline in the smallest degree from this object, towards which it ought to be directed, it no longer retains its own nature, but becomes an uncertain credulity, and an erroneous excursion of the mind. The same Divine word is the foundation by which faith is sustained and supported, from which it cannot be moved without an immediate downfall. Take away the word, then, and there will be no faith left. We are not here disputing whether the ministry of men be necessary to disseminate the word of God, by which faith is produced, which we shall discuss in another place; but we assert, that the word itself, however it may be conveyed to us, is like a mirror, in which faith may behold God. Whether, therefore, God in this instance use the agency of men, or whether he operate solely by his own power, he always discovers himself by his word to those whom he designs to draw to himself. Whence Paul defines faith as an obedience rendered to the gospel, and praises the service of faith. For the apprehension of faith is not confined to our knowing that there is a God, but chiefly consists in our understanding what is his disposition towards us. For it is not of so much importance to us to know what he is in himself, as what he is willing to be to us. We find, therefore, that faith is a knowledge of the will of God respecting us, received from his word. And the foundation of this is a previous persuasion of the Divine veracity; any doubt of which being entertained in the mind, the authority of the word will be dubious and weak, or rather it will be of no authority at all. Nor is it sufficient to believe that the veracity of God is incapable of deception or falsehood, unless you also admit, as beyond all doubt, that whatever proceeds from him is sacred and inviolable truth.

VII. But as the human heart is not excited to faith by every word of God, we must further inquire what part of the word it is, with which faith is particularly concerned. God declared to Adam, "Thou shalt surely die;" and to Cain, "The voice of thy brother's blood crieth unto me from the ground;" but these declarations are so far from being adapted to the establishment of faith, that of themselves they can only shake it. We do not deny that it is the office of faith to subscribe to the truth of God, whatever be the time, the nature, or the manner of his communications; but our present inquiry is only, what faith finds in the Divine word, upon which to rest its dependence and confidence. When our conscience beholds nothing but indignation and vengeance, how shall it not tremble with fear? And if God be the object of its terror, how should it not fly from him? But faith ought to seek God, not to fly from him. It appears, then, that we have not yet a complete definition of faith; since a knowledge of the Divine will indefinitely, ought not to be accounted faith. But suppose, instead of will,—the declaration of which is often productive of fear and sorrow,—we substitute benevolence or mercy. This will certainly bring us nearer to the nature of faith. For we are allured to seek God, after we have learned that salvation is laid up for us with him; which is confirmed to us by his declaring it to be the object of his care and affection. Therefore we need a promise of grace, to assure us that he is our propitious Father; since we cannot approach to him without it, and it is upon that alone that the human heart can securely depend. For this reason, in the Psalms, mercy and truth are generally united, as being closely connected; because it would be of no avail for us to know the veracity of God, if he did not allure us to himself by his mercy; nor should we embrace his mercy, if he did not offer it with his own mouth. "I have declared thy faithfulness and thy salvation: I have not concealed thy loving-kindness and thy truth. Let thy loving-kindness and thy truth continually preserve me." Again: "Thy mercy, O Lord, is in the heavens; and thy faithfulness reacheth unto the clouds." Again: "All the paths of the Lord are mercy and truth unto such as keep his covenant." Again: "His merciful kindness is great towards us; and the truth of the Lord endureth for ever." Again: "I will praise thy name for thy loving-kindness, and for thy truth." I forbear to quote what we read in the prophets to the same purport, that God is merciful and faithful in his promises. For it will be temerity to conclude that God is propitious to us, unless he testify concerning himself, and anticipate us by his invitation, that his will respecting us may be neither ambiguous nor obscure. But we have already seen, that Christ is the only pledge of his love, without whom the tokens of his hatred and wrath are manifest both above and below. Now, since the knowledge of the Divine goodness will not be attended with much advantage, unless it lead us to rely upon it, we must exclude that apprehension of it which is mixed with doubts, which is not uniform and steady, but wavering and undecided. Now, the human mind, blinded and darkened as it is, is very far from being able to penetrate and attain to a knowledge of the Divine will; and the heart also, fluctuating in perpetual hesitation, is far from continuing unshaken in that persuasion. Therefore our mind must be illuminated, and our heart established by some exterior power, that the word of God may obtain full credit with us. Now, we shall have a complete definition of faith, if we say, that it is a steady and certain knowledge of the Divine benevolence towards us, which, being founded on the truth of the gratuitous promise in Christ, is both revealed to our minds, and confirmed to our hearts, by the Holy Spirit.

VIII. But before I proceed any further, it will be necessary to make some preliminary observations, for the solution of difficulties, which otherwise might prove obstacles in the way of the reader.

And first, we must refute the nugatory distinction, which prevails in the schools, of formal and informal faith. For they imagine, that such as are not impressed with any fear of God, or with any sense of piety, believe all that is necessary to be known in order to salvation; as though the Holy Spirit, in illuminating our hearts to faith, were not a witness to us of our adoption. Yet, in opposition to the whole tenor of Scripture, they presumptuously dignify such a persuasion, destitute of the fear of God, with the name of faith. We need not contend with this definition any further than by simply describing the nature of faith, as it is represented in the Divine word. And this will clearly evince the ignorance and insipidity of their clamour concerning it. I have treated it in part already, and shall subjoin what remains in its proper place. At present, I affirm, that a greater absurdity than this figment of theirs, cannot possibly be imagined. They maintain faith to be a mere assent, with which every despiser of God may receive as true whatever is contained in the Scripture. But first it should be examined, whether every man acquires faith for himself by his own power, or whether it is by faith that the Holy Spirit becomes the witness of adoption. They betray puerile folly, therefore, in inquiring whether faith, which is formed by the superaddition of a quality, be the same, or whether it be a new and different faith. It clearly appears, that while they have been trifling in this manner, they never thought of the peculiar gift of the Spirit; for the commencement of faith contains in it the reconciliation by which man draws near to God. But, if they would duly consider that declaration of Paul, "With the heart man believeth unto righteousness," they would cease their trifling about this superadded quality. If we had only this one reason, it ought to be sufficient to terminate the controversy—that the assent which we give to the Divine word, as I have partly suggested before, and shall again more largely repeat, is from the heart rather than the head, and from the affections rather than the understanding. For which reason it is called "the obedience of faith," to which the Lord prefers no other obedience; because nothing is more precious to him than his own truth; which, according to the testimony of John the Baptist, believers, as it were, subscribe and seal. As this is by no means a dubious point, we conclude at once, that it is an absurdity to say, that faith is formed by the addition of a pious affection to an assent of the mind; whereas, even this assent consists in a pious affection, and is so described in the Scriptures. But another argument offers itself, which is still plainer. Since faith accepts Christ, as he is offered to us by the Father; and he is offered, not only for righteousness, remission of sins, and peace, but also for sanctification and as a fountain of living water; it is certain, that no man can ever know him aright, unless he at the same time receive the sanctification of the Spirit. Or, if any one would wish it to be more clearly expressed, Faith consists in a knowledge of Christ. Christ cannot be known without the sanctification of his Spirit. Consequently, faith is absolutely inseparable from a pious affection.

IX. This passage of Paul, "Though I have all faith, so that I could remove mountains, and have not charity, I am nothing," is generally adduced by them to support the notion of an informal faith unaccompanied with charity; but they overlook the sense in which the apostle uses the word "faith" in this place. For having, in the preceding Chapter, treated of the various gifts of the Spirit, among which he has enumerated "divers kinds of tongues, the working of miracles and prophecy," and having exhorted the Corinthians to "covet earnestly the best gifts," from which the greatest benefit and advantage would accrue to the whole body of the Church, he adds, "yet show I unto you a more excellent way;" implying, that all such gifts, whatever be their intrinsic excellence, are yet to be deemed worthless, unless they be subservient to charity; for that, being given for the edification of the Church, if not employed for that purpose, they lose their beauty and value. To prove this, he particularly specifies them, repeating the same gifts, which he had before enumerated, but under other names. He uses the word "faith" to denote what he had before called powers, (δυναμεις, *potestates, virtutes,*) that is, a power of working miracles. This, then, whether it be called power or faith, being a particular gift of God, which any impious man may both possess and abuse, as the gift of tongues, or prophecy, or other gifts, we need not wonder if it be separated from charity. But the mistake of such persons arises wholly from this—that though the word "faith" is used in many senses, not observing this diversity of signification, they argue as if it had always the same meaning. The passage which they adduce from James in support of the same error, shall be discussed in another place. Now, although, for the sake of instruction, when we design to show the nature of that knowledge of God, which is possessed by the impious, we allow that there are various kinds of faith, yet we acknowledge and preach only one faith in the pious, according to the doctrine of the Scripture. Many men certainly believe that there is a God; they admit the evangelical history and the other parts of Scripture to be true; just as we form an opinion of transactions which are narrated as having occurred in former times, or of which we have ourselves been spectators. There are some who go further; esteeming the word of God as an undoubted revelation from heaven, not wholly disregarding its precepts, and being in some measure affected both by its denunciations and by its promises. To such persons, indeed, faith is attributed; but by a catachresis, a tropical or improper form of expression; because they do not with open impiety resist, or reject, or contemn the word of God, but rather exhibit some appearance of obedience to it.

X. But this shadow or image of faith, as it is of no importance, so is unworthy of the name of faith; its great distance from the substantial truth of which, though we shall show more at large hereafter, there can be no objection to its being briefly pointed out here. Simon Magus is said to have believed, who, nevertheless, just after, betrays his unbelief. When faith is attributed to him, we do not apprehend, with some, that he merely pretended to it with his lips, while he had none in his heart; but we rather think, that being overcome with the majesty of the gospel, he did exercise a kind of faith, and perceived Christ to be the author of life and salvation, so as freely to profess himself one of his followers. Thus, in the Gospel of Luke, those persons are said to believe for a time, in whom the seed of the word is prematurely choked before it fructifies, and those in whom it takes no root, but soon dries up and perishes. We doubt not but such persons, being attracted with some taste of the word, receive it with avidity, and begin to perceive something of its Divine power; so that by the fallacious counterfeit of faith, they impose not only on the eyes of men, but even on their own minds. For they persuade themselves, that the reverence which they show for the word of God, is real piety; supposing that there is no impiety but a manifest and acknowledged abuse or contempt of it. But, whatever be the nature of that assent, it penetrates not to the heart, so as to fix its residence there; and though it sometimes appears to have shot forth roots, yet there is no life in them. The heart of man has so many recesses of vanity, and so many retreats of falsehood, and is so enveloped with fraudulent hypocrisy, that it frequently deceives even himself. But let them, who glory in such phantoms of faith, know, that in this respect they are not at all superior to devils. Persons of the former description, who hear and understand without any emotion those things, the knowledge of which makes devils tremble, are certainly far inferior to the fallen spirits; and the others are equal to them in this respect—that the sentiments with which they are impressed, finally terminate in terror and consternation.

XI. I know that it appears harsh to some, when faith is attributed to the reprobate; since Paul affirms it to be the fruit of election. But this difficulty is easily solved; for, though none are illuminated to faith, or truly feel the efficacy of the gospel, but such as are preordained to salvation, yet experience shows, that the reprobate are sometimes affected with emotions very similar to those of the elect, so that, in their own opinion, they in no respect differ from the elect. Wherefore, it is not at all absurd, that a taste of heavenly gifts is ascribed to them by the apostle, and a temporary faith by Christ: not that they truly perceive the energy of spiritual grace and clear light of faith, but because the Lord, to render their guilt more manifest and inexcusable, insinuates himself into their minds, as far as his goodness can be enjoyed without the Spirit of adoption. If any one object, that there remains, then, no further evidence by which the faithful can certainly judge of their adoption, I reply, that although there is a great similitude and affinity between the elect of God and those who are endued with a frail and transitory faith, yet the elect possess that confidence, which Paul celebrates, so as boldly to "cry, Abba, Father." Therefore, as God regenerates for ever the elect alone with incorruptible seed, so that the seed of life planted in their hearts never perishes, so he firmly seals within them the grace of his adoption, that it may be confirmed and ratified to their minds. But this by no means prevents that inferior operation of the Spirit from exerting itself even in the reprobate. In the mean time the faithful are taught to examine themselves with solicitude and humility, lest carnal security insinuate itself, instead of the assurance of faith. Besides, the reprobate have only a confused perception of grace, so that they embrace the shadow rather than the substance; because the Spirit properly seals remission of sins in the elect alone, and they apply it by a special faith to their own benefit. Yet the reprobate are justly said to believe that God is propitious to them, because they receive the gift of reconciliation, though in a confused and too indistinct manner: not that they are partakers of the same faith or regeneration with the sons of God, but because they appear, under the disguise of hypocrisy, to have the principle of faith in common with them. Nor do I deny, that God so far enlightens their minds, that they discover his grace; but he so distinguishes that perception from the peculiar testimony, which he gives to his elect, that they never attain any solid effect and enjoyment. For he does not, therefore, show himself propitious to them, by truly delivering them from death, and receiving them under his protection; but he only manifests to them present mercy. But he vouchsafes to the elect alone, the living root of faith, that they may persevere even to the end. Thus we have refuted the objection, that if God truly discovers his grace, it remains for ever; because nothing prevents God from illuminating some with a present perception of his grace, which afterwards vanishes away.

XII. Moreover, though faith is a knowledge of the benevolence of God towards us, and a certain persuasion of his veracity, yet it is not to be wondered at, that the subjects of these temporary impressions lose the sense of Divine love, which, notwithstanding its affinity to faith, is yet widely different from it. The will of God, I confess, is immutable, and his truth always consistent with itself. But I deny that the reprobate ever go so far as to penetrate to that secret revelation, which the Scripture confines to the elect. I deny, therefore, that they either apprehend the will of God, as it is immutable, or embrace his truth with constancy; because they rest in a fugitive sentiment. Thus a tree, not planted deeply enough to shoot forth living roots, in process of time withers; though for some years it may produce not only leaves and blossoms, but even fruits. Finally, as the defection of the first man was sufficient to obliterate the Divine image from his mind and soul, so we need not wonder if God enlightens the reprobate with some beams of his grace, which he afterwards suffers to be extinguished. Nor does any thing prevent him from slightly tincturing some with the knowledge of his gospel, and thoroughly imbuing others with it. It must, nevertheless, be remembered, that how diminutive and weak soever faith may be in the elect, yet, as the Spirit of God is a certain pledge and seal to them of their adoption, his impression can never be erased from their hearts; but that the reprobate have only a few scattered rays of light, which are afterwards lost; yet that the Spirit is not chargeable with deception, because he infuses no life into the seed which he drops in their hearts, that it may remain for ever incorruptible, as in the elect. I go still further; for since it is evident from the tenor of the Scripture, and from daily experience, that the reprobate are sometimes affected with a sense of Divine grace, some desire of mutual love must necessarily be excited in their hearts. Thus Saul had for a time a pious disposition to love God, from whom experiencing paternal kindness, he was allured by the charms of his goodness. But as the persuasion of the paternal love of God is not radically fixed in the reprobate, so they love him not reciprocally with the sincere affection of children, but are influenced by a mercenary disposition; for the spirit of love was given to Christ alone, that he might instil it into his members. And this observation of Paul certainly extends to none but the elect: "The love of God is shed abroad in our hearts by the Holy Ghost, which is given unto us;" the same love, which generates that confidence of invocation which I have before mentioned. Thus, on the contrary, we see that God is wonderfully angry with his children, whom he ceases not to love: not that he really hates them, but because he designs to terrify them with a sense of his wrath, to humble their carnal pride, to shake off their indolence, and to excite them to repentance. Therefore they apprehend him to be both angry with them, or at least with their sins, and propitious to them at the same time; for they sincerely deprecate his wrath, and yet resort to him for succour with tranquillity and confidence. Hence it appears, that faith is not hypocritically counterfeited by some, who nevertheless are destitute of true faith; but, while they are hurried away with a sudden impetuosity of zeal, they deceive themselves by a false opinion. Nor is it to be doubted, that indolence preoccupies them, and prevents them from properly examining their hearts as they ought to do. It is probable that those persons were of this description, to whom, according to John, "Jesus did not commit himself," notwithstanding that they believed in him, "because he knew all men: he knew what was in man." If multitudes did not depart from the common faith, (I style it common, because there is a great similitude and affinity between temporary faith and that which is living and perpetual,) Christ would not have said to his disciples, "If ye continue in my word, then are ye my disciples indeed, and ye shall know the truth, and the truth shall make you free." For he addresses those who have embraced his doctrine, and exhorts them to an increase of faith, that the light which they have received may not be extinguished by their own supineness. Therefore Paul claims faith as peculiar to the elect, indicating that many decay, because they have had no living root. Thus also Christ says in Matthew, "Every plant, which my heavenly Father hath not planted, shall be rooted up." There is a grosser deception in others, who are not ashamed to attempt to deceive both God and men. James inveighs against this class of men, who impiously profane faith by hypocritical pretensions to it. Nor would Paul require from the children of God, a "faith unfeigned," but because multitudes presumptuously arrogate to themselves what they possess not, and with their vain pretences deceive others, and sometimes even themselves. Therefore he compares a good conscience to a vessel in which faith is kept; because many, "having put away a good conscience, concerning faith have made shipwreck."

XIII. We must also remember the ambiguous signification of the word *faith*; for frequently faith signifies the sound doctrine of piety, as in the place which we have just cited, and in the same Epistle, where Paul says, that deacons must hold "the mystery of the faith in a pure conscience." Also where he predicts the apostasy of some "from the faith." But, on the contrary, he says, that Timothy had been "nourished up in the words of faith." Again, where he says, "avoiding profane and vain babblings, and oppositions of science, falsely so called; which some professing, have erred concerning the faith;" whom in another place he styles "reprobates concerning the faith." Thus, also, when he directs Titus to "rebuke them, that they may be sound in the faith," by soundness, he means nothing more than that purity of doctrine, which is so liable to be corrupted and to degenerate through the instability of men. Since "all the treasures of wisdom and knowledge are hidden in Christ," whom faith possesses, faith is justly extended to the whole summary of heavenly doctrines, with which it is inseparably connected. On the contrary, it is sometimes restricted to a particular object; as when Matthew says, that "Jesus saw their faith," who let down the paralytic man through the roof; and when Christ exclaimed respecting the centurion, "I have not found so great faith, no, not in Israel." But it is probable, that the centurion was wholly intent on the recovery of his son, a concern for whom wholly occupied his mind; yet, because he was contented with the mere answer of Christ, without being importunate for his corporeal presence, it is on account of this circumstance that his faith is so greatly extolled. And we have lately shown, that Paul uses faith for the gift of miracles; which is possessed by those who are neither regenerated by the Spirit of God, nor serious worshippers of him. In another place, also, he uses it to denote the instruction by which we are edified in the faith; for, when he suggests that faith will be abolished, it must undoubtedly be referred to the ministry of the Church, which is, at present, useful to our infirmity. In these forms of expression, however, there is an evident analogy. But when the word "faith" is in an improper sense transferred to a hypocritical profession, or to that which falsely assumes the name, it should not be accounted a harsher catachresis, than when the fear of God is used for a corrupt and perverse worship; as when it is frequently said in the sacred history, that the foreign nations, which had been transplanted to Samaria and its vicinity, feared the fictitious deities and the God of Israel; which is like confounding together heaven and earth. But our present inquiry is, what is that faith by which the children of God are distinguished from unbelievers, by which we invoke God as our Father, by which we pass from death to life, and by which Christ, our eternal life and salvation, dwells in us? The force and nature of it, I conceive, I have concisely and clearly explained.

XIV. Now, let us again examine all the parts of that definition; a careful consideration of which, I think, will leave nothing doubtful remaining. When we call it knowledge, we intend not such a comprehension as men commonly have of those things which fall under the notice of their senses. For it is so superior, that the human mind must exceed and rise above itself, in order to attain to it. Nor does the mind which attains it comprehend what it perceives, but being persuaded of that which it cannot comprehend, it understands more by the certainty of this persuasion, than it would comprehend of any human object by the exercise of its natural capacity. Wherefore Paul beautifully expresses it in these terms: "to comprehend what is the breadth, and length, and depth, and height; and to know the love of Christ, which passeth knowledge." For he meant to suggest, that what our mind apprehends by faith is absolutely infinite, and that this kind of knowledge far exceeds all understanding. Yet, because God has revealed to his saints the secret of his will, "which had been hidden from ages and from generations," therefore *faith* is in Scripture justly styled "an acknowledgment;" and by John, "knowledge," when he asserts, that believers know that they are the sons of God. And they have indeed a certain knowledge of it; but are rather confirmed by a persuasion of the veracity of God, than taught by any demonstration of reason. The language of Paul also indicates this: "whilst we are at home in the body, we are absent from the Lord; for we walk by faith, not by sight." By this he shows that the things which we understand through faith, are at a distance from us, and beyond our sight. Whence we conclude, that the knowledge of faith consists more in certainty than in comprehension.

XV. To express the solid constancy of the persuasion, we further say, that it is a certain and steady knowledge. For, as faith is not content with a dubious and versatile opinion, so neither with an obscure and perplexed conception; but requires a full and fixed certainty, such as is commonly obtained respecting things that have been tried and proved. For unbelief is so deeply rooted in our hearts, and such is our propensity to it, that though all men confess with the tongue, that God is faithful, no man can persuade himself of the truth of it, without the most arduous exertions. Especially when the time of trial comes, the general indecision discloses the fault which was previously concealed. Nor is it without reason that the Holy Spirit asserts the authority of the Divine word in terms of such high commendation, but with a design to remedy the disease which I have mentioned, that the promises of God may obtain full credit with us. "The words of the Lord (says David) are pure words; as silver tried in a furnace of earth purified seven times." Again: "The word of the Lord is tried: he is a buckler to all those that trust in him." And Solomon confirms the same, nearly in the same words: "Every word of God is pure." But, as the hundred and nineteenth Psalm is almost entirely devoted to this subject, it were needless to recite any more testimonies. Whenever God thus recommends his word to us, he, without doubt, obliquely reprehends our unbelief; for the design of those recommendations is no other than to eradicate perverse doubts from our hearts. There are also many, who have such conceptions of the Divine mercy, as to receive but very little consolation from it. For they are at the same time distressed with an unhappy anxiety, doubting whether he will be merciful to them; because they confine within too narrow limits that clemency, of which they suppose themselves to be fully persuaded. For they reflect with themselves thus: that his mercy is large and copious, bestowed upon many, and ready for the acceptance of all; but that it is uncertain whether it will reach them also, or, rather, whether they shall reach it. This thought, since it stops in the midst of its course, is incomplete. Therefore it does not so much confirm the mind with secure tranquillity, as disturb it with restless hesitation. But very different is the meaning of "full assurance," ($\pi\lambda\eta\rho o\phi o\rho\iota\alpha\varsigma$,) which is always attributed to faith in the Scriptures; and which places the goodness of God, that is clearly revealed to us, beyond all doubt. But this cannot take place, unless we have a real sense and experience of its sweetness in ourselves. Wherefore the apostle from faith deduces confidence, and from confidence boldness. For this is his language: "In Christ we have boldness and access, with confidence by the faith of him." These words imply that we have no right faith, but when we can venture with tranquillity into the Divine presence. This boldness arises only from a certain confidence of the Divine benevolence and our salvation; which is so true, that the word "faith" is frequently used for confidence.

XVI. The principal hinge on which faith turns is this—that we must not consider the promises of mercy, which the Lord offers, as true only to others, and not to ourselves; but rather make them our own, by embracing them in our hearts. Hence arises that confidence, which the same apostle in another place calls "peace;" unless any one would rather make peace the effect of confidence. It is a security, which makes the conscience calm and serene before the Divine tribunal, and without which it must necessarily be harassed and torn almost asunder with tumultuous trepidation, unless it happen to slumber for a moment in an oblivion of God and itself. And indeed it is but for a moment; for it does not long enjoy that wretched oblivion, but is most dreadfully wounded by the remembrance, which is perpetually recurring, of the Divine judgment. In short, no man is truly a believer, unless he be firmly persuaded, that God is a propitious and benevolent Father to him, and promise himself every thing from his goodness; unless he depend on the promises of the Divine benevolence to him, and feel an undoubted expectation of salvation; as the apostle shows in these words: "If we hold fast the beginning of our confidence steadfast unto the end." Here he supposes, that no man has a good hope in the Lord, who does not glory with confidence, in being an heir of the kingdom of heaven. He is no believer, I say, who does not rely on the security of his salvation, and confidently triumph over the devil and death, as Paul teaches us in this remarkable peroration: "I am persuaded (says he) that neither death, nor life, nor angels, nor principalities, nor powers, nor things present, nor things to come, shall be able to separate us from the love of God, which is in Christ Jesus our Lord." Thus the same apostle is of opinion, that "the eyes of our understanding" are not truly "enlightened," unless we discover what is the hope of the eternal inheritance, to which we are called. And he every where inculcates, that we have no just apprehensions of the Divine goodness, unless we derive from it a considerable degree of assurance.

XVII. But some one will object, that the experience of believers is very different from this; for that, in recognizing the grace of God towards them, they are not only disturbed with inquietude, (which frequently befalls them,) but sometimes also tremble with the most distressing terrors. The vehemence of temptations, to agitate their minds, is so great, that it appears scarcely compatible with that assurance of faith of which we have been speaking. We must therefore solve this difficulty, if we mean to support the doctrine we have advanced. When we inculcate, that faith ought to be certain and secure, we conceive not of a certainty attended with no doubt, or of a security interrupted by no anxiety; but we rather affirm, that believers have a perpetual conflict with their own diffidence, and are far from placing their consciences in a placid calm, never disturbed by any storms. Yet, on the other hand, we deny, however they may be afflicted, that they ever fall and depart from that certain confidence which they have conceived in the Divine mercy. The Scripture proposes no example of faith more illustrious or memorable than David, especially if you consider the whole course of his life. Yet that his mind was not invariably serene, appears from his innumerable complaints, of which it will be sufficient to select a few. When he rebukes his soul for turbulent emotions, is he not angry with his unbelief? "Why (says he) art thou cast down, O my soul? and why art thou disquieted in me? Hope thou in God." And, certainly, that consternation was an evident proof of diffidence, as though he supposed himself to be forsaken by God. In another place, also, we find a more ample confession: "I said, in my haste, I am cut off from before thine eyes." In another place, also, he debates with himself in anxious and miserable perplexity, and even raises a dispute concerning the nature of God: "Hath God forgotten to be gracious? Will the Lord cast off for ever?" What follows is still harsher: "And I said, I must fall; these are the changes of the right hand of the Most High." For, in a state of despair, he consigns himself to ruin; and not only confesses that he is agitated with doubts, but, as vanquished in the conflict, considers all as lost; because God has deserted him, and turned to his destruction that hand which used to support him. Wherefore it is not without reason that he says, "Return unto thy rest, O my soul;" since he had experienced such fluctuations amidst the waves of trouble. And yet, wonderful as it is, amidst these concussions, faith sustains the hearts of the pious, and truly resembles the palm-tree, rising with vigour undiminished by any burdens which may be laid upon it, but which can never retard its growth; as David, when he might appear to be overwhelmed, yet, chiding himself, ceased not to aspire towards God. Indeed, he who, contending with his own infirmity, strives in his anxieties to exercise faith, is already in a great measure victorious. Which we may infer from such passages as this: "Wait on the Lord: be of good courage, and he shall strengthen thine heart; wait, I say, on the Lord." He reproves himself for timidity, and repeating the same twice, confesses himself to be frequently subject to various agitations. In the mean time, he is not only displeased with himself for these faults, but ardently aspires towards the correction of them. Now, if we enter into a close and correct examination of his character and conduct, and compare him with Ahaz, we shall discover a considerable difference. Isaiah is sent to convey consolation to the anxiety of the impious and hypocritical king; he addresses him in these words: "Take heed, and be quiet; fear not," &c. But what effect had the message on him? As it had been before said, that "his heart was moved as the trees of the wood are moved with the wind," though he heard the promise, he ceased not to tremble. This therefore is the proper reward and punishment of infidelity—so to tremble with fear, that he who opens not the gate to himself by faith, in the time of temptation departs from God; but, on the contrary, believers, whom the weight of temptations bends and almost oppresses, constantly emerge from their distresses, though not without trouble and difficulty. And because they are conscious of their own imbecility, they pray with the Psalmist, "Take not the word of truth utterly out of my mouth." By these words we are taught, that they sometimes become dumb, as though their faith were destroyed; yet that they neither fail nor turn their backs, but persevere in their conflict, and arouse their inactivity by prayer, that they may not be stupefied by self-indulgence.

XVIII. To render this intelligible, it is necessary to recur to that division of the flesh and the spirit, which we noticed in another place, and which most clearly discovers itself in this case. The pious heart therefore perceives a division in itself, being partly affected with delight, through a knowledge of the Divine goodness; partly distressed with sorrow, through a sense of its own calamity; partly relying on the promise of the gospel; partly trembling at the evidence of its own iniquity; partly exulting in the apprehension of life; partly alarmed by the fear of death. This variation happens through the imperfection of faith; since we are never so happy, during the present life, as to be cured of all diffidence, and entirely filled and possessed by faith. Hence those conflicts, in which the diffidence which adheres to the relics of the flesh, rises up in opposition to the faith formed in the heart. But if, in the mind of a believer, assurance be mixed with doubts, do we not always come to this point, that faith consists not in a certain and clear, but only in an obscure and perplexed knowledge of the Divine will respecting us? Not at all. For, if we are distracted by various thoughts, we are not therefore entirely divested of faith; neither, though harassed by the agitations of diffidence, are we therefore immerged in its abyss; nor, if we be shaken, are we therefore overthrown. For the invariable issue of this contest is, that faith at length surmounts those difficulties, from which, while it is encompassed with them, it appears to be in danger.

XIX. Let us sum it up thus: As soon as the smallest particle of grace is infused into our minds, we begin to contemplate the Divine countenance as now placid, serene, and propitious to us: it is indeed a very distant prospect, but so clear, that we know we are not deceived. Afterwards, in proportion as we improve,—for we ought to be continually improving by progressive advances,—we arrive at a nearer, and therefore more certain view of him, and by continual habit he becomes more familiar to us. Thus we see, that a mind illuminated by the knowledge of God, is at first involved in much ignorance, which is removed by slow degrees. Yet it is not prevented either by its ignorance of some things, or by its obscure view of what it beholds, from enjoying a clear knowledge of the Divine will respecting itself, which is the first and principal exercise of faith. For, as a man who is confined in a prison, into which the sun shines only obliquely and partially through a very small window, is deprived of a full view of that luminary, yet clearly perceives its splendour, and experiences its beneficial influence,—thus we, who are bound with terrestrial and corporeal fetters, though surrounded on all sides with great obscurity, are nevertheless illuminated, sufficiently for all the purposes of real security, by the light of God shining ever so feebly to discover his mercy.

XX. The apostle beautifully inculcates both these ideas in various places. For when he says, that "we know in part, and we prophesy in part, and see through a glass darkly," he indicates, how very slender a portion of that wisdom which is truly Divine, is conferred upon us in the present life. For although these words imply, not only that faith remains imperfect as long as we groan under the burden of the flesh, but that our imperfection renders it necessary for us to be unremittingly employed in acquiring further knowledge, yet he suggests, that it is impossible for our narrow capacity to comprehend that which is infinite. And this Paul predicates concerning the whole Church; though every individual of us is obstructed and retarded, by his own ignorance, from making that progress which might be wished. But what a sure and certain experience, of itself, even the smallest particle of faith gives us, the same apostle shows in another place, where he asserts, that "we, with open face, beholding as in a glass the glory of the Lord, are changed into the same image." Such profound ignorance must necessarily involve much doubt and trepidation; especially as our hearts are, by a kind of natural instinct, inclined to unbelief. Besides, temptations, various and innumerable, frequently assail us with great violence. Above all, our own conscience, oppressed by its incumbent load of sin, sometimes complains and groans within itself, sometimes accuses itself, sometimes murmurs in secret, and sometimes is openly disturbed. Whether, therefore, adversity discover the wrath of God, or the conscience find in itself any reason or cause of it, thence unbelief derives weapons to oppose faith, which are perpetually directed to this object, to persuade us, that God is angry with us, and inimical to us; that we may not hope for any assistance from him, but may dread him as our irreconcilable enemy.

XXI. To sustain these attacks, faith arms and defends itself with the word of the Lord. And when such a temptation as this assails us,—that God is our enemy, because he is angry with us,—faith, on the contrary, objects, that he is merciful even when he afflicts, because chastisement proceeds rather from love than from wrath. When it is pressed with this thought, that God is an avenger of iniquities, it opposes the pardon provided for all offences, whenever the sinner makes application to the Divine clemency. Thus the pious mind, how strangely soever it may be agitated and harassed, rises at length superior to all difficulties, nor ever suffers its confidence in the Divine mercy to be shaken. The various disputes which exercise and fatigue it, terminate rather in the confirmation of that confidence. It is a proof of this, that when the saints conceive themselves to feel most the vengeance of God, they still confide their complaints to him, and when there is no appearance of his hearing them, they continue to call upon him. For what end would be answered by addressing complaint to him from whom they expected no consolation? And they would never be disposed to call upon him, unless they believed him to be ready to assist them. Thus the disciples, whom Christ reprehends for the weakness of their faith, complained indeed that they were perishing, but still they implored his assistance. Nor, when he chides them on account of their weak faith, does he reject them from the number of his children, or class them with unbelievers; but he excites them to correct that fault. Therefore we repeat the assertion already made, that faith is never eradicated from a pious heart, but continues firmly fixed, however it may be shaken, and seem to bend this way or that; that its light is never so extinguished or smothered, but that it lies at least concealed under embers; and that this is an evident proof, that the word, which is an incorruptible seed, produces fruit similar to itself, whose germ never entirely perishes. For, though it is the last cause of despair that can happen to saints, to perceive, according to their apprehension of present circumstances, the hand of God lifted up for their destruction, yet Job asserts the extent of his hope to be such, that though he should be slain by him, he would continue to trust in him. This, then, is the real state of the case: Unbelief is not inwardly predominant in the hearts of the pious, but it assails them from without; nor do its weapons mortally wound them; they only molest them, or at least inflict such wounds as are curable. For faith, according to Paul, serves us as a shield, which, being opposed to hostile weapons, receives their blows, and entirely repels them, or at least breaks their force, so that they penetrate no vital part. When faith is shaken, therefore, it is just as if a soldier, otherwise bold, were constrained, by a violent stroke of a javelin, to change his position and retreat a little; but when faith itself is wounded, it is just as if his shield were broken by a blow, yet not pierced through. For the pious mind will always recover so far as to say, with David, "Though I walk through the valley of the shadow of death, I will fear no evil; for thou art with me." To walk in the gloom of death is certainly terrible; and believers, whatever degree of firmness they have, cannot but dread it. But when this thought prevails, that God is present with them, and concerned for their salvation, fear at once gives way to security. But, as Augustine says, whatever powerful engines the devil erects against us, when he possesses not the heart, which is the residence of faith, he is kept at a distance. Thus, if we judge from the event, believers not only escape in safety from every battle, so that, receiving an accession of vigour, they are soon after prepared to enter the field again, but we see the accomplishment of what John says, in his canonical Epistle: "This is the victory that overcometh the world, even our faith." For he affirms, that it will be not only victorious in one or in a few battles, or against some particular assault, but that it will overcome the whole world, though it should be attacked a thousand times.

XXII. There is another species of fear and trembling, by which, nevertheless, the assurance of faith is so far from being impaired, that it is more firmly established. That is, when believers, considering the examples of the Divine vengeance against the impious as lessons given to them, are solicitously cautious not to provoke the wrath of God against themselves by the same crimes; or when, feeling their own misery, they learn to place all their dependence on the Lord, without whom they perceive themselves to be more inconstant and transient than the wind. For when the apostle, by a representation of the punishments which the Lord formerly inflicted on the Israelitish nation, alarms the fears of the Corinthians, lest they should involve themselves in the same calamities, he in no respect weakens their confidence, but shakes off the indolence of the flesh, by which faith is rather impaired than confirmed. Nor when, from the fall of the Jews, he takes an occasion to exhort him that standeth to beware lest he fall, does he direct us to waver, as though we were uncertain of our stability; but only forbids all arrogance and presumptuous, overweening confidence in our own strength, that the Gentiles may not proudly insult over the expelled Jews, into whose place they have been received. In that passage, however, he not only addresses believers, but in his discourse also includes hypocrites, who gloried merely in external appearance. For he admonishes not men individually, but instituting a comparison between the Jews and the Gentiles, after having shown that the rejection of the former was a righteous punishment for their unbelief and ingratitude, he exhorts the latter not to lose, by pride and haughtiness, the grace of adoption recently transferred to them. But as, in the general rejection of the Jews, there remained some of them who fell not from the covenant of adoption, so among the Gentiles there might possibly arise some, who, destitute of true faith, would only be inflated with foolish and carnal confidence, and thus abuse the goodness of God to their own ruin. But though you should understand this to be spoken to the elect and believers, no inconvenience would result from it. For it is one thing to repress the temerity, which from remaining carnality sometimes discovers itself in the saints, that it may not produce vain confidence; and another to strike the conscience with fear, that it may not rely with full security on the mercy of God.

XXIII. Moreover, when he teaches us to "work out our own salvation with fear and trembling," he only requires us to accustom ourselves, with great self-humiliation, to look up to the power of the Lord. For nothing arouses us to repose all confidence and assurance of mind on the Lord, so much as diffidence of ourselves, and anxiety arising from a consciousness of our own misery. In which sense, we must understand this declaration of the Psalmist, "I will come into thy house in the multitude of thy mercy, and in thy fear will I worship." Whence he beautifully connects the confidence of faith, which relies on the mercy of God, with that religious fear by which we ought to be affected, whenever we come into the presence of the Divine Majesty, and from its splendour, discover our extreme impurity. Solomon also truly pronounces, "Happy is the man who feareth alway; but he that hardeneth his heart shall fall into mischief." But he intends that fear which will render us more cautious, not such as would afflict and ruin us, such as, when the mind, confounded in itself, recovers itself in God; dejected in itself, finds consolation in him; and despairing of itself, revives with confidence in him. Wherefore nothing prevents believers from being distressed with fear, and at the same time enjoying the most serene consolation; as they now turn their eyes towards their own vanity, and now direct the attention of their mind to the truth of God. How can fear and faith, it will be asked, both reside in the same mind? Just as, on the contrary, insensibility and anxiety. For though the impious endeavour to acquire a habit of insensibility, that they may not be disquieted by the fear of God, the judgment of God follows them so closely, that they cannot attain the object of their desires. So nothing prevents God from training his people to humility, that in their valiant warfare they may restrain themselves within the bounds of modesty. And that this was the design of the apostle appears from the context, where, as the cause of fear and trembling, he assigns the good pleasure of God, by which he gives to his people both rightly to will, and strenuously to perform. In the same sense we should understand this prediction: "The children of Israel shall fear the Lord and his goodness;" for not only piety produces a reverence of God, but also the sweetness of grace fills a man that is dejected in himself, with fear and admiration; causing him to depend upon God, and humbly submit himself to his power.

XXIV. Yet we give no encouragement to the very pestilent philosophy, begun to be broached by some semi-Papists in the present day. For, being unable to defend that gross notion of faith as a doubtful opinion, which has been taught in the schools, they resort to another invention, and propose a confidence mixed with unbelief. They confess, that whenever we look to Christ, we find in him a sufficient ground of comfortable hope; but because we are always unworthy of all those blessings which are offered to us in Christ, they wish us to fluctuate and hesitate in the view of our own unworthiness. In short, they place the conscience in such a state between hope and fear, that it alternately inclines to both. They also connect hope and fear together, so that when the former rises, it depresses the latter, and when the latter lifts its head, the former falls. Thus Satan, finding that those open engines, which he heretofore employed to destroy the assurance of faith, are now no longer of any avail, secretly endeavours to undermine it. But what kind of confidence would that be, which should frequently give way to despair? If you consider Christ, (say they,) salvation is certain; if you return to yourself, condemnation is certain. Diffidence and good hope, therefore, must of necessity alternately prevail in your mind. As though we ought to consider Christ as standing apart from us, and not rather as dwelling within us. For we therefore expect salvation from him, not because he appears to us at a great distance, but because, having ingrafted us into his body, he makes us partakers not only of all his benefits, but also of himself. Wherefore I thus retort their own argument: If you consider yourself, condemnation is certain; but since Christ, with all his benefits, is communicated to you, so that all that he has becomes yours, and you become a member of him, and one with him,—his righteousness covers your sins; his salvation supersedes your condemnation; he interposes with his merit, that your unworthiness may not appear in the Divine presence. Indeed, the truth is, that we ought by no means to separate Christ from us, or ourselves from him; but, with all our might, firmly to retain that fellowship by which he has united us to himself. Thus the apostle teaches us: "The body (says he) is dead because of sin; but the spirit is life because of righteousness." According to this frivolous notion of these persons, he ought to have said, Christ indeed has life in himself; but you, being sinners, remain obnoxious to death and condemnation. But he speaks in a very different manner; for he states, that the condemnation which we demerit in ourselves is swallowed up by the salvation of Christ; and in confirmation of this, uses the same argument as I have adduced, that Christ is not without us, but dwells within us; and not only adheres to us by an indissoluble connection of fellowship, but by a certain wonderful communion coalesces daily more and more into one body with us, till he becomes altogether one with us. Nor do I deny, what I have lately said, that some interruptions of faith at times occur, as its imbecility is by the force of violence inclined to this or the other direction, Thus, in the thick gloom of temptations, its light is smothered; but, whatever befalls it, it never discontinues its efforts in seeking God.

XXV. Bernard reasons in a similar manner, when he professedly discusses this subject, in the Fifth Homily, on the Dedication of the Temple. "By the goodness of God, meditating sometimes on the soul, I think I discover in it, as it were, two opposite characters. If I view it as it is in itself and of itself, I cannot utter a greater truth concerning it, than that it is reduced to nothing. What need is there at present to enumerate all its miseries, how it is loaded with sins, enveloped in darkness, entangled with allurements, inflamed with inordinate desires, subject to the passions, filled with illusions, always prone to evil, inclined to every vice, and finally full of ignominy and confusion? Now, if even our righteousnesses, when viewed in the light of truth, be found to be 'as filthy rags,' what judgment will be formed of our acknowledged unrighteousness? 'If the light that is in' us 'be darkness, how great is that darkness!'

What then? Man is undoubtedly become like vanity; man is reduced to nothing; man is nothing. Yet how is he entirely nothing, whom God magnifies? How is he nothing, on whom the heart of God is fixed? Brethren, let us revive again. Although we are nothing in our own hearts, perhaps there may be something for us latent in the heart of God. O Father of mercies, O Father of the miserable, how dost thou fix thine heart on us! For thine heart is where thy treasure is. But how are we thy treasure, if we are nothing? All nations are before thee as though they existed not; they must be considered as nothing. That is, before thee; not within thee; thus it is in the judgment of thy truth; but not thus in the affection of thy clemency. Thou callest things which are not, as though they were; and therefore they are not, because thou callest things which are not; yet they are, because thou callest them. For though they are not, with reference to themselves, yet with thee they are; according to this expression of Paul: 'Not of works, but of him that calleth.' " After this, Bernard says, that there is a wonderful connection between these two considerations. Things which are connected with each other, certainly do not reciprocally destroy each other; which he also more plainly declares in the following conclusion: "Now, if we diligently examine what we are in both considerations,—how in one view we are nothing, and in the other how we are magnified,—I conceive that our boasting appears to be restrained; but perhaps it is more increased, and indeed established, that we may glory not in ourselves, but in the Lord. If we reflect, if he has decreed to save us, we shall shortly be delivered; this is sufficient to recover us. But ascending to a loftier and more extensive prospect, let us seek the city of God, let us seek his temple, let us seek his palace, let us seek his spouse. I have not forgotten, but with fear and reverence I say, We are; but in the heart of God. We are; but by his condescending favour, not by our own merit."

XXVI. Now, the fear of the Lord, which is universally ascribed to all the saints, and which is called sometimes "the beginning of wisdom," sometimes "wisdom" itself, although it be but one, proceeds from a twofold apprehension of him. For God requires the reverence of a Father and of a Master. Therefore he who truly desires to worship him, will study to pay him the obedience of a son and the submission of a servant. The Lord, by the prophet, distinguishes the obedience which is paid to him as a father, by the appellation of honour; and the service which he receives as a master, by that of fear. "A son (says he) honoureth his father, and a servant his master. If, then, I be a father, where is mine honour? And if I be a master, where is my fear?" But notwithstanding his distinction between them, you see how he confounds them together. Let the fear of the Lord therefore with us be a reverence mingled with this honour and fear. Nor is it surprising, that the same mind cherishes both these affections; for he who considers what a Father God is to us, has ample reason, even though there were no hell, to dread his displeasure more than any death. But, such is the propensity of our nature to the licentiousness of transgression, that in order to restrain it by every possible method, we should at the same time indulge this reflection, that all iniquity is an abomination to the Lord, under whose power we live, and whose vengeance they will not escape, who provoke his wrath against them by the wickedness of their lives.

XXVII. Now, the assertion of John, that "there is no fear in love, but perfect love casteth out fear, because fear hath torment," is not at all repugnant to what we have advanced. For he speaks of the terror of unbelief, between which and the fear of believers there is a wide difference. For the impious fear not God from a dread of incurring his displeasure, if they could do it with impunity; but because they know him to be armed with vindictive power, they tremble with horror at hearing of his wrath. And thus also they fear his wrath, because they apprehend it to be impending over them, because they every moment expect it to fall on their heads. But the faithful, as we have observed, fear his displeasure more than punishment, and are not disturbed with the fear of punishment, as though it were impending over them, but are rendered more cautious that they may not incur it. Thus the apostle, when addressing believers, says, "Let no man deceive you with vain words; for, because of these things cometh the wrath of God upon the children of disobedience [or unbelief.]" He threatens not its descending on them; but admonishes them to consider the wrath of the Lord prepared for the impious, on account of the crimes which he had enumerated, that they may avoid tempting it. It seldom happens, however, that the reprobate are aroused merely by simple threatenings; but, on the contrary, being already obdurate and insensible, when God thunders from heaven, if it be only in words, they rather harden themselves in rebellion; but when they feel the stroke of his hand, they are compelled to fear him, whether they will or not. This is commonly called a servile fear, in opposition to a filial fear, which is ingenuous and voluntary. Some persons curiously introduce an intermediate species of fear; because that servile and constrained affection sometimes subdues men's minds, so that they voluntarily approach to the fear of God.

XXVIII. Now, in the Divine benevolence, which is affirmed to be the object of faith, we apprehend the possession of salvation and everlasting life to be obtained. For, if no good can be wanting when God is propitious, we have a sufficient certainty of salvation, when he himself assures us of his love. "O God, cause thy face to shine, and we shall be saved," says the Psalmist. Hence the Scriptures represent this as the sum of our salvation, that he has "abolished" all "enmity," and received us into his favour. In which they imply, that since God is reconciled to us, there remains no danger, but that all things will prosper with us. Wherefore faith, having apprehended the love of God, has promises for the present life and the life to come, and a solid assurance of all blessings; but it is such an assurance as may be derived from the Divine word. For faith certainly promises itself neither longevity, nor honour, nor wealth, in the present state; since the Lord has not been pleased to appoint any of these things for us; but is contented with this assurance, that whatever we may want of the conveniences or necessaries of this life, yet God will never leave us. But its principal security consists in an expectation of the future life, which is placed beyond all doubt by the word of God. For whatever miseries and calamities may on earth await those who are the objects of the love of God, they cannot prevent the Divine benevolence from being a source of complete felicity. Therefore, when we meant to express the perfection of blessedness, we have mentioned the grace of God, as the fountain from which every species of blessings flows down to us. And we may generally observe in the Scriptures, that when they treat not only of eternal salvation, but of any blessing we enjoy, our attention is recalled to the love of God. For which reason David says, that "The loving-kindness of God," when experienced in a pious heart, "is better" and more desirable "than life" itself. Finally, if we have an abundance of all things to the extent of our desires, but are uncertain of the love or hatred of God, our prosperity will be cursed, and therefore miserable. But if the paternal countenance of God shine on us, even our miseries will be blessed, because they will be converted into aids of our salvation. Thus Paul, after an enumeration of all possible adversities, glories that they can never separate us from the love of God; and in his prayers, he always begins with the grace of God, from which all prosperity proceeds. David likewise opposes the Divine favour alone against all the terrors which disturb us: "Though I walk through the valley of the shadow of death, (says he,) I will fear no evil, for thou art with me." And we always feel our minds wavering, unless, contented with the grace of God, they seek their peace in it, and are deeply impressed with the sentiment of the Psalmist: "Blessed is the nation whose God is the Lord; and the people whom he hath chosen for his own inheritance."

XXIX. We make the foundation of faith to be the gratuitous promise; for on that faith properly rests. For, although faith admits the veracity of God in all things, whether he command or prohibit, whether he promise or threaten; though it obediently receives his injunctions, carefully observes his prohibitions, and attends to his threatenings,— yet with the promise it properly begins, on that it stands, and in that it ends. For it seeks in God for life, which is found, not in precepts nor in denunciations of punishments, but in the promise of mercy, and in that only which is gratuitous; for a conditional promise, which sends us back to our own works, promises life to us only if we find it in ourselves. Therefore, if we wish our faith not to tremble and waver, we must support it with the promise of salvation, which is voluntarily and liberally offered us by the Lord, rather in consideration of our misery, than in respect of our worthiness. Wherefore the apostle denominates the gospel "the word of faith;" a character which he denies both to the precepts and to the promises of the law; since there is nothing that can establish faith, but that liberal embassy by which God reconciles the world to himself. Hence also the same apostle frequently connects faith with the gospel; as when he states, that "the ministry of the gospel was committed to him for obedience to the faith;" that it is "the power of God unto salvation to every one that believeth;" that therein is the "righteousness of God revealed from faith to faith." Nor is this to be wondered at; for the gospel being "the ministry of reconciliation," there is no other sufficient testimony of the Divine benevolence towards us, the knowledge of which is necessary to faith. When we assert, therefore, that faith rests on the gratuitous promise, we deny not that believers embrace and revere every part of the Divine word, but we point out the promise of mercy as the peculiar object of faith. Thus believers ought to acknowledge God as a judge and avenger of crimes; yet they fix their eyes peculiarly on his clemency; described for their contemplation as "gracious and full of compassion; slow to anger, and of great mercy; good to all, and diffusing his tender mercies over all his works."

XXX. Nor do I regard the clamours of Pighius, or any such snarlers, who censure this restriction, as though it divided faith, and comprehended only one branch of it. I grant that, as I have already said, the general object of faith (as they express themselves) is the veracity of God, whether he threaten, or give us a hope of his grace. Wherefore the apostle attributes this to faith, that Noah feared the destruction of the world while it was yet unseen. If the fear of impending punishment was the work of faith, threatenings ought not to be excluded from the definition of it. This indeed is true; but these cavillers unjustly charge us with denying that faith respects every part of the word of God. For we only intend to establish these two points; first, that it never stands firmly till it comes to the gratuitous promise; secondly, that we are reconciled to God only as it unites us to Christ. Both these points are worthy of observation. We are inquiring for a faith which may distinguish the sons of God from the reprobate, and believers from unbelievers. If any man believes the justice of the Divine commands and the truth of the Divine threatenings, must he therefore be called a believer? By no means. Therefore faith can have no stability, unless it be placed on the Divine mercy. Now, to what purpose do we argue concerning faith? Is it not that we may understand the way of salvation? But how is faith saving, but by ingrafting us into the body of Christ? There will be no absurdity, then, if, in the definition of it, we insist on its principal effect, and as a difference, add to the genus that character which separates believers from unbelievers. In a word, these malevolent men have nothing to carp at in this doctrine, without involving in the same reprehension with us, the apostle Paul, who particularly styles the gospel "the word of faith."

XXXI. Hence, again, we infer, what has been before stated, that the word is as necessary to faith, as the living root of the tree is to the fruit; because, according to David, none can trust in God but those who know his name. But this knowledge proceeds not from every man's own imagination, but from the testimony which God himself gives of his own goodness. This the same Psalmist confirms in another place: "Thy salvation according to thy word." Again: "Save me: I hoped in thy word." Where we must observe the relation of faith to the word, and that salvation is the consequence of it. Yet we exclude not the Divine power, by a view of which, unless faith be supported, it will never ascribe to God the honour that is due to him. Paul seems to relate a trifling or uninteresting circumstance concerning Abraham, when he says, that he was persuaded that God, who had promised him the blessed seed, "was able also to perform." In another place, respecting himself he says, "I know whom I have believed, and am persuaded that he is able to keep that which I have committed unto him against that day." But if any one considers, how many doubts respecting the power of God frequently intrude themselves, he will fully acknowledge, that they who magnify it as it deserves, have made no small progress in faith. We shall all confess, that God is able to do whatever he pleases; but whilst the smallest temptation strikes us with consternation and terror, it is evident that we derogate from the Divine power, to which we prefer the menaces of Satan in opposition to the promises of God. This is the reason why Isaiah, when he would impress the hearts of the people with an assurance of salvation, discourses in so magnificent a manner concerning the infinite power of God. He frequently appears, after having begun to treat of the hope of pardon and reconciliation, to digress to another subject, and to wander through prolix and unnecessary circumlocutions, celebrating the wonders of the Divine government in the machine of heaven and earth, and the whole order of nature: yet there is nothing but what is applicable to the present subject; for, unless the omnipotence of God be presented to our eyes, our ears will not attend to his word, or not esteem it according to its worth. Moreover, the Scripture there speaks of his effectual power; for piety, as we have elsewhere seen, always makes a useful and practical application of the power of God; and particularly proposes to itself those of his works in which he has discovered himself as a father. Hence the frequent mention of redemption in the Scriptures, from which the Israelites might learn, that God, who had once been the author of salvation, would be its everlasting preserver. David also teaches us by his own example, that the private benefits which God has conferred on an individual, conduce to the confirmation of his faith for the future: even when he seems to have deserted us, we ought to extend our views further, so as to derive encouragement from his ancient benefits, as it is said in another psalm: "I remember the days of old; I meditate on all thy works," &c. Again: "I will remember the works of the Lord: surely I will remember thy wonders of old." But since, without the word, all our conceptions of the power and works of God are unprofitable and transient, we have sufficient reason for asserting, that there can be no faith, without the illumination of Divine grace. But here a question might be raised—What must be thought of Sarah and Rebecca, both of whom, apparently impelled by the zeal of faith, transgressed the limits of the word? Sarah, when she ardently desired the promised son, gave her maid-servant to her husband. That she sinned in many respects, is not to be denied; but I now refer to her error in being carried away by her zeal, and not restraining herself within the bounds of the Divine word. Yet it is certain, that this desire proceeded from faith. Rebecca, having been divinely assured of the election of her son Jacob, procures him the benediction by a sinful artifice; she deceives her husband, the witness and minister of the grace of God; she constrains her son to utter falsehoods; she corrupts the truth of God by various frauds and impostures; finally, by exposing his promise to ridicule, she does all in her power to destroy it. And yet this transaction, however criminal and reprehensible, was not unaccompanied with faith; because she had to overcome many obstacles, that she might aspire earnestly to that which, without any expectation of worldly advantage, was pregnant with great troubles and dangers. So we must not pronounce the holy patriarch Isaac to be entirely destitute of faith, because, after having been divinely apprized of the translation of the honour to his younger son, he nevertheless ceases not to be partial to Esau, his first-born. These examples certainly teach that errors are frequently mixed with faith, yet that faith, when real, always retains the preëminence. For, as the particular error of Rebecca did not annul the effect of the benediction, so neither did it destroy the faith which generally predominated in her mind, and was the principle and cause of that action. Nevertheless, Rebecca, in this instance, has discovered how liable the human mind is to error, as soon as it allows itself the smallest license. But though our deficiency or imbecility obscures faith, yet it does not extinguish it: in the mean time it reminds us how solicitously we ought to attend to the declarations of God; and confirms what we have said, that faith decays unless it be supported by the word; as the minds of Sarah, Isaac, and Rebecca, would have been lost in their obliquities, if they had not, by the secret restraint of God, been kept in obedience to the word.

XXXII. Again: it is not without reason that we include all the promises in Christ; as the apostle in the knowledge of him includes the whole gospel; and in another place teaches, that "all the promises of God in him are yea, and in him amen." The reason of this is plain. For, if God promises any thing, he gives a proof of his benevolence; so that there is no promise of his which is not a testimony of his love. Nor does it affect the argument, that the impious, when they are loaded with great and continual benefits from the Divine goodness, render themselves obnoxious to a heavier judgment. For since they neither think nor acknowledge that they receive those things from the hand of the Lord,—or if ever they acknowledge it, yet they never reflect within themselves on his goodness,—they cannot thereby be instructed concerning his mercy, any more than the brutes, who, according to the circumstances of their condition, receive the same effusion of his liberality, but never perceive it. Nor is it any more repugnant to our argument, that by generally rejecting the promises designed for them, they draw down on themselves severer vengeance. For although the efficacy of the promises is manifested only when they have obtained credit with us, yet their force and propriety are never extinguished by our unbelief or ingratitude. Therefore, when the Lord by his promises invites a man not only to receive, but also to meditate on the effects of his goodness, he at the same time gives him a declaration of his love. Whence we must return to this principle, that every promise is an attestation of the Divine love to us. But it is beyond all controversy, that no man is loved by God but in Christ; he is the "beloved Son," in whom the love of the Father perpetually rests, and then from him diffuses itself to us; as Paul says, that we are "accepted in the beloved." It must therefore be communicated to us by his mediation. Wherefore the apostle, in another place, calls him "our peace," and elsewhere represents him as the bond by which God is united to us in his paternal love. It follows, that whenever any promise is presented to us, our eyes must be directed to him; and that Paul is correct in stating, that all the promises of God are confirmed and accomplished in him. This is opposed by some examples. For it is not credible that Naaman the Syrian, when he inquired of the prophet respecting the right method of worshipping God, was instructed concerning the Mediator; yet his piety is commended. Cornelius, a Gentile and Roman, could scarcely be acquainted with what was not universally or clearly known among the Jews; yet his benefactions and prayers were acceptable to God; and the sacrifices of Naaman received the approbation of the prophet, which neither of these persons could have obtained without faith. Similar was the case of the eunuch to whom Philip was conducted; who, unless he had been possessed of some faith, would never have incurred the labour and expense of a long and difficult journey, for the sake of worshipping at Jerusalem. Yet we see how, on being interrogated by Philip, he betrayed his ignorance of the Mediator. I confess, indeed, that their faith was in some measure implicit, not only with respect to the person of Christ, but with respect to the power and office assigned him by the Father. At the same time it is certain that they had imbibed principles which afforded them some notion of Christ, however slight; nor should this be thought strange; for the eunuch would not have hastened from a remote country to Jerusalem to adore an unknown God; nor did Cornelius spend so much time, after having once embraced the Jewish religion, without acquainting himself with the rudiments of sound doctrine. With regard to Naaman, it would have been extremely absurd for Elisha, who directed him concerning the minutest particulars, to have been silent on the most important subject. Although their knowledge of Christ, therefore, was obscure, yet to suppose that they had none is unreasonable; because they practised the sacrifices of the law, which must have been distinguished by their end, that is, Christ, from the illegitimate sacrifices of the heathen.

XXXIII. This simple and external demonstration of the Divine word ought, indeed, to be fully sufficient for the production of faith, if it were not obstructed by our blindness and perverseness. But such is our propensity to error, that our mind can never adhere to Divine truth; such is our dulness, that we can never discern the light of it. Therefore nothing is effected by the word, without the illumination of the Holy Spirit. Whence it appears, that faith is far superior to human intelligence. Nor is it enough for the mind to be illuminated by the Spirit of God, unless the heart also be strengthened and supported by his power. On this point, the schoolmen are altogether erroneous, who, in the discussion of faith, regard it as a simple assent of the understanding, entirely neglecting the confidence and assurance of the heart. Faith, therefore, is a singular gift of God in two respects; both as the mind is enlightened to understand the truth of God, and as the heart is established in it. For the Holy Spirit not only originates faith, but increases it by degrees, till he conducts us by it all the way to the heavenly kingdom. "That good thing," says Paul, "which was committed unto thee, keep, by the Holy Ghost which dwelleth in us." If it be urged, that Paul declares the Spirit to be given to us "by the hearing of faith," this objection is easily answered. If there were only one gift of the Spirit, it would be absurd to represent the Spirit as the effect of faith, of which he is the author and cause; but when the apostle is treating of the gifts with which God adorns his Church, to lead it, by advancements in faith, forwards to perfection, we need not wonder that he ascribes those gifts to faith, which prepares us for their reception. It is accounted by the world exceedingly paradoxical, when it is affirmed, that no one can believe in Christ, but he to whom it is given. But this is partly for want of considering the depth and sublimity of heavenly wisdom, and the extreme dulness of man in apprehending the mysteries of God, and partly from not regarding that firm and steadfast constancy of heart, which is the principal branch of faith.

XXXIV. But if, as Paul tells us, no one is acquainted with the will of a man but "the spirit of a man which is in him," how could man be certain of the will of God? And if we are uncertain respecting the truth of God in those things which are the subjects of our present contemplation, how should we have a greater certainty of it, when the Lord promises such things as no eye sees and no heart conceives? Human sagacity is here so completely lost, that the first step to improvement, in the Divine school, is to forsake it. For, like an interposing veil, it prevents us from discovering the mysteries of God, which are revealed only to babes. "For flesh and blood hath not revealed," and "the natural man receiveth not the things of the Spirit of God; for they are foolishness unto him; neither can he know them, because they are spiritually discerned." The aids of the Spirit therefore are necessary, or rather it is his influence alone that is efficacious here. "Who hath known the mind of the Lord? or who hath been his counsellor?" but "the Spirit searcheth all things, yea, the deep things of God;" and through him, "we have the mind of Christ." "No man can come to me (says he) except the Father, which hath sent me, draw him. Every man therefore that hath heard and hath learned of the Father, cometh unto me. Not that any man hath seen the Father, save he which is of God." Therefore, as we can never come to Christ, unless we are drawn by the Spirit of God, so when we are drawn, we are raised both in mind and in heart above the reach of our own understanding. For illuminated by him, the soul receives, as it were, new eyes for the contemplation of heavenly mysteries, by the splendour of which it was before dazzled. And thus the human intellect, irradiated by the light of the Holy Spirit, then begins to relish those things which pertain to the kingdom of God, for which before it had not the smallest taste. Wherefore Christ's two disciples receive no benefit from his excellent discourse to them on the mysteries of his kingdom, till he opens their understanding that they may understand the Scriptures. Thus, though the apostles were taught by his Divine mouth, yet the Spirit of Truth must be sent to them, to instil into their minds the doctrine which they had heard with their ears. The word of God is like the sun shining on all to whom it is preached; but without any benefit to the blind. But in this respect we are all blind by nature; therefore it cannot penetrate into our minds, unless the internal teacher, the Spirit, make way for it by his illumination.

XXXV. In a former part of this work, relating to the corruption of nature, we have shown more at large the inability of men to believe; therefore I shall not fatigue the reader by a repetition of the same things. Let it suffice that faith itself, which we possess not by nature, but which is given us by the Spirit, is called by Paul "the spirit of faith." Therefore he prays "that God would fulfil," in the Thessalonians, "all the good pleasure of his goodness, and the work of faith with power." By calling faith "the work" of God, and "the good pleasure of his goodness," he denies it to be the proper effect of human exertion; and not content with that, he adds that it is a specimen of the Divine power. When he says to the Corinthians, that faith stands "not in the wisdom of men, but in the power of God," he speaks indeed of external miracles; but because the reprobate have no eyes to behold them, he comprehends also the inward seal which he elsewhere mentions. And that he may more illustriously display his liberality in so eminent a gift, God deigns not to bestow it promiscuously on all, but by a singular privilege imparts it to whom he will. We have already cited testimonies to prove this point. Augustine, who is a faithful expositor of them, says, "It was in order to teach us that the act of believing is owing to the Divine gift, not to human merit, that our Saviour declared, 'No man can come to me, except the Father which hath sent me draw him; and except it were given unto him of my Father.' It is wonderful, that two persons hear; one despises, the other ascends. Let him who despises, impute it to himself; let him who ascends, not arrogate it to himself." In another place he says, "Wherefore is it given to one, not to another? I am not ashamed to reply, This is a depth of the cross. From I know not what depth of the Divine judgments, which we cannot scrutinize, proceeds all our ability. That I can, I see; whence I can, I see not; unless that I see thus far, that it is of God. But why one, and not another? It is too much for me; it is an abyss, a depth of the cross. I can exclaim with admiration, but not demonstrate it in disputation." The sum of the whole is this—that Christ, when he illuminates us with faith by the power of his Spirit, at the same time ingrafts us into his body, that we may become partakers of all his benefits.

XXXVI. It next remains, that what the mind has imbibed, be transfused into the heart. For the word of God is not received by faith, if it floats on the surface of the brain; but when it has taken deep root in the heart, so as to become an impregnable fortress to sustain and repel all the assaults of temptation. But if it be true that the right apprehension of the mind proceeds from the illumination of the Spirit, his energy is far more conspicuous in such a confirmation of the heart; the diffidence of the heart being greater than the blindness of the mind; and the furnishing of the heart with assurance being more difficult than the communication of knowledge to the understanding. Therefore the Spirit acts as a seal, to seal on our hearts those very promises, the certainty of which he has previously impressed on our minds, and serves as an earnest to confirm and establish them. "After that ye believed," says the apostle, "ye were sealed with that Holy Spirit of promise, which is the earnest of our inheritance." Do you see how he shows that the hearts of believers are impressed by the Spirit, as by a seal? How, for this reason, he calls him "the Spirit of promise," because he ratifies the gospel to us? So, to the Corinthians, he says, "He which hath anointed us, is God; who hath also sealed us, and given the earnest of the Spirit in our hearts." And in another place, where he speaks of the confidence and boldness of hope, he makes "the earnest of the Spirit" the foundation of it.

XXXVII. I have not forgotten what I have already observed, and the remembrance of which experience incessantly renews, that faith is agitated with various doubts; so that the minds of the pious are seldom at ease, or at best enjoy not a state of perpetual tranquillity. But whatever assaults they may sustain, they either emerge from the very gulf of temptation, or remain firm in their station. This assurance alone nourishes and supports faith, while we are satisfied of what is declared by the Psalmist, "God is our refuge and strength, a very present help in trouble. Therefore will we not fear, though the earth be removed, and the mountains be carried into the midst of the sea." This most delightful repose is celebrated also in another psalm: "I laid me down and slept; I awaked; for the Lord sustained me." Not that David enjoyed a happy cheerfulness of soul perpetually flowing on in one even tenor; but having tasted the grace of God according to the proportion of his faith, he glories in intrepidly despising whatever could disquiet the peace of his mind. Therefore the Scripture, intending to exhort us to faith, commands us to "be quiet." In Isaiah, "In quietness and in confidence shall be your strength." In the Psalms, "Rest in the Lord, and wait patiently for him." With which corresponds the observation of the apostle to the Hebrews, "Ye have need of patience."

XXXVIII. Hence we may judge, how pernicious that dogma of the schoolmen is, that it is impossible to decide concerning the favour of God towards us, any otherwise than from moral conjecture, as every individual may deem himself not unworthy of it. If it must be determined by our works how the Lord is affected towards us, I admit we cannot attain this object even by a very slight conjecture; but as faith ought to correspond to the simple and gratuitous promise, there remains no room for doubting. For with what confidence, pray, shall we be armed, if we reason that God is propitious to us on this condition, provided the purity of our life deserve it? But having determined on a separate discussion of these points, I shall pursue them no further at present; especially since it is manifest that nothing is more opposite to faith than either conjecture or any thing else approaching to doubt. And they very mischievously pervert to this purpose the observation of the Preacher, which is frequently in their mouths: "No man knoweth whether he is worthy of hatred or of love." For not to observe that this passage is falsely rendered in the Vulgate translation, yet the meaning of Solomon, in such expressions, must be clear even to children; it is, that if any one wishes, from the present state of things, to judge who are the objects of Divine love or hatred, he labours in vain, and distresses himself to no good purpose; since "there is one event to the righteous and to the wicked; to him that sacrificeth, and to him that sacrificeth not." Whence it follows that God neither testifies his love to those whom he prospers with success, nor invariably discovers his hatred against those whom he plunges into affliction. And this observation is designed to reprove the vanity of the human understanding; since it is so extremely stupid respecting things most necessary to be known. He had just before said, "That which befalleth the sons of men, befalleth beasts; as the one dieth, so dieth the other; yea, they have all one breath; so that a man hath no preëminence above a beast." If any one would infer from this, that the opinion which we hold of the immortality of the soul rests upon mere conjecture, would he not be deservedly deemed insane? Are those persons, then, in a state of sanity, who conclude that there is no certainty of the favour of God, because it cannot be attained from the carnal contemplation of present things?

XXXIX. But they plead that it is rash presumption in men to arrogate to themselves an undoubted knowledge of the Divine will. This, indeed, I would concede to them, if we pretended to subject the incomprehensible counsel of God to the slenderness of our understanding. But when we simply assert with Paul, that "we have received, not the spirit of the world, but the Spirit which is of God, that we might know the things that are freely given to us of God," what opposition can they make to us, without at the same time insulting the Spirit of God? But if it be a horrible sacrilege to accuse the revelation which proceeds from him either of falsehood, or of uncertainty, or of ambiguity, wherein do we err in affirming its certainty? But they exclaim, that we betray great temerity, in thus presuming to boast of the Spirit of Christ. Who could believe the stupidity of men desirous of being esteemed teachers of the world, to be so extreme as to stumble in this shameful manner at the first elements of religion? It would certainly be incredible to me, if it were not proved by the writings which they have published. Paul pronounces them alone to be the sons of God, who are led by his Spirit: these men will have those who are the sons of God to be led by their own spirit, but to be destitute of the Spirit of God. He teaches, that we call God our Father at the suggestion of the Spirit, who "beareth witness with our spirit, that we are the children of God:" these men, though they forbid not all invocation of God, yet deprive us of the Spirit, by whose influence alone he can be rightly invoked. He denies them to be the servants of Christ, who are not led by the Spirit of Christ: these men invent a sort of Christianity, to which the Spirit of Christ is not necessary. He admits no hope of a happy resurrection, unless we experience the Spirit dwelling in us: these men fabricate a hope unattended by such experience. But perhaps they will answer, that they deny not the necessity of our being endued with the Spirit; but that it is the part of modesty and humility not to acknowledge our possession of him. What, then, is the meaning of the apostle in this exhortation to the Corinthians—"Examine yourselves, whether ye be in the faith; prove your own selves; know ye not yourselves, how that Jesus Christ is in you, except ye be reprobates?" But says John, "We know that he abideth in us, by the Spirit which he hath given us." And do we not call in question the promises of Christ, when we wish to be accounted the servants of God without the possession of his Spirit, whom he has announced that he will pour out upon all his people? Do we not injure the Holy Spirit, if we separate faith from him, which is his peculiar work? These being the first rudiments of piety, it is a proof of most miserable blindness, that Christians are censured as arrogant for presuming to glory in the presence of the Holy Spirit, without which glorying Christianity itself cannot exist. But they exemplify the truth of Christ's assertion, "The world knoweth not the Spirit of truth; but ye know him; for he dwelleth with you, and shall be in you."

XL. Not satisfied with one attempt to destroy the stability of faith, they assail it again from another quarter; by arguing, that although we may form a judgment concerning the favour of God from the present state of our righteousness, yet the knowledge of final perseverance remains in suspense. Truly we are left in possession of an admirable confidence of salvation, if we can only conclude from mere conjecture that we are in the favour of God at the present instant, but are utterly ignorant what may be our fate to-morrow. The apostle expresses a very different opinion: "I am persuaded (says he) that neither life, nor death, nor angels, nor principalities, nor powers, nor things present, nor things to come, nor height, nor depth, nor any other creature, shall be able to separate us from the love of God, which is in Christ Jesus our Lord." They attempt to evade the force of this, by a frivolous pretence that the apostle had it from a particular revelation; but they are too closely pressed to avail themselves of this evasion. For he is there treating of the benefits resulting from faith to all believers in common, not of any which were peculiar to his own experience. But the same apostle, they say, in another place, excites fear in us, by the mention of our imbecility and inconstancy. "Let him (says he) that thinketh he standeth, take heed lest he fall." It is true; but not a fear by which we may be thrown into consternation, but from which we may learn to "humble ourselves," as Peter expresses it, "under the mighty hand of God." Besides, how preposterous is it to limit to a moment of time the assurance of faith, whose nature it is to go beyond the bounds of the present life, and reach forward to a future immortality! Since believers, then, ascribe it to the grace of God that they are illuminated by his Spirit, and enjoy through faith a contemplation of the heavenly life, such a glorying is so remote from arrogance, that, if any one be ashamed to confess it, he rather betrays extreme ingratitude by a criminal suppression of the Divine goodness, than gives an evidence of modesty or humility.

XLI. Because we thought that the nature of faith could not be better or more clearly expressed than by the substance of the promise, which is the proper foundation on which it rests, and the removal of which would occasion its fall or annihilation,—it is from the promise, therefore, that we have taken our definition, which, nevertheless, is not at all at variance with that definition, or rather description, of the apostle, which he accommodates to his argument; where he says, that "faith is the substance of things hoped for, the evidence of things not seen." For by ὑπόστασις, which is the word he uses, and which is rendered substance, he intends a prop, as it were, on which the pious mind rests and reclines; as though he had said, that faith is a certain and secure possession of those things which are promised to us by God. Unless any one would rather understand ὑπόστασις of confidence, to which I shall not object, though I adopt that idea which is the more generally received. Again: to signify that even till the last day, when the books shall be opened, these objects are too sublime to be perceived by our senses, seen with our eyes, or handled with our hands; and that, in the mean time, they are enjoyed by us only as we exceed the capacity of our own understanding, extend our views beyond all terrestrial things, and even rise above ourselves; he has added, that this security of possession relates to things which are the objects of hope, and therefore invisible. For "hope that is seen (as Paul observes) is not hope; for what a man seeth, why doth he yet hope for?" But when he calls it an evidence, or proof, or (as Augustine has frequently rendered it) a conviction of things not seen, (for the Greek word is ἔλεγχος,) it is just as though he had called it the evidence of things not apparent, the vision of things not seen, the perspicuity of things obscure, the presence of things absent, the demonstration of things concealed. For the mysteries of God, of which description are the things that pertain to our salvation, cannot be discerned in themselves, and in their own nature; we only discover them in his word, of whose veracity we ought to be so firmly persuaded, as to consider all that he speaks as though it were already performed and accomplished. But how can the mind elevate itself to receive such a taste of the Divine goodness, without being all inflamed with mutual love to God? For the plenitude of happiness, which God has reserved for them who fear him, cannot be truly known, but it must at the same time excite a vehement affection. And those whom it has once affected, it draws and elevates towards itself. Therefore we need not wonder if a perverse and malicious heart never feel this affection, which conducts us to heaven itself, and introduces us to the most secret treasures of God and the most sacred recesses of his kingdom, which must not be profaned by the entrance of an impure heart. For what the schoolmen advance concerning the priority of charity to faith and hope, is a mere reverie of a distempered imagination, since it is faith alone which first produces charity in us. How much more accurately Bernard speaks! "I believe," says he, "that the testimony of conscience, which Paul calls the rejoicing of the pious, consists in three things. For it is necessary to believe, first of all, that you cannot have remission of sins but through the mercy of God; secondly, that you cannot have any good work, unless he bestow this also; lastly, that you cannot by any works merit eternal life, unless that also be freely given." Just after he adds, "that these things are not sufficient, but are a beginning of faith; because in believing that sins can only be forgiven by God, we ought at the same time to consider that they are forgiven us, till we are also persuaded, by the testimony of the Holy Spirit, that salvation is laid up for us; because God forgives sins; he also bestows merits; he likewise confers rewards; it is not possible to remain in this beginning." But these and other things must be treated in the proper places; it may suffice, at present, to ascertain wherein faith itself consists.

XLII. Now, wherever this living faith shall be found, it must necessarily be attended with the hope of eternal salvation as its inseparable concomitant, or rather must originate and produce it; since the want of this hope would prove us to be utterly destitute of faith, however eloquently and beautifully we might discourse concerning it. For if faith be, as has been stated, a certain persuasion of the truth of God, that it can neither lie, nor deceive us, nor be frustrated,—they who have felt this assurance, likewise expect a period to arrive when God will accomplish his promises, which, according to their persuasion, cannot but be true; so that, in short, hope is no other than an expectation of those things which faith has believed to be truly promised by God. Thus faith believes the veracity of God, hope expects the manifestation of it in due time; faith believes him to be our Father, hope expects him always to act towards us in this character; faith believes that eternal life is given to us, hope expects it one day to be revealed; faith is the foundation on which hope rests, hope nourishes and sustains faith. For as no man can have any expectations from God, but he who has first believed his promises, so also the imbecility of our faith must be sustained and cherished by patient hope and expectation, lest it grow weary and faint. For which reason, Paul rightly places our salvation in hope. For hope, while it is silently expecting the Lord, restrains faith, that it may not be too precipitate; it confirms faith, that it may not waver in the Divine promises, or begin to doubt of the truth of them; it refreshes it, that it may not grow weary; it extends it to the farthest goal, that it may not fail in the midst of the course, or even at the entrance of it. Finally, hope, by continually renewing and restoring faith, causes it frequently to persevere with more vigour than hope itself. But in how many cases the assistance of hope is necessary to the establishment of faith, will better appear, if we consider how many species of temptations assail and harass those who have embraced the word of God. First, the Lord, by deferring the execution of his promises, frequently keeps our minds in suspense longer than we wish; here it is the office of hope to obey the injunction of the prophet—"though it tarry, wait for it." Sometimes he not only suffers us to languish, but openly manifests his indignation: in this case it is much more necessary to have the assistance of hope, that, according to the language of another prophet, we may "wait upon the Lord that hideth his face from Jacob." Scoffers also arise, as Peter says, and inquire, "Where is the promise of his coming? for since the fathers fell asleep, all things continue as they were from the beginning of the creation." And the flesh and the world whisper the same things into our ears. Here faith must be supported by the patience of hope, and kept fixed on the contemplation of eternity, that it may consider "a thousand years as one day."

XLIII. On account of this union and affinity, the Scripture sometimes uses the words faith and hope without any distinction. For when Peter says that we "are kept by the power of God through faith unto salvation, ready to be revealed," he attributes to faith, what was more applicable to hope; and not without reason, since we have already shown, that hope is no other than the nourishment and strength of faith. Sometimes they are joined together, as in a passage of the same Epistle—"that your faith and hope might be in God." But Paul, in the Epistle to the Philippians, deduces expectation from hope; because in patient hope we suspend our desires till the arrival of God's appointed time. All which may be better understood from the tenth Chapter of the Epistle to the Hebrews, which I have already cited. In another place, Paul, though with some impropriety of expression, conveys the very same idea in these words: "We, through the Spirit, wait for the hope of righteousness by faith;" because, having embraced the testimony of the gospel concerning his gratuitous love, we wait till God openly manifests what is now concealed under hope. Now, it is easy to see the absurdity of Peter Lombard, in laying a twofold foundation of hope; the grace of God, and the merit of works. Hope can have no other object than faith; and the only object of faith, we have very clearly stated to be the mercy of God; to which both its eyes, if I may be allowed the expression, ought to be directed. But it may be proper to hear what kind of a reason he advances. If, says he, you venture to hope for any thing without merits, it must not be called hope, but presumption. Who is there that will not justly detest such teachers, who pronounce a confidence in the veracity of God to be temerity and presumption? For whereas it is the will of the Lord that we should expect every thing from his goodness, they assert that it is presumption to depend and rely upon it. Such a master is worthy of such disciples as he has found in the schools of wranglers! But, as for us, since we see that sinners are enjoined by the oracles of God to entertain a hope of salvation, let us joyfully presume so far on his veracity as to reject all confidence in our own works, to depend solely on his mercy, and venture to cherish a hope of happiness. He who said, "According to your faith be it unto you," will not deceive us.

7.

Justification by Faith.
The Name and Thing Defined.

I think I have already explained, with sufficient care, how that men, being subject to the curse of the law, have no means left of attaining salvation but through faith alone; and also what faith itself is, what Divine blessings it confers on man, and what effects it produces in him. The substance of what I have advanced is, that Christ, being given to us by the goodness of God, is apprehended and possessed by us by faith, by a participation of whom we receive especially two benefits. In the first place, being by his innocence reconciled to God, we have in heaven a propitious father instead of a judge; in the next place, being sanctified by his Spirit, we devote ourselves to innocence and purity of life. Of regeneration, which is the second benefit, I have said what I thought was sufficient. The method of justification has been but slightly touched, because it was necessary, first to understand that the faith, by which alone we attain gratuitous justification through the Divine mercy, is not unattended with good works, and what is the nature of the good works of the saints, in which part of this question consists. The subject of justification, therefore, must now be fully discussed, and discussed with the recollection that it is the principal hinge by which religion is supported, in order that we may apply to it with the greater attention and care. For unless we first of all apprehend in what situation we stand with respect to God, and what his judgment is concerning us, we have no foundation either for a certainty of salvation, or for the exercise of piety towards God. But the necessity of knowing this subject will be more evident from the knowledge itself.

II. But that we may not stumble at the threshold, (which would be the case were we to enter on a disputation concerning a subject not understood by us,) let us first explain the meaning of these expressions. *To be justified in the sight of God, To be justified by faith or by works.* He is said to be *justified in the sight of God* who in the Divine judgment is reputed righteous, and accepted on account of his righteousness; for as iniquity is abominable to God, so no sinner can find favour in his sight, as a sinner, or so long as he is considered as such. Wherever sin is, therefore, it is accompanied with the wrath and vengeance of God. He is justified who is considered not as a sinner, but as a righteous person, and on that account stands in safety before the tribunal of God, where all sinners are confounded and ruined. As, if an innocent man be brought under an accusation before the tribunal of a just judge, when judgment is passed according to his innocence, he is said to be justified or acquitted before the judge, so he is justified before God, who, not being numbered among sinners, has God for a witness and asserter of his righteousness. Thus he must be said, therefore, to be *justified by works,* whose life discovers such purity and holiness, as to deserve the character of righteousness before the throne of God; or who, by the integrity of his works, can answer and satisfy the divine judgment. On the other hand, he will be *justified by faith,* who, being excluded from the righteousness of works, apprehends by faith the righteousness of Christ, invested in which, he appears, in the sight of God, not as a sinner, but as a righteous man. Thus we simply explain justification to be an acceptance, by which God receives us into his favour, and esteems us as righteous persons; and we say that it consists in the remission of sins and the imputation of the righteousness of Christ.

III. For the confirmation of this point there are many plain testimonies of Scripture. In the first place, that this is the proper and most usual signification of the word, cannot be denied. But since it would be too tedious to collect all the passages and compare them together, let it suffice to have suggested it to the reader; for he will easily observe it of himself. I will only produce a few places, where this justification, which we speak of, is expressly handled. First, where Luke relates that "the people that heard Christ justified God;" and where Christ pronounces that "wisdom is justified of all her children." *To justify God*, in the former passage, does not signify to confer righteousness, which always remains perfect in him, although the whole world endeavour to rob him of it; nor, in the latter passage, does *the justifying of wisdom* denote making the doctrine of salvation righteous, which is so of itself; but both passages imply an ascription to God and to his doctrine of the praise which they deserve. Again, when Christ reprehends the Pharisees for "justifying themselves," he does not mean that they attained righteousness by doing what was right, but that they ostentatiously endeavoured to gain the character of righteousness, of which they were destitute. This is better understood by persons who are skilled in the Hebrew language; which gives the appellation of *sinners*, not only to those who are conscious to themselves of sin, but to persons who fall under a sentence of condemnation. For Bathsheba, when she says, "I and my son Solomon shall be counted offenders," or sinners, confesses no crime, but complains, that she and her son will be exposed to the disgrace of being numbered among condemned criminals. And it appears from the context, that this word, even in the translation, cannot be understood in any other than a relative sense, and that it does not denote the real character. But with respect to the present subject, where Paul says, "The Scripture foresaw that God would justify the heathen through faith," what can we understand, but that God imputes righteousness through faith? Again, when he says that God "justifieth the ungodly which believeth in Jesus," what can be the meaning, but that he delivers him by the blessing of faith from the condemnation deserved by his ungodliness? He speaks still more plainly in the conclusion, when he thus exclaims: "Who shall lay any thing to the charge of God's elect? It is God that justifieth. Who is he that condemneth? It is Christ that died, yea rather, that is risen again, who also maketh intercession for us." For it is just as if he had said, Who shall accuse them whom God absolves? Who shall condemn those for whom Christ intercedes? Justification, therefore, is no other than an acquittal from guilt of him who was accused, as though his innocence had been proved. Since God, therefore, justifies us through the mediation of Christ, he acquits us, not by an admission of our personal innocence, but by an imputation of righteousness; so that we, who are unrighteous in ourselves, are considered as righteous in Christ. This is the doctrine preached by Paul in the thirteenth Chapter of the Acts: "Through this man is preached unto you the forgiveness of sins; and by him all that believe are justified from all things, from which ye could not be justified by the law of Moses." We see that after remission of sins, this justification is mentioned, as if by way of explanation: we see clearly that it means an acquittal; that it is separated from the works of the law; that it is a mere favour of Christ; that it is apprehended by faith: we see, finally, the interposition of a satisfaction, when he says that we are justified from sins by Christ.

Thus, when it is said, that the publican "went down to his house justified," we cannot say that he obtained righteousness by any merit of works. The meaning therefore is, that after he had obtained the pardon of his sins, he was considered as righteous in the sight of God. He was righteous, therefore, not through any approbation of his works, but through God's gracious absolution. Wherefore Ambrose beautifully styles confession of sins, a legitimate justification.

IV. But leaving all contention about the term, if we attend to the thing itself, as it is described to us, every doubt will be removed. For Paul certainly describes justification as an acceptance, when he says to the Ephesians, "God hath predestinated us to the adoption of children by Jesus Christ to himself, according to the good pleasure of his will, to the praise of the glory of his grace, wherein he hath made us accepted." The meaning of this passage is the same as when in another place we are said to be "justified freely by his grace." But in the fourth Chapter to the Romans, he first mentions an imputation of righteousness, and immediately represents it as consisting in remission of sins. "David," says he, "describeth the blessedness of the man unto whom God imputeth righteousness without works, saying, Blessed are they whose iniquities are forgiven," &c. He there, indeed, argues not concerning a branch, but the whole of justification. He also adduces the definition of it given by David, when he pronounces them to be blessed who receive the free forgiveness of their sins; whence it appears, that this righteousness of which he speaks is simply opposed to guilt. But the most decisive passage of all on this point, is where he teaches us that the grand object of the ministry of the gospel is, that we may "be reconciled to God," because he is pleased to receive us into his favour through Christ, "not imputing" our "trespasses unto" us. Let the reader carefully examine the whole context; for when, by way of explanation, he just after adds, in order to describe the method of reconciliation, that Christ, "who knew no sin," was "made sin for us," he undoubtedly means by the term "reconciliation," no other than justification. Nor would there be any truth in what he affirms in another place, that we are "made righteous by the obedience of Christ," unless we are reputed righteous before God, in him, and out of ourselves.

V. But since Osiander has introduced I know not what monstrous notion of essential righteousness, by which, though he had no intention to destroy justification by grace, yet he has involved it in such obscurity as darkens pious minds, and deprives them of a serious sense of the grace of Christ,—it will be worth while, before I pass to any thing else, to refute this idle notion. In the first place, this speculation is the mere fruit of insatiable curiosity. He accumulates, indeed, many testimonies of Scripture, to prove that Christ is one with us, and we one with him, of which there is no proof necessary; but for want of observing the bond of this union, he bewilders himself. For us, however, who hold that we are united to Christ by the secret energy of his Spirit, it will be easy to obviate all his sophisms. He had conceived a notion similar to what was held by the Manichæans, so that he wished to transfuse the Divine essence into men. Hence another discovery of his, that Adam was formed in the image of God, because, even antecedently to the fall, Christ had been appointed the exemplar of the human nature. But for the sake of brevity, I shall only insist on the subject now before us. He says that we are one with Christ. This we admit; but we at the same time deny that Christ's essence is blended with ours. In the next place, we assert that this principle—that Christ is our righteousness because he is the eternal God, the fountain of righteousness, and the essential righteousness of God—is grossly perverted to support his fallacies. The reader will excuse me, if I now just hint at these things, which the order of the treatise requires to be deferred to another place. But though he alleges, in vindication of himself, that by the term *essential righteousness* he only intends to oppose the opinion that we are reputed righteous for the sake of Christ, yet he manifestly shows, that, not content with that righteousness which has been procured for us by the obedience and sacrificial death of Christ, he imagines that we are substantially righteous in God, by the infusion of his essence as well as his character. For this is the reason why he so vehemently contends, that not only Christ, but the Father and the Holy Spirit also dwell in us; which, though I allow it to be a truth, yet I maintain that he has grossly perverted. For he ought to have fully considered the nature of this inhabitation; namely, that the Father and the Spirit are in Christ; and that as "all the fulness of the Godhead dwelleth in him," so in him we possess the whole Deity. Whatever, therefore, he advances concerning the Father and the Spirit separately, has no other tendency but to seduce the simple from Christ. In the next place, he introduces a mixture of substances, by which God, transfusing himself into us, makes us, as it were, a part of himself. For he considers it as of no importance, that the power of the Holy Spirit unites us to Christ, so that he becomes our head and we become his members, unless his essence be blended with ours. But when speaking of the Father and the Spirit, he more openly betrays his opinion; which is, that we are not justified by the sole grace of the Mediator, and that righteousness is not simply or really offered to us in his person; but that we are made partakers of the Divine righteousness when God is essentially united with us.

VI. If he had only said, that Christ in justifying us becomes ours by an essential union, and that he is our head not only as man, but that the essence of his Divine nature also is infused into us,—he might have entertained himself with his fancies with less mischief, nor perhaps would so great a contention have been excited about this reverie. But as this principle is like a cuttlefish, which, by the emission of black and turbid blood, conceals its many tails, there is a necessity for a vigorous opposition to it, unless we mean to submit to be openly robbed of that righteousness which alone affords us any confidence concerning our salvation. For throughout this discussion, the terms *righteousness* and *justify* are extended by him to two things. First, he understands that "to be justified" denotes not only to be reconciled to God by a free pardon, but also to be made righteous; and that righteousness is not a gratuitous imputation, but a sanctity and integrity inspired by the Divine essence which resides in us. Secondly, he resolutely denies that Christ is our righteousness, as having, in the character of a priest, expiated our sins and appeased the Father on our behalf, but as being the eternal God and everlasting life. To prove the first assertion, that God justifies not only by pardoning, but also by regenerating, he inquires whether God leaves those whom he justifies in their natural state, without any reformation of their manners. The answer is very easy; as Christ cannot be divided, so these two blessings, which we receive together in him, are also inseparable. Whomsoever, therefore, God receives into his favour, he likewise gives them the Spirit of adoption, by whose power he renews them in his own image. But if the brightness of the sun be inseparable from his heat, shall we therefore say that the earth is warmed by his light, and illuminated by his heat? Nothing can be more apposite to the present subject than this similitude. The beams of the sun quicken and fertilize the earth, his rays brighten and illuminate it. Here is a mutual and indivisible connection. Yet reason itself prohibits us to transfer to one what is peculiar to the other. In this confusion of two blessings which Osiander obtrudes on us, there is a similar absurdity. For as God actually renews to the practice of righteousness those whom he gratuitously accepts as righteous, Osiander confounds that gift of regeneration with this gracious acceptance, and contends that they are one and the same. But the Scripture, though it connects them together, yet enumerates them distinctly, that the manifold grace of God may be the more evident to us. For that passage of Paul is not superfluous, that "Christ is made unto us righteousness and sanctification." And whenever he argues, from the salvation procured for us, from the paternal love of God, and from the grace of Christ, that we are called to holiness and purity, he plainly indicates that it is one thing to be justified, and another thing to be made new creatures. When Osiander appeals to the Scripture, he corrupts as many passages as he cites. The assertion of Paul, that "to him that worketh not, but believeth on him that justifieth the ungodly, his faith is counted for righteousness," is explained by Osiander to denote making a man righteous. With the same temerity he corrupts the whole of that fourth Chapter to the Romans, and hesitates not to impose the same false gloss on the passage just cited, "Who shall lay any thing to the charge of God's elect? It is God that justifieth;" where it is evident that the apostle is treating simply of accusation and absolution, and that his meaning wholly rests on the antithesis. His folly, therefore, betrays itself both in his arguments and in his citations of Scripture proofs. With no more propriety does he treat of the word righteousness, when he says, "that faith was reckoned to Abraham for righteousness," because that after having embraced Christ, (who is the righteousness of God, and God himself,) he was eminent for the greatest virtues. Whence it appears, that of two good parts, he erroneously makes one corrupt whole; for the righteousness there mentioned does not belong to the whole course of Abraham's life; but rather the Spirit testifies that, notwithstanding the singular eminence of Abraham's virtues, and his laudable and persevering advancement in them, yet he did not please God any otherwise than in receiving by faith the grace offered in the promise. Whence it follows, that in justification there is no regard paid to works, as Paul conclusively argues in that passage.

VII. His objection, that the power of justifying belongs not to faith of itself, but only as it receives Christ, I readily admit. For if faith were to justify of itself, or by an intrinsic efficacy, as it is expressed, being always weak and imperfect, it never could effect this but in part; and thus it would be a defective justification, which would only confer on us a partial salvation. Now, we entertain no such notion as the objection supposes; on the contrary, we affirm that, strictly speaking, "it is God that justifies;" and then we transfer this to Christ, because he is given to us for righteousness. Faith we compare to a vessel; for unless we come empty with the mouth of our soul open to implore the grace of Christ, we cannot receive Christ. Whence it may be inferred, that we do not detract from Christ the power of justifying, when we teach that faith receives him before it receives his righteousness. Nevertheless, I cannot admit the intricate comparisons of this sophist, when he says that faith is Christ; as though an earthen vessel were a treasure, because gold is concealed in it. For faith, although intrinsically it is of no dignity or value, justifies us by an application of Christ, just as a vessel full of money constitutes a man rich. Therefore I maintain that faith, which is only the instrument by which righteousness is received, cannot without absurdity be confounded with Christ, who is the material cause, and at once the author and dispenser of so great a benefit. We have now removed the difficulty as to the sense in which the word *faith* ought to be understood, when it is applied to justification.

VIII. Respecting the reception of Christ, he goes still greater lengths; asserting that the internal word is received by the ministry of the external word, by which he would divert us from the priesthood of Christ and the person of the Mediator, to his eternal divinity. We do not divide Christ, but we maintain that the same person, who, by reconciling us to the Father in his own flesh, has given us righteousness, is the eternal Word of God; and we confess that he could not otherwise have discharged the office of Mediator, and procured righteousness for us, if he were not the eternal God. But the opinion of Osiander is, that since Christ is both God and man, he is made righteousness to us, in respect of his Divine, not his human nature. Now, if this properly belong to the Divinity, it will not be peculiar to Christ, but common also to the Father and the Spirit; since the righteousness of one is the same as that of the others. Besides, what has been naturally eternal, cannot with propriety be said to be "made unto us." But though we grant that God is made righteousness unto us, how will it agree with the clause which is inserted, that "of God," he "is made unto us righteousness?" This is certainly peculiar to the character of the Mediator, who, though he contains in himself the Divine nature, yet is designated by this appropriate title, by which he is distinguished from the Father and the Spirit. But he ridiculously triumphs in that single expression of Jeremiah, where he promises that "the Lord," *Jehovah*, will be "our righteousness." He can deduce nothing from this, but that Christ, who is our righteousness, is God manifested in the flesh. We have elsewhere recited from Paul's sermon, that "God hath purchased the Church with his own blood." If any should infer from this, that the blood by which our sins were expiated, was Divine, and part of the Divine nature, who could bear so monstrous an error? But Osiander thinks he has gained every thing by this very puerile cavil; he swells, exults, and fills many pages with his swelling words, though the passage is simply and readily explained, by saying that Jehovah, when he should become the seed of David, would be the righteousness of the pious; and in the same sense Isaiah informs us, "by his knowledge shall my righteous servant justify many." Let us remark, that the speaker here is the Father; that he attributes to his Son the office of justifying; that he adds as a reason, that he is righteous; and that he places the mode or means of effecting this, in the doctrine by which Christ is made known. For it is more suitable to understand the word תעד in a passive sense. Hence I conclude, first, that Christ was made righteousness when he assumed the form of a servant; secondly, that he justifies us by his own obedience to the Father; and, therefore, that he does this for us, not according to his Divine nature, but by reason of the dispensation committed to him. For though God alone is the fountain of righteousness, and we are righteous only by a participation of him, yet, because we have been alienated from his righteousness through the unhappy breach occasioned by the fall, we are under the necessity of descending to this inferior remedy, to be justified by Christ, by the efficacy of his death and resurrection.

IX. If Osiander object, that the excellence of this work surpasses the nature of man, and therefore can be ascribed only to the Divine nature,—the former part of the objection I admit, but in the latter I maintain that he is grossly mistaken. For although Christ could neither purify our souls with his blood, nor appease the Father by his sacrifice, nor absolve us from guilt, nor, in short, perform the functions of a priest, if he were not truly God, because human power would have been unequal to so great a burden, yet it is certain that he performed all these things in his human nature. For if it be inquired, How are we justified? Paul replies, "By the obedience" of Christ. But has he obeyed in any other way than by assuming the form of a servant? Hence we infer, that righteousness is presented to us in his flesh. In the other passage also, which I much wonder that Osiander is not ashamed to quote so frequently, Paul places the source of righteousness wholly in the humanity of Christ. "He hath made him to be sin for us, who knew no sin, that we might be made the righteousness of God in him." Osiander lays great stress on "the righteousness of God," and triumphs as though he had evinced it to be his notion of essential righteousness; whereas the words convey a very different idea,—that we are righteous through the expiation effected by Christ. That "the righteousness of God" means that which God approves, ought to have been known to the youngest novices; just as in John "the praise of God" is opposed to "the praise of men." I know that "the righteousness of God" sometimes denotes that of which he is the author, and which he bestows upon us; but, without any observation of mine, the judicious reader will perceive that the meaning of this passage is only, that we stand before the tribunal of God supported by the atoning death of Christ. Nor is the term of such great importance, provided that Osiander coincides with us in this, that we are justified in Christ, inasmuch as he was made an expiatory sacrifice for us; which is altogether incompatible with his Divine nature. For this reason, when Christ designs to seal the righteousness and salvation which he has presented to us, he exhibits a certain pledge of it in his flesh. He calls himself, indeed, "living bread;" but adds, by way of explanation, "my flesh is meat indeed, and my blood is drink indeed." This method of instruction is discovered in the sacraments; which, although they direct our faith to the whole of the person of Christ, not to a part of him only, yet at the same time teach that the matter of justification and salvation resides in his human nature; not that he either justifies or vivifies, of himself as a mere man, but because it has pleased God to manifest in the Mediator that which was incomprehensible and hidden in himself. Wherefore I am accustomed to say, that Christ is, as it were, a fountain opened to us, whence we may draw what were otherwise concealed and useless in that secret and deep fountain which flows to us in the person of the Mediator. In this manner, and in this sense, provided he will submit to the clear and forcible arguments which I have adduced, I do not deny that Christ justifies us, as he is God and man, and that this work is common also to the Father and the Spirit; and, finally, that the righteousness of which Christ makes us partakers, is the eternal righteousness of the eternal God.

X. Moreover, that his cavils may not deceive the inexperienced, I confess that we are destitute of this incomparable blessing, till Christ becomes ours. I attribute, therefore, the highest importance to the connection between the head and members; to the inhabitation of Christ in our hearts; in a word, to the mystical union by which we enjoy him, so that being made ours, he makes us partakers of the blessings with which he is furnished. We do not, then, contemplate him at a distance out of ourselves, that his righteousness may be imputed to us; but because we have put him on, and are ingrafted into his body, and because he has deigned to unite us to himself, therefore we glory in a participation of his righteousness. Thus we refute the cavil of Osiander, that faith is considered by us as righteousness; as though we despoiled Christ of his right, when we affirm, that by faith we come to him empty, that he alone may fill us with his grace. But Osiander, despising this spiritual connection, insists on a gross mixture of Christ with believers; and therefore invidiously gives the appellation of Zuinglians to all who do not subscribe to his fanatical error concerning essential righteousness; because they are not of opinion that Christ is substantially eaten in the sacred supper. As for myself, indeed, I consider it the highest honour to be thus reproached by a man so proud and so absorbed in his own delusions; although he attacks not me alone, but other writers well known in the world, whom he ought to have treated with modest respect. But this does not at all affect me, who am supporting no private interest; wherefore I the more unreservedly advocate this cause, conscious that I am free from every sinister motive. His great importunity in insisting on essential righteousness, and an essential inhabitation of Christ in us, goes to this length—first, that God transfuses himself into us by a gross mixture of himself with us, as he pretends that there is a carnal eating in the sacred supper; secondly, that God inspires his righteousness into us, by which we are really righteous with him, since, according to this man, such righteousness is as really God himself, as the goodness, or holiness, or perfection of God. I shall not take much trouble to refute the testimonies adduced by him, which he violently perverts from the celestial to the present state. By Christ, says Peter, "are given unto us exceeding great and precious promises; that by these ye might be partakers of the Divine nature." As though we were now such as the gospel promises we shall be at the second advent of Christ; nay, John apprizes us, that *then* "we shall be like God; for we shall see him as he is." I have thought proper to give the reader only a small specimen, and endeavoured to pass over these impertinences, not that it is difficult to refute them, but because I am unwilling to be tedious in labouring to no purpose.

XI. There is yet more latent poison in the second particular, in which he maintains, that we are righteous together with God. I think I have already sufficiently demonstrated, that although this dogma were not so pestiferous, yet because it is weak and unsatisfactory, and evaporates through its own inanity, it ought justly to be rejected by all judicious and pious readers. But this is an impiety not to be tolerated—under the pretext of a twofold righteousness to weaken the assurance of salvation, and to elevate us above the clouds, that we may not embrace by faith the grace of expiation, and call upon God with tranquillity of mind. Osiander ridicules those who say that justification is a forensic term, because it is necessary for us to be actually righteous: nor is there any thing that he more dislikes than the doctrine that we are justified by gratuitous imputation. Now, if God do not justify by absolving and pardoning us, what is the meaning of this declaration of Paul? "God was in Christ, reconciling the world unto himself, not imputing their trespasses unto them. For he hath made him to be sin for us, who knew no sin; that we might be made the righteousness of God in him." First I find, that they are accounted righteous who are reconciled to God: the manner is specified, that God justifies by pardoning; just as, in another passage, justification is opposed to accusation; which antithesis clearly demonstrates, that the form of expression is borrowed from the practice of courts. Nor is there any one, but tolerably versed in the Hebrew language, provided at the same time that he be in his sound senses, who can be ignorant that this is the original of the phrase, and that this is its import and meaning. Now, let Osiander answer me whether, where Paul says that "David describeth righteousness without works, saying, Blessed are they whose iniquities are forgiven," whether, I say, this be a complete definition or a partial one. Certainly Paul does not adduce the testimony of the Psalmist, as teaching that pardon of sins is a part of righteousness, or concurs to the justification of a man; but he includes the whole of righteousness in a free remission, pronouncing, "Blessed are they whose iniquities are forgiven, and whose sins are covered. Blessed is the man to whom the Lord will not impute sin." He thence estimates and judges of the felicity of such a man, because in this way he becomes righteous, not actually, but by imputation. Osiander objects, that it would be dishonourable to God, and contrary to his nature, if he justified those who still remain actually impious. But it should be remembered that, as I have already observed, the grace of justification is inseparable from regeneration, although they are distinct things. But since it is sufficiently known from experience, that some relics of sin always remain in the righteous, the manner of their justification must of necessity be very different from that of their renovation to newness of life. For the latter God commences in his elect, and as long as they live carries it on gradually, and sometimes slowly, so that they are always obnoxious at his tribunal to the sentence of death. He justifies them, however, not in a partial manner, but so completely, that they may boldly appear in heaven, as being invested with the purity of Christ. For no portion of righteousness could satisfy our consciences, till we have ascertained that God is pleased with us, as being unexceptionably righteous before him. Whence it follows, that the doctrine of justification is perverted and totally overturned, when doubts are injected into the mind, when the confidence of salvation is shaken, when bold and fearless worship is interrupted, and when quiet and tranquillity with spiritual joy are not established. Whence Paul argues from the incompatibility of things contrary to each other, that the inheritance is not of the law, because then faith would be rendered vain; which, if it be fixed upon works, must inevitably fall; since not even the most holy of all saints will find them afford any ground of confidence. This difference between justification and regeneration (which Osiander confounds together, and denominates a twofold righteousness) is beautifully expressed by Paul; for, speaking of his real righteousness, or of the integrity which he possessed, to which Osiander gives the appellation of essential righteousness, he sorrowfully exclaims, "O wretched man that I am! who shall deliver me from the body of this death?" But resorting to the righteousness which is founded in the Divine mercy alone, he nobly triumphs over life, and death, and reproaches, and famine, and the sword, and all adverse things and persons. "Who shall lay any thing to the charge of God's elect? It is God that justifieth. For I am persuaded, that nothing shall be able to separate us from the love of God, which is in Christ Jesus our Lord." He plainly declares himself to be possessed of that righteousness, which alone is fully sufficient for salvation in the sight of God; so that the miserable servitude, in a consciousness of which he was just before bewailing his condition, neither diminishes, nor in the smallest degree interrupts, the confidence with which he triumphs. This diversity is sufficiently known, and is even familiar to all the saints, who groan under the burden of their iniquities, and yet with victorious confidence rise superior to every fear. But the objection of Osiander, that it is incongruous to the nature of God, recoils upon himself; for, although he invests the saints with a twofold righteousness, as with a garment covered with skins, he is, notwithstanding, constrained to acknowledge that no man can please God without the remission of his sins. If this be true, he should at least grant that they who are not actually righteous, are accounted righteous in proportion, as it is expressed, to the degree of imputation. But how far shall a sinner extend this gracious acceptance, which is substituted in the place of righteousness? Shall he estimate it by the weight? Truly he will be in great uncertainty to which side to incline the balance; because he will not be able to assume to himself as much righteousness as may be necessary to his confidence. It is well that he, who would wish to prescribe laws to God, is not the arbiter of this cause. But this address of David to God will remain: "That thou mightest be justified when thou speakest, and be clear when thou judgest." And what extreme arrogance it is to condemn the supreme Judge when he freely absolves, and not to be satisfied with this answer, "I will show mercy on whom I will show mercy!" And yet the intercession of Moses, which God checked with this reply, was not that he would spare none, but that, though they were guilty, he would remove their guilt and absolve them all at once. We affirm, therefore, that those who were undone are justified before God by the obliteration of their sins; because, sin being the object of his hatred, he can love none but those whom he justifies. But this is a wonderful method of justification, that sinners, being invested with the righteousness of Christ, dread not the judgment which they have deserved; and that, while they justly condemn themselves, they are accounted righteous out of themselves.

XII. But the readers must be cautioned to pay a strict attention to the mystery which Osiander boasts that he will not conceal from them. For, after having contended with great prolixity, that we do not obtain favour with God solely through the imputation of the righteousness of Christ, because it would be impossible for him to esteem those as righteous who are not so, (I use his own words,) he at length concludes, that Christ is given to us for righteousness, not in respect of his human, but of his Divine nature; and that, though this righteousness can only be found in the person of the Mediator, yet it is the righteousness, not of man, but of God. He does not combine two righteousnesses, but evidently deprives the humanity of Christ of all concern in the matter of justification. It is worth while, however, to hear what arguments he adduces. It is said in the passage referred to, that "Christ is made unto us wisdom," which is applicable only to the eternal Word. Neither, therefore, is Christ, considered as man our righteousness. I reply, that the only begotten Son of God was indeed his eternal wisdom; but this title is here ascribed to him by Paul in a different sense, because "in him are hid all the treasures of wisdom and knowledge." What, therefore, he had with the Father, he has manifested to us; and so what Paul says, refers not to the essence of the Son of God, but to our benefit, and is rightly applied to the humanity of Christ; because, although he was a light shining in darkness before his assumption of the flesh, yet he was a hidden light till he appeared in the nature of man "as the Sun of righteousness;" wherefore he calls himself "the light of the world." Osiander betrays his folly likewise in objecting, that justification exceeds the power of angels and men; since it depends not upon the dignity of any creature, but upon the appointment of God. If angels were desirous to offer a satisfaction to God, it would be unavailing; because they have not been appointed to it. This was peculiar to the man Christ, who was "made under the law, to redeem us from the curse of the law." He likewise very unjustly accuses those who deny that Christ is our righteousness according to his Divine nature, of retaining only one part of Christ, and (what is worse) making two Gods; because, though they acknowledge that God dwells in us, yet they flatly deny that we are righteous through the righteousness of God. For if we call Christ the author of life in consequence of his having suffered death, "that he might destroy him that had the power of death," it is not to be inferred that we deny this honour to his complete person, as God manifested in the flesh: we only state with precision the means by which the righteousness of God is conveyed to us, so that we may enjoy it. In this, Osiander has fallen into a very pernicious error. We do not deny, that what is openly exhibited to us in Christ flows from the secret grace and power of God; nor do we refuse to admit, that the righteousness conferred on us by

Christ is the righteousness of God as proceeding from him; but we constantly maintain that we have righteousness and life in the death and resurrection of Christ. I pass over that shameful accumulation of passages, with which, without any discrimination, and even without common sense, he has burdened the reader, in order to evince, that wherever mention is made of righteousness, it ought to be understood of this essential righteousness; as where David implores the righteousness of God to assist him; which as he does above a hundred times, Osiander hesitates not to pervert such a great number of passages. Nor is there any thing more solid in his other objection, that the term "righteousness" is properly and rightly applied to that by which we are excited to rectitude of conduct, and that God alone "worketh in us both to will and to do." Now, we do not deny, that God renews us by his Spirit to holiness and righteousness of life; but it should first be inquired, whether he does this immediately by himself, or through the medium of his Son, with whom he has deposited all the plenitude of his Spirit, that with his abundance he might relieve the necessities of his members. Besides, though righteousness flows to us from the secret fountain of the Divinity, yet it does not follow that Christ, who in the flesh sanctified himself for our sakes, is our righteousness with respect to his Divine nature. Equally frivolous is his assertion, that Christ himself was righteous with the righteousness of God; because, if he had not been influenced by the will of the Father, not even he could have performed the part assigned him. For though it has been elsewhere observed, that all the merit of Christ himself flows from the mere favour of God, yet this affords no countenance to the fanciful notion with which Osiander fascinates his own eyes and those of the injudicious. For who would admit the inference, that because God is the original source of our righteousness, we are therefore essentially righteous, and have the essence of the Divine righteousness residing in us? In redeeming the Church (Isaiah says) God "put on righteousness as a breastplate;" but was it to spoil Christ of the armour which he had given him, and to prevent his being a perfect Redeemer? The prophet only meant that God borrowed nothing extrinsic to himself, and had no assistance in the work of our redemption. Paul has briefly intimated the same in other words, saying that he has given us salvation in order "to declare his righteousness." Nor does this at all contradict what he states in another place, "that by the obedience of one we are made righteous." To conclude: whoever fabricates a twofold righteousness, that wretched souls may not rely wholly and exclusively on the Divine mercy, makes Christ an object of contempt, and crowns him with platted thorns.

XIII. But as many persons imagine righteousness to be composed of faith and works, let us also prove, before we proceed, that the righteousness of faith is so exceedingly different from that of works, that if one be established, the other must necessarily be subverted. The apostle says, "I count all things but dung, that I may win Christ, and be found in him, not having mine own righteousness, which is of the law, but that which is through the faith of Christ, the righteousness which is of God by faith." Here we see a comparison of two opposites, and an implication that his own righteousness must be forsaken by him who wishes to obtain the righteousness of Christ. Wherefore, in another place, he states this to have been the cause of the ruin of the Jews, that, "going about to establish their own righteousness, they have not submitted themselves unto the righteousness of God." If, by establishing our own righteousness, we reject the righteousness of God, then, in order to obtain the latter, the former must doubtless be entirely renounced. He conveys the same sentiment when he asserts, that "boasting is excluded. By what law? of works? Nay; but by the law of faith." Whence it follows, that as long as there remains the least particle of righteousness in our works, we retain some cause for boasting. But if faith excludes all boasting, the righteousness of works can by no means be associated with the righteousness of faith. To this purpose he speaks so clearly in the fourth Chapter to the Romans, as to leave no room for cavil or evasion. "If Abraham (says he) were justified by works, he hath whereof to glory." He adds, "but" he hath "not" whereof to glory "before God." It follows, therefore, that he was not justified by works. Then he advances another argument from two opposites. "To him that worketh is the reward not reckoned of grace, but of debt." But righteousness is attributed to faith through grace. Therefore it is not from the merit of works. Adieu, therefore, to the fanciful notion of those who imagine a righteousness compounded of faith and works.

XIV. The sophists, who amuse and delight themselves with perversion of the Scripture and vain cavils, think they have found a most excellent subterfuge, when they explain *works*, in these passages, to mean those which men yet unregenerate perform without the grace of Christ, merely through the unassisted efforts of their own free-will; and deny that they relate to spiritual works. Thus, according to them, a man is justified both by faith and by works, only the works are not properly his own, but the gifts of Christ and the fruits of regeneration. For they say that Paul spoke in this manner, only that the Jews, who relied on their own strength, might be convinced of their folly in arrogating righteousness to themselves, whereas it is conferred on us solely by the Spirit of Christ, not by any exertion properly our own. But they do not observe, that in the contrast of legal and evangelical righteousness, which Paul introduces in another place, all works are excluded, by what title soever they may be distinguished. For he teaches that this is the righteousness of the law, that he who has fulfilled the command of the law shall obtain salvation; but that the righteousness of faith consists in believing that Christ has died and is risen again. Besides, we shall see, as we proceed, in its proper place, that sanctification and righteousness are separate blessings of Christ. Whence it follows, that even spiritual works are not taken into the account, when the power of justifying is attributed to faith. And the assertion of Paul, in the place just cited, that Abraham has not whereof to glory before God, since he was not justified by works, ought not to be restricted to any literal appearance or external display of virtue, or to any efforts of free-will; but though the life of the patriarch was spiritual, and almost angelic, yet his works did not possess sufficient merit to justify him before God.

XV. The errors of the schoolmen, who mingle their preparations, are rather more gross; but they instil into the simple and incautious a doctrine equally corrupt, while under the pretext of the Spirit and of grace, they conceal the mercy of God, which alone can calm the terrors of the conscience. We confess, indeed, with Paul, that "the doers of the law are justified before God;" but since we are all far from being observers of the law, we conclude, that those works which should be principally available to justification, afford us no assistance, because we are destitute of them. With respect to the common Papists, or schoolmen, they are in this matter doubly deceived; both in denominating faith a certainty of conscience in expecting from God a reward of merit, and in explaining the grace of God to be, not an imputation of gratuitous righteousness, but the Spirit assisting to the pursuit of holiness. They read in the apostle, "He that cometh to God must believe that he is, and that he is a rewarder of them that diligently seek him." But they do not consider the manner of seeking him. And that they mistake the sense of the word "grace," is evident from their writings. For Lombard represents justification by Christ as given us in two ways. He says, "The death of Christ justifies us, first, because it excites charity in our hearts, by which we are made actually righteous; secondly, because it destroys sin, by which the devil held us in captivity, so that now it cannot condemn us." We see how he considers the grace of God in justification to consist in our being directed to good works by the grace of the Holy Spirit. He wished, indeed, to follow the opinion of Augustine; but he follows him at a great distance, and even deviates considerably from a close imitation of him; for whatever he finds clearly stated by him, he obscures, and whatever he finds pure in him, he corrupts. The schools have always been running into worse and worse errors, till at length they have precipitated themselves into a kind of Pelagianism. Nor, indeed, is the opinion of Augustine, or at least his manner of expression, to be altogether admitted. For though he excellently despoils man of all the praise of righteousness, and ascribes the whole to the grace of God, yet he refers grace to sanctification, in which we are regenerated by the Spirit to newness of life.

XVI. The Scripture, when speaking of the righteousness of faith, leads us to something very different. It teaches us, that being diverted from the contemplation of our own works, we should regard nothing but the mercy of God and the perfection of Christ. For it states this to be the order of justification; that from the beginning God deigns to embrace sinful man with his pure and gratuitous goodness, contemplating nothing in him to excite mercy, but his misery; (for God beholds him utterly destitute of all good works;) deriving from himself the motive for blessing him, that he may affect the sinner himself with a sense of his supreme goodness, who, losing all confidence in his own works, rests the whole of his salvation on the Divine mercy. This is the sentiment of faith, by which the sinner comes to the enjoyment of his salvation, when he knows from the doctrine of the gospel that he is reconciled to God; that having obtained remission of sins, he is justified by the intervention of the righteousness of Christ; and though regenerated by the Spirit of God, he thinks on everlasting righteousness reserved for him, not in the good works to which he devotes himself, but solely in the righteousness of Christ. When all these things shall have been particularly examined, they will afford a perspicuous explication of our opinion. They will, however, be better digested in a different order from that in which they have been proposed. But it is of little importance, provided they are so connected with each other, that we may have the whole subject rightly stated and well confirmed.

XVII. Here it is proper to recall to remembrance the relation we have before stated between faith and the gospel; since the reason why faith is said to justify, is, that it receives and embraces the righteousness offered in the gospel. But its being offered by the gospel absolutely excludes all consideration of works. This Paul very clearly demonstrates on various occasions; and particularly in two passages. In his Epistle to the Romans, contrasting the law and the gospel, he says, "Moses describeth the righteousness which is of the law, that the man which doeth those things shall live by them. But the righteousness which is of faith speaketh on this wise: That if thou shalt confess with thy mouth the Lord Jesus, and shalt believe in thine heart that God hath raised him from the dead, thou shalt be saved." Do you perceive how he thus discriminates between the law and the gospel, that the former attributes righteousness to works, but the latter bestows it freely, without the assistance of works? It is a remarkable passage, and may serve to extricate us from a multitude of difficulties, if we understand that the righteousness which is given us by the gospel is free from all legal conditions. This is the reason why he more than once strongly opposes the *promise* to the *law*. "If the inheritance be of the law, it is no more of promise;" and more in the same Chapter to the same purpose. It is certain that the law also has its promises. Wherefore, unless we will confess the comparison to be improper, there must be something distinct and different in the promises of the gospel. Now, what can that be, but that they are gratuitous and solely dependent on the Divine mercy, whilst the promises of the law depend on the condition of works? Nor let any one object, that it is only the righteousness which men would obtrude on God from their own natural powers and free-will that is rejected; since Paul teaches it as a universal truth, that the precepts of the law are unprofitable, because, not only among the vulgar, but even among the very best of men, there is not one who can fulfil them. Love is certainly the principal branch of the law: when the Spirit of God forms us to it, why does it not constitute any part of our righteousness, but because even in the saints it is imperfect, and therefore of itself deserves no reward?

XVIII. The other passage is as follows: "That no man is justified by the law in the sight of God, it is evident; for, The just shall live by faith. And the law is not of faith; but, The man that doeth them shall live in them." How could this argument be supported, unless it were certain that works do not come into the account of faith, but are to be entirely separated from it? The law, he says, differs from faith. Why? Because works are required to the righteousness of the law. It follows, therefore, that works are not required to the righteousness of faith. From this statement it appears, that they who are justified by faith, are justified without the merit of works, and beyond the merit of works; for faith receives that righteousness which the gospel bestows; and the gospel differs from the law in this respect, that it does not confine righteousness to works, but rests it entirely on the mercy of God. He argues in a similar manner to the Romans, that "Abraham had not whereof to glory; for he believed God, and it was counted unto him for righteousness;" and by way of confirmation he subjoins, that then there is room for the righteousness of faith when there are no works which merit any reward. He tells us, that where there are works, they receive a reward "of debt," but that what is given to faith is "of grace;" for this is the clear import of the language which he there uses. When he adds, a little after, "Therefore it is of faith" that we obtain the inheritance, in order "that it might be by grace," he infers that the inheritance is gratuitous, because it is received by faith: and why is this, but because faith, without any assistance of works, depends wholly on the Divine mercy? And in the same sense undoubtedly he elsewhere teaches us, that "the righteousness of God without the law is manifested, being witnessed by the law and the prophets;" because, by excluding the law, he denies that righteousness is assisted by works, or that we obtain it by working, but asserts that we come empty in order to receive it.

XIX. The reader will now discover, with what justice the sophists of the present day cavil at our doctrine, when we say *that a man is justified by faith only*. That a man is justified *by faith*, they do not deny, because the Scripture so often declares it; but since it is nowhere expressly said to be by faith only, they cannot bear this addition to be made. But what reply will they give to these words of Paul, where he contends that "righteousness is not of faith unless it be gratuitous?" How can any thing gratuitous consist with works? And by what cavils will they elude what he asserts in another place, that in the gospel "is the righteousness of God revealed?" If righteousness is revealed in the gospel, it is certainly not a mutilated and partial, but a complete and perfect one. The law, therefore, has no concern in it. And respecting this exclusive particle, *only*, they rest on an evasion which is not only false, but glaringly ridiculous. For does not he most completely attribute every thing to faith alone, who denies every thing to works? What is the meaning of these expressions of Paul? "Righteousness is manifested without the law," "justified freely by his grace," "justified without the deeds of the law." Here they have an ingenious subterfuge, which, though it is not of their own invention, but borrowed from Origen and some of the ancients, is nevertheless very absurd. They pretend that the works excluded are the ceremonial works of the law, not the moral works. They have made such a proficiency by their perpetual disputations, that they have forgotten the first elements of logic. Do they suppose the apostle to have been insane, when he adduced these passages in proof of his doctrine? "The man that doeth them shall live in them;" and "Cursed is every one that continueth not in all things which are written in the book of the law to do them." If they be in their sober senses, they will not assert that life was promised to the observers of ceremonies, and the curse denounced merely on the transgressors of them. If these places are to be understood of the moral law, it is beyond a doubt, that moral works likewise are excluded from the power to justify. To the same purpose are these arguments which he uses: "For by the law is the knowledge of sin;" consequently not righteousness. "Because the law worketh wrath," therefore not righteousness. Since the law cannot assure our consciences, neither can it confer righteousness. Since faith is counted for righteousness, consequently righteousness is not a reward of works, but is gratuitously bestowed. Since we are justified by faith, boasting is precluded. "If there had been a law given which could have given life, verily righteousness should have been by the law. But the Scripture hath concluded all under sin, that the promise by faith of Jesus Christ might be given to them that believe." Let them idly pretend, if they dare, that these are applicable to ceremonies, not to morals; but even children would explode such consummate impudence. We may therefore be assured, that when the power of justifying is denied to the law, the whole law is included.

XX. If any one should wonder why the apostle does not content himself with simply mentioning *works*, but says *works of the law*, the reason is obvious. For though works are so greatly esteemed, they derive their value from the Divine approbation rather than from any intrinsic excellence. For who can dare to boast to God of any righteousness of works, but what he has approved? Who can dare to claim any reward as due to them, but what he has promised? It is owing, therefore, to the Divine favour, that they are accounted worthy both of the title and of the reward of righteousness; and so they are valuable, only when they are intended as acts of obedience to God. Wherefore the apostle, in another place, in order to prove that Abraham could not be justified by works, alleges, that "the law was four hundred and thirty years after the covenant was confirmed." Ignorant persons would ridicule such an argument, because there might have been righteous works before the promulgation of the law; but knowing that works have no such intrinsic worth, independently of the testimony and esteem of God, he has taken it for granted that, antecedently to the law, they had no power to justify. We know why he expressly mentions "the works of the law," when he means to deny justification by works; it is because they alone can furnish any occasion of controversy. However, he likewise excludes all works, without any limitation, as when he says, "David describeth the blessedness of the man, unto whom God imputeth righteousness without works." They cannot, therefore, by any subtleties prevent us from retaining this general exclusive particle. It is in vain, also, that they catch at another frivolous subtlety, alleging that we are justified only by that "faith which worketh by love;" with a view to represent righteousness as depending on love. We acknowledge, indeed, with Paul, that no other faith justifies, except that "which worketh by love;" but it does not derive its power to justify from the efficacy of that love. It justifies in no other way than as it introduces us into a participation of the righteousness of Christ. Otherwise there would be no force in the argument so strenuously urged by the apostle. "To him that worketh," says he, "is the reward not reckoned of grace, but of debt. But to him that worketh not, but believeth on him that justifieth the ungodly, his faith is counted for righteousness." Was it possible for him to speak more plainly than by thus asserting, that there is no righteousness of faith, except where there are no works entitled to any reward; and that faith is imputed for righteousness, only when righteousness is conferred through unmerited grace?

XXI. Now, let us examine the truth of what has been asserted in the definition, that the righteousness of faith is a reconciliation with God, which consists solely in remission of sins. We must always return to this axiom—That the Divine wrath remains on all men, as long as they continue to be sinners. This Isaiah has beautifully expressed in the following words: "The Lord's hand is not shortened, that it cannot save; neither is his ear heavy, that it cannot hear; but your iniquities have separated between you and your God, and your sins have hid his face from you, that he will not hear." We are informed, that sin makes a division between man and God, and turns the Divine countenance away from the sinner. Nor can it be otherwise; because it is incompatible with his righteousness to have any communion with sin. Hence the apostle teaches, that man is an enemy to God, till he be reconciled to him through Christ. Whom, therefore, the Lord receives into fellowship, him he is said to justify; because he cannot receive any one into favour or into fellowship with himself, without making him from a sinner to be a righteous person. This, we add, is accomplished by the remission of sins. For if they, whom the Lord has reconciled to himself, be judged according to their works, they will still be found actually sinners; who, notwithstanding, must be absolved and free from sin. It appears, then, that those whom God receives, are made righteous no otherwise than as they are purified by being cleansed from all their defilements by the remission of their sins; so that such a righteousness may, in one word, be denominated a remission of sins.

XXII. Both these points are fully established by the language of Paul, which I have already recited. "God was in Christ, reconciling the world unto himself, not imputing their trespasses unto them; and hath committed unto us the word of reconciliation." Then he adds the substance of his ministry: "He hath made him to be sin for us, who knew no sin; that we might be made the righteousness of God in him." The terms "righteousness" and "reconciliation" are here used by him indiscriminately, to teach us that they are mutually comprehended in each other. And he states the manner of obtaining this righteousness to consist in our transgressions not being imputed to us. Wherefore we can no longer doubt how God justifies, when we hear that he reconciles us to himself by not imputing our sins to us. Thus, in the Epistle to the Romans, the apostle proves, that "God imputeth righteousness without works," from the testimony of David, who declares, "Blessed are they whose iniquities are forgiven, and whose sins are covered. Blessed is the man to whom the Lord will not impute sin." By "blessedness," in this passage, he undoubtedly means righteousness; for since he asserts it to consist in remission of sins, there is no reason for our adopting any other definition of it. Wherefore Zachariah, the father of John the Baptist, places "the knowledge of salvation" in "the remission of sins." And Paul, observing the same rule in the sermon which he preached to the people of Antioch on the subject of salvation, is stated by Luke to have concluded in the following manner: "Through this man is preached unto you the forgiveness of sins; and by him all that believe are justified from all things, from which ye could not be justified by the law of Moses." The apostle thus connects "forgiveness of sins" with "justification," to show that they are identically the same; whence he justly argues, that this righteousness which we obtain through the favour of God is gratuitously bestowed upon us. Nor should it be thought a strange expression, that believers are justified before God, not by their works, but by his gracious acceptance of them; since it occurs so frequently in the Scripture, and sometimes also in the fathers. Augustine says, "The righteousness of the saints, in this world, consists rather in the remission of their sins than in the perfection of their virtues." With which corresponds the remarkable observation of Bernard: "Not to sin at all, is the righteousness of God; but the righteousness of man is the Divine grace and mercy." He had before asserted, "that Christ is righteousness to us in absolution, and therefore that they alone are righteous who have obtained pardon through his mercy."

XXIII. Hence, also, it is evident, that we obtain justification before God, solely by the intervention of the righteousness of Christ. Which is equivalent to saying, that a man is righteous, not in himself, but because the righteousness of Christ is communicated to him by imputation; and this is a point which deserves an attentive consideration. For it supersedes that idle notion, that a man is justified by faith, because faith receives the Spirit of God by whom he is made righteous; which is too repugnant to the foregoing doctrine, ever to be reconcilable to it. For he must certainly be destitute of all righteousness of his own, who is taught to seek a righteousness out of himself. This is most clearly asserted by the apostle, when he says, "He hath made him to be sin for us, who knew no sin; that we might be made the righteousness of God in him." We see that our righteousness is not in ourselves, but in Christ; and that all our title to it rests solely on our being partakers of Christ; for in possessing him, we possess all his riches with him. Nor does any objection arise from what he states in another place, that "God, sending his own Son in the likeness of sinful flesh, and for sin, condemned sin in the flesh; that the righteousness of the law might be fulfilled in us;" where he intends no other fulfilment than what we obtain by imputation. For the Lord Christ so communicates his righteousness to us, that, with reference to the Divine judgment, he transfuses its virtue into us in a most wonderful manner. That the apostle intended no other, abundantly appears from another declaration, which he had made just before: "As by one man's disobedience many were made sinners, so by the obedience of one shall many be made righteous." What is placing our righteousness in the obedience of Christ, but asserting, that we are accounted righteous only because his obedience is accepted for us as if it were our own? Wherefore Ambrose appears to me to have very beautifully exemplified this righteousness in the benediction of Jacob; that as he, who had on his own account no claim to the privileges of primogeniture, being concealed in his brother's habit, and invested with his garment, which diffused a most excellent odour, insinuated himself into the favour of his father, that he might receive the benediction to his own advantage, under the character of another; so we shelter ourselves under the precious purity of Christ our elder brother, that we may obtain the testimony of righteousness in the sight of God. The words of Ambrose are, "That Isaac smelled the odour of the garments, perhaps indicates, that we are justified not by works, but by faith; since the infirmity of the flesh is an impediment to works, but the brightness of faith, which merits the pardon of sin, conceals the error of our actions." And such is indeed the real fact; for that we may appear before the face of God to salvation, it is necessary for us to be perfumed with his fragrance, and to have all our deformities concealed and absorbed in his perfection.

8.

Two Things Necessary to Be
Observed in Gratuitous Justification.

Here are two things to which we must always be particularly attentive; to maintain the glory of the Lord unimpaired and undiminished, and to preserve in our own consciences a placid composure and serene tranquillity with regard to the Divine judgment. We see how frequently and solicitously the Scripture exhorts us to render ascriptions of praise to God alone, when it treats of justification. And, indeed, the apostle assures us that the design of the Lord in conferring righteousness upon us in Christ, is to manifest his own righteousness. The nature of that manifestation he immediately subjoins: it is, "that he might be just, and the justifier of him which believeth in Jesus." The righteousness of God, we see, is not sufficiently illustrious, unless he alone be esteemed righteous, and communicate the grace of justification to the unworthy. For this reason it is his will "that every mouth be stopped, and all the world become guilty before him;" because, as long as man has any thing to allege in his own defence, it detracts something from the glory of God. Thus in Ezekiel he teaches us how greatly we glorify his name by an acknowledgment of our iniquity: "Ye shall remember your ways, (saith he,) and all your doings, wherein ye have been defiled; and ye shall loathe yourselves in your own sight for all your evils that ye have committed. And ye shall know that I am the Lord, when I have wrought with you for my name's sake, not according to your wicked ways, nor according to your corrupt doings." If these things are contained in the true knowledge of God, that, humbled with a consciousness of our iniquity, we should consider him as indulging us with blessings of which we are unworthy, why do we attempt, to our own serious injury, to pilfer the smallest particle of the praise due to his gratuitous goodness? Thus also when Jeremiah proclaims, "Let not the wise man glory in his wisdom, neither let the mighty man glory in his might, let not the rich man glory in his riches; but let him that glorieth glory in the Lord;" does he not suggest that the glory of God sustains some diminution, if any man glory in himself? To this use these words are clearly applied by Paul, when he states, that all the branches of our salvation are deposited with Christ, that we may not glory except in the Lord. For he intimates, that they who suppose themselves to have even the least ground for glorying in themselves, are guilty of rebelling against God, and obscuring his glory.

II. The truth, then, is, that we never truly glory in him, till we have entirely renounced all glory of our own. On the converse, this may be admitted as an axiom universally true, that they who glory in themselves, glory in opposition to God. For Paul is of opinion that the world is not "subject to the judgment of God," till men are deprived of all foundation for glorying. Therefore Isaiah, when he announces, that "in the Lord shall all the seed of Israel be justified," adds also, "and shall glory;" as though he had said, that the end of God in justifying the elect was, that they might glory in himself, and in no other. But how we should glory in the Lord, he had stated in the preceding verse: "Surely, shall one say, in the Lord have I righteousness and strength." Let us observe, that what is required is not a simple confession, but a confession confirmed by an oath; that we may not suppose any fictitious pretence of humility to be sufficient.

Here let no one plead that he does not glory at all, when without arrogance he recognizes his own righteousness; for such an opinion cannot exist without generating confidence, nor confidence without being attended with glorying. Let us remember, therefore, in the whole controversy concerning righteousness, that this end must be kept in view, that all the praise of it may remain perfect and undiminished with the Lord; because, according to the apostle's testimony, he has bestowed his grace on us in order "to declare his righteousness; that he might be just, and the justifier of him which believeth in Jesus." Wherefore, in another place, after having declared that the Lord has conferred salvation on us in order to display "the praise of the glory of his grace," repeating, as it were, the same sentiment, he adds, "By grace are ye saved through faith; and that not of yourselves; it is the gift of God; not of works, lest any man should boast." And when Peter admonishes us that we are called to the hope of salvation, "that we should show forth the praises (or virtues) of him who hath called us out of darkness into his marvellous light," he evidently means that the praises of God alone should resound in the ears of believers, so as to impose total silence on all the presumption of the flesh. The conclusion of the whole is, that man cannot without sacrilege arrogate to himself the least particle of righteousness, because it is so much detracted and diminished from the glory of the righteousness of God.

III. Now, if we inquire by what means the conscience can obtain peace before God, we shall find no other than our reception of gratuitous righteousness from his free gift. Let us always remember the inquiry of Solomon—"Who can say, I have made my heart clean, I am pure from my sin?" It is certain that there is no man who is not covered with infinite pollution. Let a man of the most perfect character, then, retire into his own conscience, and enter into a scrutiny of his actions, and what will be the result? Will he feel a high degree of satisfaction, as though there were the most entire agreement between God and him? or will he not rather be lacerated with terrible agonies, on perceiving in himself such ample cause for condemnation, if he be judged according to his works? If the conscience reflect on God, it must either enjoy a solid peace with his judgment, or be surrounded with the terrors of hell. We gain nothing, therefore, in our discussions of this point, unless we establish a righteousness, the stability of which will support our souls under the scrutiny of the Divine judgment. When our souls shall possess what will enable them to appear with boldness in the presence of God, and to await and receive his judgment without any fear, then, and not before, we may be assured that we have found a righteousness which truly deserves the name. It is not without reason, therefore, that this subject is so largely insisted on by the apostle, whose words I prefer to my own: "For if they which are of the law be heirs, faith is made void, and the promise is made of none effect." He first infers, that faith is annulled and superseded, if the promise of righteousness respect the merit of our works, or depend on our observance of the law. For no man could ever securely rely on it, since he never would be able to determine with certainty for himself that he had fulfilled the law, as in fact no man ever does completely satisfy it by any works of his own. Not to seek far for testimonies of this fact, every individual may be his own witness of it, who will enter unprejudiced into an examination of himself. And hence it appears in what deep and dark recesses hypocrisy buries the minds of men, while they indulge themselves in such great security, and hesitate not to oppose their self-adulation to the judgment of God, as though they would stop the proceedings of his tribunal. But believers, who sincerely examine themselves, are troubled and distressed with a solicitude of a very different nature. The minds of men universally, therefore, ought to feel first hesitation, and then despair, while considering, every one for himself, the magnitude of the debt with which they are still oppressed, and their immense distance from the conditions prescribed to them. Behold their confidence already broken and extinguished; for to confide is not to fluctuate, to vary, to be hurried hither and thither, to hesitate, to be kept in suspense, to stagger, and finally to despair; but it is, to strengthen the mind with content, certainty, and solid security, and to have somewhat upon which to stand and to rest.

IV. He adds likewise another consideration, that the promise would be void and of none effect. For if the fulfilment of it depend on our merit, when shall we have made such a progress as to deserve the favour of God? Besides, this second argument is a consequence of the former, since the promise will be fulfilled to those alone who shall exercise faith in it. Therefore, if faith be wanting, the promise will retain no force. "Therefore the inheritance is of faith, that it might be by grace; to the end the promise might be sure to all the seed." For it is abundantly confirmed, when it depends solely on the Divine mercy; because mercy and truth are connected by an indissoluble bond, and whatever God mercifully promises, he also faithfully performs. Thus David, before he implores salvation for himself according to the word of God, first represents it as originating in his mercy: "According to thy word unto thy servant, let thy tender mercies come unto me, that I may live." And for this there is sufficient reason, since God has no other inducement to promise than what arises from his mere mercy. Here, then, we must place, and, as it were, deeply fix, all our hopes, without regarding our own works, or seeking any assistance from them. Nor must it be supposed that we are advancing a new doctrine, for the same conduct is recommended by Augustine. "Christ," says he, "will reign in his servants for ever. God has promised this, God has said it; if that be insufficient, God has sworn it. Since the promise, therefore, is established, not according to our merits, but according to his mercy, no man ought to speak with anxiety of that which he cannot doubt." Bernard also says, "The disciples of Christ asked, Who can be saved? He replied, With men this is impossible, but not with God. This is all our confidence, this our only consolation, this the whole foundation of our hope. But certain of the possibility, what think we of his will? Who knows whether he deserve love or hatred? Who has known the mind of the Lord, or who has been his counsellor? Here, now, we evidently need faith to help us, and his truth to assist us; that what is concealed from us in the heart of the Father, may be revealed by the Spirit, and that the testimony of the Spirit may persuade our hearts that we are sons of God; that he may persuade us by calling and justifying us freely by faith; in which there is, as it were, an intermediate passage from eternal predestination to future glory." Let us draw the following brief conclusion: The Scripture declares that the promises of God have no efficacy, unless they be embraced by the conscience with a steady confidence; and whenever there is any doubt or uncertainty, it pronounces them to be made void. Again, it asserts that they have no stability if they depend on our works. Either, therefore, we must be for ever destitute of righteousness, or our works must not come into consideration, but the ground must be occupied by faith alone, whose nature it is to open the ears and shut the eyes; that is, to be intent only on the promise, and to avert the thoughts from all human dignity or merit. Thus is accomplished that remarkable prophecy of Zechariah: "I will remove the iniquity of that land in one day. In that day, saith the Lord of hosts, shall ye call every man his neighbour under the vine and under the fig-tree;" in which the prophet suggests that believers enjoy no true peace till after they have obtained the remission of their sins. For this analogy must be observed in the prophets, that when they treat of the kingdom of Christ, they exhibit the external bounties of God as figures of spiritual blessings. Wherefore also Christ is denominated "the Prince of peace," and "our Peace;" because he calms all the agitations of the conscience. If we inquire, by what means; we must come to the sacrifice by which God is appeased. For no man will ever lose his fears who shall not be assured that God is propitiated solely by that atonement which Christ has made by sustaining his wrath. In short, we must seek for peace only in the terrors of Christ our Redeemer.

V. But why do I use such an obscure testimony? Paul invariably denies that peace or tranquillity can be enjoyed in the conscience, without a certainty that we are justified by faith. And he also declares whence that certainty proceeds; it is "because the love of God is shed abroad in our hearts by the Holy Ghost;" as though he had said that our consciences can never be satisfied without a certain persuasion of our acceptance with God. Hence he exclaims in the name of all believers, "Who shall separate us from the love of God which is in Christ?" For till we have reached that port of safety, we shall tremble with alarm at every slightest breeze; but while God shall manifest himself as our Shepherd, we shall fear no evil even in the valley of the shadow of death. Whoever they are, therefore, who pretend that we are justified by faith, because, being regenerated, we are righteous by living a spiritual life, they have never tasted the sweetness of grace, so as to have confidence that God would be propitious to them. Whence also it follows, that they know no more of the method of praying aright, than the Turks or any other profane nations. For according to the testimony of Paul, faith is not genuine unless it dictate and suggest that most delightful name of Father, and unless it open our mouth freely to cry, "Abba, Father;" which he in another place expresses still more clearly: "In Christ we have boldness and access with confidence by the faith of him." This certainly arises not from the gift of regeneration; which, being always imperfect in the present state, contains in itself abundant occasion of doubting. Wherefore it is necessary to come to this remedy; that believers should conclude that they cannot hope for an inheritance in the kingdom of heaven on any other foundation, but because, being ingrafted into the body of Christ, they are gratuitously accounted righteous. For with respect to justification, faith is a thing merely passive, bringing nothing of our own to conciliate the favour of God, but receiving what we need from Christ.

9.

The Commencement and
Continual Progress of Justification.

For the further elucidation of this subject, let us examine what kind of righteousness can be found in men during the whole course of their lives. Let us divide them into four classes. For either they are destitute of the knowledge of God, and immerged in idolatry; or, having been initiated by the sacraments, they lead impure lives, denying God in their actions, while they confess him with their lips, and belong to Christ only in name; or they are hypocrites, concealing the iniquity of their hearts with vain disguises; or, being regenerated by the Spirit of God, they devote themselves to true holiness. In the first of these classes, judged of according to their natural characters, from the crown of the head to the sole of the foot there will not be found a single spark of goodness; unless we mean to charge the Scripture with falsehood in these representations which it gives of all the sons of Adam—that "the heart is deceitful above all things, and desperately wicked;" that "every imagination of man's heart is evil from his youth;" that "the thoughts of man are vanity; that there is no fear of God before his eyes;" that "there is none that understandeth, none that seeketh after God;" in a word, "that he is flesh," a term expressive of all those works which are enumerated by Paul—"adultery, fornication, uncleanness, lasciviousness, idolatry, witchcraft, hatred, variance, emulations, wrath, strife, seditions, heresies, envyings, murders," and every impurity and abomination that can be conceived. This is the dignity, in the confidence of which they must glory. But if any among them discover that integrity in their conduct which among men has some appearance of sanctity, yet, since we know that God regards not external splendour, we must penetrate to the secret springs of these actions, if we wish them to avail any thing to justification. We must narrowly examine, I say, from what disposition of heart these works proceed. Though a most extensive field of observation is now before us, yet, since the subject may be despatched in very few words, I shall be as compendious as possible.

II. In the first place, I do not deny, that whatever excellences appear in unbelievers, they are the gifts of God. I am not so at variance with the common opinion of mankind, as to contend that there is no difference between the justice, moderation, and equity of Titus or Trajan, and the rage, intemperance, and cruelty of Caligula, or Nero, or Domitian; between the obscenities of Tiberius and the continence of Vespasian; and, not to dwell on particular virtues or vices, between the observance and the contempt of moral obligation and positive laws. For so great is the difference between just and unjust, that it is visible even in the lifeless image of it. For what order will be left in the world, if these opposites be confounded together? Such a distinction as this, therefore, between virtuous and vicious actions, has not only been engraven by the Lord in the heart of every man, but has also been frequently confirmed by his providential dispensations. We see how he confers many blessings of the present life on those who practise virtue among men. Not that this external resemblance of virtue merits the least favour from him; but he is pleased to discover his great esteem of true righteousness, by not permitting that which is external and hypocritical to remain without a temporal reward. Whence it follows, as we have just acknowledged, that these virtues, whatever they may be, or rather images of virtues, are the gifts of God; since there is nothing in any respect laudable which does not proceed from him.

III. Nevertheless the observation of Augustine is strictly true—that all who are strangers to the religion of the one true God, however they may be esteemed worthy of admiration for their reputed virtue, not only merit no reward, but are rather deserving of punishment, because they contaminate the pure gifts of God with the pollution of their own hearts. For though they are instruments used by God for the preservation of human society, by the exercise of justice, continence, friendship, temperance, fortitude, and prudence, yet they perform these good works of God very improperly; being restrained from the commission of evil, not by a sincere attachment to true virtue, but either by mere ambition, or by self-love, or by some other irregular disposition. These actions, therefore, being corrupted in their very source by the impurity of their hearts, are no more entitled to be classed among virtues, than those vices which commonly deceive mankind by their affinity and similitude to virtues. Besides, when we remember that the end of what is right is always to serve God, whatever is directed to any other end, can have no claim to that appellation. Therefore, since they regard not the end prescribed by Divine wisdom, though an act performed by them be externally and apparently good, yet, being directed to a wrong end, it becomes sin. He concludes, therefore, that all the Fabricii, Scipios, and Catos, in all their celebrated actions, were guilty of sin, inasmuch as, being destitute of the light of faith, they did not direct those actions to that end to which they ought to have directed them; that consequently they had no genuine righteousness; because moral duties are estimated not by external actions, but by the ends for which such actions are designed.

IV. Besides, if there be any truth in the assertion of John, that "he that hath not the Son of God, hath not life;" they who have no interest in Christ, whatever be their characters, their actions, or their endeavours, are constantly advancing, through the whole course of their lives, towards destruction and the sentence of eternal death. On this argument is founded the following observation of Augustine: "Our religion discriminates between the righteous and the unrighteous, not by the law of works, but by that of faith, without which works apparently good are perverted into sins." Wherefore the same writer, in another place, strikingly compares the exertions of such men to a deviation in a race from the prescribed course. For the more vigorously any one runs out of the way, he recedes so much the further from the goal, and becomes so much the more unfortunate. Wherefore he contends, that it is better to halt in the way, than to run out of the way. Finally, it is evident that they are evil trees, since without a participation of Christ there is no sanctification. They may produce fruits fair and beautiful to the eye, and even sweet to the taste, but never any that are good. Hence we clearly perceive that all the thoughts, meditations, and actions of man, antecedent to a reconciliation to God by faith, are accursed, and not only of no avail to justification, but certainly deserving of condemnation. But why do we dispute concerning it as a dubious point, when it is already proved by the testimony of the apostle, that "without faith it is impossible to please God?"

V. But the proof will be still clearer, if the grace of God be directly opposed to the natural condition of man. The Scripture invariably proclaims, that God finds nothing in men which can incite him to bless them, but that he prevents them by his gratuitous goodness. For what can a dead man do to recover life? But when God illuminates us with the knowledge of himself, he is said to raise us from death, and to make us new creatures. For under this character we find the Divine goodness towards us frequently celebrated, especially by the apostle. "God," says he, "who is rich in mercy, for his great love wherewith he loved us, even when we were dead in sins, hath quickened us together with Christ," &c. In another place, when, under the type of Abraham, he treats of the general calling of believers, he says, It is "God, who quickeneth the dead, and calleth those things which be not as though they were." If we are nothing, what can we do? Wherefore God forcibly represses this presumption, in the Book of Job, in the following words: "Who hath prevented me, that I should repay him? Whatsoever is under the whole heaven is mine." Paul, explaining this passage, concludes from it, that we ought not to suppose we bring any thing to the Lord but ignominious indigence and emptiness. Wherefore, in the passage cited above, in order to prove that we attain to the hope of salvation, not by works, but solely by the grace of God, he alleges, that "we are his workmanship, created in Christ Jesus unto good works, which God hath before ordained that we should walk in them." As though he would say, Who of us can boast that he has influenced God by his righteousness, since our first power to do well proceeds from regeneration? For, according to the constitution of our nature, oil might be extracted from a stone sooner than we could perform a good work. It is wonderful, indeed, that man, condemned to such ignominy, dares to pretend to have any thing left. Let us confess, therefore, with that eminent servant of the Lord, that "God hath saved us, and called us with a holy calling, not according to our works, but according to his own purpose and grace;" and that "the kindness and love of God our Saviour towards man appeared," because "not by works of righteousness which we have done, but according to his mercy he saved us; that being justified by his grace, we should be made heirs of eternal life." By this confession we divest man of all righteousness, even to the smallest particle, till through mere mercy he has been regenerated to the hope of eternal life; for if a righteousness of works contributed any thing to our justification, we are not truly said to be "justified by grace." The apostle, when he asserted justification to be by grace, had certainly not forgotten his argument in another place, that "if it be of works, then it is no more grace." And what else does our Lord intend, when he declares, "I am not come to call the righteous, but sinners?" If sinners only are admitted, why do we seek to enter by a counterfeit righteousness?

VI. The same thought frequently recurs to me, that I am in danger of injuring the mercy of God, by labouring with so much anxiety in the defence of this doctrine, as though it were doubtful or obscure. But such being our malignity, that, unless it be most powerfully subdued, it never allows to God that which belongs to him, I am constrained to dwell a little longer upon it. But as the Scripture is sufficiently perspicuous on this subject, I shall use its language in preference to my own. Isaiah, after having described the universal ruin of mankind, properly subjoins the method of recovery. "The Lord saw it, and it displeased him that there was no judgment. And he saw that there was no man, and wondered that there was no intercessor: therefore his own arm brought salvation unto him; and his righteousness it sustained him." Where are our righteousnesses, if it be true, as the prophet says, that no one assists the Lord in procuring his salvation? So another prophet introduces the Lord speaking of the reconciliation of sinners to himself, saying, "I will betroth thee unto me for ever, in righteousness, and in judgment, and in loving-kindness, and in mercies. I will have mercy upon her that had not obtained mercy." If this covenant, which is evidently our first union with God, depend on his mercy, there remains no foundation for our righteousness. And I should really wish to be informed by those, who pretend that man advances to meet God with some righteousness of works, whether there be any righteousness at all, but that which is accepted by God. If it be madness to entertain such a thought, what that is acceptable to God can proceed from his enemies, who, with all their actions, are the objects of his complete abhorrence? And that we are all the inveterate and avowed enemies of our God, till we are justified and received into his friendship, is an undeniable truth. If justification be the principle from which love originates, what righteousnesses of works can precede it? To destroy that pestilent arrogance, therefore, John carefully apprizes us that "we did not first love him." And the Lord had by his prophet long before taught the same truth: "I will love them freely," saith he, "for mine anger is turned away." If his love was spontaneously inclined towards us, it certainly is not excited by works. But the ignorant mass of mankind have only this notion of it—that no man has merited that Christ should effect our redemption; but that towards obtaining the possession of redemption, we derive some assistance from our own works. But however we may have been redeemed by Christ, yet till we are introduced into communion with him by the calling of the Father, we are both heirs of darkness and death, and enemies to God. For Paul teaches, that we are not purified and washed from our pollutions by the blood of Christ, till the Spirit effects that purification within us. This is the same that Peter intends, when he declares that the "sanctification of the Spirit" is effectual "unto obedience, and sprinkling of the blood of Jesus Christ." If we are sprinkled by the Spirit with the blood of Christ for purification, we must not imagine that before this ablution we are in any other state than that of sinners destitute of Christ. We may be certain, therefore, that the commencement of our salvation is, as it were, a resurrection from death to life; because, when "on the behalf of Christ it is given to us to believe on him," we then begin to experience a transition from death to life.

VII. The same reasoning may be applied to the second and third classes of men in the division stated above. For the impurity of the conscience proves, that they are neither of them yet regenerated by the Spirit of God; and their unregeneracy betrays also their want of faith: whence it appears, that they are not yet reconciled to God, or justified in his sight, since these blessings are only attained by faith. What can be performed by sinners alienated from God, that is not execrable in his view? Yet all the impious, and especially hypocrites, are inflated with this foolish confidence. Though they know that their heart is full of impurity, yet if they perform any specious actions, they esteem them too good to be despised by God. Hence that pernicious error, that though convicted of a polluted and impious heart, they cannot be brought to confess themselves destitute of righteousness; but while they acknowledge themselves to be unrighteous, because it cannot be denied, they still arrogate to themselves some degree of righteousness. This vanity the Lord excellently refutes by the prophet. "Ask now," saith he, "the priests, saying, If one bear holy flesh in the skirt of his garment, and with his skirt do touch bread, or any meat, shall it be holy? And the priests answered and said, No. Then said Haggai, If one that is unclean by a dead body touch any of these, shall it be unclean? And the priests answered and said, It shall be unclean. Then answered Haggai, and said, So is this people, and so is this nation before me, saith the Lord; and so is every work of their hands; and that which they offer there is unclean." I wish that this passage might either obtain full credit with us, or be deeply impressed on our memory. For there is no one, however flagitious his whole life may be, who can suffer himself to be persuaded of what the Lord here plainly declares. The greatest sinner, as soon as he has performed two or three duties of the law, doubts not but they are accepted of him for righteousness; but the Lord positively denies that any sanctification is acquired by such actions, unless the heart be previously well purified; and not content with this, he asserts that all the works of sinners are contaminated by the impurity of their hearts. Let the name of righteousness, then, no longer be given to these works which are condemned for their pollution by the lips of God. And by what a fine similitude does he demonstrate this! For it might have been objected that what the Lord had enjoined was inviolably holy. But he shows, on the contrary, that it is not to be wondered at, if those things which are sanctified by the law of the Lord, are defiled by the pollution of the wicked; since an unclean hand cannot touch any thing that has been consecrated, without profaning it.

VIII. He excellently pursues the same argument also in Isaiah: "Bring no more vain oblations; incense is an abomination unto me; your new moons and your appointed feasts my soul hateth; they are a trouble unto me; I am weary to bear them. When ye spread forth your hands, I will hide mine eyes from you; yea, when ye make many prayers, I will not hear: your hands are full of blood. Wash you, make you clean; put away the evil of your doings." What is the reason that the Lord is so displeased at an obedience to his law? But, in fact, he here rejects nothing that arises from the genuine observance of the law; the beginning of which, he every where teaches, is an unfeigned fear of his name. If that be wanting, all the oblations made to him are not merely trifles, but nauseous and abominable pollutions. Let hypocrites go now, and, retaining depravity concealed in their hearts, endeavour by their works to merit the favour of God. But by such means they will add provocation to provocation; for "the sacrifice of the wicked is an abomination to the Lord; but the prayer of the upright" alone "is his delight." We lay it down, therefore, as an undoubted truth, which ought to be well known to such as are but moderately versed in the Scriptures, that even the most splendid works of men not yet truly sanctified, are so far from righteousness in the Divine view, that they are accounted sins. And therefore they have strictly adhered to the truth, who have maintained that the works of a man do not conciliate God's favour to his person; but, on the contrary, that works are never acceptable to God, unless the person who performs them has previously found favour in his sight. And this order, to which the Scripture directs us, is religiously to be observed. Moses relates, that "The Lord had respect unto Abel and to his offering." Does he not plainly indicate that the Lord is propitious to men, before he regards their works? Wherefore the purification of the heart is a necessary prerequisite, in order that the works which we perform may be favourably received by God; for the declaration of Jeremiah is always in force, that the "eyes of the Lord are upon the truth." And the Holy Spirit has asserted by the mouth of Peter, that it is "by faith" alone that the "heart" is "purified," which proves that the first foundation is laid in a true and living faith.

IX. Let us now examine what degree of righteousness is possessed by those whom we have ranked in the fourth class. We admit, that when God, by the interposition of the righteousness of Christ, reconciles us to himself, and having granted us the free remission of our sins, esteems us as righteous persons, to this mercy he adds also another blessing; for he dwells in us by his Holy Spirit, by whose power our carnal desires are daily more and more mortified, and we are sanctified, that is, consecrated to the Lord unto real purity of life, having our hearts moulded to obey his law, so that it is our prevailing inclination to submit to his will, and to promote his glory alone by all possible means. But even while, under the guidance of the Holy Spirit, we are walking in the ways of the Lord,—that we may not forget ourselves, and be filled with pride, we feel such remains of imperfection, as afford us abundant cause for humility. The Scripture declares, that "there is not a just man upon earth, that doeth good and sinneth not." What kind of righteousness, then, will even believers obtain from their own works? In the first place, I assert, that the best of their performances are tarnished and corrupted by some carnal impurity and debased by a mixture of some alloy. Let any holy servant of God select from his whole life that which he shall conceive to have been the best of all his actions, and let him examine it with attention on every side; he will undoubtedly discover in it some taint of the corruption of the flesh; since our alacrity to good actions is never what it ought to be, but our course is retarded by great debility. Though we perceive that the blemishes which deform the works of the saints, are not difficult to be discovered, yet suppose we admit them to be very diminutive spots, will they not be at all offensive in the sight of God, in which even the stars are not pure? We have now ascertained, that there is not a single action performed by the saints, which, if judged according to its intrinsic merit, does not justly deserve to be rewarded with shame.

X. In the next place, even though it were possible for us to perform any works completely pure and perfect, yet one sin is sufficient to extinguish and annihilate all remembrance of antecedent righteousness, as is declared by the prophet. With him James also agrees: "Whosoever shall offend," says he, "in one point, he is guilty of all." Now, since this mortal life is never pure or free from sin, whatever righteousness we might acquire being perpetually corrupted, overpowered, and destroyed by subsequent sins, it would neither be admitted in the sight of God, nor be imputed to us for righteousness. Lastly, in considering the righteousness of works, we should regard, not any action commanded in the law, but the commandment itself. Therefore, if we seek righteousness by the law, it is in vain for us to perform two or three works; a perpetual observance of the law is indispensably necessary. Wherefore God does not impute to us for righteousness that remission of sins, of which we have spoken, once only, (as some foolishly imagine,) in order that, having obtained pardon for our past lives, we may afterwards seek righteousness by the law; which would be only sporting with us, and deluding us by a fallacious hope. For since perfection is unattainable by us, as long as we are in this mortal body, and the law denounces death and judgment on all whose works are not completely and universally righteous, it will always have matter of accusation and condemnation against us, unless it be prevented by the Divine mercy continually absolving us by a perpetual remission of our sins. Wherefore it will ever be true, as we asserted at the beginning, that if we be judged according to our demerits, whatever be our designs or undertakings, we are nevertheless with all our endeavours and all our pursuits, deserving of death and destruction.

XI. We must strenuously insist on these two points—first, that there never was an action performed by a pious man, which, if examined by the scrutinizing eye of Divine justice, would not deserve condemnation; and secondly, if any such thing be admitted, (though it cannot be the case with any individual of mankind,) yet being corrupted and contaminated by the sins, of which its performer is confessedly guilty, it loses every claim to the Divine favour. And this is the principal hinge on which our controversy [with the Papists] turns. For concerning the beginning of justification, there is no dispute between us and the sounder schoolmen, but we all agree, that a sinner being freely delivered from condemnation obtains righteousness, and that by the remission of his sins; only they, under the term *justification*, comprehend that renovation in which we are renewed by the Spirit of God to an obedience to the law, and so they describe the righteousness of a regenerate man as consisting in this—that a man, after having been once reconciled to God through faith in Christ, is accounted righteous with God on account of his good works, the merit of which is the cause of his acceptance. But the Lord, on the contrary, declares, "that faith was reckoned to Abraham for righteousness," not during the time while he yet remained a worshipper of idols, but after he had been eminent during many years for the sanctity of his life. Abraham, then, had for a long time worshipped God from a pure heart, and performed all that obedience to the law, which a mortal man is capable of performing; yet, after all, his righteousness consisted in faith. Whence we conclude, according to the argument of Paul, that it was not of works. So when the prophet says, "The just shall live by his faith," he is not speaking of the impious and profane, whom the Lord justifies by converting them to the faith; but his address is directed to believers, and they are promised life by faith. Paul also removes every doubt, when, in confirmation of this sentiment, he adduces the following passage of David: "Blessed are they whose iniquities are forgiven." But it is certain that David spake not of impious men, but of believers, whose characters resembled his own; for he spoke from the experience of his own conscience. Wherefore it is necessary for us, not to have this blessing for once only, but to retain it as long as we live. Lastly, he asserts, that the message of a free reconciliation with God, is not only promulgated for a day or two, but is perpetual in the church. Believers, therefore, even to the end of their lives, have no other righteousness than that which is there described. For the mediatorial office is perpetually sustained by Christ, by whom the Father is reconciled to us; and the efficacy of whose death is perpetually the same, consisting in ablution, satisfaction, expiation, and perfect obedience, which covers all our iniquities. And Paul does not tell the Ephesians that they are indebted to grace merely for the beginning of their salvation, but that they "are saved by grace, not of works, lest any man should boast."

XII. The subterfuges, by which the schoolmen endeavour to evade these arguments, are unavailing. They say, that the sufficiency of good works to justification arises not from their intrinsic merit, but from the grace through which they are accepted. Secondly, because they are constrained to acknowledge the righteousness of works to be always imperfect in the present state, they admit, that as long as we live we need the remission of our sins, in order to supply the defects of our works; but that our deficiencies are compensated by works of supererogation. I reply, that what they denominate the grace through which our works are accepted, is no other than the free goodness of the Father, with which he embraces us in Christ, when he invests us with the righteousness of Christ, and accepts it as ours, in order that, in consequence of it, he may treat us as holy, pure, and righteous persons. For the righteousness of Christ (which, being the only perfect righteousness, is the only one that can bear the Divine scrutiny) must be produced on our behalf, and judicially presented, as in the case of a surety. Being furnished with this, we obtain by faith the perpetual remission of our sins. Our imperfections and impurities, being concealed by its purity, are not imputed to us, but are as it were buried, and prevented from appearing in the view of Divine justice, till the advent of that hour, when the old man being slain and utterly annihilated in us, the Divine goodness shall receive us into a blessed peace with the new Adam, in that state to wait for the day of the Lord, when we shall receive incorruptible bodies, and be translated to the glories of the celestial kingdom.

XIII. If these things are true, surely no works of ours can render us acceptable to God; nor can the actions themselves be pleasing to him, any otherwise than as a man, who is covered with the righteousness of Christ, pleases God and obtains the remission of his sins. For God has not promised eternal life as a reward of certain works; he only declares, that "he that doeth these things shall live," denouncing, on the contrary, that memorable curse against all who continue not in the observance of every one of his commands. This abundantly refutes the erroneous notion of a partial righteousness, since no other righteousness is admitted into heaven but an entire observance of the law. Nor is there any more solidity in their pretence of a sufficient compensation for imperfections by works of supererogation. For are they not by this perpetually recurring to the subterfuge, from which they have already been driven, that the partial observance of the law constitutes, as far as it goes, a righteousness of works? They unblushingly assume as granted, what no man of sound judgment will concede. The Lord frequently declares, that he acknowledges no righteousness of works, except in a perfect obedience to his law. What presumption is it for us, who are destitute of this, in order that we may not appear to be despoiled of all our glory, or, in other words, to submit entirely to the Lord—what presumption is it for us to boast of I know not what fragments of a few actions, and to endeavour to supply deficiencies by other satisfactions! *Satisfactions* have already been so completely demolished, that they ought not to occupy even a transient thought. I only remark, that those who trifle in this manner, do not consider what an execrable thing sin is in the sight of God; for indeed they ought to know, that all the righteousness of all mankind, accumulated in one mass, is insufficient to compensate for a single sin. We see that man on account of one offence was rejected and abandoned by God, so that he lost all means of regaining salvation. They are deprived, therefore, of the power of satisfaction, with which, however they flatter themselves, they will certainly never be able to render a satisfaction to God, to whom nothing will be pleasing or acceptable that proceeds from his enemies. Now, his enemies are all those to whom he determines to impute sin. Our sins, therefore, must be covered and forgiven, before the Lord can regard any of our works. Whence it follows that the remission of sins is absolutely gratuitous, and that it is wickedly blasphemed by those who obtrude any *satisfactions*. Let us, therefore, after the example of the apostle, "forgetting those things which are behind, and reaching forth unto those things which are before, press toward the mark for the prize of our high calling."

XIV. But how is the pretence of works of supererogation consistent with this injunction—"When ye shall have done all those things which are commanded you, say, We are unprofitable servants; we have done that which was our duty to do?" This direction does not inculcate an act of simulation or falsehood, but a decision in our mind respecting that of which we are certain. The Lord, therefore, commands us sincerely to think and consider with ourselves, that our services to him are none of them gratuitous, but merely the performance of indispensable duties; and that justly; for we are servants under such numerous obligations as we could never discharge; even though all our thoughts and all our members were devoted to the duties of the law. In saying, therefore, "When ye shall have done all those things which are commanded," he supposes a case of one man having attained to a degree of righteousness beyond what is attained by all the men in the world. How, then, while every one of us is at the greatest distance from this point, can we presume to glory that we have completely attained to that perfect standard? Nor can any one reasonably object, that there is nothing to prevent his efforts from going beyond his necessary obligations, who in any respect fails of doing the duty incumbent on him. For we must acknowledge, that we cannot imagine any thing pertaining either to the service of God or to the love of our neighbour, which is not comprehended in the Divine law. But if it is a part of the law, let us not boast of voluntary liberality, where we are bound by necessity.

XV. It is irrelevant to this subject, to allege the boasting of Paul, that among the Corinthians he voluntarily receded from what, if he had chosen, he might have claimed as his right, and not only did what was incumbent on him to do, but afforded them his gratuitous services beyond the requisitions of duty. They ought to attend to the reason there assigned, that he acted thus, "lest he should hinder the gospel of Christ." For wicked and fraudulent teachers recommended themselves by this stratagem of liberality, by which they endeavoured, both to conciliate a favourable reception to their own pernicious dogmas, and to fix an odium on the gospel; so that Paul was necessitated either to endanger the doctrine of Christ, or to oppose these artifices. Now, if it be a matter of indifference to a Christian to incur an offence when he may avoid it, I confess that the apostle performed for the Lord a work of supererogation; but if this was justly required of a prudent minister of the gospel, I maintain that he did what was his duty to do. Even if no such reason appeared, yet the observation of Chrysostom is always true—that all that we have is on the same tenure as the possessions of slaves, which the law pronounces to be the property of their masters. And Christ has clearly delivered the same truth in the parable, where he inquires whether we thank a servant, when he returns home in the evening, after the various labours of the day. But it is possible that he may have laboured with greater diligence than we had ventured to require. This may be granted; yet he has done no more than, by the condition of servitude, he was under an obligation to do; since he belongs to us, with all the ability he has. I say nothing of the nature of the supererogations which these men wish to boast of before God; for they are contemptible trifles, which he has never commanded, which he does not approve, nor, when they render up their account to him, will he accept them. We cannot admit that there are any works of supererogation, except such as those of which it is said by the prophet, "Who hath required this at your hand?" But let them remember the language of another passage respecting these things: "Wherefore do ye spend money for that which is not bread? and your labour for that which satisfieth not?" It is easy, indeed, for these idle doctors to dispute concerning these things in easy chairs; but when the Judge of all shall ascend the judgment seat, all such empty notions must vanish away. The object of our inquiries ought to be, what plea we may bring forward with confidence at his tribunal, not what we can invent in schools and cloisters.

XVI. On this subject our minds require to be guarded chiefly against two pernicious principles—That we place no confidence in the righteousness of our works, and that we ascribe no glory to them. The Scriptures every where drive us from all confidence, when they declare that all our righteousnesses are odious in the Divine view, unless they are perfumed with the holiness of Christ; and that they can only excite the vengeance of God, unless they are supported by his merciful pardon. Thus they leave us nothing to do, but to deprecate the wrath of our Judge with the confession of David, "Enter not into judgment with thy servant; for in thy sight shall no man living be justified." And where Job says, "If I be wicked, woe unto me; and if I be righteous, yet will I not lift up my head;" though he refers to that consummate righteousness of God, compared to which even the angels are deficient, yet he at the same time shows, that when God comes to judgment, all men must be dumb. For he not only means that he would rather freely recede, than incur the danger of contending with the rigour of God, but signifies that he experiences in himself no other righteousness than what would instantaneously vanish before the Divine presence. When confidence is destroyed, all boasting must of necessity be relinquished. For who can give the praise of righteousness to his works, in which he is afraid to confide in the presence of God? We must therefore have recourse to the Lord, in whom we are assured, by Isaiah, that "all the seed of Israel shall be justified, and shall glory;" for it is strictly true, as he says in another place, that we are "the planting of the Lord, that he might be glorified." Our minds therefore will then be properly purified, when they shall in no degree confide nor glory in our works. But foolish men are led into such a false and delusive confidence, by the error of always considering their works as the cause of their salvation.

XVII. But if we advert to the four kinds of causes, which the philosophers direct us to consider in the production of effects, we shall find none of them consistent with works in the accomplishment of our salvation. For the Scripture every where proclaims, that the efficient cause of eternal life being procured for us, was the mercy of our heavenly Father, and his gratuitous love towards us; that the material cause is Christ and his obedience, by which he obtained a righteousness for us; and what shall we denominate the formal and instrumental cause, unless it be faith? These three John comprehends in one sentence, when he says, that "God so loved the world that he gave his only begotten Son, that whosoever believeth in him should not perish, but have everlasting life." The final cause the apostle declares to be, both the demonstration of the Divine righteousness and the praise of the Divine goodness, in a passage in which he also expressly mentions the other three causes. For this is his language to the Romans: "All have sinned, and come short of the glory of God, being justified freely by his grace:" here we have the original source of our salvation, which is the gratuitous mercy of God towards us. It follows, "through the redemption that is in Christ Jesus:" here we have the matter of our justification. "Through faith in his blood:" here he points out the instrumental cause, by which the righteousness of Christ is revealed to us. Lastly, he subjoins the end of all, when he says, "To declare his righteousness; that he might be just, and the justifier of him which believeth in Jesus." And to suggest, by the way, that this righteousness consists in reconciliation or propitiation, he expressly asserts that Christ was "set forth to be a propitiation." So also in the first Chapter to the Ephesians, he teaches that we are received into the favour of God through his mere mercy; that it is accomplished by the mediation of Christ; that it is apprehended by faith; and that the end of all is, that the glory of the Divine goodness may be fully displayed. When we see that every part of our salvation is accomplished without us, what reason have we to confide or to glory in our works? Nor can even the most inveterate enemies of Divine grace raise any controversy with us concerning the efficient or the final cause, unless they mean altogether to renounce the authority of the Scripture. Over the material and formal causes they superinduce a false colouring; as if our own works were to share the honour of them with faith and the righteousness of Christ. But this also is contradicted by the Scripture, which affirms that Christ is the sole author of our righteousness and life, and that this blessing of righteousness is enjoyed by faith alone.

XVIII. The saints often confirm and console themselves with the remembrance of their own innocence and integrity, and sometimes even refrain not from proclaiming it. Now, this is done for two reasons; either that, in comparing their good cause with the bad cause of the impious, they derive from such comparison an assurance of victory, not so much by the commendation of their own righteousness, as by the just and merited condemnation of their adversaries; or that, even without any comparison with others, while they examine themselves before God, the purity of their consciences affords them some consolation and confidence. To the former of these reasons we shall advert hereafter; let us now briefly examine the consistency of the latter with what we have before asserted, that in the sight of God we ought to place no reliance on the merit of works, nor glory on account of them. The consistency appears in this—that for the foundation and accomplishment of their salvation, the saints look to the Divine goodness alone, without any regard to works. And they not only apply themselves to it above all things, as the commencement of their happiness, but likewise depend upon it as the consummation of their felicity. A conscience thus founded, built up, and established, is also confirmed by the consideration of works; that is, as far as they are evidences of God dwelling and reigning in us. Now, this confidence of works being found in none but those who have previously cast all the confidence of their souls on the mercy of God, it ought not to be thought contrary to that upon which it depends. Wherefore, when we exclude the confidence of works, we only mean that the mind of a Christian should not be directed to any merit of works as a mean of salvation; but should altogether rely on the gratuitous promise of righteousness. We do not forbid him to support and confirm this faith by marks of the Divine benevolence to him. For if, when we call to remembrance the various gifts which God has conferred on us, they are all as so many rays from the Divine countenance, by which we are illuminated to contemplate the full blaze of supreme goodness,—much more the grace of good works, which demonstrates that we have received the Spirit of adoption.

XIX. When the saints, therefore, confirm their faith, or derive matter of rejoicing from the integrity of their consciences, they only conclude, from the fruits of vocation, that they have been adopted by the Lord as his children. The declaration of Solomon, that "In the fear of the Lord is strong confidence;" and the protestation sometimes used by the saints to obtain a favourable audience from the Lord, that "they have walked before" him "in truth and with a perfect heart;" these things have no concern in laying the foundation for establishing the conscience; nor are they of any value, except as they are consequences of the Divine vocation. For there nowhere exists that fear of God which can establish a full assurance, and the saints are conscious that their integrity is yet accompanied with many relics of corruption. But as the fruits of regeneration evince that the Holy Spirit dwells in them, this affords them ample encouragement to expect the assistance of God in all their necessities, because they experience him to be their Father in an affair of such vast importance. And even this they cannot attain, unless they have first apprehended the Divine goodness, confirmed by no other assurance but that of the promise. For if they begin to estimate it by their good works, nothing will be weaker or more uncertain; for, if their works be estimated in themselves, their imperfection will menace them with the wrath of God, as much as their purity, however incomplete, testifies his benevolence. In a word, they declare the benefits of God, but in such a way as not to turn away from his gratuitous favour, in which Paul assures us there is "length, and breadth, and depth, and height;" as though he had said, Which way soever the pious turn their views, how high soever they ascend, how widely soever they expatiate, yet they ought not to go beyond the love of Christ, but employ themselves wholly in meditating on it, because it comprehends in itself all dimensions. Therefore he says that it "passeth knowledge," and that when we know how much Christ has loved us, we are "filled with all the fulness of God." So also in another place, when he glories that believers are victorious in every conflict, he immediately adds, as the reason of it, "through him that loved us."

XX. We see now, that the confidence which the saints have in their works is not such as either ascribes any thing to the merit of them, (since they view them only as the gifts of God, in which they acknowledge his goodness, and as marks of their calling, whence they infer their election,) or derogates the least from the gratuitous righteousness which we obtain in Christ; since it depends upon it, and cannot subsist without it. This is concisely and beautifully represented by Augustine, when he says, "I do not say to the Lord, Despise not the works of my hands. I have sought the Lord with my hands, and I have not been deceived. But I commend not the works of my hands; for I fear that when thou hast examined them, thou wilt find more sin than merit. This only I say, this I ask, this I desire; Despise not the works of thy hands. Behold in me thy work, not mine. For if thou beholdest mine, thou condemnest me; if thou beholdest thine own, thou crownest me. Because whatever good works I have, they are from thee." He assigns two reasons why he ventured not to boast of his works to God; first, that if he has any good ones, he sees nothing of his own in them; secondly, that even these are buried under a multitude of sins. Hence the conscience experiences more fear and consternation than security. Therefore he desires God to behold his best performances, only that he may recognize in them the grace of his own calling, and perfect the work which he has begun.

XXI. The remaining objection is, that the Scripture represents the good works of believers as the causes for which the Lord blesses them. But this must be understood so as not to affect what we have before proved, that the efficient cause of our salvation is the love of God the Father; the material cause, the obedience of the Son; the instrumental cause, the illumination of the Spirit, that is, faith; and the final cause, the glory of the infinite goodness of God. No obstacle arises from these things to prevent good works being considered by the Lord as inferior causes. But how does this happen? Because those whom his mercy has destined to the inheritance of eternal life, he, in his ordinary dispensations, introduces to the possession of it by good works. That which, in the order of his dispensations, precedes, he denominates the cause of that which follows. For this reason he sometimes deduces eternal life from works; not that the acceptance of it is to be referred to them; but because he justifies the objects of his election, that he may finally glorify them; he makes the former favour, which is a step to the succeeding one, in some sense the cause of it. But whenever the true cause is to be assigned, he does not direct us to take refuge in works, but confines our thoughts entirely to his mercy. For what does he teach us by the apostle? "The wages of sin is death; but the gift of God is eternal life through Jesus Christ our Lord." Why does he not oppose righteousness to sin, as well as life to death? Why does he not make righteousness the cause of life, as well as sin the cause of death? For then the antithesis would have been complete, whereas by this variation it is partly destroyed. But the apostle intended by this comparison to express a certain truth—that death is due to the demerits of men, and that life proceeds solely from the mercy of God. Lastly, these phrases denote rather the order of the Divine gifts, than the cause of them. In the accumulation of graces upon graces, God derives from the former a reason for adding the next, that he may not omit any thing necessary to the enrichment of his servants. And while he thus pursues his liberality, he would have us always to remember his gratuitous election, which is the source and original of all. For although he loves the gifts which he daily confers, as emanations from that fountain, yet it is our duty to adhere to that gratuitous acceptance, which alone can support our souls, and to connect the gifts of his Spirit, which he afterwards bestows on us, with the first cause, in such a manner as will not be derogatory to it.

10.

Boasting of the Merit of Works, Equally Subversive of God's Glory in the Gift of Righteousness, and of the Certainty of Salvation.

We have now discussed the principal branch of this subject; that because righteousness, if dependent on works, must inevitably be confounded in the sight of God, therefore it is contained exclusively in the mercy of God and the participation of Christ, and consequently in faith alone. Now, it must be carefully remarked that this is the principal hinge on which the argument turns, that we may not be implicated in the common delusion, which equally affects the learned and the vulgar. For as soon as justification by faith or works becomes the subject of inquiry, they have immediate recourse to those passages which seem to attribute to works some degree of merit in the sight of God; as though justification by works would be fully evinced, if they could be proved to be of any value before God. We have already clearly demonstrated that the righteousness of works consists only in a perfect and complete observance of the law. Whence it follows, that no man is justified by works, but he who, being elevated to the summit of perfection, cannot be convicted even of the least transgression. This, therefore, is a different and separate question, whether, although works be utterly insufficient for the justification of men, they do not, nevertheless, merit the grace of God.

II. In the first place, with respect to the term *merit*, it is necessary for me to premise, that whoever first applied it to human works, as compared with the Divine judgment, showed very little concern for the purity of the faith. I gladly abstain from all controversies about mere words; but I could wish that this sobriety had always been observed by Christian writers, that they had avoided the unnecessary adoption of terms not used in the Scriptures, and calculated to produce great offence, but very little advantage. For what necessity was there for the introduction of the word *merit*, when the value of good works might be significantly expressed without offence by a different term? But the great offence contained in it, appears in the great injury the world has received from it. The consummate haughtiness of its import can only obscure the Divine grace, and taint the minds of men with presumptuous arrogance. I confess, the ancient writers of the Church have generally used it, and I wish that their misuse of one word had not been the occasion of error to posterity. Yet they also declare in some places that they did not intend any thing prejudicial to the truth. For this is the language of Augustine in one passage: "Let human merit, which was lost by Adam, here be silent, and let the grace of God reign through Jesus Christ." Again: "The saints ascribe nothing to their own merits; they will ascribe all, O God, only to thy mercy." In another place: "And when a man sees that whatever good he has, he has it not from himself, but from his God, he sees that all that is commended in him proceeds not from his own merits, but from the Divine mercy." We see how, by divesting man of the power of performing good actions, he likewise destroys the dignity of merit. Chrysostom says, "Our works, if there be any consequent on God's gratuitous vocation, are a retribution and a debt; but the gifts of God are grace, beneficence, and immense liberality." Leaving the name, however, let us rather attend to the thing. I have before cited a passage from

Bernard: "As not to presume on our merits is sufficiently meritorious, so to be destitute of merits is sufficient for the judgment." But by the explanation immediately annexed, he properly softens the harshness of these expressions, when he says, "Therefore you should be concerned to have merits; and if you have them, you should know that they are given to you; you should hope for the fruit, the mercy of God; and you have escaped all danger of poverty, ingratitude, and presumption. Happy the Church which is not destitute, either of merits without presumption, or of presumption without merits." And just before he had fully shown how pious his meaning was. "For concerning merits," he says, "why should the Church be solicitous, which has a more firm and secure foundation for glorying in the purpose of God? For God cannot deny himself; he will perform what he has promised. Thus you have no reason for inquiring, on account of what merits we may hope for blessings, especially when you read, 'Not for your sakes, but for my sake;' it is sufficiently meritorious to know that merits are insufficient."

III. The Scripture shows what all our works are capable of meriting, when it represents them as unable to bear the Divine scrutiny, because they are full of impurity; and in the next place, what would be merited by the perfect observance of the law, if this could any where be found, when it directs us, "When ye shall have done all those things which are commanded you, say, We are unprofitable servants;" because we shall not have conferred any favour on God, but only have performed the duties incumbent on us, for which no thanks are due. Nevertheless, the good works which the Lord has conferred on us, he denominates our own, and declares that he will not only accept, but also reward them. It is our duty to be animated by so great a promise, and to stir up our minds that we "be not weary in well doing," and to be truly grateful for so great an instance of Divine goodness. It is beyond a doubt, that whatever is laudable in our works proceeds from the grace of God; and that we cannot properly ascribe the least portion of it to ourselves. If we truly and seriously acknowledge this truth, not only all confidence, but likewise all idea of merit, immediately vanishes. We, I say, do not, like the sophists, divide the praise of good works between God and man, but we preserve it to the Lord complete, entire, and uncontaminated. All that we attribute to man, is, that those works which were otherwise good are tainted and polluted by his impurity. For nothing proceeds from the most perfect man, which is wholly immaculate. Therefore let the Lord sit in judgment on the best of human actions, and he will indeed recognize in them his own righteousness, but man's disgrace and shame. Good works, therefore, are pleasing to God, and not unprofitable to the authors of them; and they will moreover receive the most ample blessings from God as their reward; not because they merit them, but because the Divine goodness has freely appointed them this reward. But what wickedness is it, not to be content with that Divine liberality which remunerates works destitute of merit with unmerited rewards, but with sacrilegious ambition still to aim at more, that what entirely originates in the Divine munificence may appear to be a compensation of the merit of works! Here I appeal to the common sense of every man. If he who, by the liberality of another, enjoys the use and profit of an estate, usurp to himself also the title of proprietor, does he not by such ingratitude deserve to lose the possession which he had? So also if a slave, manumitted by his master, conceal his mean condition as a freed-man, and boast that he was free by birth, does he not deserve to be reduced to his former servitude? For this is the legitimate way of enjoying a benefit, if we neither arrogate more than is given us, nor defraud our benefactor of his due praise; but, on the contrary, conduct ourselves in such a manner, that what he has conferred on us may appear, as it were, to continue with himself. If this moderation ought to be observed towards men, let every one examine and consider what is due to God.

IV. I know that the sophists abuse some texts in order to prove that the term *merit* is found in the Scriptures with reference to God. They cite a passage from Ecclesiasticus: "Mercy shall make place for every man according to the merit of his works." And from the Epistle to the Hebrews: "To do good, and to communicate, forget not; for with such sacrifices men merit of God." My right to reject the authority of Ecclesiasticus I at present relinquish; but I deny that they faithfully cite the words of the writer of Ecclesiasticus, whoever he might be; for in the Greek copy it is as follows: Παση ελεημοσυνη ποιησει τοπον· εκαστος γαρ κατα τα εργα αυτου ευρησει. "He shall make place for every mercy; and every man shall find according to his works." And that this is the genuine reading, which is corrupted in the Latin version, appears both from the complexion of the words themselves and from the preceding context. In the passage quoted from the Epistle to the Hebrews, there is no reason why they should endeavour to insnare us by a single word, when the apostle's words in the Greek imply nothing more than that "with such sacrifices God is well pleased." This alone ought to be abundantly sufficient to repress and subdue the insolence of our pride, that we transgress not the scriptural rule by ascribing any dignity to human works. Moreover, the doctrine of the Scripture is, that our good works are perpetually defiled with many blemishes, which might justly offend God and incense him against us; so far are they from being able to conciliate his favour, or to excite his beneficence towards us; yet that, because in his great mercy he does not examine them according to the rigour of his justice, he accepts them as though they were immaculately pure, and therefore rewards them, though void of all merit, with infinite blessings both in this life and in that which is to come. For I cannot admit the distinction laid down by some, who are otherwise men of learning and piety, that good works merit the graces which are conferred on us in this life, and that eternal salvation is the reward of faith alone; because the Lord almost always places the reward of labours and the crown of victory in heaven. Besides, to ascribe the accumulation of graces upon graces, given us by the Lord, to the merit of works, in such a manner as to detract it from grace, is contrary to the doctrine of the Scripture. For though Christ says, that "to every one that hath shall be given," and that "the good and faithful servant, who hath been faithful over a few things, shall be made ruler over many things," yet he likewise shows in another place, that the improvements of believers are the gifts of his gratuitous kindness. "Ho, every one that thirsteth," says he, "come ye to the waters, and he that hath no money; come ye, buy, and eat; yea, come, buy wine and milk without money and without price." Whatever, therefore, is now conferred on believers to promote their salvation as well as their future blessedness, flows exclusively from the beneficence of God; nevertheless he declares, that both in the latter and in the former, he has respect to our works, because, to demonstrate the magnitude of his love to us, he dignifies with such honour, not only ourselves, but even the gifts which he has bestowed on us.

V. If these points had been handled and digested in proper order in former ages, there would never have arisen so many debates and dissensions. Paul says, that in erecting the superstructure of Christian doctrine, it is necessary to retain that foundation which he had laid among the Corinthians, other than which no man can lay, which is Jesus Christ. What kind of a foundation have we in Christ? Has he begun our salvation, that we may complete it ourselves? and has he merely opened a way for us to proceed in by our own powers? By no means; but, as the apostle before stated, when we acknowledge him, he is "made unto us righteousness." No man, therefore, is properly founded on Christ, but he who has complete righteousness in him; since the apostle says, that he was sent, not to assist us in the attainment of righteousness, but to be himself our righteousness; that is to say, that we were chosen in him from eternity, before the formation of the world, not on account of any merit of ours, but according to the purpose of the Divine will; that by the death of Christ we are redeemed from the sentence of death, and liberated from perdition; that in him we are adopted as sons and heirs by the heavenly Father, to whom we have been reconciled by his blood; that being committed to his protection, we are not in the least danger of perishing; that being thus ingrafted into him, we are already, as it were, partakers of eternal life, and entered by hope into the kingdom of God; and moreover, that having obtained such a participation of him, however foolish we may be in ourselves, he is our wisdom before God; that however impure we are, he is our purity; that though we are weak and exposed to Satan, yet that power is ours which is given to him in heaven and in earth, by which he defeats Satan for us, and breaks the gates of hell; that though we still carry about with us a body of death, yet he is our life; in short, that all that is his belongs to us, and that we have every thing in him, but nothing in ourselves. On this foundation, I say, it is necessary for us to build, if we wish to "grow unto a holy temple in the Lord."

VI. But the world has long been taught a different lesson; for I know not what good works of morality have been invented to render men acceptable to God, before they are ingrafted into Christ. As though the Scripture were false in asserting, that "he that hath not the Son of God, hath not life." If they are destitute of life, how could they generate any cause of life? As though there were no truth in the declaration, that "whatsoever is not of faith, is sin!" as though an evil tree could produce good fruits! But what room have these most pestilent sophists left to Christ for the exertion of his power? They say that he has merited for us the first grace; that is, the opportunity of meriting; and that now it is our part not to miss the offered opportunity. What extreme impudence and impiety! Who would have expected that any persons professing the name of Christ, would presume thus to rob him of his power, and almost to trample him under their feet? It is every where testified of him, that all who believe in him are justified: these men tell us, that the only benefit received from him is, that a way is opened for all men to justify themselves. But I wish that they had experienced what is contained in these passages: "He that hath the Son, hath life;" "he that believeth is passed from death unto life;" "justified by his grace," that we might "be made heirs of eternal life;" that believers have Christ abiding in them, by whom they are united to God; that they are partakers of his life, and sit with him "in heavenly places;" that they are translated into the kingdom of God, and have obtained salvation; and innumerable places of similar import. For they do not signify that by faith in Christ we merely gain the ability to attain righteousness or effect our salvation, but that both are bestowed on us. Therefore, as soon as we are ingrafted into Christ by faith, we are already become sons of God, heirs of heaven, partakers of righteousness, possessors of life, and (the better to refute their falsehoods) we have attained, not the opportunity of meriting, but all the merits of Christ; for they are all communicated to us.

VII. Thus the Sorbonic schools, those sources of all kinds of errors, have deprived us of justification by faith, which is the substance of all piety. They grant, indeed, in words, that a man is justified by faith formed; but this they afterwards explain to be, because faith renders good works effectual to justification; so that their mention of faith has almost the appearance of mockery, since it could not be passed over in silence, while the Scripture is so full of it, without exposing them to great censure. And not content with this, they rob God of part of the praise of good works, and transfer it to man. Perceiving that good works avail but little to the exaltation of man, and that they cannot properly be denominated merits if they be considered as the effects of Divine grace, they derive them from the power of free-will; which is like extracting oil from a stone. They contend, that though grace be the principal cause of them, yet that this is not to the exclusion of free-will, from which all merit originates. And this is maintained not only by the latter sophists, but likewise by their master, Lombard, whom, when compared with them, we may pronounce to be sound and sober. Truly wonderful was their blindness, with Augustine so frequently in their mouths, not to see how solicitously he endeavoured to prevent men from arrogating the least degree of glory on account of good works. Before, when we discussed the question of free-will, we cited from him some testimonies to this purpose; and similar ones frequently recur in his writings; as when he forbids us ever to boast of our merits, since even they are the gifts of God; and when he says, "that all our merit proceeds from grace alone; that it is not obtained by our sufficiency, but is produced entirely by grace," &c. That Lombard was blind to the light of Scripture, in which he appears not to have been so well versed, need not excite so much surprise. Yet nothing could be wished for more explicit, in opposition to him and his disciples, than this passage of the apostle; who, having interdicted Christians from all boasting, subjoins as a reason why boasting is unlawful, that "we are his (God's) workmanship, created in Christ Jesus unto good works, which God hath before ordained that we should walk in them." Since nothing good, then, can proceed from us but as we are regenerated, and our regeneration is, without exception, entirely of God, we have no right to arrogate to ourselves the smallest particle of our good works. Lastly, while they assiduously inculcate good works, they at the same time instruct the consciences of men in such a manner, that they can never dare to be confident that God is propitious and favourable to their works. But, on the contrary, our doctrine, without any mention of merit, animates the minds of believers with peculiar consolation, while we teach them that their works are pleasing to God, and that their persons are undoubtedly accepted by him. And we likewise require, that no man attempt or undertake any work without faith; that is, unless he can previously determine, with a certain confidence of mind, that it will be pleasing to God.

VIII. Wherefore let us not suffer ourselves to be seduced even a hair's breadth from the only foundation, on which, when it is laid, wise architects erect a firm and regular superstructure. For if there be a necessity for doctrine and exhortation, they apprize us, that "for this purpose the Son of God was manifested, that he might destroy the works of the devil; whosoever is born of God doth not commit sin:" "the time past of our life may suffice us to have wrought the will of the Gentiles;" the elect of God are vessels of mercy selected to honour, and therefore ought to be cleansed from all impurity. But every thing is said at once, when it is shown that Christ chooses such for his disciples as will deny themselves, take up their cross, and follow him. He who has denied himself, has laid the axe to the root of all evils, that he may no longer seek those things which are his own; he who has taken up his cross, has prepared himself for all patience and gentleness. But the example of Christ comprehends not only these, but all other duties of piety and holiness. He was obedient to his Father, even to death; he was entirely occupied in performing the works of God; he aspired with his whole soul to promote the glory of his Father; he laid down his life for his brethren; he both acted and prayed for the benefit of his enemies. But if there be need of consolation, these passages will afford it in a wonderful degree: "We are troubled on every side, yet not distressed; we are perplexed, but not in despair; persecuted, but not forsaken; cast down, but not destroyed; always bearing about in the body the dying of the Lord Jesus, that the life also of Jesus might be made manifest in our body." "If we be dead with him, we shall also live with him; if we suffer, we shall also reign with him." "Being made conformable unto his death; if by any means I might attain unto the resurrection of the dead." The Father has predestinated all whom he has chosen in his Son "to be conformed to his image, that he might be the first-born among many brethren;" and therefore "neither death, nor life, nor things present, nor things to come, shall separate us from the love of God which is in Christ Jesus;" but "all things shall work together for good" to us, and conduce to our salvation. We do not justify men by works before God; but we say, that all who are of God are regenerated and made new creatures, that they may depart from the kingdom of sin into the kingdom of righteousness; and that by this testimony they ascertain their vocation, and, like trees, are judged by their fruits.

11.

On Prayer, The Principal Exercise Of Faith, And The Medium Of Our Daily Reception Of Divine Blessings.

From the subjects already discussed, we clearly perceive how utterly destitute man is of every good, and in want of all the means of salvation. Wherefore, if he seek for relief in his necessities, he must go out of himself, and obtain it from some other quarter. It has been subsequently stated, that the Lord voluntarily and liberally manifests himself in his Christ, in whom he offers us all felicity instead of our misery, and opulence instead of our poverty; in whom he opens to our view the treasures of heaven, that our faith may be wholly engaged in the contemplation of his beloved Son, that all our expectation may depend upon him, and that in him all our hope may rest and be fully satisfied. This, indeed, is that secret and recondite philosophy, which cannot be extracted from syllogisms; but is well understood by those whose eyes God has opened, that in his light they may see light. But since we have been taught by faith to acknowledge, that whatever we want for the supply of our necessities is in God and our Lord Jesus Christ, in whom it has pleased the Father all the fulness of his bounty should dwell, that we may all draw from it, as from a most copious fountain, it remains for us to seek in him, and by prayers to implore of him, that which we have been informed resides in him. Otherwise to know God as the Lord and Giver of every good, who invites us to supplicate him, but neither to approach him nor to supplicate him, would be equally unprofitable, as for a man to neglect a treasure discovered to him buried in the earth. Wherefore the apostle, to show that true faith cannot but be engaged in calling upon God, has laid down this order—that, as faith is produced by the gospel, so by faith our hearts are brought to invoke the name of the Lord. And this is the same as he had a little before said, that the "Spirit of adoption," who seals the testimony of the gospel in our hearts, encourages our spirits, so that they venture to pour out their desires before God, excite "groanings that cannot be uttered," and cry with confidence, "Abba, Father." This last subject, therefore, having been before only cursorily mentioned and slightly touched, requires now to be treated more at large.

II. By means of prayer, then, we penetrate to those riches which are reserved with our heavenly Father for our use. For between God and men there is a certain communication; by which they enter into the sanctuary of heaven, and in his immediate presence remind him of his promises, in order that his declarations, which they have implicitly believed, may in time of necessity be verified in their experience. We see, therefore, that nothing is revealed to us, to be expected from the Lord, for which we are not likewise enjoined to pray; so true is it, that prayer digs out those treasures, which the gospel of the Lord discovers to our faith. Now, the necessity and various utility of the exercise of prayer no language can sufficiently explain. It is certainly not without reason that our heavenly Father declares, that the only fortress of salvation consists in invocation of his name; by which we call to our aid the presence of his providence, which watches over all our concerns; of his power, which supports us when weak and ready to faint; and of his goodness, which receives us into favour, though miserably burdened with sins; in which, finally, we call upon him to manifest his presence with us in all his attributes. Hence our consciences derive peculiar peace and tranquillity; for when the affliction which oppressed us is represented to the Lord, we feel abundant composure even from this consideration—that none of our troubles are concealed from him, whom we know to possess both the greatest readiness and the greatest ability to promote our truest interest.

III. But some will say, Does he not, without information, know both our troubles and our necessities; so that it may appear unnecessary to solicit him with our prayers, as if he were inattentive or sleeping, till aroused by our voice? But such reasoners advert not to the Lord's end in teaching his people to pray; for he has appointed it not so much for his own sake as for ours. It is his pleasure indeed, as is highly reasonable, that his right be rendered to him, by their considering him as the Author of all that is desired and found useful by men, and by their acknowledgments of this in their prayers. But the utility of this sacrifice, by which he is worshipped, returns to us. The greater the confidence, therefore, with which the ancient saints gloried in the Divine benefits to themselves and others, with so much the more earnestness were they incited to pray. The single example of Elijah shall suffice, who, though certain of God's design, having already with sufficient authority promised rain to king Ahab, yet anxiously prays between his knees, and sends his servant seven times to look for it; not with an intention to discredit the Divine oracle, but under a conviction of his duty to prevent his faith becoming languid and torpid, by pouring out his prayers before God. Wherefore, although, when we are stupid and insensible to our own miseries, he vigilantly watches and guards us, and sometimes affords us unsolicited succour, yet it highly concerns us assiduously to supplicate him, that our heart may be always inflamed with a serious and ardent desire of seeking, loving, and worshipping him, while we accustom ourselves in all our necessities to resort to him as our sheet anchor. Further, that no desire or wish, which we should be ashamed for him to know, may enter our minds; when we learn to present our wishes, and so to pour out our whole heart in his presence. Next, that we may be prepared to receive his blessings with true gratitude of soul, and even with grateful acknowledgments; being reminded by our praying that they come from his hand. Moreover, that when we have obtained what we sought, the persuasion that he has answered our requests may excite us to more ardent meditations on his goodness, and produce a more joyful welcome of those things which we acknowledge to be the fruits of our prayers. Lastly, that use and experience itself may yield our minds a confirmation of his providence in proportion to our imbecility, while we apprehend that he not only promises never to forsake us, and freely opens a way of access for our addressing him in the very moment of necessity; but that his hand is always extended to assist his people, whom he does not feed with mere words, but supports with present aid. On these accounts our most merciful Father, though liable to no sleep or languor, yet frequently appears as if he were sleepy or languid, in order to exercise us, who are otherwise slothful and inactive, in approaching, supplicating, and earnestly importuning him to our own advantage. It is extremely absurd, therefore, in them who, with a view to divert the minds of men from praying to God, pretend that it is useless for us by our interruptions to weary the Divine Providence, which is engaged in the conservation of all things; whereas the Lord declares, on the contrary, that he "is nigh to all that call upon him in truth." And equally nugatory is the objection of others, that it is superfluous to petition for those things which the Lord is ready voluntarily to bestow; whereas even those very things, which flow to us from his spontaneous liberality, he wishes us to consider as granted to our prayers. This is evinced by that memorable passage in the Psalms, as well as by many other correspondent texts,—"The eyes of the Lord are upon the righteous, and his ears are open unto their cry;" which celebrates the Divine Providence as spontaneously engaged to accomplish the salvation of believers; yet does not omit the exercise of faith, by which sloth is expelled from the minds of men. The eyes of God, then, are vigilant to succour the necessity of the blind; but he is likewise willing to hear our groans, to give a better proof of his love towards us. And thus it is equally true, that "he that keepeth Israel neither slumbers nor sleeps," and yet that he remains, as it were, forgetful of us, while he beholds us slothful and dumb.

IV. Now, for conducting prayer in a right and proper manner, the first rule is, that our heart and mind be composed to a suitable frame, becoming those who enter into conversation with God. This state of mind we shall certainly attain, if, divested of all carnal cares and thoughts, that tend to divert and seduce it from a right and clear view of God, it not only devotes itself entirely to the solemn exercise, but is likewise as far as possible elevated and carried above itself. Nor do I here require a mind so disengaged as to be disturbed by no solicitude; since there ought, on the contrary, most anxiously to be kindled within us a fervency of prayer, (as we see the holy servants of God discover great solicitude, and even anguish, when they say they utter their complaints to the Lord from the deep abysses of affliction and the very jaws of death.) But I maintain the necessity of dismissing all foreign and external cares, by which the wandering mind may be hurried hither and thither, and dragged from heaven down to earth. It ought to be elevated above itself, that it may not intrude into the Divine presence any of the imaginations of our blind and foolish reason, nor confine itself within the limits of its own vanity, but rise to purity worthy of God.

V. Both these things are highly worthy of observation—first, that whoever engages in prayer, should apply all his faculties and attention to it, and not be distracted, as is commonly the case, with wandering thoughts; nothing being more contrary to a reverence for God than such levity, which indicates a licentious spirit, wholly unrestrained by fear. In this case our exertions must be great in proportion to the difficulty we experience. For no man can be so intent on praying, but he may perceive many irregular thoughts intruding on him, and either interrupting, or by some oblique digression retarding, the course of his devotions. But here let us consider what an indignity it is, when God admits us to familiar intercourse with him, to abuse such great condescension by a mixture of things sacred and profane, while our thoughts are not confined to him by reverential awe; but as if we were conversing with a mean mortal, we quit him in the midst of our prayer, and make excursions on every side. We may be assured, therefore, that none are rightly prepared for the exercise of prayer, but those who are so affected by the Divine Majesty as to come to it divested of all earthly cares and affections. And this is indicated by the ceremony of lifting up the hands, that men may remember that they are at a great distance from God, unless they lift up their thoughts on high. As it is also expressed in the psalm, "Unto thee do I lift up my soul." And the Scripture frequently uses this mode of expression, "to lift up one's prayer;" that they, who desire to be heard by God, may not sink into lethargic inactivity. To sum up the whole, the greater the liberality of God towards us, in gently inviting us to disburden ourselves of our cares by casting them on him, the less excusable are we, unless his signal and incomparable favour preponderate with us beyond every thing else, and attract us to him in a serious application of all our faculties and attention to the duty of prayer; which cannot be done unless our mind by strenuous exertion rise superior to every impediment. Our second proposition is, that we must pray for no more than God permits. For though he enjoins us to pour out our hearts before him, yet he does not carelessly give the reins to affections of folly and depravity; and when he promises to "fulfil the desire" of believers, he does not go to such an extreme of indulgence, as to subject himself to their caprice. But offences against both these rules are common and great; for most men not only presume, without modesty or reverence, to address God concerning their follies, and impudently to utter at his tribunal whatever has amused them in their reveries or dreams, but so great is their folly or stupidity, that they dare to obtrude upon God all their foulest desires, which they would be exceedingly ashamed to reveal to men. Some heathens have ridiculed and even detested this presumption, but the vice itself has always prevailed; and hence it was that the ambitious chose Jupiter as their patron; the avaricious, Mercury; the lovers of learning, Apollo and Minerva; the warlike, Mars; and the libidinous, Venus; just as in the present age (as I have lately hinted) men indulge a greater license to their unlawful desires in their prayers, than if they were conversing in a jocular manner with their equals. God suffers not his indulgence to be so mocked, but asserts his power, and subjects our devotions to his commands. Therefore we ought to remember this passage in John: "This is the confidence that we have in him, that, if we ask any thing according to his will, he heareth us." But as our abilities are very unequal to such great perfection, we must seek some remedy to relieve us. As the attention of the mind ought to be fixed on God, so it is necessary that it should be followed by the affection of the heart. But they both remain far below this elevation; or rather, to speak more consistently with truth, they grow weary and fail in the ascent, or are carried a contrary course. Therefore, to assist this imbecility, God gives us the Spirit, to be the director of our prayers, to suggest what is right, and to regulate our affections. For "the Spirit helpeth our infirmities; for we know not what we should pray for as we ought; but the Spirit itself maketh intercession for us with groanings which cannot be uttered;" not that he really prays or groans; but he excites within us confidence, desires, and sighs, to the conception of which our native powers were altogether inadequate. Nor is it without reason that Paul terms those "groanings," which arise from believers under the influence of the Spirit, "unutterable;" because they who are truly engaged in prayers, are not ignorant that they are so perplexed with dubious anxieties, that they can scarcely decide what it is expedient to utter; and even while they are attempting to lisp, they stammer and hesitate; whence it follows that the ability of praying rightly is a peculiar gift. These things are not said in order that we may indulge our own indolence, resigning the office of prayer to the Spirit of God, and growing torpid in that negligence to which we are too prone; according to the impious errors of some, that we should wait in indolent supineness till he call our minds from other engagements and draw them to himself; but rather that, wearied with our sloth and inactivity, we may implore such assistance of the Spirit. Nor does the apostle, when he exhorts us to "pray in the Holy Ghost," encourage us to remit our vigilance; signifying, that the inspiration of the Spirit operates in the formation of our prayers, so as not in the least to impede or retard our own exertions; since it is the will of God to prove in this instance the efficacious influence of faith on our hearts.

VI. Let this be the second rule: That in our supplications we should have a real and permanent sense of our indigence, and seriously considering our necessity of all that we ask, should join with the petitions themselves a serious and ardent desire of obtaining them. For multitudes carelessly recite a form of prayer, as though they were discharging a task imposed on them by God; and though they confess that this is a remedy necessary for their calamities, since it would be certain destruction to be destitute of the Divine aid which they implore, yet that they perform this duty merely in compliance with custom, is evident from the coldness of their hearts, and their inattention to the nature of their petitions. They are led to this by some general and confused sense of their necessity, which nevertheless does not excite them to implore a relief for their great need as a case of present urgency. Now, what can we imagine more odious or execrable to God than this hypocrisy, when any man prays for the pardon of sins, who at the same time thinks he is not a sinner, or at least does not think that he is a sinner? which is an open mockery of God himself. But such depravity, as I have before observed, pervades the whole human race, that as a matter of form they frequently implore of God many things which they either expect to receive from some other source independent of his goodness, or imagine themselves already to possess. The crime of some others appears to be smaller, but yet too great to be tolerated; who, having only imbibed this principle, that God must be propitiated by devotions, mutter over their prayers without meditation. But believers ought to be exceedingly cautious, never to enter into the presence of God to present any petition, without being inflamed with a fervent affection of soul, and feeling an ardent desire to obtain it from him. Moreover, although in those things which we request only for the Divine glory, we do not at the first glance appear to regard our own necessity, yet it is incumbent on us to pray for them with equal fervour and vehemence of desire. As when we pray that his name may be hallowed, or sanctified, we ought (so to speak) ardently to hunger and thirst for that sanctification.

VII. If any man object, that we are not always urged to pray by the same necessity, this I grant, and this distinction is usefully represented to us by James: "Is any among you afflicted? let him pray. Is any merry? let him sing psalms." Common sense itself therefore dictates, that because of our extreme indolence, we are the more vigorously stimulated by God to earnestness in prayer according to the exigencies of our condition. And this David calls "a time when God may be found," because (as he teaches in many other places) the more severely we are oppressed by troubles, disasters, fears, and other kinds of temptations, we have the greater liberty of access to God, as though he then particularly invited us to approach him. At the same time, it is equally true that we ought to be, as Paul says, "praying always," because, how great soever we may believe the prosperity of our affairs, and though we are surrounded on every side by matter of joy, yet there is no moment of time in which our necessity does not furnish incitements to prayer. Does any one abound in wine and corn? Since he cannot enjoy a morsel of bread but by the continual favour of God, his cellars or barns afford no objection to his praying for daily bread. Now, if we reflect how many dangers threaten us every moment, fear itself will teach us that there is no time in which prayer is unsuitable to us. Yet this may be discovered still better in spiritual concerns. For when will so many sins, of which we are conscious, suffer us to remain in security, without humbly deprecating both the guilt and the punishment? When will temptations grant us a truce, so that we need not be in haste to obtain assistance? Besides, an ardent desire of the

Divine kingdom and glory ought irresistibly to attract us, not by intervals, but without intermission, rendering every season equally suitable. It is not in vain, therefore, that assiduity in prayer is so frequently enjoined. I speak not yet of perseverance, which shall be mentioned hereafter; but the scriptural admonitions to "pray without ceasing" are so many reproofs of our sloth; because we feel not our need of this care and diligence. This rule precludes and banishes from prayer, hypocrisy, subtilty, and falsehood. God promises that he will be near to all who call upon him in truth, and declares he will be found by those who seek him with their whole heart. But to this, persons pleased with their own impurity never aspire. Legitimate prayer, therefore, requires repentance. Whence it is frequently said in the Scriptures, that God hears not the wicked, and that their prayers are an abomination; as are also their sacrifices; for it is reasonable, that they who shut up their own hearts, should find the ears of God closed against them; and God should be inflexible to them who provoke his rigour by their obduracy. In Isaiah, he threatens thus: "When ye make many prayers, I will not hear: your hands are full of blood." Again in Jeremiah: "I protested, yet they inclined not their ear. Therefore, though they shall cry unto me, I will not hearken unto them." Because he considers himself grossly insulted by the wicked boasting of his covenant, while they are continually dishonouring his sacred name. Wherefore he complains, in Isaiah, "This people draw near me with their mouth, but have removed their heart far from me." He does not restrict this solely to prayer; but asserts his abhorrence of hypocrisy in every branch of his worship. Which is the meaning of this passage in James: "Ye ask, and receive not, because ye ask amiss, that ye may consume it upon your lusts." It is true, indeed, (as we shall presently again see,) that the prayers of the faithful depend not on their personal worthiness; yet this does not supersede the admonition of John: "Whatsoever we ask, we receive of him, because we keep his commandments;" because an evil conscience shuts the gate against us. Whence it follows, that none pray aright, and that no others are heard, but the sincere worshippers of God. Whosoever therefore engages in prayer, should be displeased with himself on account of his sins, and assume, what he cannot do without repentance, the character and disposition of a beggar.

VIII. To these must be added a third rule—That whoever presents himself before God for the purpose of praying to him, must renounce every idea of his own glory, reject all opinion of his own merit, and, in a word, relinquish all confidence in himself, giving, by this humiliation of himself, all the glory entirely to God; lest, arrogating any thing, though ever so little, to ourselves, we perish from his presence in consequence of our vanity. Of this submission, which prostrates every high thought, we have frequent examples in the servants of God; of whom the most eminent for holiness feel the greatest consternation on entering into the presence of the Lord. Thus Daniel, whom the Lord himself has so highly commended, said, "We do not present our supplications before thee for our righteousness, but for thy great mercies. O Lord, hear; O Lord, forgive; O Lord, hearken and do; defer not, for thine own sake, O my God; for thy city and thy people are called by thy name." Nor does he, as is generally the case, confound himself with the multitude, as one of the people; but makes a separate confession of his own guilt, resorting as a suppliant to the asylum of pardon; as he expressly declares, "Whilst I was confessing my sin, and the sin of my people." We are taught the same humility also by the example of David: "Enter not into judgment with thy servant; for in thy sight shall no man living be justified." In this manner Isaiah prays: "Behold, thou art wroth; for we have sinned: in thy ways is continuance, and we shall be saved. For we are all as an unclean thing, and all our righteousnesses are as filthy rags; and we all do fade as a leaf; and our iniquities, like the wind, have taken us away. And there is none that calleth upon thy name, that stirreth up himself to take hold of thee; for thou hast hid thy face from us, and hast consumed us, because of our iniquities. But now, O Lord, thou art our Father; we are the clay, and thou our potter; and we all are the work of thy hand. Be not wroth very sore, O Lord, neither remember iniquity for ever; behold, see, we beseech thee, we are all thy people." Observe, they have no dependence but this; that considering themselves as God's children, they despair not of his future care of them. Thus Jeremiah: "Though our iniquities testify against us, do thou it for thy name's sake." For that is equally consistent with the strictest truth and holiness, which was written by an uncertain author, but is ascribed to the prophet Baruch: "A soul sorrowful and desolate for the greatness of its sin, bowed down and infirm, a hungry soul and fainting eyes give glory to thee, O Lord. Not according to the righteousnesses of our fathers do we pour out our prayers in thy sight, and ask mercy before thy face, O Lord, our God; but because thou art merciful, have mercy upon us, for we have sinned against thee."

IX. Finally, the commencement and even introduction to praying rightly is a supplication for pardon with an humble and ingenuous confession of guilt. For neither is there any hope that even the holiest of men can obtain any blessing of God till he be freely reconciled to him, nor is it possible for God to be propitious to any, but those whom he pardons. It is no wonder, then, if believers with this key open to themselves the gate of prayer; as we learn from many places in the Psalms. For David, when requesting another thing, says, "Remember not the sins of my youth, nor my transgressions: according to thy mercy remember thou me, for thy goodness' sake, O Lord." Again: "Look upon mine affliction and my pain; and forgive all my sins." Where we likewise perceive, that it is not sufficient for us to call ourselves to a daily account for recent sins, unless we remember those which might seem to have been long buried in oblivion. For the same Psalmist, in another place, having confessed one grievous crime, takes occasion thence to revert to his mother's womb, where he had contracted his original pollution; not in order to extenuate his guilt by the corruption of his nature, but that, accumulating all the sins of his life, he may find God the more ready to listen to his prayers in proportion to the severity of his self-condemnation. But though the saints do not always in express terms pray for remission of sins, yet if we diligently examine their prayers recited in the Scriptures, it will easily appear, as I assert, that they derived their encouragement to pray from the mere mercy of God, and so always began by deprecating his displeasure; for if every man examine his own conscience, he is so far from presuming familiarly to communicate his cares to God, that he trembles at every approach to him, except in a reliance on his mercy and forgiveness. There is also, indeed, another special confession, when they wish for an alleviation of punishments, which is tacitly praying for the pardon of their sins; because it were absurd to desire the removal of an effect, while the cause remains. For we must beware of imitating foolish patients, who are only solicitous for the cure of the symptoms, but neglect the radical cause of the disease. Besides, we should first seek for God to be propitious to us, previously to any external testimonies of his favour; because it is his own will to observe this order, and it would be of little advantage to us to receive benefits from him, unless a discovery to the conscience of his being appeased towards us rendered him altogether amiable in our view. Of this we are likewise apprized by the reply of Christ; for when he had determined to heal a paralytic person, he said, "Thy sins be forgiven thee;" thereby calling our attention to that which ought to be the chief object of desire, that God may receive us into his favour, and then, by affording us assistance, discover the effect of reconciliation. But beside the special confession of present guilt, in which believers implore the pardon of every sin and the remission of every punishment, that general preface, which conciliates a favourable attention to our prayers, is never to be omitted; because, unless they be founded on God's free mercy, they will all be unavailing. To this topic we may refer that passage of John—"If we confess our sins, he is faithful and just to forgive us our sins, and to cleanse us from all unrighteousness." Wherefore, under the law, prayers are required to be consecrated by an atonement of blood, to render them acceptable, and to remind the people that they were unworthy of so great and honourable a privilege, till, purified from their pollutions, they should derive confidence in prayer from the mere mercy of God.

X. But when the saints sometimes appear to urge their own righteousness as an argument in their supplications with God,—as when David says, "Preserve my soul; for I am holy;" and Hezekiah, "I beseech thee, O Lord, remember now how I have walked before thee in truth, and have done that which is good in thy sight,"—their only design in such modes of expression is, from their regeneration to prove themselves to be servants and sons of God, to whom he declares he will be propitious. He tells us by the Psalmist, (as we have already seen,) that "his eyes are upon the righteous, and that his ears are open unto their cry;" and again, by the apostle, that "whatsoever we ask, we receive of him, because we keep his commandments;" in which passages he does not determine the value of prayer according to the merit of works; but intends by them to establish the confidence of those who are conscious to themselves, as all believers ought to be, of unfeigned integrity and innocence. For the observation in John, made by the blind man who received his sight, that "God heareth not sinners," is a principle of Divine truth, if we understand the word *sinners*, in the common acceptation of Scripture, to signify those who are all asleep and content in their sins, without any desire of righteousness; since no heart can ever break out into a sincere invocation of God, unaccompanied with aspirations after piety. To such promises, therefore, correspond those declarations of the saints, in which they introduce the mention of their own purity or innocence, that they may experience a manifestation to themselves of what is to be expected by all the servants of God. Besides, they are generally found in the use of this species of prayer, when before the Lord they compare themselves with their enemies, from whose iniquity they desire him to deliver them. Now, in this comparison, we need not wonder, if they produce their righteousness and simplicity of heart, in order to prevail upon him by the justice of their cause to yield the more ready assistance. We object not, therefore, to the pious heart of a good man making use before the Lord of the consciousness of his own purity for his confirmation in the promises which the Lord has given for the consolation and support of his true worshippers; but his confidence of success we wish to be independent of every consideration of personal merit, and to rest solely on the Divine clemency.

XI. The fourth and last rule is, That thus prostrate with true humility, we should nevertheless be animated to pray by the certain hope of obtaining our requests. It is indeed an apparent contradiction, to connect a certain confidence of God's favour with a sense of his righteous vengeance; though these two things are perfectly consistent, if persons oppressed by their own guilt be encouraged solely by the Divine goodness. For as we have before stated, that repentance and faith, of which one terrifies, and the other exhilarates, are inseparably connected, so their union is necessary in prayer. And this agreement is briefly expressed by David: "I will come (says he) into thy house in the multitude of thy mercy; and in thy fear will I worship toward thy holy temple." Under the "goodness of God," he comprehends faith, though not to the exclusion of fear; for his majesty not only commands our reverence, but our own unworthiness makes us forget all pride and security, and fills us with fear. I do not mean a confidence which delivers the mind from all sense of anxiety, and soothes it into pleasant and perfect tranquillity; for such a placid satisfaction belongs to those whose prosperity is equal to their wishes, who are affected by no care, corroded by no desire, and alarmed by no fear. And the saints have an excellent stimulus to calling upon God, when their necessities and perplexities harass and disquiet them, and they are almost despairing in themselves, till faith opportunely relieves them; because, amidst such troubles, the goodness of God is so glorious in their view, that though they groan under the pressure of present calamities, and are likewise tormented with the fear of greater in future, yet a reliance on it alleviates the difficulty of bearing them, and encourages a hope of deliverance. The prayers of a pious man, therefore, must proceed from both these dispositions, and must also contain and discover them both; though he must groan under present evils, and is anxiously afraid of new ones, yet at the same time he must resort for refuge to God, not doubting his readiness to extend the assistance of his hand. For God is highly incensed by our distrust, if we supplicate him for blessings which we have no expectation of receiving. There is nothing, therefore, more suitable to the nature of prayers, than that they be conformed to this rule—not to rush forward with temerity, but to follow the steps of faith. To this principle Christ calls the attention of us all in the following passage: "I say unto you, What things soever ye desire, when ye pray, believe that ye receive them, and ye shall have them." This he confirms also in another place: "Whatsoever ye shall ask in prayer, believing, ye shall receive." With which James agrees: "If any of you lack wisdom, let him ask of God, that giveth to all men liberally, and upbraideth not. But let him ask in faith, nothing wavering." Where, by opposing "faith" to "wavering," he very aptly expresses its nature. And equally worthy of attention is what he adds, that they avail nothing, who call upon God in perplexity and doubt, and are uncertain in their minds whether they shall be heard or not; whom he even compares to waves, which are variously tossed and driven about with the wind. Whence he elsewhere calls a legitimate prayer "the prayer of faith." Besides, when God so frequently affirms, that he will give to every man according to his faith, he implies that we can obtain nothing without faith. Finally, it is faith that obtains whatever is granted in answer to prayer. This is the meaning of that famous passage of Paul, to which injudicious men pay little attention: "How shall they call on him, in whom they have not believed? And how shall they believe in him, of whom they have not heard? So then faith cometh by hearing, and hearing by the word of God." For by a regular deduction of prayer originally from faith, he evidently contends, that God cannot be sincerely invoked by any, but those to whom his clemency and gentleness have been revealed and familiarly discovered by the preaching of the gospel.

XII. This necessity our adversaries never consider. Therefore, when we inculcate on believers a certain confidence of mind that God is propitious and benevolent towards them, they consider us as advancing the greatest of all absurdities. But if they were in the habit of true prayer, they would certainly understand, that there can be no proper invocation of God without such a strong sense of the Divine benevolence. But since no man can fully discover the power of faith without an experience of it in his heart, what advantage can arise from disputing with such men, who plainly prove that they never had any other than a vain imagination? For the value and necessity of that assurance which we require, is chiefly learned by prayer; and he who does not perceive this, betrays great stupidity of conscience. Leaving, then, this class of blinded mortals, let us ever abide by the decision of Paul, that God cannot be called upon, but by those who receive from the gospel a knowledge of his mercy, and a certain persuasion that it is prepared for them. For what kind of an address would this be? "O Lord, I am truly in doubt, whether thou be willing to hear me; but since I am oppressed with anxiety, I flee to thee, that if I be worthy thou mayest assist me." This does not resemble the solicitude of the saints, whose prayers we read in the Scriptures. Nor is it agreeable to the teaching of the Holy Spirit by the apostle, who commands us "to come boldly to the throne of grace, that we may find grace;" and informs us, that "we have boldness and access, with confidence, by the faith of Christ." This assurance of obtaining what we implore, therefore, which is both commanded by the Lord himself, and taught by the example of the saints, it becomes us to hold fast with all our might, if we would pray to any good purpose. For that prayer alone is accepted by God, which arises (if I may use the expression) from such a presumption of faith, and is founded on an undaunted assurance of hope. He might, indeed, have contented himself with the simple mention of "faith;" yet he has not only added "confidence," but furnished that confidence with liberty or "boldness" to distinguish by this criterion between us and unbelievers, who do indeed pray to God in common with us, but entirely at an uncertainty. For which reason, the whole Church prays in the psalm, "Let thy mercy, O Lord, be upon us, according as we hope in thee." The Psalmist elsewhere introduces the same idea: "This I know; for God is for me." Again: "In the morning will I direct my prayer unto thee, and will look up." For from these words we gather, that prayers are but empty sounds, if unattended by hope, from which, as from a watch-tower, we quietly look out for God. With which corresponds the order of Paul's exhortation; for before exhorting believers to "pray always with all prayer and supplication in the Spirit," he first directs them to "take the shield of faith, the helmet of salvation, and the sword of the Spirit, which is the word of God." Now, let the reader recollect, what I have before asserted, that faith is not at all weakened by being connected with an acknowledgment of our misery, poverty, and impurity. For believers feel themselves oppressed by a grievous load of sins, while destitute of every thing which could conciliate the favour of God, and burdened with much guilt, which might justly render him an object of their dread; yet they cease not to present themselves before him; nor does this experience terrify them from resorting to him, since there is no other way of access to him. For prayer was instituted, not that we might arrogantly exalt ourselves in the presence of God, or form a high opinion of any thing of our own; but that we might confess our guilt to him, and deplore our miseries with the familiarity of children confiding their complaints to their parents. The immense accumulation of our distresses should operate as so many incitements to urge us to pray; as we are taught likewise by the example of the Psalmist: "Heal my soul; for I have sinned against thee." I confess, indeed, that the operation of such incentives would be fatal, were it not for the Divine aid; but our most benevolent Father, in his incomparable mercy, has afforded a timely remedy, that allaying all perturbation, alleviating all cares, and dispelling all fears, he might gently allure us to himself, and facilitate our approach to him, by the removal of every obstacle and every doubt.

XIII. And in the first place, when he enjoins us to pray, the commandment itself implies a charge of impious contumacy, if we disobey it. No command can be more precise than that in the psalm: "Call upon me in the day of trouble." But as the Scripture recommends no one of the duties of piety more frequently, it is unnecessary to dwell any longer upon it. "Ask, (says our Lord,) and it shall be given you; knock, and it shall be opened unto you." To this precept, however, there is also annexed a promise, which is very necessary; for though all men acknowledge obedience to be due to a precept, yet the greater part of them would neglect the calls of God, if he did not promise to be propitious to them, and even to advance to meet them. These two positions being proved, it is evident that all those who turn their backs on God, or do not directly approach him, are not only guilty of disobedience and rebellion, but also convicted of unbelief; because they distrust the promises; which is the more worthy of observation, since hypocrites, under the pretext of humility and modesty, treat the command of God with such haughty contempt as to give no credit to his kind invitation, and even defraud him of a principal part of his worship. For after having refused sacrifices, in which all holiness then appeared to consist, he declares the principal and most acceptable part of his service to be, "calling upon him in the day of trouble." Wherefore, when he requires what is due to him, and animates us to a cheerful obedience, there are no pretexts for diffidence or hesitation sufficiently specious to excuse us. The numerous texts of Scripture, therefore, which enjoin us to call upon God, are as so many banners placed before our eyes to inspire us with confidence. It were temerity to rush into the presence of God, without a previous invitation from him. He therefore opens a way for us by his own word: "I will say, It is my people; and they shall say, The Lord is my God." We see how he leads his worshippers, and desires them to follow him; and therefore that there is no reason to fear lest the melody, which he dictates, should not be agreeable to him. Let us particularly remember this remarkable character of God, by a reliance on which we shall easily surmount every obstacle: "O thou that hearest prayer, unto thee shall all flesh come." For what is more amiable or attractive than for God to bear this character, which assures us, that nothing is more agreeable to his nature, than to grant the requests of humble suppliants? Hence the Psalmist concludes that the way is open, not to a few only, but to all men; because he addresses all in these words: "Call upon me in the day of trouble: I will deliver thee, and thou shalt glorify me." According to this rule, David, in order to obtain his request, pleads the promise that had been given him: "Thou, O Lord, hast revealed to thy servant—; therefore hath thy servant found in his heart to pray." Whence we conclude that he would have been fearful, had he not been encouraged by the promise. So in another place he furnishes himself with this general doctrine: "He will fulfil the desire of them that fear him." In the Psalms we may likewise observe the connection of prayer as it were interrupted, and sudden transitions made, sometimes to the power of God, sometimes to his goodness, and sometimes to the truth of his promises. It might appear as though David mutilated his prayers by an unseasonable introduction of such passages; but believers know by experience, that the ardour of devotion languishes, unless it be supported by fresh supplies; and therefore a meditation on the nature and the word of God is far from being useless in the midst of our prayers. Let us not hesitate, then, to follow the example of David in the introduction of topics calculated to reanimate languid souls with new vigour.

XIV. And it is wonderful that we are no more affected with promises so exceedingly sweet; that the generality of men, wandering through a labyrinth of errors, after having forsaken the fountain of living waters, prefer hewing out for themselves cisterns incapable of containing any water, to embracing the free offers of Divine goodness. "The name of the Lord (says Solomon) is a strong tower: the righteous runneth into it, and is safe." And Joel, after having predicted the speedy approach of a dreadful destruction, adds this memorable sentence: "Whosoever shall call on the name of the Lord, shall be delivered;" which we know properly refers to the course of the gospel. Scarcely one man in a hundred is induced to advance to meet the Lord. He proclaims by Isaiah, "Before they call, I will answer; and while they are yet speaking, I will hear." And in another place he dignifies the whole Church in general with the same honour; as it belongs to all the members of Christ: "He shall call upon me, and I will answer him: I will be with him in trouble: I will deliver him." As I have before said, however, my design is not to enumerate all the texts, but to select the most remarkable, from which we may perceive the condescending kindness of God in inviting us to him, and the circumstances of aggravation attending our ingratitude, while our indolence still lingers in the midst of such powerful incitements. Wherefore let these words perpetually resound in our ears: "The Lord is nigh unto all them that call upon him, to all that call upon him in truth;" as well as those which we have cited from Isaiah and Joel; in which God affirms, that he is inclined to hear prayers, and is delighted, as with a sacrifice of a sweet savour, when we cast our cares upon him. We derive this singular benefit from the Divine promises, when our prayers are conceived without doubt or trepidation; but in reliance on his word, whose majesty would otherwise terrify us, we venture to call upon him as our Father, because he deigns to suggest to us this most delightful appellation. Favoured with such invitations, it remains for us to know that they furnish us with sufficient arguments to enforce our petitions; since our prayers rest on no intrinsic merit; but all their worthiness, as well as all our hope of obtaining our requests, is founded in, and dependent upon, the Divine promises; so that there is no need of any other support or further anxiety. Therefore we may be fully assured, that though we equal not the sanctity so celebrated in holy patriarchs, prophets, and apostles, yet, since the command to pray is common to us as well as to them, and we are partakers of the same common faith, if we rely on the Divine word, we are associated with them in this privilege. For God's declaration, (already noticed,) that he will be gentle and merciful to all, gives all, even the most miserable, a hope of obtaining the objects of their supplications; and therefore we should remark the general forms of expression, by which no man, from the greatest to the least, is excluded; only let him possess sincerity of heart, self-abhorrence, humility, and faith; and let not our hypocrisy profane the name of God by a pretended invocation of him; our most merciful Father will not reject those whom he exhorts to approach him, and even urges by every possible mode of solicitation. Hence the argument of David's prayer, just recited: "Thou, O Lord, hast revealed to thy servant——; therefore hath thy servant found in his heart to pray this prayer unto thee. And now, O Lord God, thou art that God, and thy words be true, and thou hast promised this goodness unto thy servant:" begin therefore and do it. As also in another place: "Let thy kindness be according to thy word unto thy servant." And all the Israelites together, whenever they fortify themselves with a recollection of the covenant, sufficiently declare that fear ought to be banished from our devotions, because it is contrary to the Divine injunction; and in this respect they imitated the examples of the patriarchs, particularly of Jacob, who, after having confessed himself "not worthy of the least of all the mercies" he had received from the hand of God, yet declares himself animated to pray for still greater blessings, because God had promised to grant them. But whatever be the pretences of unbelievers, for not applying to God under the pressure of every necessity, for not seeking him or imploring his aid, they are equally chargeable with defrauding him of the honour due to him, as if they had fabricated for themselves new gods and idols; for by this conduct, they deny him to be the Author of all their blessings. On the contrary, there is nothing more efficacious to deliver believers from every scruple, than this consideration, that no impediment ought to prevent their acting according to the command of God, who declares that nothing is more agreeable to him than obedience. These observations tend more fully to elucidate what I have advanced before; that a spirit of boldness in prayer is perfectly consistent with fear, reverence, and solicitude; and that there is no absurdity in God's exalting those who are abased. This establishes an excellent agreement between those apparently repugnant forms of expression. Both Jeremiah and Daniel use this phrase: "Make prayers fall" before God; for so it is in the original. Jeremiah also: "Let our supplication fall before thee." Again: believers are frequently said to "lift up their prayer." So says Hezekiah, when requesting the prophet to intercede for him. And David desires that his prayer may ascend "as incense." For though, under a persuasion of God's fatherly love, they cheerfully commit themselves to his faithfulness, and hesitate not to implore the assistance he freely promises, yet they are not impudently elated with careless security, but ascend upwards by the steps of the promises, yet in such a manner, that they still continue to be suppliant and self-abased.

XV. Here several questions are started. The Scripture relates that the Lord has complied with some prayers, which nevertheless did not arise from a calm or well-regulated heart. Jotham, for a just cause indeed, but from the impulse of rage, resentment, and revenge, devoted the inhabitants of Shechem to the destruction which afterwards fell upon them: the Lord, by fulfilling this curse, seems to approve of such disorderly sallies of passion. Samson also was hurried away by similar fervour when he said, "O Lord, strengthen me, that I may be avenged of the Philistines." For though there was some mixture of honest zeal, yet it was a violent, and therefore sinful, avidity of revenge which predominated. God granted the request. Whence it seems deducible, that prayers not conformable to the rules of the Divine word, are nevertheless efficacious. I reply, first, that a permanent rule is not annulled by particular examples; secondly, that peculiar emotions have sometimes been excited in a few individuals, causing a distinction between them and men in general. For the answer of Christ to his disciples, who inconsiderately wished to emulate the example of Elias, "that they knew not what spirit they were of," is worthy of observation. But we must remark, further, that God is not always pleased with the prayers which he grants; but that, as far as examples are concerned, there are undeniable evidences of the Scripture doctrine, that he succours the miserable, and hears the groans of those who under the pressure of injustice implore his aid; that he therefore executes his judgments, when the complaints of the poor arise to him, though they are unworthy of the least favourable attention. For how often, by punishing the cruelty, rapine, violence, lust, and other crimes of the impious, by restraining their audacity and fury, and even subverting their tyrannical power, has he manifestly assisted the victims of unrighteous oppression, though they have been beating the air with supplications to an unknown God! And one of the Psalmists clearly teaches that some prayers are not ineffectual, which nevertheless do not penetrate into heaven by faith. For he collects those prayers which necessity naturally extorts from unbelievers as well as from believers, but to which the event shows God to be propitious. Does he by such condescension testify that they are acceptable to him? No; he designs to amplify or illustrate his mercy by this circumstance, that even the requests of unbelievers are not refused; and likewise to stimulate his true worshippers to greater diligence in prayer, while they see that even the lamentations of the profane are not unattended with advantage. Yet there is no reason why believers should deviate from the rule given them by God, or envy unbelievers, as though they had made some great acquisition when they have obtained the object of their wishes. In this manner we have said that the Lord was moved by the hypocritical penitence of Ahab, in order to prove by this example how ready he is to grant the prayers of his own elect, when they seek reconciliation with him by true conversion. Therefore in the Psalms he expostulates with the Jews, because, after having experienced his propitiousness to their prayers, they had almost immediately returned to their native perverseness. It is evident, also, from the history of the Judges, that whenever they wept, though their tears were hypocritical, yet they were delivered from the hands of their enemies. As the Lord, therefore, "maketh his sun to rise on the evil and on the good," promiscuously, so he despises not the lamentations of those whose cause is just, and whose afflictions deserve relief. At the same time his attention to them is no more connected with salvation, than his furnishing food to the despisers of his goodness. The question relative to Abraham and Samuel is attended with more difficulty; the former of whom prayed for the inhabitants of Sodom without any Divine direction, and the latter for Saul even contrary to a plain prohibition. The same is the case of Jeremiah, who deprecated the destruction of the city. For though they suffered a repulse, yet it seems harsh to deny them to have been under the influence of faith. But the modest reader will, I hope, be satisfied with this solution; that mindful of the general principles by which God enjoins them to be merciful even to the unworthy, they were not entirely destitute of faith, though in a particular instance their opinion may have disappointed them. Augustine has somewhere this judicious observation: "How do the saints pray in faith, when they implore of God that which is contrary to his decrees? It is because they pray according to his will, not that hidden and immutable will, but that with which he inspires them, that he may hear them in a different way, as he wisely discriminates." This is an excellent remark; because, according to his incomprehensible designs, he so regulates the events of things, that the prayers of the saints, which contain a mixture of faith and error, are not in vain. Yet this no more affords an example for imitation, than a sufficient plea to excuse the saints themselves, whom I admit to have transgressed the bounds of duty. Wherefore, when no certain promise can be found, we should present our supplications to God in a conditional way; which is implied in this petition of David: "Awake to the judgment that thou hast commanded;" because he suggests that he was directed by a particular revelation to pray for a temporal blessing.

XVI. It will also be of use to remark, that the things I have delivered concerning the four rules for praying aright, are not required by God with such extreme rigour as to cause the rejection of all prayers, in which he does not find a perfection of faith or repentance, united with ardent zeal and well-regulated desires. We have said, that although prayer is a familiar intercourse between God and pious men, yet reverence and modesty must be preserved, that we may not give a loose to all our wishes, nor even in our desires exceed the Divine permission; and to prevent the majesty of God being lessened in our view, our minds must be raised to a pure and holy veneration of him. This no man has ever performed with the purity required; for, to say nothing of the multitude, how many complaints of David savour of intemperance of spirit! not that he would designedly remonstrate with God, or murmur at his judgments; but he faints in consequence of his infirmity, and finds no better consolation than to pour his sorrows into the Divine bosom. Moreover, God bears with our lisping, and pardons our ignorance, whenever any inconsiderate expressions escape us; and certainly without this indulgence there could be no freedom of prayer. But though it was David's intention to submit himself wholly to the Divine will, and his patience in prayer was equal to his desire of obtaining his requests, yet we sometimes perceive the appearance and ebullition of turbulent passions, very inconsistent with the first rule we have laid down. We may discover, particularly from the conclusion of the thirty-ninth psalm, with what vehemence of grief this holy man was hurried away beyond all the bounds of propriety. "O spare me (says he) before I go hence, and be no more." One might be ready to say, that the man, being in despair, desires nothing but the removal of God's hand, that he may putrefy in his own iniquities and miseries. He does not intend to rush into intemperance of language, or, as is usual with the reprobate, desire God to depart from him; he only complains that he cannot bear the Divine wrath. In these temptations, also, the saints often drop petitions, not sufficiently conformable to the rule of God's word, and without due reflection on what is right and proper. All prayers polluted with these blemishes deserve to be rejected; yet if the saints mourn, correct themselves, and return to themselves again, God forgives them. Thus they offend likewise against the second rule; because they frequently have to contend with their own indifference; nor do their poverty and misery sufficiently incite them to seriousness of devotion. Now, their minds frequently wander, and are almost absorbed in vanity; and they also need pardon in this respect, lest languid, or mutilated, or interrupted and desultory prayers should meet with a repulse. God has naturally impressed the minds of men with a conviction that prayers require to be attended with an elevation of heart. Hence the ceremony of elevating the hands, as before observed, which has been common in all ages and nations, and still continues; but where is the person, who, while lifting up the hands, is not conscious of dulness, because his heart cleaves to the earth? As to praying for the remission of sins, though none of the faithful omit this article, yet they who have been truly engaged in prayers, perceive that they scarcely offer the tenth part of the sacrifices mentioned by David: "The sacrifices of God are a broken spirit; a broken and a contrite heart, O God, thou wilt not despise." Thus they have always to pray for a twofold forgiveness; both because they are conscious of many transgressions, with which they are not so deeply affected as to be sufficiently displeased with themselves, and as they are enabled to advance in repentance and the fear of God, humbled with just sorrow for their offences, they deprecate the vengeance of the Judge. But above all, the weakness or imperfection of their faith would vitiate the prayers of believers, were it not for the Divine indulgence; but we need not wonder that this defect is forgiven by God, who frequently exercises his children with severe discipline, as if he fully designed to annihilate their faith. It is a very sharp temptation, when believers are constrained to cry, "How long wilt thou be angry against the prayer of thy people?" as though even their prayers were so many provocations of Divine wrath. So when Jeremiah says, "God shutteth out my prayer," he was undoubtedly agitated with severe trouble. Innumerable examples of this kind occur in the Scriptures, from which it appears that the faith of the saints is often mingled and agitated with doubts, so that amidst the exercises of faith and hope, they nevertheless betray some remains of unbelief; but since they cannot attain all that is to be wished, it becomes them to be increasingly diligent, in order that, correcting their faults, they may daily make nearer approaches to the perfect rule of prayer, and at the same time to consider into what an abyss of evils they must have been plunged, who even in their very remedies contract new diseases; since there is no prayer which God would not justly disdain, if he did not overlook the blemishes with which they are all deformed. I mention these things, not that believers may securely forgive themselves any thing sinful, but that, by severely correcting themselves, they may strive to surmount these obstacles; and that, notwithstanding the endeavours of Satan to obstruct them in all their ways, with a view to prevent them from praying, they may nevertheless break through all opposition, certainly persuaded, that, though they experience many impediments, yet God is pleased with their efforts, and approves of their prayers, provided they strenuously aim at that which they do not immediately attain.

XVII. But since there is no one of the human race worthy to present himself to God, and to enter into his presence, our heavenly Father himself, to deliver us at once from shame and fear, which might justly depress all our minds, has given us his Son Jesus Christ our Lord to be our Advocate and Mediator with him; introduced by whom we may boldly approach him, confident, with such an Intercessor, that nothing we ask in his name will be denied us, as nothing can be denied to him by his Father. And to this must be referred all that we have hitherto advanced concerning faith; because, as the promise recommends Christ to us as the Mediator, so, unless our hope of success depend on him, it deprives itself of all the benefit of prayer. For as soon as we reflect on the terrible majesty of God, we cannot but be exceedingly afraid, and driven away from him by a consciousness of our unworthiness, till we discover Christ as the Mediator, who changes the throne of dreadful glory into a throne of grace; as the apostle also exhorts us to "come boldly unto the throne of grace, that we may obtain mercy, and find grace to help in time of need." And as there is a rule given for calling upon God, as well as a promise that they shall be heard who call upon him, so we are particularly enjoined to invoke him in the name of Christ; and we have an express promise, that what we ask in his name we shall obtain. "Hitherto (says he) ye have asked nothing in my name: ask, and ye shall receive. At that day ye shall ask in my name; and whatsoever ye shall ask in my name, that will I do, that the Father may be glorified in the Son." Hence it is plain beyond all controversy, that they who call upon God in any other name than that of Christ, are guilty of a contumacious neglect of his precepts, and a total disregard of his will; and that they have no promise of any success. For, as Paul says of Christ, "All the promises of God in him are yea, and in him amen;" that is, are confirmed and fulfilled.

XVIII. And we must carefully remark the circumstance of the time when Christ commands his disciples to apply to his intercession, which was to be after his ascension to heaven; "At that day (says he) ye shall ask in my name." It is certain that from the beginning no prayers had been heard but for the sake of the Mediator. For this reason the Lord had appointed in the law, that the priest alone should enter the sanctuary, bearing on his shoulders the names of the tribes of Israel and the same number of precious stones before his breast; but that the people should stand without in the court, and there unite their prayers with those of the priest. The use of the sacrifice was to render their prayers effectual. The meaning, therefore, of that shadowy ceremony of the law was, that we are all banished from the presence of God, and therefore need a mediator to appear in our name, to bear us on his shoulders, and bind us to his breast, that we may be heard in his person; and, moreover, that the sprinkling of his blood purifies our prayers, which have been asserted to be otherwise never free from defilement. And we see that the saints, when they wished to obtain any thing by prayer, founded their hope on the sacrifices; because they knew them to be the confirmations of all their prayers. David says, "The Lord remember all thy offerings, and accept thy burnt-sacrifice." Hence we conclude, that God has from the beginning been appeased by the intercession of Christ, so as to accept the devotions of believers. Why, then, does Christ assign a new period, when his disciples shall begin to pray in his name, but because this grace, being now become more illustrious, deserves to be more strongly recommended to us? In this same sense he had just before said, "Hitherto ye have asked nothing in my name; ask." Not that they were totally unacquainted with the office of the Mediator, (since all the Jews were instructed in these first principles,) but because they did not yet clearly understand that Christ, on his ascension to heaven, would be more evidently the advocate of the Church than he was before. Therefore, to console their sorrow for his absence with some signal advantage, he claims the character of an advocate, and teaches them that they have hitherto wanted the principal benefit, which it shall be given them to enjoy, when they shall call upon God with greater freedom in a reliance on his intercession; as the apostle says that this new way is consecrated by his blood. So much the more inexcusable is our perverseness, unless we embrace with the greatest alacrity such an inestimable benefit, which is particularly destined for us.

XIX. Moreover, since he is the only way of access by which we are permitted to approach God, to them who deviate from this road, and desert this entrance, there remains no other way of access to God, nor any thing on his throne but wrath, judgment, and terror. Finally, since the Father has appointed him to be our Head and Leader, they who in any respect decline or turn aside from him, endeavour, as far as they can, to deface and obliterate a character impressed by God. Thus Christ is appointed as the one Mediator, by whose intercession the Father is rendered propitious and favourable to us. The saints have likewise their intercessions, in which they mutually commend each other's interests to God, and which are mentioned by the apostle; but these are so far from detracting any thing from the intercession of Christ, that they are entirely dependent on it. For as they arise from the affection of love, reciprocally felt by us towards each other as members of one body, so likewise they are referred to the unity of the Head. Being made also in the name of Christ, what are they but a declaration, that no man can be benefited by any prayers at all, independently of Christ's intercession? And as the intercession of Christ is no objection to our mutually pleading for each other, in our prayers in the Church, so let it be considered as a certain maxim, that all the intercessions of the whole Church should be directed to that principal one. We ought to beware of ingratitude particularly on this head, because God, pardoning our unworthiness, not only permits us to pray each one for himself, but even admits us as intercessors for one another. For, when those who richly deserve to be rejected, if they should privately pray each for himself, are appointed by God as advocates of his Church, what pride would it betray to abuse this liberality to obscure the honour of Christ!

XX. Now, the cavil of the sophists is quite frivolous, that Christ is the Mediator of redemption, but believers of intercession; as if Christ, after performing a temporary mediation, had left to his servants that which is eternal and shall never die. They who detract so diminutive a portion of honour from him, treat him, doubtless, very favourably. But the Scripture, with the simplicity of which a pious man, forsaking these impostors, ought to be contented, speaks very differently; for when John says, "If any man sin, we have an Advocate with the Father, Jesus Christ," does he only mean that he has been heretofore an Advocate for us, or does he not rather ascribe to him a perpetual intercession? What is intended by the assertion of Paul, that he "is even at the right hand of God, and also maketh intercession for us?" And when he elsewhere calls him the "one Mediator between God and man," does he not refer to prayers, which he has mentioned just before?" For having first asserted that intercessions should be made for all men, he immediately adds, in confirmation of that idea, that all have one God and one Mediator. Consistent with which is the explanation of Augustine, when he thus expresses himself: "Christian men in their prayers mutually recommend each other to the Divine regard. That person, for whom no one intercedes, while he intercedes for all, is the true and only Mediator. The apostle Paul, though a principal member under the Head, yet because he was a member of the body of Christ, and knew the great and true High Priest of the Church had entered, not typically, into the recesses within the veil, the holy of holies, but truly and really into the interior recesses of heaven, into a sanctuary not emblematical, but eternal,—Paul, I say, recommends himself to the prayers of believers. Neither does he make himself a mediator between God and the people, but exhorts all the members of the body of Christ mutually to pray for one another; since the members have a mutual solicitude for each other; and if one member suffers, the rest sympathize with it. And so should the mutual prayers of all the members, who are still engaged in the labours of the present state, ascend on each other's behalf to the Head, who is gone before them into heaven, and who is the propitiation for our sins. For if Paul were a mediator, the other apostles would likewise sustain the same character; and so there would be many mediators; and Paul's argument could not be supported, when he says, 'For there is one God, and one Mediator between God and men, the man Christ Jesus; in whom we also are one, if we keep the unity of the Spirit in the bond of peace.'" Again, in another place: "But if you seek a priest, he is above the heavens, where he now intercedes for you, who died for you on earth." Yet we do not dream that he intercedes for us in suppliant prostration at the Father's feet; but we apprehend, with the apostle, that he appears in the presence of God for us in such a manner, that the virtue of his death avails as a perpetual intercession for us; yet so as that, being entered into the heavenly sanctuary, he continually, till the consummation of all things, presents to God the prayers of his people, who remain, as it were, at a distance in the court.

XXI. With respect to the saints who are dead in the flesh, but live in Christ, if we attribute any intercession to them, let us not imagine that they have any other way of praying to God than by Christ, who is the only way, or that their prayers are accepted by God in any other name. Therefore, since the Scripture calls us away from all others to Christ alone,—since it is the will of our heavenly Father to gather together all things in him,—it would be a proof of great stupidity, not to say insanity, to be so desirous of procuring an admission by the saints, as to be seduced from him, without whom they have no access themselves. But that this has been practised in some ages, and is now practised wherever Popery prevails, who can deny? Their merits are frequently obtruded to conciliate the Divine favour; and in general Christ is totally neglected, and God is addressed through their names. Is not this transferring to them that office of exclusive intercession, which we have before asserted to be peculiar to Christ? Again, who, either angel or demon, ever uttered to any of the human race a syllable concerning such an intercession as they pretend? for the Scripture is perfectly silent respecting any such thing. What reason, then, was there for its invention? Certainly, when the human mind thus seeks assistances for itself, in which it is not warranted by the word of God, it evidently betrays its want of faith. Now, if we appeal to the consciences of all the advocates for the intercession of saints, we shall find that the only cause of it is, an anxiety in their minds, as if Christ could fail of success, or be too severe in this business. By which perplexity they, in the first place, dishonour Christ, and rob him of the character of the only Mediator, which, as it has been given by the Father as his peculiar prerogative, ought therefore not to be transferred to any other. And by this very conduct they obscure the glory of his nativity, and frustrate the benefit of his cross; in a word, they divest and defraud him of the praise which is due to him for all his actions and all his sufferings; since the end of them all is, that he may really be, and be accounted, the sole Mediator. They at the same time reject the goodness of God, who exhibits himself as their Father; for he is not a father to them, unless they acknowledge Christ as their brother. Which they plainly deny, unless they believe themselves to be the objects of his fraternal affection, than which nothing can be more mild or tender. Wherefore the Scripture offers him alone to us, sends us to him, and fixes us in him. "He," says Ambrose, "is our mouth, with which we address the Father; our eye, by which we behold the Father; our right hand, by which we present ourselves to the Father. Without whose mediation, neither we, nor any of all the saints, have the least intercourse with God." If they reply, that the public prayers in the churches are finished by this conclusion, "through Christ our Lord," it is a frivolous subterfuge; because the intercession of Christ is not less profaned when it is confounded with the prayers and merits of the dead, than if it were wholly omitted, and the dead alone mentioned. Besides, in all their litanies, both verse and prose, where every honour is ascribed to dead saints, there is no mention of Christ.

XXII. But their folly rises to such a pitch, that we have here a striking view of the genius of superstition, which, when it has once shaken off the reins, places in general no limits to its excursions. For after men had begun to regard the intercession of saints, they by degrees gave to each his particular attributes, so that sometimes one, sometimes another, might be invoked as intercessor, according to the difference of the cases; then they chose each his particular saint, to whose protection they committed themselves as to the care of tutelary gods. Thus they not only set up (as the prophet anciently accused Israel) gods according to the number of their cities, but even according to the multitude of persons. But, since the saints refer all their desires solely to the will of God, and observe it, and acquiesce in it, he must entertain foolish and carnal, and even degrading thoughts of them, who ascribes to them any other prayer, than that in which they pray for the advent of the kingdom of God; very remote from which is what they pretend concerning them—that every one of them is disposed by a private affection more particularly to regard his own worshippers. At length multitudes fell even into horrid sacrilege, by invoking them, not as subordinate promoters, but as principal agents, in their salvation. See how low wretched mortals fall, when they wander from their lawful station, the word of God. I omit the grosser monstrosities of impiety, for which, though they render them detestable to God, angels, and men, they do not yet feel either shame or grief. Prostrate before the statue or picture of Barbara, Catharine, and others, they mutter *Pater Noster*, "Our Father." This madness the pastors are so far from endeavouring to remedy or to restrain, that, allured by the charms of lucre, they approve and applaud it. But though they attempt to remove from themselves the odium of so foul a crime, yet what plea will they urge in defence of this, that Eligius and Medardus are supplicated to look down from heaven on their servants, and to assist them? and the holy Virgin to command her Son to grant their petitions? It was anciently forbidden at the Council of Carthage, that at the altar any prayers should be made directly to the saints; and it is probable that, when those holy men could not wholly subdue the force of depraved custom, they imposed this restraint, that the public prayers might not be deformed by this phrase, "Saint Peter, pray for us." But to how much greater lengths of diabolical absurdity have they proceeded, who hesitate not to transfer to dead men what exclusively belongs to God and Christ!

XXIII. But when they attempt to make this intercession appear to be founded on the authority of Scripture, they labour in vain. We frequently read, they say, of the prayers of angels; and not only so, but the prayers of believers are said to be carried by their hands into the presence of God. But if they would compare saints deceased to angels, they ought to prove that they are the ministering spirits who are delegated to superintend the concerns of our salvation, whose province it is to keep us in all our ways, who surround us, who advise and comfort us, who watch over us; all of which offices are committed to angels, but not to departed saints. How preposterously they include dead saints with angels, fully appears from so many different functions, by which the Scripture distinguishes some from others. No man will presume, without previous permission, to act the part of an advocate before an earthly judge: whence, then, have worms so great a license to obtrude on God as intercessors those who are not recorded to have been appointed to that office? God has been pleased to appoint the angels to attend to our salvation, whence they frequent the sacred assemblies, and the Church is to them a theatre, in which they admire the various and "manifold wisdom of God." Those who transfer to others that which is peculiar to them, certainly confound and pervert the order established by God, which ought to be inviolable. With equal dexterity they proceed to cite other testimonies. God said to Jeremiah, "Though Moses and Samuel stood before me, yet my mind could not be toward this people." How, they say, could he thus have spoken concerning persons deceased, unless he knew that they were accustomed to intercede for the living? But I, on the contrary, deduce this conclusion—That since it appears that neither Moses nor Samuel interceded for the Israelites, there was then no intercession of the dead. For who of the saints must we believe to be concerned for the salvation of the people, when this ceases to be the case with Moses, who far surpassed all others in this respect while alive? But if they pursue such minute subtleties, that the dead intercede for the living, because the Lord has said, "Though they interceded," I shall argue, with far greater plausibility, in this manner—In the people's extreme necessity, no intercession was made by Moses, of whom it is said, Though he interceded. Therefore it is highly probable, that no intercession is made by any other, since they are all so far from possessing the gentleness, kindness, and paternal solicitude of Moses. This is indeed the consequence of their cavilling, that they are wounded with the same weapons with which they thought themselves admirably defended. But it is very ridiculous, that a plain sentence should be so distorted; only because the Lord declares that he will not spare the crimes of the people, even though their cause had been pleaded by Moses or Samuel, to whose prayers he had shown himself so very propitious. This idea is very clearly deduced from a similar passage of Ezekiel—"Though these three men, Noah, Daniel, and Job, were in the land, they should deliver but their own souls by their righteousness, saith the Lord God;" where he undoubtedly meant to signify, if two of them should return to life again; for the third was then alive, namely, Daniel, who is well known to have given an incomparable specimen of his piety, even in the flower of his youth. Let us then leave them, whom the Scripture clearly shows to have finished their course. Therefore Paul, when speaking of David, does not say that he assists posterity by his prayers, but only that "he served his own generation."

XXIV. They further object—Shall we then divest them of every benevolent wish, who through the whole course of their lives breathed only benevolence and mercy? Truly, as I do not wish too curiously to inquire into their actions or thoughts, so it is by no means probable that they are agitated by the impulse of particular wishes, but rather that with fixed and permanent desires they aspire after the kingdom of God; which consists no less in the perdition of the impious, than in the salvation of believers. If this be true, their charity also is comprehended within the communion of the body of Christ, and extends no further than the nature of that communion permits. But though I grant that in this respect they pray for us, yet they do not therefore relinquish their own repose, to be distracted with earthly cares; and much less are they therefore to be the objects of our invocation. Neither is it a necessary consequence of this, that they must imitate the conduct of men on earth by mutually praying for one another. For this conduces to the cultivation of charity among them, while they divide, as it were, between them, and reciprocally bear their mutual necessities. And in this, indeed, they act according to God's precept, and are not destitute of his promise; which two are always the principal points in prayer. No such considerations have any relation to the dead; whom when the Lord has removed from our society, he has left us no intercourse with them, nor them, indeed, as far as our conjectures can reach, any with us. But if any one plead, that they cannot but retain the same charity towards us, as they are united with us by the same faith, yet who has revealed that they have ears long enough to reach our voices, and eyes so perspicacious as to watch over our necessities? They talk in the schools of I know not what refulgence of the Divine countenance irradiating them, in which, as in a mirror, they behold from heaven the affairs of men. But to affirm this, especially with the presumption with which they dare to assert it, what is it but an attempt, by the infatuated dreams of our own brains, forcibly to penetrate into the secret appointments of God, without the authority of his word, and to trample the Scripture under our feet? which so frequently pronounces our carnal wisdom to be hostile to the wisdom of God; totally condemns the vanity of our mind; and directs all our reason to be laid in the dust, and the Divine will to be the sole object of our regard.

XXV. The other testimonies of Scripture which they adduce in defence of this false doctrine, they distort with the greatest perverseness. But Jacob (they say) prays that his own name, and the name of his fathers, Abraham and Isaac, might be named on his posterity. Let us first inquire the form of this naming, or calling on their names, among the Israelites; for they do not invoke their fathers to assist them; but they beseech God to remember his servants Abraham, Isaac, and Jacob. Their example, therefore, is no vindication of those who address the saints themselves. But as these stupid mortals understand neither what it is to name the name of Jacob, nor for what reason it should be named, we need not wonder that they so childishly err even in the form itself. This phraseology more than once occurs in the Scriptures. For Isaiah says, that the name of the husband is "called upon" the wife who lives under his care and protection. The naming or calling, therefore, of the name of Abraham upon the Israelites, consists in their deducing their genealogy from him, and revering and celebrating his memory as their great progenitor. Neither is Jacob actuated by a solicitude for perpetuating the celebrity of his name, but by a knowledge that all the happiness of his posterity consisted in the inheritance of that covenant which God had made with him: and perceiving that this would be the greatest of all blessings to them, he prays that they may be numbered among his children; which is only transmitting to them the succession of the covenant. They, on their part, when they introduce the mention of this in their prayers, do not recur to the intercessions of the dead, but put the Lord in remembrance of his covenant, in which their most merciful Father has engaged to be propitious and beneficent to them, for the sake of Abraham, Isaac, and Jacob. How little the saints depended in any other sense on the merits of their fathers, is evinced by the public voice of the Church in the prophet: "Thou art our Father, though Abraham be ignorant of us, and Israel acknowledge us not: thou, O Lord, art our Father, our Redeemer." And when they thus express themselves, they add at the same time, "O Lord, return, for thy servants' sake;" yet not entertaining a thought of any intercession, but adverting to the blessing of the covenant. But now, since we have the Lord Jesus, in whose hand the eternal covenant of mercy is not only made but confirmed to us,—whose name should we rather plead in our prayers? And since these good doctors contend that the patriarchs are in these words represented as intercessors, I wish to be informed by them, why, in such a vast multitude, no place, not even the lowest among them, is allotted to Abraham, the father of the Church? From what vile source they derive their advocates, is well known. Let them answer me by proving it right, that Abraham, whom God has preferred to all others, and elevated to the highest degree of honour, should be neglected and suppressed. The truth is, that since this practice was unknown in the ancient Church, they thought proper, in order to conceal its novelty, to be silent respecting the ancient fathers; as though the difference of names were a valid excuse for a recent and corrupt custom. But the objection urged by some, that God is entreated to have mercy on the people for the sake of David, is so far from supporting their error, that it is a decisive refutation of it. For if we consider the character sustained by David, he is selected from the whole company of the saints, that God may fulfil the covenant which he made with him; so that it refers to the covenant, rather than to the person, and contains a figurative declaration of the sole intercession of Christ. For it is certain that what was peculiar to David, as being a type of Christ, is inapplicable to any others.

XXVI. But it seems that some are influenced by the frequent declarations which we read, that the prayers of the saints are heard. Why? Truly because they have prayed.

"They cried unto thee," says the Psalmist, "and were delivered; they trusted in thee, and were not confounded." Therefore, let us likewise pray after their example, that we may obtain a similar audience. But these men preposterously argue, that none will be heard but such as have been once already heard. How much more properly does James say, "Elias was a man subject to like passions as we are, and he prayed earnestly that it might not rain; and it rained not on the earth by the space of three years and six months. And he prayed again, and the heaven gave rain, and the earth brought forth her fruit." What! does he infer any peculiar privilege of Elias, to which we should have recourse? Not at all; but he shows the perpetual efficacy of pure and pious prayer, to exhort us to pray in a similar manner. For we put a mean construction on the promptitude and benignity of God in hearing them, unless we be encouraged by such instances to a firmer reliance on his promises; in which he promises to hear, not one or two, or even a few, but all who call upon his name. And this ignorance is so much the less excusable, because they appear almost professedly to disregard so many testimonies of Scripture. David experienced frequent deliverances by the Divine power; was it that he might arrogate it to himself, in order to deliver us by his interposition? He makes some very different declarations: "The righteous shall compass me about; for thou shalt deal bountifully with me." Again: "They looked unto him, and were lightened; and their faces were not ashamed. This poor man cried, and the Lord heard him, and saved him out of all his troubles." The Psalms contain many such prayers, in which he implores God to grant his requests from this consideration, that the righteous may not be put to shame, but may be encouraged by his example to entertain a good hope. Let us be contented at present with one instance: "For this shall every one that is godly pray unto thee in a time when thou mayest be found;" a text which I have the more readily cited, because the hireling and cavilling advocates of Popery have not been ashamed to plead it to prove the intercession of the dead. As though David had any other design than to show the effect which would proceed from the Divine clemency and goodness when his prayers should be heard. And in general it must be maintained, that an experience of the grace of God, both to ourselves and to others, affords no small assistance to confirm our faith in his promises. I do not recite numerous passages, where he proposes to himself the past blessings of God as a ground of present and future confidence, since they will naturally occur to those who peruse the Psalms. Jacob by his example had long before taught the same lesson: "I am not worthy of the least of all the mercies, and of all the truth, which thou hast showed unto thy servant; for with my staff I passed over this Jordan; and now I am become two bands." He mentions the promise indeed, but not alone; he likewise adds the effect, that he may in future confide with the greater boldness in the continuance of the Divine goodness towards him. For God is not like mortals, who grow weary of their liberality, or whose wealth is exhausted; but is to be estimated by his own nature, as is judiciously done by David, when he says, "Thou hast redeemed me, O Lord God of truth." After ascribing to him the praise of his salvation, he adds, that he is a God of truth; because, unless he were perpetually and uniformly consistent with himself, there could not be derived from his benefits a sufficient argument for confiding in him, and praying to him. But when we know that every act of assistance, which he affords us, is a specimen and proof of his goodness and faithfulness, we shall have no reason to fear lest our hopes be confounded or our expectations disappointed.

XXVII. Let us conclude this argument in the following manner: Since the Scripture represents the principal part of Divine worship to be an invocation of God, as he, in preference to all sacrifices, requires of us this duty of piety, no prayer can without evident sacrilege be directed to any other. Wherefore also the Psalmist says, "If we have stretched out our hands to a strange god, shall not God search this out?" Besides, since God will only be invoked in faith, and expressly commands prayers to be conformed to the rule of his word; finally, since faith founded on the word is the source of true prayer,—as soon as the least deviation is made from the word, there must necessarily be an immediate corruption of prayer. But it has been already shown, that if the whole Scripture be consulted, this honour is there claimed for God alone. With respect to the office of intercession, we have also seen, that it is peculiar to Christ, and that no prayer is acceptable to God, unless it be sanctified by this Mediator. And though believers mutually pray to God for their brethren, we have proved that this derogates nothing from the sole intercession of Christ; because they all commend both themselves and others to God in a reliance upon it. Moreover we have argued, that this is injudiciously applied to the dead, of whom we nowhere read that they are commanded to pray for us. The Scripture frequently exhorts us to the mutual performance of this duty for each other; but concerning the dead there is not even a syllable; and James, by connecting these two things, "Confess your faults one to another, and pray one for another," tacitly excludes the dead. Wherefore, to condemn this error, this one reason is sufficient, that right prayer originates in faith, and that faith is produced by hearing the word of God, where there is no mention of this fictitious intercession; for the temerity of superstition has chosen itself advocates, who were not of Divine appointment. For whilst the Scripture abounds with many forms of prayer, there is not to be found an example of this advocacy, without which the Papists believe there can be no prayer at all. Besides, it is evident that this superstition has arisen from a want of faith, because they either were not content with Christ as their intercessor, or entirely denied him this glory. The latter of these is easily proved from their impudence; for they adduce no argument more valid to show that we need the mediation of the saints, than when they object that we are unworthy of familiar access to God. Which indeed we acknowledge to be strictly true; but we thence conclude, that they rob Christ of every thing, who consider his intercession as unavailing without the assistance of George and Hippolytus, and other such phantasms.

XXVIII. But though prayer is properly restricted to wishes and petitions, yet there is so great an affinity between petition and thanksgiving, that they may be justly comprehended under the same name. For the species which Paul enumerates, fall under the first member of this division. In requests and petitions we pour out our desires before God, imploring those things which tend to the propagation of his glory and the illustration of his name, as well as those benefits which conduce to our advantage. In thanksgiving we celebrate his beneficence towards us with due praises, acknowledging all the blessings we have received as the gifts of his liberality. Therefore David has connected these two parts together: "Call upon me in the day of trouble: I will deliver thee, and thou shalt glorify me." The Scripture, not without reason, enjoins us the continual use of both; for we have elsewhere said that our want is so great, and experience itself proclaims that we are molested and oppressed on every side with such numerous and great perplexities, that we all have sufficient cause for unceasing sighs, and groans, and ardent supplications to God. For though they enjoy a freedom from adversity, yet the guilt of their sins, and the innumerable assaults of temptation, ought to stimulate even the most eminent saints to pray for relief. But of the sacrifice of praise and thanksgiving there can be no interruption, without guilt; since God ceases not to accumulate on us his various benefits, according to our respective cases, in order to constrain us, inactive and sluggish as we are, to the exercise of gratitude. Finally, we are almost overwhelmed with such great and copious effusions of his beneficence; we are surrounded, whithersoever we turn our eyes, by such numerous and amazing miracles of his hand, that we never want matter of praise and thanksgiving. And to be a little more explicit on this point, since all our hopes and all our help are in God, (which has already been sufficiently proved,) so that we cannot enjoy prosperity, either in our persons or in any of our affairs, without his benediction,—it becomes us assiduously to commend to him ourselves and all our concerns. Further, whatever we think, speak, or act, let all our thoughts, words, and actions be under his direction, subject to his will, and finally in hope of his assistance. For the curse of God is denounced on all, who deliberate and decide on any enterprise in a reliance on themselves or on any other, who engage in or attempt to begin any undertaking independently of his will, and without invoking his aid. And since it has already been several times observed, that he is justly honoured when he is acknowledged to be the Author of all blessings, it thence follows that they should all be so received from his hand, as to be attended with unceasing thanksgiving; and that there is no other proper method of using the benefits which flow to us from his goodness, but by continual acknowledgments of his praise, and unceasing expressions of our gratitude. For Paul, when he declares that they are "sanctified by the word of God and prayer," at the same time implies, that they are not at all holy and pure to us without the word and prayer; the word being metonymically used to denote faith. Wherefore David, after experiencing the goodness of the Lord, beautifully declares, "He hath put a new song in my mouth;" in which he certainly implies that we are guilty of a criminal silence, if we omit to praise him for any benefit; since, in every blessing he bestows on us, he gives us additional cause to bless his name. Thus also Isaiah, proclaiming the unparalleled grace of God, exhorts believers to a new and uncommon song. In which sense David elsewhere says, "O Lord, open thou my lips; and my mouth shall show forth thy praise." Hezekiah likewise, and Jonah, declare that the end of their deliverance shall be to sing the Divine goodness in the temple. David prescribes the same general rule for all the saints. "What shall I render (says he) unto the Lord for all his benefits towards me? I will take the cup of salvation, and call upon the name of the Lord." And this is followed by the Church in another psalm: "Save us, O Lord our God, to give thanks unto thy holy name, and to triumph in thy praise." Again: "He will regard the prayer of the destitute, and not despise their prayer. This shall be written for the generation to come; and the people which shall be created shall praise the Lord. To declare the name of the Lord in Zion, and his praise in Jerusalem." Moreover, whenever believers entreat the Lord to do any thing "for his name's sake," as they profess themselves unworthy to obtain any blessing on their own account, so they lay themselves under an obligation to thanksgiving; and promise that the Divine beneficence shall be productive of this proper effect on them, even to cause them to celebrate its fame. Thus Hosea, speaking of the future redemption of the Church, addresses the Lord: "Take away all iniquity, and receive us graciously; so will we render the calves of our lips." Nor do the Divine blessings only claim the praises of the tongue, but naturally conciliate our love. "I love the Lord (says David) because he hath heard my voice and my supplications." In another place also, enumerating the assistances he had experienced, "I will love thee, O Lord, my strength." Nor will any praises ever please God, but such as flow from this ardour of love. We must likewise remember the position of Paul, that all petitions, to which thanksgiving is not annexed, are irregular and faulty. For thus he speaks: "In every thing by prayer and supplication with thanksgiving, let your requests be made known unto God." For since moroseness, weariness, impatience, pungent sorrow and fear, impel many to mutter petitions, he enjoins such a regulation of the affections, that believers may cheerfully bless God, even before they have obtained their requests. If this connection ought to exist in circumstances apparently adverse, God lays us under a still more sacred obligation to sing his praises, whenever he grants us the enjoyment of our wishes. But as we have asserted that our prayers, which had otherwise been defiled, are consecrated by the intercession of Christ, so the apostle, when he exhorts us "by Christ to offer the sacrifice of praise," admonishes us that our lips are not sufficiently pure to celebrate the name of God, without the intervention of the priesthood of Christ. Whence we infer, how prodigious must be the fascination of the Papists, the majority of whom wonder that Christ is called an Advocate. This is the reason why Paul directs to "pray without ceasing," and "in every thing to give thanks;" because he desires that all men, with all possible assiduity, at every time and in every place, and in all circumstances and affairs, may direct their prayers to God, expecting all from him, and ascribing to him the praise of all, since he affords us perpetual matter of prayer and praise.

XXIX. But this diligence in prayer, although it chiefly respects the particular and private devotions of each individual, has, notwithstanding, some reference also to the public prayers of the Church. But these cannot be unceasing, nor ought they to be conducted otherwise than according to the polity which is appointed by the common consent. This, indeed, I confess. For therefore also certain hours are fixed and prescribed, though indifferent with God, yet necessary to the customs of men, that the benefit of all may be regarded, and all the affairs of the Church be administered, according to the direction of Paul, "decently and in order." But this by no means prevents it from being the duty of every Church often to stimulate themselves to a greater frequency of prayer, and also to be inflamed with more ardent devotion on the pressure of any necessity unusually great. But the place to speak of perseverance, which is nearly allied to unceasing diligence, will be towards the end. Moreover these things afford no encouragement to those vain repetitions which Christ has chosen to interdict us; for he does not forbid us to pray long or frequently, or with great fervour of affection; but he forbids us to confide in our ability to extort any thing from God by stunning his ears with garrulous loquacity, as though he were to be influenced by the arts of human persuasion. For we know that hypocrites, who do not consider that they are concerned with God, are as pompous in their prayers as in a triumph. For that Pharisee, who thanked God that he was not like other men, undoubtedly flattered himself in the eyes of men, as if he wished to gain by his prayer the reputation of sanctity. Hence that βαττολογια (*vain repetition*) which from a similar cause at present prevails among the Papists; while some vainly consume the time by reiterating the same oraisons, and others recommend themselves among the vulgar by a tedious accumulation of words. Since this garrulity is a puerile mocking of God, we need not wonder that it is prohibited in the Church, that nothing may be heard there but what is serious, and proceeds from the very heart. Very similar to this corrupt practice is another, which Christ condemns at the same time; that hypocrites, for the sake of ostentation, seek after many witnesses of their devotions, and rather pray in the market-place, than that their prayers should want the applause of the world. But as it has been already observed that the end of prayer is to elevate our minds towards God, both in a confession of his praise and in a supplication of his aid, we may learn from this that its principal place is in the mind and heart; or, rather, that prayer itself is the desire of the inmost heart, which is poured out and laid before God the searcher of hearts. Wherefore our heavenly Teacher, as has already been mentioned, when he intended to deliver the best rule respecting prayer, gave the following command: "Enter into thy closet, and when thou hast shut thy door, pray to thy Father which is in secret; and thy Father which seeth in secret shall reward thee openly." For when he has dissuaded from imitating the example of hypocrites, who endeavoured by the ambitious ostentation of their prayers to gain the favour of men, he immediately adds a better direction, which is, to enter into our closet, and there to pray with the door shut. In which words, as I understand them, he has taught us to seek retirement, that we may be enabled to descend into our own hearts, with all our powers of reflection, and promised us that God, whose temples our bodies ought to be, will accede to the desires of our souls. For he did not intend to deny the expediency of praying also in other places; but shows that prayer is a kind of secret thing, which lies principally in the heart, and requires a tranquillity of mind undisturbed by all cares. It was not without reason, therefore, that the Lord himself, when he would engage in an unusual vehemence of devotion, retired to some solitary place, far from the tumult of men; but with a view to admonish us by his own example, that we ought not to neglect these helps, by which our hearts, naturally too inconstant, are more intensely fixed on the devotional exercise. But notwithstanding, as he did not refrain from praying even in the midst of a multitude, if at any time the occasion required it, so we, in all places where it may be necessary, should "lift up holy hands." And so it is to be concluded, that whoever refuses to pray in the solemn assembly of the saints, knows nothing of private prayer, either solitary or domestic. And again, that he who neglects solitary and private prayer, how sedulously soever he may frequent the public assemblies, only forms there such as are mere wind, because he pays more deference to the opinion of men than to the secret judgment of God. In the mean time, that the common prayers of the Church might not sink into contempt, God anciently distinguished them by splendid titles, especially when he called the temple a "house of prayer." For by this expression he taught both that the duty of prayer is a principal part of his worship, and that the temple had been erected as a standard for believers, in order that they might engage in it with one consent. There was also added a remarkable promise: "Praise waiteth for thee, O God, in Sion; and unto thee shall the vow be performed;" in which words the Psalmist informs us that the prayers of the Church are never in vain, because the Lord supplies his people with perpetual matter of praise and joy. But though the legal shadows have ceased, yet since it has been the Divine will by this ceremony to maintain a unity of faith among us also, the same promise undoubtedly belongs to us, Christ having confirmed it with his own mouth, and Paul having represented it as perpetually valid.

XXX. Now, as God in his word commands believers to unite in common prayers, so also it is necessary that public temples be appointed for performing them; where they who refuse to join with the people of God in their devotions, have no just reason for abusing this pretext, that they enter into their closets, in obedience to the Divine mandate. For he who promises to grant whatever shall be implored by two or three persons convened in his name, proves that he is far from despising prayers offered in public; provided they be free from ostentation and a desire of human applause, and accompanied with a sincere and real affection dwelling in the secret recesses of the heart. If this be the legitimate use of temples, as it certainly is, there is need of great caution, lest we either consider them as the proper habitations of the Deity, where he may be nearer to us to hear our prayers,—an idea which has begun to be prevalent for several ages,—or ascribe to them I know not what mysterious sanctity, which might be supposed to render our devotions more holy in the Divine view. For since we are ourselves the true temples of God, we must pray within ourselves, if we wish to invoke him in his holy temple. But let us, who are directed to worship the Lord "in spirit and in truth," without any difference of place, relinquish those gross ideas of religion to the Jews or pagans. There was, indeed, anciently a temple dedicated, by Divine command, to the oblation of prayers and sacrifices: at that time the truth was figuratively concealed under such shadows; but now, having been plainly discovered to us, it no longer permits an exclusive attachment to any material temple. Nor, indeed, was the temple recommended to the Jews that they might enclose the Divine presence within its walls, but that they might be employed in contemplating a representation of the true temple. Therefore Isaiah and Stephen have sharply reprehended those who suppose that God dwells in any respect "in temples made with hands."

XXXI. Hence it is moreover clearly evident, that neither voice nor singing, if used in prayer, has any validity, or produces the least benefit with God, unless it proceed from the inmost desire of the heart. But they rather provoke his wrath against us, if they be only emitted from the lips and throat; since that is an abuse of his sacred name, and a derision of his majesty; as we conclude from the words of Isaiah, which, though their meaning be more extensive, contain also a reproof of this offence: "The Lord said, Forasmuch as this people draw near me with their mouth, and with their lips do honour me, but have removed their heart far from me, and their fear toward me is taught by the precept of men,—therefore, behold, I will proceed to do a marvellous work among this people, even a marvellous work and a wonder; for the wisdom of their wise men shall perish, and the understanding of their prudent men shall be hid." Nor do we here condemn the use of the voice, or singing, but rather highly recommend them, provided they accompany the affection of the heart. For they exercise the mind in Divine meditation, and fix the attention of the heart; which by its lubricity and versatility is easily relaxed and distracted to a variety of objects, unless it be supported by various helps. Besides, as the glory of God ought in some respect to be manifested in every part of our bodies, to this service, both in singing and in speaking, it becomes us especially to addict and devote our tongues, which were created for the express purpose of declaring and celebrating the Divine praises. Nevertheless the principal use of the tongue is in the public prayers which are made in the congregations of believers; the design of which is, that with one common voice, and as it were with the same mouth, we may all at once proclaim the glory of God, whom we worship in one spirit and with the same faith; and this is publicly done, that all interchangeably, each one of his brother, may receive the confession of faith, and be invited and stimulated by his example.

XXXII. Now, the custom of singing in churches (to speak of it by the way) not only appears to be very ancient, but that it was even used by the apostles, may be concluded from these words of Paul: "I will sing with the spirit, and I will sing with the understanding also." Again, to the Colossians: "Teaching and admonishing one another in psalms, and hymns, and spiritual songs, singing with grace in your hearts to the Lord." For in the former passage he inculcates singing with the voice and with the heart; and in the latter he recommends spiritual songs, which may conduce to the mutual edification of the saints. Yet that it was not universal is proved by Augustine, who relates that in the time of Ambrose, the church at Milan first adopted the practice of singing, when, during the persecution of the orthodox faith by Justina, the mother of Valentinian, the people were unusually assiduous in their vigils; and that the other Western churches followed. For he had just before mentioned that this custom had been derived from the churches of the East. He signifies also, in the second book of his Retractations, that in his time it was received in Africa. "One Hilary, (says he,) who held the tribunitial office, took every opportunity of loading with malicious censures the custom which was then introduced at Carthage, that hymns from the Book of Psalms should be sung at the altar, either before the oblation, or while that which had been offered was distributed to the people. In obedience to the commands of my brethren, I answered him." And certainly if singing be attempered to that gravity which becomes the presence of God and of angels, it adds a dignity and grace to sacred actions, and is very efficacious in exciting the mind to a true concern and ardour of devotion. Yet great caution is necessary, that the ears be not more attentive to the modulation of the notes, than the mind to the spiritual import of the words. With which danger Augustine confesses himself to have been so affected, as sometimes to have wished for the observance of the custom instituted by Athanasius, who directed that the reader should sound the words with such a gentle inflection of voice, as would be more nearly allied to rehearsing than to singing. But when he recollected the great benefit which himself had received from singing, he inclined to the other side. With the observance, therefore, of this limitation, it is without doubt an institution of great solemnity and usefulness. As, on the reverse, whatever music is composed only to please and delight the ear, is unbecoming the majesty of the Church, and cannot but be highly displeasing to God.

XXXIII. Hence also it plainly appears, that public prayers are to be composed, not in Greek among the Latins, nor in Latin among the French or English, as has hitherto been universally practised; but in the vernacular tongue, which may be generally understood by the whole congregation; for it ought to be conducted to the edification of the whole Church, to whom not the least benefit can result from sounds which they do not understand. But they who disregard the voice both of charity and of humanity, ought at least to discover some little respect for the authority of Paul, whose words are free from all ambiguity: "When thou shalt bless with the Spirit, how shall he that occupieth the room of the unlearned say Amen at thy giving of thanks, seeing he understandeth not what thou sayest? For thou verily givest thanks well, but the other is not edified." Who, then, can sufficiently wonder at the unbridled license of the Papists, who, notwithstanding this apostolic caution against it, are not afraid to bellow their verbose prayers in a foreign language, of which they neither sometimes understand a syllable themselves, nor wish a syllable to be understood by others! But Paul directs to a different practice: "What is it then? (says he) I will pray with the spirit, and I will pray with the understanding also: I will sing with the spirit, and I will sing with the understanding also." Signifying by the word *spirit* the peculiar gift of tongues, which was abused by some of its possessors, when they separated it from understanding. Thus it must be fully admitted, that both in public and in private prayer, the tongue, unaccompanied by the heart, cannot but be highly displeasing to God; and likewise that the mind ought to be incited, in the ardour of meditation, to rise to a much higher elevation than can ever be attained by the expression of the tongue; lastly, that the tongue is indeed not necessary to private prayer, any further than as the mind is insufficient to arouse itself, or as the vehemence of its emotions irresistibly carries the tongue along with them. For though some of the best prayers are not vocal, yet it is very common, under strong emotions, for the tongue to break forth into sounds, and the other members into gestures, without the least ostentation. Hence the uncertain muttering of Hannah, somewhat similar to which is experienced by the saints in all ages, when they break forth into abrupt and imperfect sounds. The corporeal gestures usually observed in prayer, such as kneeling and uncovering the head, are customs designed to increase our reverence of God.

XXXIV. Now, we must learn not only a certain rule, but also the form of praying; even that which our heavenly Father has given us by his beloved Son; in which we may recognize his infinite goodness and clemency. For beside advising and exhorting us to seek him in all our necessities, as children, whenever they are afflicted with any distress, are accustomed to have recourse to the protection of their parents; seeing that we did not sufficiently perceive how great was our poverty, what it was right to implore, or what would be suitable to our condition, he has provided a remedy even for this our ignorance, and abundantly supplied the deficiencies of our capacity. For he has prescribed for us a form, in which he gives a statement of all that it is lawful to desire of him, all that is conducive to our benefit, and all that it is necessary to ask. From this kindness of his, we derive great consolation in the persuasion that we pray for nothing absurd, nothing injurious or unseasonable; in a word, nothing but what is agreeable to him; since our petitions are almost in his own words. Plato, observing the ignorance of men in presenting their supplications to God, which if granted were frequently very detrimental to them, pronounces this to be the best method of praying, borrowed from an ancient poet: "King Jupiter, give us those things which are best, whether we pray for them or not; but command evil things to remain at a distance from us, even though we implore them." And indeed the wisdom of that heathen is conspicuous in this instance, since he considers it as very dangerous to supplicate the Lord to gratify all the dictates of our appetites; and at the same time discovers our infelicity, who cannot, without danger, even open our mouths in the presence of God, unless we be instructed by the Spirit in the right rule of prayer. And this privilege deserves to be the more highly valued by us, since the only begotten Son of God puts words into our mouths, which may deliver our minds from all hesitation.

XXXV. This form or rule of prayer, whichever appellation be given to it, is composed of six petitions. For my reason for not agreeing with those who divide it into seven parts is, that the Evangelist appears, by the insertion of the adversative conjunction, to connect together these two clauses; as though he had said, Suffer us not to be oppressed with temptation, but rather succour our weakness, and deliver us, that we may not fall. The ancient writers of the Church also are of our opinion; so that what is now added in Matthew in the seventh place, must be explained as belonging to the sixth petition. Now, though the whole prayer is such, that in every part of it the principal regard must be paid to the glory of God, yet to this the first three petitions are particularly devoted, and to this alone we ought to attend in them, without any consideration of our own interest. The remaining three concern ourselves, and are expressly assigned to supplications for those things which tend to our benefit. As when we pray that God's name may be hallowed, since he chooses to prove whether our love and worship of him be voluntary, or dictated by mercenary motives, we must then think nothing of our own interest, but his glory must be proposed as the only object of our fixed attention; nor is it lawful for us to be differently affected in the other petitions of this class. And this indeed conduces to our great benefit; because, when the Divine name is hallowed or sanctified as we pray, it becomes likewise our sanctification. But our eyes should overlook, and be, as it were, blind to such advantage, so as not to pay the least regard to it. And even if we were deprived of all hope of private benefit, yet this hallowing, and the other things which pertain to the glory of God, ought still to be the objects of our desires and of our prayers. This is conspicuous in the examples of Moses and Paul, who felt a pleasure in averting their minds and eyes from themselves, and in praying with vehement and ardent zeal for their own destruction, that they might promote the kingdom and glory of God even at the expense of their own happiness. On the other hand, when we pray that our daily bread may be given us, although we wish for what is beneficial to ourselves, yet here also we ought principally to aim at the glory of God, so as not even to ask it, unless it tend to his glory. Now, let us attempt an explanation of the prayer itself.

XXXVI. Our Father, who art in heaven, &c. The first idea that occurs is, what we have before asserted, that we ought never to present a prayer to God but in the name of Christ, since no other name can recommend it to his regard. For by calling God our Father, we certainly plead the name of Christ. For with what confidence could any one call God his Father? who could proceed to such a degree of temerity, as to arrogate to himself the dignity of a son of God, if we had not been adopted as the children of his grace in Christ? who, being his true Son, has been given by him to us as our brother, that the character which properly belongs to him by nature, may become ours by the blessing of adoption, if we receive this inestimable favour with a steady faith; as John says, that to them is given "power to become the sons of God, even to them that believe on the name of the only begotten of the Father." Therefore he denominates himself our Father, and wishes us to give him the same appellation; delivering us from all diffidence by the great sweetness of this name, since the affection of love can nowhere be found in a stronger degree than in the heart of a father. Therefore he could not give us a more certain proof of his infinite love towards us, than by our being denominated the sons of God. But his love to us is as much greater and more excellent than all the love of our parents, as he is superior to all men in goodness and mercy; so that though all the fathers in the world, divested of every emotion of paternal affection, should leave their children destitute, he will never forsake us, because "he cannot deny himself." For we have his promise, "If ye, then, being evil, know how to give good gifts unto your children, how much more shall your Father which is in heaven?" Again, in the prophet: "Can a woman forget her child? Yea, they may forget, yet will I not forget thee." But if we are his sons, then, as a son cannot commit himself to the protection of a stranger and an alien, without at the same time complaining of the cruelty or poverty of his father, so neither can we seek supplies for our wants from any other quarter than from him, without charging him with indigence and inability, or with cruelty and excessive austerity.

XXXVII. Neither let us plead that we are justly terrified by a consciousness of our sins, which may cause even a merciful, kind Father to be daily offended with us. For if, among men, a son can conduct his cause with his father by no better advocate, can conciliate and recover his lost favour by no better mediator, than by approaching him as an humble suppliant, acknowledging his own guilt, and imploring his father's mercy, (for the bowels of a father could not conceal their emotions at such supplications,) what will he do, who is "the Father of mercies, and the God of all comfort?" Will he not hear the cries and groans of his children when they deprecate his displeasure for themselves, especially since it is to this that he invites and exhorts us; rather than attend to any intercessions of others, to which they resort in great consternation, not without some degree of despair, arising from a doubt of the kindness and clemency of their Father? Of this exuberance of paternal kindness, he gives us a beautiful representation in a parable; where a father meets and embraces a son who had alienated himself from his family, who had dissolutely lavished his substance, who had grievously offended him in every respect: nor does he wait till he actually supplicates for pardon, but anticipates him, recognizes him when returning at a great distance, voluntarily runs to meet him, consoles him, and receives him into favour. For by proposing to our view an example of such great kindness in a man, he intended to teach us how much more abundant compassion we ought, notwithstanding our ingratitude, rebellion, and wickedness, to expect from him, who is not only our Father, but the most benevolent and merciful of all fathers, provided we only cast ourselves on his mercy. And to give us the more certain assurance that he is such a Father, if we be Christians, he will be called not only "Father," but expressly "Our Father;" as though we might address him in the following manner: O Father, whose affection towards thy children is so strong, and whose readiness to pardon them is so great, we thy children invoke thee and pray to thee, under the assurance and full persuasion that thou hast no other than a paternal affection towards us, how unworthy soever we are of such a Father. But because the contracted capacities of our minds cannot conceive of a favour of such immense magnitude, we not only have Christ as the pledge and earnest of adoption, but as a witness of this adoption he gives us the Spirit, by whom we are enabled with a loud voice freely to cry, "Abba, Father." Whenever, therefore, we may be embarrassed by any difficulty, let us remember to supplicate him, that he will correct our timidity, and give us this spirit of magnanimity to enable us to pray with boldness.

XXXVIII. But since we are not instructed, that every individual should appropriate him to himself exclusively as his Father, but rather that we should all in common call him Our Father, we are thereby admonished how strong a fraternal affection ought to prevail among us, who, by the same privilege of mercy and free grace, are equally the children of such a Father. For if we all have one common Father, from whom proceeds every blessing we enjoy, there ought to be nothing exclusively appropriated by any among us, but what we should be ready to communicate to each other with the greatest alacrity of heart, whenever necessity requires. Now, if we desire, as we ought, to exert ourselves for our mutual assistance, there is nothing in which we can better promote the interests of our brethren, than by commending them to the providential care of our most benevolent Father, with whose mercy and favour no other want can be experienced. And, indeed, this is a debt which we owe to our Father himself. For as he who truly and cordially loves any father of a family, feels likewise a love and friendship for his whole household, in the same manner, our zeal and affection towards this heavenly Father must be shown towards his people, his family, his inheritance, whom he has dignified with the honourable appellation of the "fulness" of his only begotten Son. Let a Christian, then, regulate his prayers by this rule, that they be common, and comprehend all who are his brethren in Christ; and not only those whom he at present sees and knows to be such, but all men in the world; respecting whom, what God has determined is beyond our knowledge; only that to wish and hope the best concerning them, is equally the dictate of piety and of humanity. It becomes us, however, to exercise a peculiar and superior affection "unto them who are of the household of faith;" whom the apostle has in every case recommended to our particular regards. In a word, all our prayers ought to be such, as to respect that community which our Lord has established in his kingdom and in his family.

XXXIX. Yet this is no objection to the lawfulness of particular prayers, both for ourselves and for other certain individuals; provided our minds be not withdrawn from a regard to this community, nor even diverted from it, but refer every thing to this point. For though the words of them be singular, yet as they are directed to this end, they cease not to be common. All this may be rendered very intelligible by a similitude. God has given a general command to relieve the wants of all the poor; and yet this is obeyed by them who to that end succour the indigence of those whom they either know or see to be labouring under poverty; even though they pass by multitudes who are oppressed with necessities equally severe, because neither their knowledge nor ability can extend to all. In the same manner, no opposition is made to the Divine will by them who, regarding and considering this common society of the Church, present such particular prayers, in which, with a public spirit, but in particular terms, they recommend to God themselves or others, whose necessity he has placed within their more immediate knowledge. However, there is not a perfect similarity in every respect between prayer and donation of alms, for munificence cannot be exercised but towards them whose wants we have perceived; but we may assist by our prayers even the greatest strangers, and those with whom we are the most unacquainted, how distant soever they may be from us. This is done by that general form of prayer, which comprehends all the children of God, among whom they also are numbered. To this may be referred the exhortation which Paul gives believers of his age, "that men pray every where, lifting up holy hands without wrath;" because by admonishing them, that discord shuts the gate against prayers, he advises them unanimously to unite all their petitions together.

XL. It is added, That he is in heaven. From which it is not hastily to be inferred, that he is included and circumscribed within the circumference of heaven, as by certain barriers. For Solomon confesses, that "the heaven of heavens cannot contain" him. And he says himself, by the prophet, "The heaven is my throne, and the earth is my footstool." By which he clearly signifies that he is not limited to any particular region, but diffused throughout all space. But because the dulness of our minds could not otherwise conceive of his ineffable glory, it is designated to us by the heaven, than which we can behold nothing more august or more majestic. Since, then, wherever our senses apprehend any thing, there they are accustomed to fix it, God is represented as beyond all place, that when we seek him we may be elevated above all reach of both body and soul. Moreover, by this form of expression, he is exalted above all possibility of corruption or mutation: finally, it is signified, that he comprehends and contains the whole world, and governs the universe by his power. Wherefore, this is the same as if he had been said to be possessed of an incomprehensible essence, infinite magnitude or sublimity, irresistible power, and unlimited immortality. But when we hear this, our thoughts must be raised to a higher elevation when God is mentioned; that we may not entertain any terrestrial or carnal imaginations concerning him, that we may not measure him by our diminutive proportions, or judge of his will by our affections. We should likewise be encouraged to place the most implicit reliance on him, by whose providence and power we understand both heaven and earth to be governed. To conclude: under the name of "Our Father" is represented to us, that God who has appeared to us in his own image, that we might call upon him with a steady faith; and the familiar appellation of Father is not only adapted to produce confidence, but also efficacious to prevent our minds from being seduced to dubious or fictitious deities, and to cause them to ascend from the only begotten Son to the common Father of angels and of saints; moreover, when his throne is placed in heaven, we are reminded by his government of the world, that it is not in vain for us to approach to him who makes us the objects of his present and voluntary care. "He that cometh to God (says the apostle) must believe that he is, and that he is a rewarder of them that diligently seek him." Christ asserts both these of his Father, that we may have first a firm faith in his existence, and then a certain persuasion that, since he deigns to extend his providence to us, he will not neglect our salvation. By these principles, Paul prepares us for praying in right manner; for his exhortation, "Let your requests be made known unto God," is thus prefaced: "The Lord is at hand. Be careful for nothing." Whence it appears, that their prayers must be attended with great doubt and perplexity of mind, who are not well established in this truth, that "the eyes of the Lord are upon the righteous."

XLI. The first petition is, That God's name may be hallowed; the necessity of which is connected with our great disgrace. For what is more shameful, than that the Divine glory should be obscured partly by our ingratitude, partly by our malignity, and, as far as possible, obliterated by our presumption, infatuation, and perverseness? Notwithstanding all the sacrilegious rage and clamours of the impious, yet the refulgence of holiness still adorns the Divine name. Nor does the Psalmist without reason exclaim, "According to thy name, O God, so is thy praise unto the ends of the earth." For wherever God may be known, there must necessarily be a manifestation of his perfections of power, goodness, wisdom, righteousness, mercy, and truth, which command our admiration and excite us to celebrate his praise. Therefore, because God is so unjustly robbed of his holiness on earth, if it is not in our power to assert it for him, we are at least commanded to regard it in our prayers. The substance of it is, that we wish God to receive all the honour that he deserves, that men may never speak or think of him but with the highest reverence; to which is opposed that profanation, which has always been too common in the world, as it continues to be in the present age. And hence the necessity of this petition, which, if we were influenced by only a tolerable degree of piety, ought to be superfluous. But if the name of God be truly hallowed, when separated from all others it breathes pure glory, we are here commanded to pray, not only that God will vindicate his holy name from all contempt and ignominy, but also that he will constrain all mankind to revere it. Now, as God manifests himself to us partly by his word, and partly by his works, he is no otherwise hallowed by us, than if we attribute to him in both instances that which belongs to him, and so receive whatever proceeds from him; ascribing, moreover, equal praise to his severity and to his clemency; since on the multiplicity and variety of his works he has impressed characters of his glory, which should draw from every tongue a confession of his praise. Thus will the Scripture obtain a just authority with us, nor will any event obstruct the benedictions which God deserves in the whole course of his government of the world. The tendency of the petition is, further, that all impiety which sullies this holy name, may be utterly abolished; that whatever obscures or diminishes this hallowing, whether detraction or derision, may disappear; and that while God restrains all sacrilege, his majesty may shine with increasing splendour.

XLII. The second petition is, That the kingdom of God may come; which, though it contains nothing new, is yet not without reason distinguished from the first; because, if we consider our inattention in the most important of all concerns, it is useful for that which ought of itself to have been most intimately known to us, to be inculcated in a variety of words. Therefore, after we have been commanded to pray to God to subdue, and at length utterly to destroy, every thing that sullies his holy name, there is now added another petition, similar and almost identically the same—That his kingdom may come. Now, though we have already given a definition of this kingdom, I now briefly repeat, that God reigns when men, renouncing themselves and despising the world and the present state, submit themselves to his righteousness, so as to aspire to the heavenly state. Thus this kingdom consists of two parts; the one, God's correcting by the power of his Spirit all our carnal and depraved appetites, which oppose him in great numbers; the other, his forming all our powers to an obedience to his commands. No others therefore observe a proper order in this petition, but they who begin from themselves, that is, that they may be purified from all corruptions which disturb the tranquillity, or violate the purity, of God's kingdom. Now, since the Divine word resembles a royal sceptre, we are commanded to pray that he will subdue the hearts and minds of all men to a voluntary obedience to it. This is accomplished, when, by the secret inspiration of his Spirit, he displays the efficacy of his word, and causes it to obtain the honour it deserves. Afterwards, it is our duty to descend to the impious, by whom his authority is resisted with the perseverance of obstinacy and the fury of despair. God therefore erects his kingdom on the humiliation of the whole world, though his methods of humiliation are various; for he restrains the passions of some, and breaks the unsubdued arrogance of others. It ought to be the object of our daily wishes, that God would collect churches for himself from all the countries of the earth, that he would enlarge their numbers, enrich them with gifts, and establish a legitimate order among them; that, on the contrary, he would overthrow all the enemies of the pure doctrine and religion, that he would confound their counsels, and defeat their attempts. Whence it appears that the desire of a daily progress is not enjoined us in vain; because human affairs are never in such a happy situation, as that all defilement of sin is removed, and purity can be seen in full perfection. This perfection is deferred till the last advent of Christ, when, the apostle says, "God will be all in all." And so this petition ought to withdraw us from all the corruptions of the world, which separate us from God, and prevent his kingdom from flourishing within us; it ought likewise to inflame us with an ardent desire of mortifying the flesh, and finally to teach us to bear the cross; since these are the means which God chooses for the extension of his kingdom. Nor should we be impatient that the outward man is destroyed, provided the inward man be renewed. For this is the order of the kingdom of God, that, when we submit to his righteousness, he makes us partakers of his glory. This is accomplished, when, discovering his light and truth with perpetual accession of splendour, before which the shades and falsehoods of Satan and of his kingdom vanish and become extinct, he by the aids of his Spirit directs his children into the path of rectitude, and strengthens them to perseverance; but defeats the impious conspiracies of his enemies, confounds their insidious and fraudulent designs, disappoints their malice, and represses their obstinacy, till at length "he" will "consume" Antichrist "with the spirit of his mouth, and destroy" all impiety "with the brightness of his coming."

XLIII. The third petition is, That the will of God may be done on earth as it is in heaven; which, though it is an appendage to his kingdom, and cannot be disjoined from it, is yet not without reason separately mentioned, on account of our ignorance, which does not apprehend with facility what it is for God to reign in the world. There will be nothing absurd, then, in understanding this as an explanation, that God's kingdom will then prevail in the world, when all shall submit to his will. Now, we speak not here of his secret will, by which he governs all things, and appoints them to fulfil his own purposes. For though Satan and men oppose him with all the violence of rage, yet his incomprehensible wisdom is able, not only to divert their impetuosity, but to overrule it for the accomplishment of his decrees. But the Divine will here intended, is that to which voluntary obedience corresponds; and therefore heaven is expressly compared with the earth, because the angels, as the Psalmist says, spontaneously "do his commandments, hearkening unto the voice of his word." We are therefore commanded to desire that, as in heaven nothing is done but according to the Divine will, and the angels are placidly conformed to every thing that is right, so the earth, all obstinacy and depravity being annihilated, may be subject to the same government. And in praying for this, we renounce our own carnal desires; because, unless we resign all our affections to God, we are guilty of all the opposition in our power to his will, for nothing proceeds from us but what is sinful. And we are likewise habituated by this petition to a renunciation of ourselves, that God may rule us according to his own pleasure; and not only so, but that he may also create in us new minds and new hearts, annihilating our own, that we may experience no emotion of desire within us, but a mere consent to his will; in a word, that we may have no will of our own, but that our hearts may be governed by his Spirit, by whose internal teachings we may learn to love those things which please him, and to hate those which he disapproves; consequently, that he may render abortive all those desires which are repugnant to his will. These are the three first clauses of this prayer, in praying which we ought solely to have in view the glory of God, omitting all consideration of ourselves, and not regarding any advantage of our own, which, though they largely contribute to it, should not be our end in these petitions. But though all these things, even if we never think of them, nor wish for them, nor request them, must nevertheless happen in their appointed time, yet they ought to be the objects of our wishes, and the subjects of our prayers. And such petitions it will be highly proper for us to offer, that we may testify and profess ourselves to be the servants and sons of God; manifesting the sincerest devotedness, and making the most zealous efforts in our power for advancing the honour which is due to him, both as a Master and as a Father. Persons, therefore, who are not incited, by this ardent zeal for promoting the glory of God, to pray, that his name may be hallowed, that his kingdom may come, and that his will may be done, are not to be numbered among his sons and servants; and as all these things will be accomplished in opposition to their inclinations, so they will contribute to their confusion and destruction.

XLIV. Next follows the second part of the prayer, in which we descend to our own interests; not that we must dismiss all thoughts of the Divine glory, (which, according to Paul, should be regarded even in eating and drinking,) and only seek what is advantageous to ourselves; but we have already announced that this is the distinction—that God, by exclusively claiming three petitions, absorbs us entirely in the consideration of himself, that thus he may prove our piety; afterwards he permits us to attend to our own interests, yet on this condition, that the end of all our requests be the illustration of his glory, by whatever benefits he confers on us, since nothing is more reasonable than that we live and die to him. But the first petition of the second part, Give us this day our daily bread, is a general request to God for a supply of all our corporeal wants in the present state, not only for food and clothing, but also for every thing which he sees to be conducive to our good, that we may eat our bread in peace. By this we briefly surrender ourselves to his care, and commit ourselves to his providence, that he may feed, nourish, and preserve us. For our most benevolent Father disdains not to receive even our body into his charge and protection, that he may exercise our faith in these minute circumstances, while we expect every thing from him, even down to a crumb of bread and a drop of water. For since it is a strange effect of our iniquity, to be affected and distressed with greater solicitude for the body than for the soul, many, who venture to confide to God the interests of their souls, are nevertheless still solicitous concerning the body, still anxious what they shall eat and what they shall wear; and unless they have an abundance of corn, wine, and oil, for the supply of their future wants, tremble with fear. Of so much greater importance to us is the shadow of this transitory life, than that eternal immortality. But they who, confiding in God, have once cast off that anxiety for the concerns of the body, expect likewise to receive from him superior blessings, even salvation and eternal life. It is therefore no trivial exercise of faith, to expect from God those things which otherwise fill us with so much anxiety; nor is it a small proficiency when we have divested ourselves of this infidelity, which is almost universally interwoven with the human constitution. The speculations of some, concerning supernatural bread, appear to me not very consonant to the meaning of Christ; for if we did not ascribe to God the character of our Supporter even in this transitory life, our prayer would be defective. The reason which they allege has too much profanity; that it is unbecoming for the children of God, who ought to be spiritual, not only to devote their own attention to terrestrial cares, but also to involve God in the same anxieties with themselves; as though, truly, his benediction and paternal favour were not conspicuous even in our sustenance; or there were no meaning in the assertion, that "godliness hath promise of the life that now is, and of that which is to come." Now, though remission of sins is of much greater value than corporeal aliments, yet Christ has given the first place to the inferior blessing, that he might gradually raise us to the two remaining petitions, which properly pertain to the heavenly life; in which he has consulted our dulness. We are commanded to ask "our bread," that we may be content with the portion which our heavenly Father deigns to allot us, nor practise any illicit arts for the love of lucre. In the mean time, it must be understood that it becomes ours by a title of donation; because neither our industry, nor our labour, nor our hands, as is observed by Moses, acquire any thing for us of themselves, when unattended by the Divine blessing; and that even an abundance of bread would not be of the least service to us, unless it were by the Divine power converted into nourishment. And therefore this liberality of God is equally as necessary to the rich as to the poor; for though their barns and cellars were full, they would faint with hunger and thirst, unless through his goodness they enjoyed their food. The expression "this day," or "day by day," as it is in the other Evangelist, and the epithet *daily*, restrain the inordinate desire of transitory things, with which we are often violently inflamed, and which leads to other evils; since if we have a greater abundance, we fondly lavish it away in pleasure, delights, ostentation, and other kinds of luxury. Therefore we are enjoined to ask only as much as will supply our necessity, and as it were for the present day, with this confidence, that our heavenly Father, after having fed us to-day, will not fail us to-morrow. Whatever affluence, then, we possess, even when our barns and cellars are full, yet it behoves us always to ask for our daily bread; because it must be considered as an undeniable truth, that all property is nothing, any further than the Lord, by the effusions of his favour, blesses it with continual improvement; and that even what we have in our possession is not our own, any further than as he hourly bestows on us some portion of it, and grants us the use of it. Since the pride of man does not easily suffer itself to be convinced of this, the Lord declares that he has given to all ages an eminent proof of it, by feeding his people with manna in the desert, in order to apprize us "that man doth not live by bread only, but by every word that proceedeth out of his mouth;" which implies, that it is his power alone by which our life and strength are sustained, although he communicates it to us by corporeal means; as he is accustomed to teach us likewise by an opposite example, when he breaks, at his pleasure, the strength (and, as he himself calls it, "the staff") of bread, so that though men eat they pine with hunger, and though they drink are parched with thirst. Now, they who are not satisfied with daily bread, but whose avidity is insatiable, and whose desires are unbounded, and they who are satiated with their abundance, and think themselves secure amid their immense riches, and who nevertheless supplicate the Divine Being in this petition, are guilty of mocking him. For the former ask what they would not wish to obtain, and even what most of all they abominate, that is, daily bread only; they conceal from God, as much as they can, their avaricious disposition; whereas true prayer ought to pour out before him the whole mind, and all the inmost secrets of the soul; and the latter implore what they are far from expecting to receive from him, what they think they have in their own possession. In its being called "ours," the Divine goodness is, as we have observed, the more conspicuous, since it makes that *ours*, to which we have no claim of right. Yet we must not reject the explanation which I have likewise hinted at, that it intends also such as is acquired by just and innocent labour, and not procured by acts of deception and rapine; because, whatever we acquire by any criminal methods, is never our own, but belongs to others. Our praying that it may be "given" to us signifies that it is the simple and gratuitous donation of God, from what quarter soever we receive it; even when it most of all appears to be obtained by our own skill and industry, and to be procured by our own hands; since it is solely the effect of his blessing, that our labours are attended with success.

XLV. It follows—Forgive us our debts; in which petition, and the next, Christ has comprised whatever relates to the heavenly life; as in these two parts consists the spiritual covenant which God has made for the salvation of his Church—"I will write my law in their hearts, and will pardon their iniquities." Here Christ begins with remission of sins: immediately after, he subjoins a second favour—that God would defend us by the power, and support us by the aid, of his Spirit, to enable us to stand unconquered against all temptations. Sins he calls debts, because we owe the penalty of them—a debt we are altogether incapable of discharging, unless we are released by this remission, which is a pardon flowing from his gratuitous mercy, when he freely cancels these debts without any payment from us, being satisfied by his own mercy in Christ, who has once given himself for our redemption. Those, therefore, who rely on God's being satisfied with their own merits, or the merits of others, and persuade themselves that remission of sins is purchased by these satisfactions, have no interest in this gratuitous forgiveness; and while they call upon God in this form, they are only subscribing their own accusation, and even sealing their condemnation with their own testimony. For they confess themselves debtors, unless they are discharged by the benefit of remission, which nevertheless they accept not, but rather refuse, while they obtrude upon God their own merits and satisfactions. For in this way they do not implore his mercy, but appeal to his judgment. They who amuse themselves with dreams of perfection, superseding the necessity of praying for pardon, may have disciples whom itching ears lead into delusions; but it must be clear that all whom they gain are perverted from Christ, since he teaches all to confess their guilt, and receives none but sinners; not that he would flatter and encourage sins, but because he knew that believers are never wholly free from the vices of their flesh, but always remain obnoxious to the judgment of God. It ought, indeed, to be the object of our desires and strenuous exertions, that, having fully discharged every part of our duty, we may truly congratulate ourselves before God on being pure from every stain; but as it pleases God to restore his image within us by degrees, so that some contagion always remains in our flesh, the remedy ought never to be neglected. Now, if Christ, by the authority given him by the Father, enjoins us, as long as we live, to have recourse to prayer for the pardon of guilt, who will tolerate the new teachers, who endeavour to dazzle the eyes of the simple with a visionary phantom of perfect innocence, and fill them with a confidence in the possibility of their being delivered from all sin? which, according to John, is no other than making God a liar. At the same time, also, these worthless men, by obliterating one article, mutilate, and so totally invalidate, the covenant of God, in which we have seen our salvation is contained; being thus guilty not only of sacrilege by separating things so united, but also of impiety and cruelty, by overwhelming miserable souls with despair, and of treachery to themselves and others, by contracting a habit of carelessness, in diametrical opposition to the Divine mercy. The objection of some, that in wishing the advent of God's kingdom, we desire at the same time the abolition of sin, is too puerile; because, in the first part of the prayer, we have an exhibition of the highest perfection, but here of infirmity. Thus these two things are perfectly consistent, that in aspiring towards the mark we may not neglect the remedies required by our necessity. Lastly, we pray that we may be forgiven AS WE FORGIVE OUR DEBTORS; that is, as we forgive and pardon all who have ever injured us, either by unjust actions or by contumelious language. Not that it is our province to forgive the guilt of sin and transgression; this is the prerogative of God alone: our forgiveness consists in divesting the mind of anger, enmity, and desire of revenge, and losing the memory of injuries by a voluntary forgetfulness. Wherefore we must not pray to God for forgiveness of sins, unless we also forgive all the offences and injuries of others against us, either present or past. But if we retain any enmities in our minds, meditate acts of revenge, and seek opportunities of annoyance, and even if we do not endeavour to obtain reconciliation with our enemies, to oblige them by all kind offices, and to render them our friends,—we beseech God, by this petition, not to grant us remission of sins. For we supplicate him to grant to us what we grant to others. This is praying him not to grant it to us, unless we grant it also. What do persons of this description gain by their prayers but a heavier judgment? Lastly, it must be observed, that this is not a condition, that he would forgive us as we forgive our debtors, because we can merit his forgiveness of us by our forgiveness of others, as though it described the cause of his forgiveness; but, by this expression, the Lord intended, partly to comfort the weakness of our faith; for he has added this as a sign, that we may be as certainly assured of remission of sins being granted us by him, as we are certain and conscious of our granting it to others; if, at the same time, our minds be freed and purified from all hatred, envy, and revenge; partly by this, as a criterion, he expunges from the number of his children, those who, hasty to revenge and difficult to forgive, maintain inveterate enmities, and cherish in their own hearts towards others, that indignation which they deprecate from themselves, that they may not presume to invoke him as their Father. Which is also clearly expressed by Luke in Christ's own words.

XLVI. The sixth petition is, Lead us not into temptation, but deliver us from evil. This, as we have said, corresponds to the promise respecting the law of God to be engraven in our hearts. But because our obedience to God is not without continual warfare, and severe and arduous conflicts, we here pray for arms, and assistance to enable us to gain the victory. This suggests to us our necessity, not only of the grace of the Spirit within us to soften, bend, and direct our hearts to obedience to God, but also of his aid to render us invincible, in opposition to all the stratagems and violent assaults of Satan. Now, the forms of temptations are many and various. For the corrupt conceptions of the mind, provoking us to transgressions of the law, whether suggested by our own concupiscence or excited by the devil, are temptations; and things not evil in themselves, nevertheless become temptations through the subtlety of the devil, when they are obtruded on our eyes in such a manner that their intervention occasions our seduction or declension from God. And these temptations are either from prosperous, or from adverse events. From prosperous ones, as riches, power, honours; which generally dazzle men's eyes by their glitter and external appearance of goodness, and insnare them with their blandishments, that, caught with such delusions and intoxicated with such delights, they forget their God. From unpropitious ones, as poverty, reproaches, contempt, afflictions, and other things of this kind; overcome with the bitterness and difficulty of which, they fall into despondency, cast away faith and hope, and at length become altogether alienated from God. To both these kinds of temptations which assail us, whether kindled within us by our concupiscence, or presented to us by the craft of Satan, we pray our heavenly Father not to permit us to yield, but rather to sustain and raise us up with his hand, that, strong in his might, we may be able to stand firm against all the assaults of our malignant enemy, whatever imaginations he may inject into our minds; and also, that whatever is presented to us on either quarter, we may convert it to our benefit; that is, by not being elated with prosperity or dejected with adversity. Yet we do not here pray for an entire exemption from all temptations, which we very much need, to excite, stimulate, and animate us, lest we should grow torpid with too much rest. For it was not without reason that David wished to be tempted or tried; nor is it without cause that the Lord daily tries his elect, chastising them by ignominy, poverty, tribulation, and the cross in various forms. But the temptations of God are widely different from those of Satan. Satan tempts to overthrow, condemn, confound, and destroy. But God, that, by proving his people, he may make a trial of their sincerity, to confirm their strength by exercising it, to mortify, purify, and refine their flesh, which, without such restraints, would run into the greatest excesses. Besides, Satan attacks persons unarmed and unprepared, to overwhelm the unwary. "God, with the temptation, also makes a way to escape, that they may be able to bear" whatever he brings upon them. By the word *evil*, whether we understand the devil or sin, is of little importance. Satan himself, indeed, is the enemy that lies in wait for our life; but sin is the weapon with which he seeks our destruction. Our petition therefore is, that we may not be overwhelmed and conquered by any temptations, but that we may stand, strong in the power of the Lord, against all adverse powers that assault us, which is not to submit to temptations; that being taken into his custody and charge, and being secure in his protection, we may persevere unconquered, and rise superior to sin, death, the gates of hell, and the whole kingdom of the devil. This is being delivered from evil. Here it must also be carefully remarked, that it is not in our power to contend with so powerful an enemy as the devil, and sustain the violence of his assaults. Otherwise it would be useless, or insulting, to supplicate from God what we already possessed in ourselves. Certainly, they who prepare themselves for such a combat with self-confidence, are not sufficiently aware of the skill and prowess of the enemy that they have to meet. Now, we pray to be delivered from his power, as from the mouth of a ravenous and raging lion, just about to tear us with his teeth and claws, and to swallow us down his throat, unless the Lord snatch us from the jaws of death; knowing, at the same time, that if the Lord shall be present and fight for us while we are silent, in his strength "we shall do valiantly." Let others confide as they please in the native abilities and powers of free-will, which they suppose themselves to possess,—let it be sufficient for us, to stand and be strong in the power of God alone. But this petition comprehends more than at first appears. For if the Spirit of God is our strength for fighting the battle with Satan, we shall not be able to gain the victory, till, being full of him, we shall have laid aside all the infirmity of our flesh. When we pray for deliverance from Satan and sin, therefore, we pray to be frequently enriched with new accessions of Divine grace; till, being quite filled with them, we may be able to triumph over all evil. To some there appears a difficulty and harshness in our petition to God, that he will not lead us into temptation, whereas, according to James, it is contrary to his nature for him to tempt us. But this objection has already been partly answered, because our own lust is properly the cause of all the temptations that overcome us, and therefore we are charged with the guilt. Nor does James intend any other than to assert the futility and injustice of transferring to God the vices which we are constrained to impute to ourselves, because we are conscious of our being guilty of them. But notwithstanding this, God may, when he sees fit, deliver us to Satan, abandon us to a reprobate mind and sordid passions, and so lead us into temptations, by a righteous yet often secret judgment; the cause being frequently concealed from man, but, at the same time, well known to him. Whence it is inferred, that there is no impropriety in this mode of expression, if we are persuaded that there is any meaning in his frequent threatenings, that he will manifest his vengeance on the reprobate, by smiting them with blindness and hardness of heart.

XLVII. These three petitions, in which we particularly commend to God ourselves and all our concerns, evidently prove, what we have before asserted, that the prayers of Christians ought to be public, and to regard the public edification of the Church, and the advancement of the communion of believers. For each individual does not supplicate the gift of any favour to himself in particular; but we all in common pray for our bread, the remission of our sins, that we may not be led into temptation, that we may be delivered from evil. The cause is likewise subjoined, which gives us such great boldness in asking, and confidence of obtaining; which, though not to be found in the Latin copies, yet appears too apposite to this place to be omitted—namely, His is the kingdom, and the power, and the glory for ever. This is a solid and secure basis for our faith; for if our prayers were to be recommended to God by our own merit, who could dare to utter a word in his presence? Now, all miserable, unworthy, and destitute as we are of every recommendation, yet we shall never want an argument or plea for our prayers: our confidence can never forsake us; for our Father can never be deprived of his kingdom, power, and glory. The whole is concluded with Amen; which expresses our ardent desire to obtain the blessings supplicated of God, and confirms our hope that all these things are already obtained, and will certainly be granted to us; because they are promised by God, who is incapable of deception. And this agrees with that form of petition already quoted—"Do this, O Lord, for thy name's sake, not for our sake, or for our righteousness;" in which the saints not only express the end of their prayers, but acknowledge that they are unworthy to obtain it, unless God derive the cause from himself, and that their confidence of success arises solely from his nature.

XLVIII. Whatever we ought, or are even at liberty, to seek from God, is stated to us in this model and directory for prayer, given by that best of masters, Christ, whom the Father has set over us as our Teacher, and to whom alone he has enjoined us to listen. For he was always his eternal wisdom, and being made man, was given to men as the Angel of great counsel. And this prayer is so comprehensive and complete, that whatever addition is made of any thing extraneous or foreign, not capable of being referred to it, is impious and unworthy of the approbation of God. For in this summary he has prescribed what is worthy of him, what is acceptable to him, what is necessary for us, and, in a word, what he chooses to bestow. Wherefore those who presume to go beyond it, and to ask of God any thing else, in the first place, are determined to make some addition of their own to the wisdom of God, which cannot be done without folly and blasphemy; in the next place, despising the limits fixed by the will of God, they are led far astray by their own irregular desires; and in the last place, they will never obtain any thing, since they pray without faith. And there is no doubt that all prayers of this kind are made without faith, because they are not sanctioned by the word of God, the only basis on which faith can stand. But they who neglect the Master's rule, and indulge their own desires, not only deviate from the word of God, but make all possible opposition against it. With equal beauty and truth, therefore, Tertullian has called this a *legitimate prayer*, tacitly implying, that all others are irregular and unlawful.

XLIX. We would not here be understood, as if we were confined to this form of prayer, without the liberty of changing a word or syllable. For the Scriptures contain many prayers, expressed in words very different from this, yet written by the same Spirit, and very profitable for our use. Many, which have little verbal resemblance to it, are continually suggested to believers by the same Spirit. We only mean by these observations, that no one should even seek, expect, or ask for any thing that is not summarily comprehended in this prayer, though there may be a diversity of expression, without any variation of sense. As it is certain that all the prayers contained in the

Scriptures, or proceeding from pious hearts, are referred to this, so it is impossible to find one any where which can surpass or even equal the perfection of this. Here is nothing omitted which ought to be recollected for the praises of God, nothing that should occur to the mind of man for his own advantage; and the whole is so complete, as justly to inspire universal despair of attempting any improvement. To conclude; let us remember, that this is the teaching of Divine wisdom, which taught what it willed, and willed what is needful.

L. But though we have before said that we ought to be always aspiring towards God with our minds, and praying without intermission, yet as our weakness requires many assistances, and our indolence needs to be stimulated, we ought every one of us, for the sake of regularity, to appoint particular hours which should not elapse without prayer, and which should witness all the affections of the mind entirely engaged in this exercise; as, when we rise in the morning, before we enter on the business of the day, when we sit down to meat, when we have been fed by the Divine blessing, when we retire to rest. This must not be a superstitious observance of hours, by which, as if discharging our debt to God, we may fancy ourselves discharged from all obligation for the remaining hours; but a discipline for our weakness, which may thus, from time to time, be exercised and stimulated. It must especially be the object of our solicitous care, whenever we are oppressed, or see others oppressed, with adversity, immediately to resort to him with celerity, not of body, but of mind; secondly, to suffer no prosperity of our own or others to pass without testifying our acknowledgment of his hand by praise and thanksgiving; lastly, we must carefully observe this in every prayer, that we entertain not the thought of binding God to certain circumstances, or prescribing to him the time, the place, or the manner of his proceedings. As we are taught by this prayer to fix no law, to impose no condition on him, but to leave it to his will to do what he intends, in the manner, at the time, and in the place he pleases, therefore, before we form a petition for ourselves, we first pray that his will may be done; thereby submitting our will to his, that, being, as it were, bridled and restrained, it may not presume to regulate God, but may constitute him the arbiter and ruler of all its desires.

LI. If, with minds composed to this obedience, we suffer ourselves to be governed by the laws of Divine Providence, we shall easily learn to persevere in prayer, and with suspended desires to wait patiently for the Lord; assured, though he does not discover himself, yet that he is always near us, and in his own time will declare that his ears have not been deaf to those prayers which, to human apprehension, seemed to be neglected. Now, this, if God do not at any time answer our first prayers, will be an immediate consolation, to prevent our sinking into despair, like those who, actuated only by their own ardour, call upon God in such a manner, that if he do not attend to their first transports, and afford them present aid, they at once imagine him to be displeased and angry with them, and, casting away all hope of succeeding in their prayers, cease to call upon him. But deferring our hope with a well-tempered equanimity, let us rather practise the perseverance so highly recommended to us in the Scriptures. For in the Psalms we may frequently observe how David and other faithful men, when, almost wearied with praying, they seemed to beat the air, and God seemed deaf to their petitions, yet did not desist from praying; because the authority of the Divine word is not maintained, unless it be fully credited, notwithstanding the appearance of any circumstances to the contrary. Nor let us tempt God, and provoke him against us by wearying him with our presumption; which is the practice of many who merely bargain with God on a certain condition, and as though he were subservient to their passions, bind him with laws of their own stipulation; with which unless he immediately complies, they give way to anger and fretfulness, to cavils, and murmurs, and rage. To such persons, therefore, he frequently grants in his wrath what he denies in mercy to others. This is exemplified in the children of Israel, for whom it had been better for the Lord not to have heard them, than for them to swallow his indignation with the meat that he sent them.

LII. But if, after long waiting, our sense neither understands what advance we have made by praying, nor experiences any advantage resulting from it, yet our faith will assure us, what cannot be perceived by sense, that we have obtained what was expedient for us, since the Lord so frequently and so certainly promises to take care of our troubles when they have been once deposited in his bosom. And thus he will cause us to possess abundance in poverty, and consolation in affliction. For though all things fail us, yet God will never forsake us; he cannot disappoint the expectation and patience of his people. He will amply compensate us for the loss of all others, for he comprehends in himself all blessings, which he will reveal to us at the day of judgment, when his kingdom will be fully manifested. Besides, though God grants our prayers, he does not always answer them according to the express form of the request; but seeming to keep us in suspense, shows by unknown means that our prayers were not in vain. This is the meaning of these words of John: "If we know that he heareth us, whatsoever we ask, we know that we have the petitions that we desired of him." This seems to be a feeble superfluity of expression, but is in reality a very useful declaration, that God, even when he does not comply with our desires, is nevertheless favourable and propitious to our prayers, so that a hope depending upon his word can never disappoint us. Now, this patience is very necessary to support believers, who would not long stand unless they relied upon it. For the Lord proves his people with heavy trials, and exercises them with severity; frequently driving them to various kinds of extremities, and suffering them to remain in them a long time before he grants them any enjoyment of his grace; and as Hannah says, "The Lord killeth, and maketh alive; he bringeth down to the grave, and bringeth up." In such distresses must they not inevitably faint in their minds, and fall into despair, unless, in the midst of their affliction and desolation, and almost death, they were revived by this reflection, that God regards them, and that the end of their present evils is approaching? But though they rely on the certainty of this hope, they at the same time cease not to pray; because, without constant perseverance in prayer, we pray to no purpose.

12.

Eternal Election, or God's Predestination of Some to Salvation, And of Others to Destruction.

The covenant of life not being equally preached to all, and among those to whom it is preached not always finding the same reception, this diversity discovers the wonderful depth of the Divine judgment. Nor is it to be doubted that this variety also follows, subject to the decision of God's eternal election. If it be evidently the result of the Divine will, that salvation is freely offered to some, and others are prevented from attaining it,—this immediately gives rise to important and difficult questions, which are incapable of any other explication, than by the establishment of pious minds in what ought to be received concerning election and predestination—a question, in the opinion of many, full of perplexity; for they consider nothing more unreasonable, than that, of the common mass of mankind, some should be predestinated to salvation, and others to destruction. But how unreasonably they perplex themselves will afterwards appear from the sequel of our discourse. Besides, the very obscurity which excites such dread, not only displays the utility of this doctrine, but shows it to be productive of the most delightful benefit. We shall never be clearly convinced as we ought to be, that our salvation flows from the fountain of God's free mercy, till we are acquainted with his eternal election, which illustrates the grace of God by this comparison, that he adopts not all promiscuously to the hope of salvation, but gives to some what he refuses to others. Ignorance of this principle evidently detracts from the Divine glory, and diminishes real humility. But according to Paul, what is so necessary to be known, never can be known, unless God, without any regard to works, chooses those whom he has decreed. "At this present time also, there is a remnant according to the election of grace. And if by grace, then it is no more of works; otherwise, grace is no more grace. But if it be of works, then it is no more grace; otherwise, work is no more work." If we need to be recalled to the origin of election, to prove that we obtain salvation from no other source than the mere goodness of God, they who desire to extinguish this principle, do all they can to obscure what ought to be magnificently and loudly celebrated, and to pluck up humility by the roots. In ascribing the salvation of the remnant of the people to the election of grace, Paul clearly testifies, that it is then only known that God saves whom he will of his mere good pleasure, and does not dispense a reward to which there can be no claim. They who shut the gates to prevent any one from presuming to approach and taste this doctrine, do no less injury to man than to God; for nothing else will be sufficient to produce in us suitable humility, or to impress us with a due sense of our great obligations to God. Nor is there any other basis for solid confidence, even according to the authority of Christ, who, to deliver us from all fear, and render us invincible amidst so many dangers, snares, and deadly conflicts, promises to preserve in safety all whom the Father has committed to his care. Whence we infer, that they who know not themselves to be God's peculiar people will be tortured with continual anxiety; and therefore, that the interest of all believers, as well as their own, is very badly consulted by those who, blind to the three advantages we have remarked, would wholly remove the foundation of our salvation. And hence the Church rises to our view, which otherwise, as Bernard justly observes, could neither be discovered nor recognized among creatures, being in two respects wonderfully concealed in the bosom of a blessed predestination, and in the mass of a miserable damnation. But before I enter on the subject itself, I must address some preliminary observations to two sorts of persons. The discussion of predestination—a subject of itself rather intricate—is made very perplexed, and therefore dangerous, by human curiosity, which no barriers can restrain from wandering into forbidden labyrinths, and soaring beyond its sphere, as if determined to leave none of the Divine secrets unscrutinized or unexplored. As we see multitudes every where guilty of this arrogance and presumption, and among them some who are not censurable in other respects, it is proper to admonish them of the bounds of their duty on this subject. First, then, let them remember that when they inquire into predestination, they penetrate the inmost recesses of Divine wisdom, where the careless and confident intruder will obtain no satisfaction to his curiosity, but will enter a labyrinth from which he will find no way to depart. For it is unreasonable that man should scrutinize with impunity those things which the Lord has determined to be hidden in himself; and investigate, even from eternity, that sublimity of wisdom which God would have us to adore and not comprehend, to promote our admiration of his glory. The secrets of his will which he determined to reveal to us, he discovers in his word; and these are all that he foresaw would concern us or conduce to our advantage.

II. "We are come into the way of faith," says Augustine; "let us constantly pursue it. It conducts into the king's palace, in which are hidden all the treasures of wisdom and knowledge. For the Lord Christ himself envied not his great and most select disciples when he said, 'I have many things to say unto you, but ye cannot bear them now.' We must walk, we must improve, we must grow, that our hearts may be able to understand those things of which we are at present incapable. If the last day finds us improving, we shall then learn what we never could learn in the present state." If we only consider that the word of the Lord is the only way to lead us to an investigation of all that ought to be believed concerning him, and the only light to enlighten us to behold all that ought to be seen of him, this consideration will easily restrain and preserve us from all presumption. For we shall know that when we have exceeded the limits of the word, we shall get into a devious and darksome course, in which errors, slips, and falls, will often be inevitable. Let us, then, in the first place, bear in mind, that to desire any other knowledge of predestination than what is unfolded in the word of God, indicates as great folly, as a wish to walk through unpassable roads, or to see in the dark. Nor let us be ashamed to be ignorant of some things relative to a subject in which there is a kind of learned ignorance. Rather let us abstain with cheerfulness from the pursuit of that knowledge, the affectation of which is foolish, dangerous, and even fatal. But if we are stimulated by the wantonness of intellect, we must oppose it with a reflection calculated to repress it, that as "it is not good to eat much honey, so for men to search their own glory, is not glory." For there is sufficient to deter us from that presumption, which can only precipitate us into ruin.

III. Others, desirous of remedying this evil, will have all mention of predestination to be as it were buried; they teach men to avoid every question concerning it as they would a precipice. Though their moderation is to be commended, in judging that mysteries ought to be handled with such great sobriety, yet, as they descend too low, they have little influence on the mind of man, which refuses to submit to unreasonable restraints.

To observe, therefore, the legitimate boundary on this side also, we must recur to the word of the Lord, which affords a certain rule for the understanding. For the Scripture is the school of the Holy Spirit, in which, as nothing necessary and useful to be known is omitted, so nothing is taught which it is not beneficial to know. Whatever, therefore, is declared in the Scripture concerning predestination, we must be cautious not to withhold from believers, lest we appear either to defraud them of the favor of their God, or to reprove and censure the Holy Spirit for publishing what it would be useful by any means to suppress. Let us, I say, permit the Christian man to open his heart and his ears to all the discourses addressed to him by God, only with this moderation, that as soon as the Lord closes his sacred mouth, he shall also desist from further inquiry. This will be the best barrier of sobriety, if in learning we not only follow the leadings of God, but as soon as he ceases to teach, we give up our desire of learning. Nor is the danger they dread, sufficient to divert our attention from the oracles of God. It is a celebrated observation of Solomon, that "it is the glory of God to conceal a thing." But, as both piety and common sense suggest that this is not to be understood generally of every thing, we must seek for the proper distinction, lest we content ourselves with brutish ignorance under the pretext of modesty and sobriety. Now, this distinction is clearly expressed in a few words by Moses. "The secret things," he says, "belong unto the Lord our God; but those things which are revealed belong unto us, and to our children for ever, that we may do all the words of this law." For we see how he enforces on the people attention to the doctrine of the law only by the celestial decree, because it pleased God to promulgate it; and restrains the same people within those limits with this single reason, that it is not lawful for mortals to intrude into the secrets of God.

IV. Profane persons, I confess, suddenly lay hold of something relating to the subject of predestination, to furnish occasion for objections, cavils, reproaches, and ridicule. But if we are frightened from it by their impudence, all the principal articles of the faith must be concealed, for there is scarcely one of them which such persons as these leave unviolated by blasphemy. The refractory mind will discover as much insolence, on hearing that there are three persons in the Divine essence, as on being told, that when God created man, he foresaw what would happen concerning him. Nor will they refrain from derision on being informed, that little more than five thousand years have elapsed since the creation of the world. They will ask why the power of God was so long idle and asleep. Nothing can be advanced which they will not endeavour to ridicule. Must we, in order to check these sacrileges, say nothing of the Divinity of the Son and Spirit, or pass over in silence the creation of the world? In this instance, and every other, the truth of God is too powerful to dread the detraction of impious men; as is strenuously maintained by Augustine, in his treatise on the Perseverance of the Faithful. We see the false apostles, with all their defamation and accusation of the true doctrine of Paul, could never succeed to make him ashamed of it. Their assertion, that all this discussion is dangerous to pious minds, because it is inconsistent with exhortations, shakes their faith, and disturbs and discourages the heart itself, is without any foundation. Augustine admits, that he was frequently blamed, on these accounts, for preaching predestination too freely; but he readily and amply refutes them. But as many and various absurdities are crowded upon us here, we prefer reserving every one to be refuted in its proper place. I only desire this general admission, that we should neither scrutinize those things which the Lord has left concealed, nor neglect those which he has openly exhibited, lest we be condemned for excessive curiosity on the one hand, or for ingratitude on the other. For it is judiciously remarked by Augustine, that we may safely follow the Scripture, which proceeds as with the pace of a mother stooping to the weakness of a child, that it may not leave our weak capacities behind. But persons who are so cautious or timid, as to wish predestination to be buried in silence, lest feeble minds should be disturbed,—with what pretext, I ask, will they gloss over their arrogance, which indirectly charges God with foolish inadvertency, as though he foresaw not the danger which they suppose they have had the penetration to discover. Whoever, therefore, endeavours to raise prejudices against the doctrine of predestination, openly reproaches God, as though something had inconsiderately escaped from him that is pernicious to the Church.

V. Predestination, by which God adopts some to the hope of life, and adjudges others to eternal death, no one, desirous of the credit of piety, dares absolutely to deny. But it is involved in many cavils, especially by those who make foreknowledge the cause of it. We maintain, that both belong to God; but it is preposterous to represent one as dependent on the other. When we attribute foreknowledge to God, we mean that all things have ever been, and perpetually remain, before his eyes, so that to his knowledge nothing is future or past, but all things are present; and present in such a manner, that he does not merely conceive of them from ideas formed in his mind, as things remembered by us appear present to our minds, but really beholds and sees them as if actually placed before him. And this foreknowledge extends to the whole world, and to all the creatures. Predestination we call the eternal decree of God, by which he has determined in himself, what he would have to become of every individual of mankind. For they are not all created with a similar destiny; but eternal life is fore-ordained for some, and eternal damnation for others. Every man, therefore, being created for one or the other of these ends, we say, he is predestinated either to life or to death. This God has not only testified in particular persons, but has given a specimen of it in the whole posterity of Abraham, which should evidently show the future condition of every nation to depend upon his decision. "When the Most High divided the nations, when he separated the sons of Adam, the Lord's portion was his people; Jacob was the lot of his inheritance." The separation is before the eyes of all: in the person of Abraham, as in the dry trunk of a tree, one people is peculiarly chosen to the rejection of others: no reason for this appears, except that Moses, to deprive their posterity of all occasion of glorying, teaches them that their exaltation is wholly from God's gratuitous love. He assigns this reason for their deliverance, that "he loved their fathers, and chose their seed after them." More fully in another Chapter: "The Lord did not set his love upon you, nor choose you, because you were more in number than any people; but because the Lord loved you." He frequently repeats the same admonition: "Behold, the heaven is the Lord's thy God, the earth also, with all that therein is. Only the Lord had a delight in thy fathers to love them, and he chose their seed after them." In another place, sanctification is enjoined upon them, because they were chosen to be a peculiar people. And again, elsewhere, love is asserted to be the cause of their protection. It is declared by the united voice of the faithful, "He hath chosen our inheritance for us, the excellency of Jacob, whom he loved." For the gifts conferred on them by God, they all ascribe to gratuitous love, not only from a consciousness that these were not obtained by any merit of theirs, but from a conviction, that the holy patriarch himself was not endued with such excellence as to acquire the privilege of so great an honour for himself and his posterity. And the more effectually to demolish all pride, he reproaches them with having deserved no favour, being "a stiff-necked and rebellious people." The prophets also frequently reproach the Jews with the unwelcome mention of this election, because they had shamefully departed from it. Let them, however, now come forward, who wish to restrict the election of God to the desert of men, or the merit of works. When they see one nation preferred to all others,—when they hear that God had no inducement to be more favourable to a few, and ignoble, and even disobedient and obstinate people,—will they quarrel with him because he has chosen to give such an example of mercy? But their obstreperous clamours will not impede his work, nor will the reproaches they hurl against Heaven, injure or affect his justice; they will rather recoil upon their own heads. To this principle of the gracious covenant, the Israelites are also recalled whenever thanks are to be rendered to God, or their hopes are to be raised for futurity. "He hath made us, and not we ourselves," says the Psalmist: "we are his people, and the sheep of his pasture." It is not without reason that the negation is added, "not we ourselves," that they may know that of all the benefits they enjoy, God is not only the Author, but derived the cause from himself, there being nothing in them deserving of such great honour. He also enjoins them to be content with the mere good pleasure of God, in these words: "O ye seed of Abraham his servant, ye children of Jacob his chosen." And after having recounted the continual benefits bestowed by God as fruits of election, he at length concludes that he had acted with such liberality, "because he remembered his covenant." Consistent with this doctrine is the song of the whole Church: "Thy right hand, and thine arm, and the light of thy countenance, gave our fathers the land, because thou hadst a favour unto them." It must be observed that where mention is made of the land, it is a visible symbol of the secret separation, which comprehends adoption. David, in another place, exhorts the people to the same gratitude: "Blessed is the nation whose God is the Lord; and the people whom he hath chosen for his own inheritance." Samuel animates to a good hope: "The Lord will not forsake his people, for his great name's sake; because it hath pleased the Lord to make you his people." David, when his faith is assailed, thus arms himself for the conflict: "Blessed is the man whom thou choosest, and causest to approach unto thee; he shall dwell in thy courts." But since the election hidden in God has been confirmed by the first deliverance, as well as by the second and other intermediate blessings, the word *choose* is transferred to it in Isaiah: "The Lord will have mercy on Jacob, and will yet choose Israel;" because, contemplating a future period, he declares that the collection of the residue of the people, whom he had appeared to have forsaken, would be a sign of the stable and sure election, which had likewise seemed to fail. When he says also, in another place, "I have chosen thee, and not cast thee away," he commends the continual course of his signal liberality and paternal benevolence. The angel, in Zechariah, speaks more plainly: "The Lord shall choose Jerusalem again;" as though his severe chastisement had been a rejection, or their exile had been an interruption of election; which, nevertheless, remains inviolable, though the tokens of it are not always visible.

VI. We must now proceed to a second degree of election, still more restricted, or that in which the Divine grace was displayed in a more special manner, when of the same race of Abraham God rejected some, and by nourishing others in the Church, proved that he retained them among his children. Ishmael at first obtained the same station as his brother Isaac, for the spiritual covenant was equally sealed in him by the symbol of circumcision. He is cut off; afterwards Esau; lastly, an innumerable multitude, and almost all Israel. In Isaac the seed was called; the same calling continued in Jacob. God exhibited a similar example in the rejection of Saul, which is magnificently celebrated by the Psalmist: "He refused the tabernacle of Joseph, and chose not the tribe of Ephraim, but chose the tribe of Judah;" and this the sacred history frequently repeats, that the wonderful secret of Divine grace may be more manifest in that change. I grant, it was by their own crime and guilt that Ishmael, Esau, and persons of similar characters, fell from the adoption; because the condition annexed was, that they should faithfully keep the covenant of God, which they perfidiously violated. Yet it was a peculiar favour of God, that he deigned to prefer them to other nations; as it is said in the Psalms: "He hath not dealt so with any nation; and as for his judgments, they have not known them." But I have justly said that here are two degrees to be remarked; for in the election of the whole nation, God has already shown that in his mere goodness he is bound by no laws, but is perfectly free, so that none can require of him an equal distribution of grace, the inequality of which demonstrates it to be truly gratuitous. Therefore Malachi aggravates the ingratitude of Israel, because, though not only elected out of the whole race of mankind, but also separated from a sacred family to be a peculiar people, they perfidiously and impiously despised God their most beneficent Father. "Was not Esau Jacob's brother? saith the Lord: yet I loved Jacob, and I hated Esau." For God takes it for granted, since both were sons of a holy father, successors of the covenant, and branches from a sacred root, that the children of Jacob were already laid under more than common obligations by their admission to that honour; but Esau the first-born having been rejected, and their father, though inferior by birth, having been made the heir, he proves them guilty of double ingratitude, and complains of their violating this twofold claim.

VII. Though it is sufficiently clear, that God, in his secret counsel, freely chooses whom he will, and rejects others, his gratuitous election is but half displayed till we come to particular individuals, to whom God not only offers salvation, but assigns it in such a manner, that the certainty of the effect is liable to no suspense or doubt. These are included in that one seed mentioned by Paul; for though the adoption was deposited in the hand of Abraham, yet many of his posterity being cut off as putrid members, in order to maintain the efficacy and stability of election, it is necessary to ascend to the head, in whom their heavenly Father has bound his elect to each other, and united them to himself by an indissoluble bond. Thus the adoption of the family of Abraham displayed the favour of God, which he denied to others; but in the members of Christ there is a conspicuous exhibition of the superior efficacy of grace; because, being united to their head, they never fail of salvation. Paul, therefore, justly reasons from the passage of Malachi which I have just quoted, that where God, introducing the covenant of eternal life, invites any people to himself, there is a peculiar kind of election as to part of them, so that he does not efficaciously choose all with indiscriminate grace. The declaration, "Jacob have I loved," respects the whole posterity of the patriarch, whom the prophet there opposes to the descendants of Esau. Yet this is no objection to our having in the person of one individual a specimen of the election, which can never fail of attaining its full effect. These, who truly belong to Christ, Paul correctly observes, are called "a remnant;" for experience proves, that of a great multitude the most part fall away and disappear, so that often only a small portion remains. That the general election of a people is not always effectual and permanent, a reason readily presents itself, because, when God covenants with them, he does not also give them the spirit of regeneration to enable them to persevere in the covenant to the end; but the external call, without the internal efficacy of grace, which would be sufficient for their preservation, is a kind of medium between the rejection of all mankind and the election of the small number of believers. The whole nation of Israel was called "God's inheritance," though many of them were strangers; but God, having firmly covenanted to be their Father and Redeemer, regards that gratuitous favour rather than the defection of multitudes; by whom his truth was not violated, because his preservation of a certain remnant to himself, made it evident that his calling was without repentance. For God's collection of a Church for himself, from time to time, from the children of Abraham, rather than from the profane nations, was in consideration of his covenant, which, being violated by the multitude, he restricted to a few, to prevent its total failure. Lastly, the general adoption of the seed of Abraham was a visible representation of a greater blessing, which God conferred on a few out of the multitude. This is the reason that Paul so carefully distinguishes the descendants of Abraham according to the flesh, from his spiritual children called after the example of Isaac. Not that the mere descent from Abraham was a vain and unprofitable thing, which could not be asserted without depreciating the covenant; but because to the latter alone the immutable counsel of God, in which he predestinated whom he would, was of itself effectual to salvation. But I advise my readers to adopt no prejudice on either side, till it shall appear from adduced passages of Scripture what sentiments ought to be entertained. In conformity, therefore, to the clear doctrine of the Scripture, we assert, that by an eternal and immutable counsel, God has once for all determined, both whom he would admit to salvation, and whom he would condemn to destruction. We affirm that this counsel, as far as concerns the elect, is founded on his gratuitous mercy, totally irrespective of human merit; but that to those whom he devotes to condemnation, the gate of life is closed by a just and irreprehensible, but incomprehensible, judgment. In the elect, we consider calling as an evidence of election, and justification as another token of its manifestation, till they arrive in glory, which constitutes its completion. As God seals his elect by vocation and justification, so by excluding the reprobate from the knowledge of his name and the sanctification of his Spirit, he affords an indication of the judgment that awaits them. Here I shall pass over many fictions fabricated by foolish men to overthrow predestination. It is unnecessary to refute things which, as soon as they are advanced, sufficiently prove their own falsehood. I shall dwell only on those things which are subjects of controversy among the learned, or which may occasion difficulty to simple minds, or which impiety speciously pleads in order to stigmatize the Divine justice.

13.

The True Church, and the Necessity of Our Union with Her, Being the Mother of All the Pious.

That by the faith of the gospel Christ becomes ours, and we become partakers of the salvation procured by him, and of eternal happiness, has been explained in the preceding Book. But as our ignorance and slothfulness, and, I may add, the vanity of our minds, require external aids, in order to the production of faith in our hearts, and its increase and progressive advance even to its completion, God has provided such aids in compassion to our infirmity; and that the preaching of the gospel might be maintained, he has deposited this treasure with the Church. He has appointed pastors and teachers, that his people might be taught by their lips; he has invested them with authority; in short, he has omitted nothing that could contribute to a holy unity of faith, and to the establishment of good order. First of all, he has instituted Sacraments, which we know by experience to be means of the greatest utility for the nourishment and support of our faith. For as, during our confinement in the prison of our flesh, we have not yet attained to the state of angels, God has, in his wonderful providence, accommodated himself to our capacity, by prescribing a way in which we might approach him, notwithstanding our immense distance from him. Wherefore the order of instruction requires us now to treat of the Church and its government, orders, and power; secondly, of the Sacraments; and lastly, of Civil Government; and at the same time to call off the pious readers from the abuses of the Papacy, by which Satan has corrupted every thing that God had appointed to be instrumental to our salvation. I shall begin with the Church, in whose bosom it is God's will that all his children should be collected, not only to be nourished by her assistance and ministry during their infancy and childhood, but also to be governed by her maternal care, till they attain a mature age, and at length reach the end of their faith. For it is not lawful to "put asunder" those things "which God hath joined together;" that the Church is the mother of all those who have him for their Father; and that not only under the law, but since the coming of Christ also, according to the testimony of the apostle, who declares the new and heavenly Jerusalem to be "the mother of us all."

II. That article of the Creed, in which we profess to believe the Church, refers not only to the visible Church of which we are now speaking, but likewise to all the elect of God, including the dead as well as the living. The word BELIEVE is used, because it is often impossible to discover any difference between the children of God and the ungodly; between his peculiar flock and wild beasts. The particle IN, interpolated by many, is not supported by any probable reason. I confess that it is generally adopted at present, and is not destitute of the suffrage of antiquity, being found in the Nicene Creed, as it is transmitted to us in ecclesiastical history. Yet it is evident from the writings of the fathers, that it was anciently admitted without controversy to say, "I believe the Church," not "*in* the Church." For not only is this word not used by Augustine and the ancient writer of the work "On the Exposition of the Creed," which passes under the name of Cyprian, but they particularly remark that there would be an impropriety in the expression, if this preposition were inserted; and they confirm their opinion by no trivial reason. For we declare that we believe *in God* because our mind depends upon him as true, and our confidence rests in him. But this would not be applicable to the Church, any more than to "the remission of sins," or the "resurrection of the body." Therefore, though I am averse to contentions about words, yet I would rather adopt a proper phraseology adapted to express the subject than affect forms of expression by which the subject would be unnecessarily involved in obscurity. The design of this clause is to teach us, that though the devil moves every engine to destroy the grace of Christ, and all the enemies of God exert the most furious violence in the same attempt, yet his grace cannot possibly be extinguished, nor can his blood be rendered barren, so as not to produce some fruit. Here we must regard both the secret election of God, and his internal vocation; because he alone "knoweth them that are his;" and keeps them enclosed under his "seal," to use the expression of Paul; except that they bear his impression, by which they may be distinguished from the reprobate. But because a small and contemptible number is concealed among a vast multitude, and a few grains of wheat are covered with a heap of chaff, we must leave to God alone the knowledge of his Church whose foundation is his secret election. Nor is it sufficient to include in our thoughts and minds the whole multitude of the elect, unless we conceive of such a unity of the Church, into which we know ourselves to be truly ingrafted. For unless we are united with all the other members under Christ our Head, we can have no hope of the future inheritance. Therefore the Church is called CATHOLIC, or universal; because there could not be two or three churches, without Christ being divided, which is impossible. But all the elect of God are so connected with each other in Christ, that as they depend upon one head, so they grow up together as into one body, compacted together like members of the same body; being made truly one, as living by one faith, hope, and charity, through the same Divine Spirit, being called not only to the same inheritance of eternal life, but also to a participation of one God and Christ. Therefore, though the melancholy desolation which surrounds us, seems to proclaim that there is nothing left of the Church, let us remember that the death of Christ is fruitful, and that God wonderfully preserves his Church as it were in hiding-places; according to what he said to Elijah: "I have reserved to myself seven thousand men, who have not bowed the knee to Baal."

III. This article of the creed, however, relates in some measure to the external Church, that every one of us may maintain a brotherly agreement with all the children of God, may pay due deference to the authority of the Church, and, in a word, may conduct himself as one of the flock. Therefore we add THE COMMUNION OF SAINTS—a clause which, though generally omitted by the ancients, ought not to be neglected, because it excellently expresses the character of the Church; as though it had been said that the saints are united in the fellowship of Christ on this condition, that whatever benefits God confers upon them, they should mutually communicate to each other. This destroys not the diversity of grace, for we know that the gifts of the Spirit are variously distributed; nor does it disturb the order of civil polity, which secures to every individual the exclusive enjoyment of his property, as it is necessary for the preservation of the peace of society that men should have peculiar and distinct possessions. But the community asserted is such as Luke describes, that "the multitude of them that believed were of one heart and of one soul;" and Paul, when he exhorts the Ephesians to be "one body, and one spirit, even as they were called in one hope." Nor is it possible, if they are truly persuaded that God is a common Father to them all, and

Christ their common Head, but that, being united in brotherly affection, they should mutually communicate their advantages to each other. Now, it highly concerns us to know what benefit we receive from this. For we believe the Church, in order to have a certain assurance that we are members of it. For thus our salvation rests on firm and solid foundations, so that it cannot fall into ruin, though the whole fabric of the world should be dissolved. First, it is founded on the election of God, and can be liable to no variation or failure, but with the subversion of his eternal providence. In the next place, it is united with the stability of Christ, who will no more suffer his faithful people to be severed from him, than his members to be torn in pieces. Besides, we are certain, as long as we continue in the bosom of the Church, that we shall remain in possession of the truth. Lastly, we understand these promises to belong to us: "In mount Zion shall be deliverance." God is in the midst of her; she shall not be moved." Such is the effect of union with the Church, that it retains us in the fellowship of God. The very word *communion* likewise contains abundant consolation; for while it is certain that whatever the Lord confers upon his members and ours belong to us, our hope is confirmed by all the benefits which they enjoy. But in order to embrace the unity of the Church in this manner, it is unnecessary, as we have observed, to see the Church with our eyes, or feel it with our hands; on the contrary, from its being an object of faith, we are taught that it is no less to be considered as existing, when it escapes our observation, than if it were evident to our eyes. Nor is our faith the worse, because it acknowledges the Church which we do not fully comprehend; for we are not commanded here to distinguish the reprobate from the elect, which is not our province, but that of God alone; we are only required to be assured in our minds, that all those who, by the mercy of God the Father, through the efficacious influence of the Holy Spirit, have attained to the participation of Christ, are separated as the peculiar possession and portion of God; and that being numbered among them, we are partakers of such great grace.

IV. But as our present design is to treat of the *visible* Church, we may learn even from the title of *mother*, how useful and even necessary it is for us to know her; since there is no other way of entrance into life, unless we are conceived by her, born of her, nourished at her breast, and continually preserved under her care and government till we are divested of this mortal flesh, and "become like the angels." For our infirmity will not admit of our dismission from her school; we must continue under her instruction and discipline to the end of our lives. It is also to be remarked, that out of her bosom there can be no hope of remission of sins, or any salvation, according to the testimony of Joel and Isaiah; which is confirmed by Ezekiel, when he denounces that those whom God excludes from the heavenly life, shall not be enrolled among his people. So, on the contrary, those who devote themselves to the service of God, are said to inscribe their names among the citizens of Jerusalem. For which reason the Psalmist says, "Remember me, O Lord, with the favour that thou bearest unto thy people: O visit me with thy salvation; that I may see the good of thy chosen; that I may rejoice in the gladness of thy nation; that I may glory with thine inheritance." In these words the paternal favour of God, and the peculiar testimony of the spiritual life, are restricted to his flock, to teach us that it is always fatally dangerous to be separated from the Church.

V. But let us proceed to state what belongs to this subject. Paul writes, that Christ, "that he might fill all things, gave some apostles, and some prophets, and some evangelists, and some pastors and teachers; for the perfecting of the saints, for the work of the ministry, for the edifying of the body of Christ: till we all come in the unity of the faith, and of the knowledge of the Son of God, unto a perfect man, unto the measure of the stature of the fulness of Christ." We see that though God could easily make his people perfect in a single moment, yet it was not his will that they should grow to mature age, but under the education of the Church. We see the means expressed; the preaching of the heavenly doctrine is assigned to the pastors. We see that all are placed under the same regulation, in order that they may submit themselves with gentleness and docility of mind to be governed by the pastors who are appointed for this purpose. Isaiah had long before described the kingdom of Christ by this character: "My Spirit that is upon thee, and my words which I have put in thy mouth, shall not depart out of thy mouth, nor out of the mouth of thy seed, nor out of the mouth of thy seed's seed, from henceforth and for ever." Hence it follows, that all who reject the spiritual food for their souls, which is extended to them by the hands of the Church, deserve to perish with hunger and want. It is God who inspires us with faith, but it is through the instrumentality of the gospel, according to the declaration of Paul, "that faith cometh by hearing." So also the power to save resides in God, but, as the same apostle testifies in another place, he displays it in the preaching of the gospel. With this design, in former ages he commanded solemn assemblies to be held in the sanctuary, that the doctrine taught by the mouth of the priest might maintain the unity of the faith; and the design of those magnificent titles, where the temple is called God's "rest," his "sanctuary," and "dwelling-place," where he is said to "dwell between the cherubim," was no other than to promote the esteem, love, reverence, and dignity of the heavenly doctrine; which the view of a mortal and despised man would otherwise greatly diminish. That we may know, therefore, that we have an inestimable treasure communicated to us from earthen vessels, God himself comes forward, and as he is the Author of this arrangement, so he will be acknowledged as present in his institution. Therefore, after having forbidden his people to devote themselves to auguries, divinations, magical arts, necromancy, and other superstitions, he adds, that he will give them what ought to be sufficient for every purpose, namely, that he will never leave them without prophets. Now, as he did not refer his ancient people to angels, but raised up earthly teachers, who truly discharged the office of angels, so, in the present day, he is pleased to teach us by the instrumentality of men. And as formerly he was not content with the written law, but appointed the priests as interpreters, at whose lips the people might inquire its true meaning, so, in the present day, he not only requires us to be attentive to reading, but has appointed teachers for our assistance. This is attended with a twofold advantage. For on the one hand, it is a good proof of our obedience when we listen to his ministers, just as if he were addressing us himself; and on the other, he has provided for our infirmity, by choosing to address us through the medium of human interpreters, that he may sweetly allure us to him, rather than to drive us away from him by his thunders. And the propriety of this familiar manner of teaching, is evident to all the pious, from the terror with which the majesty of God justly alarms them. Those who consider the authority of the doctrine as weakened by the meanness of the men who are called to teach it, betray their ingratitude; because among so many excellent gifts with which God has adorned mankind, it is a peculiar privilege, that he deigns to consecrate men's lips and tongues to his service, that his voice may be heard in them. Let us not therefore, on our parts, be reluctant to receive and obey the doctrine of salvation proposed to us at his express command; for though the power of God is not confined to external means, yet he has confined us to the ordinary manner of teaching, the fanatical rejecters of which necessarily involve themselves in many fatal snares. Many are urged by pride, or disdain, or envy, to persuade themselves that they can profit sufficiently by reading and meditating in private, and so to despise public assemblies, and consider preaching as unnecessary. But since they do all in their power to dissolve and break asunder the bond of unity, which ought to be preserved inviolable, not one of them escapes the just punishment of this impious breach, but they all involve themselves in pestilent errors and pernicious reveries. Wherefore, in order that the pure simplicity of faith may flourish among us, let us not be reluctant to use this exercise of piety, which the Divine institution has shown to be necessary, and which God so repeatedly commends to us. There has never been found, among the most extravagant of mortals, one insolent enough to say that we ought to shut our ears against God; but the prophets and pious teachers, in all ages, have had a difficult contest with the wicked, whose arrogance can never submit to be taught by the lips and ministry of men. Now, this is no other than effacing the image of God, which is discovered to us in the doctrine. For the faithful under the former dispensation were directed to seek the face of God in the sanctuary; and this is so frequently repeated in the law, for no other reason, but because the doctrine of the law and the exhortations of the prophets exhibited to them a lively image of God; as Paul declares that his preaching displayed "the glory of God in the face of Jesus Christ." And in so much the greater detestation ought we to hold those apostates, who make it their study to cause divisions in churches, as if they would drive away the sheep from the fold, and throw them into the jaws of wolves. But let us remember what we have quoted from Paul—that the Church can only be edified by the preaching of this word, and that the saints have no common bond of union to hold them together, any longer than, while learning and profiting with one accord, they observe the order which God has prescribed for the Church. It was principally for this end, as I have already stated, that the faithful under the law were commanded to resort to the sanctuary; because Moses not only celebrates it as the residence of God, but likewise declares it to be the place where God has fixed the record of his name; which without the doctrine of piety, he plainly suggests, would be of no use. And it is undoubtedly for the same reason that David complains, with great bitterness of soul, of being prevented from access to the tabernacle by the tyrannical cruelty of his enemies. To many persons perhaps this appears to be a puerile lamentation, because it could be but a very trivial loss, and not a privation of much satisfaction to be absent from the court of the temple, provided he were in the possession of other pleasures. But by this one trouble, anxiety, and sorrow, he complains that he is grieved, tormented, and almost consumed; because nothing is more valued by believers than this assistance, by which God gradually raises his people from one degree of elevation to another. For it is also to be remarked, that God always manifested himself to the holy fathers, in the mirror of his doctrine, in such a manner that their knowledge of him was spiritual. Hence the temple was not only called his *face*, but in order to guard against all superstition, was also designated as his *footstool*. And this is that happy conjunction in the unity of the faith spoken of by Paul, when all, from the highest to the lowest, are aspiring towards the head. All the temples which the Gentiles erected to God with any other design, were nothing but a profanation of his worship—a crime which, though not to an equal extent, was also frequently committed by the Jews. Stephen reproaches them for it in the language of Isaiah: "The Most High dwelleth not in temples made with hands; as saith the prophet, Heaven is my throne, and earth is my footstool," because God alone sanctifies temples by his word, that they may be legitimately used for his worship. And if we presumptuously attempt any thing without his command, the evil beginning is immediately succeeded by further inventions, which multiply the mischief without end. Xerxes, however, acted with great indiscretion, when, at the advice of the magi, he burned or demolished all the temples of Greece, from an opinion of the absurdity that gods, to whom all space ought to be left perfectly free, should be enclosed within walls and roofs. As if it were not in the power of God to descend in any way to us, and yet at the same time not to make any change of place, or to confine us to earthly means, but rather to use them as vehicles to elevate us towards his celestial glory, which fills all things with its immensity, as well as transcends the heavens in its sublimity.

VI. Now, as the present age has witnessed a violent dispute respecting the efficacy of the ministry, some exaggerating its dignity beyond measure, and others contending that it is a criminal transfer to mortal man of what properly belongs to the Holy Spirit, to suppose that ministers and teachers penetrate the mind and heart, so as to correct the blindness of the one, and the hardness of the other,—we must proceed to a decision of this controversy. The arguments advanced on both sides may be easily reconciled by a careful observation of the passages, in which God, the Author of preaching, connecting his Spirit with it, promises that it shall be followed with success; or those in which, separating himself from all external aids, he attributes the commencement of faith, as well as its subsequent progress, entirely and exclusively to himself. The office of the second Elias, according to Malachi, was to illuminate the minds and to "turn the hearts of the fathers to the children," and the disobedient to the wisdom of the just. Christ declares that he sent his disciples, that they "should bring forth fruit" from their labours. What that fruit was, is briefly defined by Peter, when he says that we are "born again, not of corruptible seed, but of incorruptible." Therefore Paul glories that he had "begotten" the Corinthians "through the gospel," and that they were "the seal of his apostleship;" and even that he was "not a minister of the letter," merely striking the ear with a vocal sound, but that the energy of the Spirit had been given to him to render his doctrine efficacious. In the same sense, he affirms, in another Epistle, that his "gospel came not in word only, but also in power." He declares also to the Galatians, that they "received the Spirit by the hearing of faith." In short, there are several places, in which he not only represents himself as a "labourer together with God," but even attributes to himself the office of communicating salvation. He certainly never advanced all these things, in order to arrogate to himself the least praise independent of God, as he briefly states in other passages: "Our entrance in unto you was not in vain." "I labour, striving according to his working, which worketh in me mightily." "He that wrought effectually in Peter to the apostleship of the circumcision, the same was mighty in me toward the Gentiles." Besides, it is evident, from other places, that he leaves ministers possessed of nothing, considered in themselves: "Neither is he that planteth any thing, neither he that watereth; but God that giveth the increase." Again: "I laboured more abundantly than they all; yet not I, but the grace of God which was with me." And it is certainly necessary to bear in memory those passages, in which God ascribes to himself the illumination of the mind and renovation of the heart, and thereby declares it to be sacrilege for man to arrogate to himself any share in either. Yet every one who attends with docility of mind to the ministers whom God has appointed, will learn from the beneficial effect, that this mode of teaching has not in vain been pleasing to God, and that this yoke of modesty has not without reason been imposed upon believers.

VII. From what has been said, I conceive it must now be evident what judgment we ought to form respecting the Church, which is visible to our eyes, and falls under our knowledge. For we have remarked that the word *Church* is used in the sacred Scriptures in two senses. Sometimes, when they mention the Church, they intend that which is really such in the sight of God, into which none are received but those who by adoption and grace are the children of God, and by the sanctification of the Spirit are the true members of Christ. And then it comprehends not only the saints at any one time resident on earth, but all the elect who have lived from the beginning of the world. But the word *Church* is frequently used in the Scriptures to designate the whole multitude, dispersed all over the world, who profess to worship one God and Jesus Christ, who are initiated into his faith by baptism, who testify their unity in true doctrine and charity by a participation of the sacred supper, who consent to the word of the Lord, and preserve the ministry which Christ has instituted for the purpose of preaching it. In this Church are included many hypocrites, who have nothing of Christ but the name and appearance; many persons ambitious, avaricious, envious, slanderous, and dissolute in their lives, who are tolerated for a time, either because they cannot be convicted by a legitimate process, or because discipline is not always maintained with sufficient vigour. As it is necessary, therefore, to believe that Church, which is invisible to us, and known to God alone, so this Church, which is visible to men, we are commanded to honour, and to maintain communion with it.

VIII. As far, therefore, as was important for us to know it, the Lord has described it by certain marks and characters. It is the peculiar prerogative of God himself to "know them that are his," as we have already stated from Paul. And to guard against human presumption ever going to such an extreme, the experience of every day teaches us how very far his secret judgments transcend all our apprehensions. For those who seemed the most abandoned, and were generally considered past all hope, are recalled by his goodness into the right way; while some, who seemed to stand better than others, fall into perdition. "According to the secret predestination of God," therefore, as Augustine observes, "there are many sheep without the pale of the Church, and many wolves within." For he knows and seals those who know not either him or themselves. Of those who externally bear his seal, his eyes alone can discern who are unfeignedly holy, and will persevere to the end; which is the completion of salvation. On the other hand, as he saw it to be in some measure requisite that we should know who ought to be considered as his children, he has in this respect accommodated himself to our capacity. And as it was not necessary that on this point we should have an assurance of faith, he has substituted in its place a judgment of charity, according to which we ought to acknowledge as members of the Church all those who by a confession of faith, an exemplary life, and a participation of the sacraments, profess the same God and Christ with ourselves. But the knowledge of the body itself being more necessary to our salvation, he has distinguished it by more clear and certain characters.

IX. Hence the visible Church rises conspicuous to our view. For wherever we find the word of God purely preached and heard, and the sacraments administered according to the institution of Christ, there, it is not to be doubted, is a Church of God; for his promise can never deceive—"where two or three are gathered together in my name, there am I in the midst of them." But, that we may have a clear understanding of the whole of this subject, let us proceed by the following steps: That the universal Church is the whole multitude, collected from all nations, who, though dispersed in countries widely distant from each other, nevertheless consent to the same truth of Divine doctrine, and are united by the bond of the same religion; that in this universal Church are comprehended particular churches, distributed according to human necessity in various towns and villages; and that each of these respectively is justly distinguished by the name and authority of a church; and that individuals, who, on a profession of piety, are enrolled among Churches of the same description, though they are really strangers to any particular Church, do nevertheless in some respect belong to it, till they are expelled from it by a public decision. There is some difference, however, in the mode of judging respecting private persons and churches. For it may happen, in the case of persons whom we think altogether unworthy of the society of the pious, that, on account of the common consent of the Church, by which they are tolerated in the body of Christ, we may be obliged to treat them as brethren, and to class them in the number of believers. In our private opinion we approve not of such persons as members of the Church, but we leave them the station they hold among the people of God, till it be taken away from them by legitimate authority. But respecting the congregation itself, we must form a different judgment. If they possess and honour the ministry of the word, and the administration of the sacraments, they are, without all doubt, entitled to be considered as a Church; because it is certain that the word and sacraments cannot be unattended with some good effects. In this manner, we preserve the unity of the universal Church, which diabolical spirits have always been endeavouring to destroy; and at the same time without interfering with the authority of those legitimate assemblies, which local convenience has distributed in different places.

X. We have stated that the marks by which the Church is to be distinguished, are, the preaching of the word and the administration of the sacraments. For these can nowhere exist without bringing forth fruit, and being prospered with the blessing of God. I assert not that wherever the word is preached, the good effects of it immediately appear; but that it is never received so as to obtain a permanent establishment, without displaying some efficacy. However this may be, where the word is heard with reverence, and the sacraments are not neglected, there we discover, while that is the case, an appearance of the Church, which is liable to no suspicion of uncertainty, of which no one can safely despise the authority, or reject the admonitions, or resist the counsels, or slight the censures, much less separate from it and break up its unity. For so highly does the Lord esteem the communion of his Church, that he considers every one as a traitor and apostate from religion, who perversely withdraws himself from any Christian society which preserves the true ministry of the word and sacraments. He commends the authority of the Church, in such a manner as to account every violation of it an infringement of his own. For it is not a trivial circumstance, that the Church is called "the house of God, the pillar and ground of truth." For in these words Paul signifies that in order to keep the truth of God from being lost in the world, the Church is its faithful guardian; because it has been the will of God, by the ministry of the Church, to preserve the pure preaching of his word, and to manifest himself as our affectionate Father, while he nourishes us with spiritual food, and provides all things conducive to our salvation. Nor is it small praise, that the Church is chosen and separated by Christ to be his spouse, "not having spot or wrinkle," to be "his body, the fulness of him that filleth all in all." Hence it follows, that a departure from the Church is a renunciation of God and Christ. And such a criminal dissension is so much the more to be avoided, because, while we endeavour, as far as lies in our power, to destroy the truth of God, we deserve to be crushed with the most powerful thunders of his wrath. Nor is it possible to imagine a more atrocious crime, than that sacrilegious perfidy, which violates the conjugal relation that the only begotten Son of God has condescended to form with us.

XI. Let us, therefore, diligently retain those characters impressed upon our minds, and estimate them according to the judgment of God. For there is nothing that Satan labours more to accomplish, than to remove and destroy one or both of them; at one time to efface and obliterate these marks, and so to take away all true and genuine distinction of the Church; at another to inspire us with contempt of them, and so to drive us out of the Church by an open separation. By his subtlety it has happened, that in some ages the pure preaching of the word has altogether disappeared; and in the present day he is labouring with the same malignity to overturn the ministry; which, however, Christ has ordained in his Church, so that if it were taken away, the edification of the Church would be quite at an end. How dangerous, then, how fatal is the temptation, when it even enters into the heart of a man to withdraw himself from that congregation, in which he discovers those signs and characters which the Lord has deemed sufficiently descriptive of his Church! We see, however, that great caution requires to be observed on both sides. For, to prevent imposture from deceiving us, under the name of the Church, every congregation assuming this name should be brought to that proof, like gold to the touchstone. If it have the order prescribed by the Lord in the word and sacraments, it will not deceive us; we may securely render to it the honour due to all churches. On the contrary, if it pretend to the name of a Church, without the word and sacraments, we ought to beware of such delusive pretensions, with as much caution as, in the other case, we should use in avoiding presumption and pride.

XII. When we affirm the pure ministry of the word, and pure order in the celebration of the sacraments, to be a sufficient pledge and earnest, that we may safely embrace the society in which both these are found, as a true Church, we carry the observation to this point, that such a society should never be rejected as long as it continues in those things, although in other respects it may be chargeable with many faults. It is possible, moreover, that some fault may insinuate itself into the preaching of the doctrine, or the administration of the sacraments, which ought not to alienate us from its communion. For all the articles of true doctrine are not of the same description. Some are so necessary to be known, that they ought to be universally received as fixed and indubitable principles, as the peculiar maxims of religion; such as, that there is one God; that Christ is God and the Son of God; that our salvation depends on the mercy of God; and the like. There are others, which are controverted among the churches, yet without destroying the unity of the faith. For why should there be a division on this point, if one church be of opinion, that souls, at their departure from their bodies, are immediately removed to heaven; and another church venture to determine nothing respecting their local situation, but be nevertheless firmly convinced, that they live to the Lord; and if this diversity of sentiment on both sides be free from all fondness for contention and obstinacy of assertion? The language of the apostle is, "Let us therefore, as many as be perfect, be thus minded; and if in any thing ye be otherwise minded, God shall reveal even this unto you." Does not this sufficiently show, that a diversity of opinion respecting these nonessential points ought not to be a cause of discord among Christians? It is of importance, indeed, that we should agree in every thing; but as there is no person who is not enveloped with some cloud of ignorance, either we must allow of no church at all, or we must forgive mistakes in those things, of which persons may be ignorant, without violating the essence of religion, or incurring the loss of salvation. Here I would not be understood to plead for any errors, even the smallest, or to recommend their being encouraged by connivance or flattery. But I maintain, that we ought not, on account of every trivial difference of sentiment, to abandon the Church, which retains the saving and pure doctrine that insures the preservation of piety, and supports the use of the sacraments instituted by our Lord. In the mean time, if we endeavour to correct what we disapprove, we are acting in this case according to our duty. And to this we are encouraged by the direction of Paul: "If any thing be revealed to another that sitteth by, let the first hold his peace." From which it appears, that every member of the Church is required to exert himself for the general edification, according to the measure of his grace, provided he do it decently and in order; that is to say, that we should neither forsake the communion of the Church, nor, by continuing in it, disturb its peace and well regulated discipline.

XIII. But in bearing with imperfections of life, we ought to carry our indulgence a great deal further. For this is a point in which we are very liable to err, and here Satan lies in wait to deceive us with no common devices. For there have always been persons, who, from a false notion of perfect sanctity, as if they were already become disembodied spirits, despised the society of all men in whom they could discover any remains of human infirmity. Such, in ancient times, were the Cathari, and also the Donatists, who approached to the same folly. Such, in the present day, are some of the Anabaptists, who would be thought to have made advances in piety beyond all others. There are others who err, more from an inconsiderate zeal for righteousness, than from this unreasonable pride. For when they perceive, that among those to whom the gospel is preached, its doctrine is not followed by correspondent effects in the life, they immediately pronounce, that there no church exists. This is, indeed, a very just ground of offence, and one for which we furnish more than sufficient occasion in the present unhappy age; nor is it possible to excuse our abominable inactivity, which the Lord will not suffer to escape with impunity, and which he has already begun to chastise with heavy scourges. Woe to us, therefore, who, by the dissolute licentiousness of our crimes, cause weak consciences to be wounded on our account! But, on the other hand, the error of the persons of whom we now speak, consists in not knowing how to fix any limits to their offence. For where our Lord requires the exercise of mercy, they entirely neglect it, and indulge themselves in immoderate severity. Supposing it impossible for the Church to exist, where there is not a perfect purity and integrity of life, through a hatred of crimes they depart from the true Church, while they imagine themselves to be only withdrawing from the factions of the wicked. They allege, that the Church of Christ is holy. But that they may also understand, that it is composed of good and bad men mingled together, let them hear that parable from the lips of Christ, where it is compared to a net, in which fishes of all kinds are collected, and no separation is made till they are exposed on the shore. Let them hear another parable, comparing the Church to a field, which, after having been sown with good seed, is, by the craft of an enemy, corrupted with tares, from which it is never cleared till the harvest is brought into the barn. Lastly, let them hear another comparison of the Church to a threshing-floor, in which the wheat is collected in such a manner, that it lies concealed under the chaff, till, after being carefully purged, by winnowing and sifting, it is at length laid up in the garner. But if our Lord declares, that the Church is to labour under this evil, and to be encumbered with a mixture of wicked men, even till the day of judgment, it is vain to seek for a Church free from every spot.

XIV. But they exclaim, that it is an intolerable thing that the pestilence of crimes so generally prevails. I grant it would be happy if the fact were otherwise; but in reply, I would present them with the judgment of the apostle. Among the Corinthians, more than a few had gone astray, and the infection had seized almost the whole society; there was not only one species of sin, but many; and they were not trivial faults, but dreadful crimes; and there was not only a corruption of morals, but also of doctrine. In this case, what is the conduct of the holy apostle, the organ of the heavenly Spirit, by whose testimony the Church stands or falls? Does he seek to separate from them? Does he reject them from the kingdom of Christ? Does he strike them with the thunderbolt of the severest anathema? He not only does none of these things, but, on the contrary, acknowledges and speaks of them as a Church of Christ and a society of saints. If there remained a church among the Corinthians, where contentions, factions, and emulations were raging; where cupidity, disputes, and litigations were prevailing; where a crime held in execration even among the Gentiles, was publicly sanctioned; where the name of Paul, whom they ought to have revered as their father, was insolently defamed; where some ridiculed the doctrine of the resurrection, with the subversion of which the whole gospel would be annihilated; where the graces of God were made subservient to ambition, instead of charity; where many things were conducted without decency and order; and if there still remained a Church, because the ministry of the word and sacraments was not rejected—who can refuse the name of a Church to those who cannot be charged with a tenth part of those crimes? And those who display such violence and severity against the Churches of the present age, I ask, how would they have conducted themselves towards the Galatians, who almost entirely deserted the gospel, but among whom, nevertheless, the same apostle found Churches?

XV. They object that Paul bitterly reproves the Corinthians for admitting an atrocious offender into their company, and follows this reproof with a general declaration, that with a man of scandalous life it is not lawful even to eat. Here they exclaim, If it be not lawful to eat common bread with him, how can it be lawful to unite with him in eating the bread of the Lord? I confess it is a great disgrace, if persons of immoral lives occupy places among the children of God; and if the sacred body of Christ be prostituted to them, the disgrace is vastly increased. And, indeed, if Churches be well regulated, they will not suffer persons of abandoned characters among them, nor will they promiscuously admit the worthy and the unworthy to that sacred supper. But because the pastors are not always so diligent in watching over them, and sometimes exercise more indulgence than they ought, or are prevented from exerting the severity they would wish, it happens that even those who are openly wicked are not always expelled from the society of the saints. This I acknowledge to be a fault, nor have I any inclination to extenuate it, since Paul sharply reproves it in the Corinthians. But though the Church may be deficient in its duty, it does not therefore follow that it is the place of every individual to pass judgment of separation for himself. I admit that it is the duty of a pious man to withdraw himself from all private intimacy with the wicked, and not to involve himself in any voluntary connection with them. But it is one thing to avoid familiar intercourse with the wicked; and another thing, from hatred of them, to renounce the communion of the Church. And persons who deem it sacrilege to participate with them the bread of the Lord, are in this respect far more rigid than Paul. For when he exhorts us to a pure and holy participation of it, he requires not one to examine another, or every one to examine the whole Church, but each individual to prove himself. If it were unlawful to communicate with an unworthy person, Paul would certainly have enjoined us to look around us, to see whether there were not some one in the multitude by whose impurity we might be contaminated. But as he only requires every one to examine himself, he shows that it is not the least injury to us if some unworthy persons intrude themselves with us. And this is fully implied in what he afterwards subjoins: "He that eateth and drinketh unworthily, eateth and drinketh judgment to himself." He says, not to others, but to himself, and with sufficient reason. For it ought not to be left to the judgment of every individual *who* ought to be admitted into the Church, and *who* ought to be expelled from it. This authority belongs to the whole Church, and cannot be exercised without legitimate order, as will be stated more at large hereafter. It would be unjust, therefore, that any individual should be contaminated with the unworthiness of another, whose approach it is neither in his power nor his duty to prevent.

XVI. But though this temptation sometimes arises even to good men, from an inconsiderate zeal for righteousness, yet we shall generally find that excessive severity is more owing to pride and haughtiness, and a false opinion which persons entertain of their own superior sanctity, than to true holiness, and a real concern for its interests. Those, therefore, who are most daring in promoting a separation from the Church, and act, as it were, as standard-bearers in the revolt, have in general no other motive than to make an ostentatious display of their own superior excellence, and their contempt of all others. Augustine correctly and judiciously observes—"Whereas the pious rule and method of ecclesiastical discipline ought principally to regard the unity of the Spirit in the bond of peace, which the apostle enjoined to be preserved by mutual forbearance, and which not being preserved, the medicinal punishment is evinced to be not only superfluous, but even pernicious, and therefore to be no longer medicinal; those wicked children, who, not from a hatred of the iniquities of others, but from a fondness for their own contentions, earnestly endeavour to draw the simple and uninformed multitude wholly after them, by entangling them with boasting of their own characters, or at least to divide them; those persons, I say, inflated with pride, infuriated with obstinacy, insidious in the circulation of calumnies, and turbulent in raising seditions, conceal themselves under the mask of a rigid severity, lest they should be proved to be destitute of the truth; and those things which in the Holy Scriptures are commanded to be done with great moderation, and without violating the sincerity of love, or breaking the unity of peace, for the correction of the faults of our brethren, they pervert to the sacrilege of schism, and an occasion of separation from the Church." To pious and peaceable persons he gives this advice: that they should correct in mercy whatever they can; that what they cannot, they should patiently bear, and affectionately lament, till God either reform and correct it, or, at the harvest, root up the tares and sift out the chaff. All pious persons should study to fortify themselves with these counsels, lest, while they consider themselves as valiant and strenuous defenders of righteousness, they depart from the kingdom of heaven, which is the only kingdom of righteousness. For since it is the will of God that the communion of his Church should be maintained in this external society, those who, from an aversion to wicked men, destroy the token of that society, enter on a course in which they are in great danger of falling from the communion of saints. Let them consider, in the first place, that in a great multitude there are many who escape their observation, who, nevertheless, are truly holy and innocent in the sight of God. Secondly, let them consider, that of those who appear subject to moral maladies, there are many who by no means please or flatter themselves in their vices, but are oftentimes aroused, with a serious fear of God, to aspire to greater integrity. Thirdly, let them consider that judgment ought not to be pronounced upon a man from a single act, since the holiest persons have sometimes most grievous falls. Fourthly, let them consider, that the ministry of the word, and the participation of the sacraments, have too much influence in preserving the unity of the Church, to admit of its being destroyed by the guilt of a few impious men. Lastly, let them consider, that in forming an estimate of the Church, the judgment of God is of more weight than that of man.

XVII. When they allege that there must be some reason why the Church is said to be holy, it is necessary to examine the holiness in which it excels; lest by refusing to admit the existence of a Church without absolute and sinless perfection, we should leave no Church in the world. It is true, that, as Paul tells us, "Christ loved the Church, and gave himself for it, that he might sanctify and cleanse it, by the washing of water by the word, that he might present it to himself a glorious Church, not having spot, or wrinkle, or any such thing." It is nevertheless equally true, that the Lord works from day to day in smoothing its wrinkles, and purging away its spots; whence it follows, that its holiness is not yet perfect. The Church, therefore, is so far holy, that it is daily improving, but has not yet arrived at perfection; that it is daily advancing, but has not yet reached the mark of holiness; as in another part of this work will be more fully explained. The predictions of the prophets, therefore, that "Jerusalem shall be holy, and there shall no strangers pass through her any more," and that the way of God shall be a "way of holiness, over which the unclean shall not pass," are not to be understood as if there were no blemish remaining in any of the members of the Church; but because they aspire with all their souls towards perfect holiness and purity, the goodness of God attributes to them that sanctity to which they have not yet fully attained. And though such evidences of sanctification are oftentimes rarely to be found among men, yet it must be maintained, that, from the foundation of the world, there has never been a period in which God had not his Church in it; and that, to the consummation of all things, there never will be a time in which he will not have his Church. For although, in the very beginning of time, the whole human race was corrupted and defiled by the sin of Adam; yet, from this polluted mass, God always sanctifies some vessels to honour, so that there is no age which has not experienced his mercy. This he has testified by certain promises, such as the following: "I have made a covenant with my chosen: I have sworn unto David, my servant, Thy seed will I establish for ever, and build up thy throne to all generations." Again: "The Lord hath chosen Zion; he hath desired it for his habitation. This is my rest for ever." Again: "Thus saith the Lord, which giveth the sun for a light by day, and the ordinances of the moon and of the stars for a light by night: If those ordinances depart from before me, saith the Lord, then the seed of Israel also shall cease from being a nation before me for ever."

XVIII. Of this truth Christ himself, the apostles, and almost all the prophets, have given us an example. Dreadful are those descriptions in which Isaiah, Jeremiah, Joel, Habakkuk, and others, deplore the disorders of the Church of Jerusalem. There was such general and extreme corruption in the people, in the magistrates, and in the priests, that Isaiah does not hesitate to compare Jerusalem to Sodom and Gomorrah. Religion was partly despised, partly corrupted. Their manners were generally disgraced by thefts, robberies, treacheries, murders, and similar crimes. Nevertheless, the prophets on this account neither raised themselves new churches, nor built new altars for the oblation of separate sacrifices; but whatever were the characters of the people, yet because they considered that God had deposited his word among that nation, and instituted the ceremonies in which he was there worshipped, they lifted up pure hands to him even in the congregation of the impious. If they had thought that they contracted any contagion from these services, surely they would have suffered a hundred deaths rather than have permitted themselves to be dragged to them. There was nothing therefore to prevent their departure from them, but the desire of preserving the unity of the Church. But if the holy prophets were restrained by a sense of duty from forsaking the Church on account of the numerous and enormous crimes which were practised, not by a few individuals, but almost by the whole nation,—it is extreme arrogance in us, if we presume immediately to withdraw from the communion of a Church where the conduct of all the members is not compatible either with our judgment, or even with the Christian profession.

XIX. Now, what kind of an age was that of Christ and his apostles? Yet the desperate impiety of the Pharisees, and the dissolute lives every where led by the people, could not prevent *them* from using the same sacrifices, and assembling in the same temple with others, for the public exercises of religion. How did this happen, but from a knowledge that the society of the wicked could not contaminate those who with pure consciences united with them in the same solemnities? If any one pay no deference to the prophets and apostles, let him at least acquiesce in the authority of Christ. Cyprian has excellently remarked, "Although tares, or impure vessels, are found in the Church, yet this is not a reason why we should withdraw from it. It only behoves us to labour that we may be the wheat, and to use our utmost endeavours and exertions, that we may be vessels of gold or of silver. But to break in pieces the vessels of earth belongs to the Lord alone, to whom a rod of iron is also given. Nor let any one arrogate to himself what is exclusively the province of the Son of God, by pretending to fan the floor, clear away the chaff, and separate all the tares by the judgment of man. This is proud obstinacy and sacrilegious presumption, originating in a corrupt frenzy." Let these two points, then, be considered as decided; first, that he who voluntarily deserts the external communion of the Church where the word of God is preached, and the sacraments are administered, is without any excuse; secondly, that the faults either of few persons or of many, form no obstacles to a due profession of our faith in the use of the ceremonies instituted by God; because the pious conscience is not wounded by the unworthiness of any other individual, whether he be a pastor or a private person; nor are the mysteries less pure and salutary to a holy and upright man, because they are received at the same time by the impure.

XX. Their severity and haughtiness go to still greater lengths. Acknowledging no church but such as is pure from the smallest blemishes, they are even angry with honest teachers, because, by exhorting believers to progressive improvements, they teach them to groan under the burden of sins, and to seek for pardon all their lifetime. For hereby, they pretend, the people are drawn away from perfection. I confess, that in urging men to perfection, we ought to labour with unremitting ardour and diligence; but to inspire their minds with a persuasion that they have already attained it, while they are yet in the pursuit of it, I maintain to be a diabolical invention. Therefore, in the Creed, *the communion of saints* is immediately followed by *the forgiveness of sins*, which can only be obtained by the citizens and members of the Church, as we read in the prophet. The heavenly Jerusalem, therefore, ought first to be built, in which this favour of God may be enjoyed, that whoever shall enter it, their iniquity shall be blotted out. Now, I affirm that this ought first to be built; not that there can ever be any Church without remission of sins, but because God has not promised to impart his mercy, except in the communion of saints. Our first entrance, therefore, into the Church and kingdom of God, is the remission of sins, without which we have no covenant or union with God. For thus he speaks by the prophet: "In that day will I make a covenant for them with the beasts of the field, and with the fowls of heaven, and with the creeping things of the ground; and I will break the bow and the sword, and the battle out of the earth, and will make them to lie down safely. And I will betroth thee unto me for ever; yea, I will betroth thee unto me in righteousness, and in judgment, and in loving-kindness, and in mercies." We see how God reconciles us to himself by his mercy. So in another place, where he foretells the restoration of the people whom he had scattered in his wrath, he says, "I will cleanse them from all their iniquity, whereby they have sinned against me." Wherefore it is by the sign of ablution, that we are initiated into the society of his Church; by which we are taught that there is no admittance for us into the family of God, unless our pollution be first taken away by his goodness.

XXI. Nor does God only once receive and adopt us into his Church by the remission of sins; he likewise preserves and keeps us in it by the same mercy. For to what purpose would it be, if we obtained a pardon which would afterwards be of no use? And that the mercy of the Lord would be vain and delusive, if it were only granted for once, all pious persons can testify to themselves; for every one of them is all his lifetime conscious of many infirmities, which need the Divine mercy. And surely it is not without reason, that God particularly promises this grace to the members of his family, and commands the same message of reconciliation to be daily addressed to them. As we carry about with us the relics of sin, therefore, as long as we live, we shall scarcely continue in the Church for a single moment, unless we are sustained by the constant grace of the Lord in forgiving our sins. But the Lord has called his people to eternal salvation; they ought, therefore, to believe that his grace is always ready to pardon their sins. Wherefore it ought to be held as a certain conclusion, that from the Divine liberality, by the intervention of the merit of Christ, through the sanctification of the Spirit, pardon of sins has been, and is daily, bestowed upon us, who have been admitted and ingrafted into the body of the Church.

XXII. It was to dispense this blessing to us, that the keys were given to the Church. For, when Christ gave commandment to his apostles, and conferred on them the power of remitting sins, it was not with an intention that they should merely absolve from their sins those who were converted from impiety to the Christian faith, but rather that they should continually exercise this office among the faithful. This is taught by Paul, when he says, that the message of reconciliation was committed to the ministers of the Church, that in the name of Christ they might daily exhort the people to be reconciled to God. In the communion of saints, therefore, sins are continually remitted to us by the ministry of the Church, when the presbyters or bishops, to whom this office is committed, confirm pious consciences, by the promises of the gospel, in the hope of pardon and remission; and that as well publicly as privately, according as necessity requires. For there are many persons who, on account of their infirmity, stand in need of separate and private consolation. And Paul tells us that he "taught," not only publicly, but also "from house to house, testifying repentance toward God, and faith toward our Lord Jesus Christ;" and admonished every individual separately respecting the doctrine of salvation. Here are three things, therefore, worthy of our observation. First, that whatever holiness may distinguish the children of God, yet such is their condition as long as they inhabit a mortal body, that they cannot stand before God without remission of sins. Secondly, that this benefit belongs to the Church; so that we cannot enjoy it unless we continue in its communion. Thirdly, that it is dispensed to us by the ministers and pastors of the Church, either in the preaching of the gospel, or in the administration of the sacraments; and that this is the principal exercise of the power of the keys, which the Lord has conferred on the society of believers. Let every one of us, therefore, consider it as his duty, not to seek remission of sins any where but where the Lord has placed it. Of public reconciliation, which is a branch of discipline, we shall speak in its proper place.

XXIII. But as those fanatic spirits, of whom I spoke, endeavour to rob the Church of this sole anchor of salvation, our consciences ought to be still more strongly fortified against such a pestilent opinion. The Novatians disturbed the ancient Churches with this tenet; but the present age also has witnessed some of the Anabaptists, who resemble the Novatians by falling into the same follies. For they imagine that by baptism the people of God are regenerated to a pure and angelic life, which cannot be contaminated by any impurities of the flesh. And if any one be guilty of sin after baptism, they leave him no prospect of escaping the inexorable judgment of God. In short, they encourage no hope of pardon in any one who sins after having received the grace of God; because they acknowledge no other remission of sins than that by which we are first regenerated. Now, though there is no falsehood more clearly refuted in the Scripture than this, yet because its advocates find persons to submit to their impositions, as Novatus formerly had numerous followers, let us briefly show how very pernicious their error is both to themselves and to others. In the first place, when the saints obey the command of the Lord by a daily repetition of this prayer, "forgive us our debts," they certainly confess themselves to be sinners. Nor do they pray in vain, for our Lord has not enjoined the use of any petitions, but such as he designed to grant. And after he had declared that the whole prayer would be heard by the Father, he confirmed this absolution by a special promise. What do we want more? The Lord requires from the saints a confession of sins, and that daily as long as they live, and he promises them pardon. What presumption is it either to assert that they are exempt from sin, or, if they have fallen, to exclude them from all grace! To whom does he enjoin us to grant forgiveness seventy times seven times? Is it not to our brethren? And what was the design of this injunction, but that we might imitate his clemency? He pardons, therefore, not once or twice, but as often as the sinner is alarmed with a sense of his sins, and sighs for mercy.

XXIV. But to begin from the infancy of the Church: the patriarchs had been circumcised, admitted to the privileges of the covenant, and without doubt instructed in justice and integrity by the care of their father, when they conspired to murder their brother. This was a crime to be abominated even by the most desperate and abandoned robbers. At length, softened by the admonitions of Judah, they sold him for a slave. This also was an intolerable cruelty. Simon and Levi, in a spirit of nefarious revenge, condemned even by the judgment of their father, murdered the inhabitants of Sichem. Reuben was guilty of execrable incest with his father's concubine. Judah, with an intention of indulging a libidinous passion, violated the law of nature by a criminal connection with his son's wife. Yet they are so far from being expunged out of the number of the chosen people, that, on the contrary, they are constituted the heads of the nation. What shall we say of David? Though he was the official guardian of justice, how scandalously did he prepare the way for the gratification of a blind passion, by the effusion of innocent blood! He had already been regenerated, and among the regenerate had been distinguished by the peculiar commendations of the Lord; yet he perpetrated a crime even among heathens regarded with horror, and yet he obtained mercy. And not to dwell any longer on particular examples, the numerous promises which the law and the prophets contain, of Divine mercy towards the Israelites, are so many proofs of the manifestation of God's placability to the offences of his people. For what does Moses promise to the people in case of their return to the Lord, after having fallen into idolatry? "Then the Lord thy God will turn thy captivity, and have compassion upon thee, and will return and gather thee from all the nations, whither the Lord thy God hath scattered thee. If any of thine be driven out unto the outmost parts of heaven, from thence will the Lord thy God gather thee."

XXV. But I am unwilling to commence an enumeration which would have no end. For the prophets are full of such promises, which offer mercy to the people, though covered with innumerable crimes. What sin is worse than rebellion? It is described as a divorce between God and the Church: yet this is overcome by the goodness of God. Hear his language by the mouth of Jeremiah: "If a man put away his wife, and she go from him, and become another man's, shall he return unto her again? Shall not that land be greatly polluted? But thou hast played the harlot with many lovers, and thou hast polluted the land with thy whoredoms and with thy wickedness. Yet return again to me, thou backsliding Israel, saith the Lord, and I will not cause mine anger to fall upon you; for I am merciful, saith the Lord, and will not keep anger for ever." And surely there cannot possibly be any other disposition in him who affirms, that he "hath no pleasure in the death of the wicked, but that the wicked turn from his way and live." Therefore, when Solomon dedicated the temple, he appointed it also for this purpose, that prayers, offered to obtain pardon of sins, might there be heard and answered. His words are, "If they sin against thee, (for there is no man that sinneth not,) and thou be angry with them, and deliver them to the enemy, so that they carry them away captives unto the land of the enemy, far or near; yet if they shall bethink themselves, and repent in the land whither they were carried captives, and repent and make supplication unto thee in the land of those that carried them captives, saying, We have sinned, and have done perversely, we have committed wickedness; and pray unto thee toward the land which thou gavest unto their fathers, the city which thou hast chosen, and the house which I have built for thy name; then hear thou their prayer and their supplication in heaven, and forgive thy people that have sinned against thee, and all their transgressions wherein they have transgressed against thee." Nor was it without cause that in the law the Lord ordained daily sacrifices for sins; for unless he had foreseen that his people would be subject to the maladies of daily sins, he would never have appointed these remedies.

XXVI. Now, I ask whether, by the advent of Christ, in whom the fulness of grace was displayed, believers have been deprived of this benefit, so that they can no longer presume to supplicate for the pardon of their sins; so that if they offend against the Lord, they can obtain no mercy. What would this be but to affirm, that Christ came for the destruction of his people, and not for their salvation; if the loving-kindness of God, in the pardon of sins, which was continually ready to be exercised to the saints under the Old Testament, be maintained to be now entirely withdrawn? But if we give any credit to the Scriptures, which proclaim that in Christ the grace and philanthropy of God have at length been fully manifested, that his mercy has been abundantly diffused, and reconciliation between God and man accomplished, we ought not to doubt that the clemency of our heavenly Father is displayed to us in greater abundance, rather than restricted or diminished. Examples to prove this are not wanting. Peter, who had been warned that he who would not confess the name of Christ before men would be denied by him before angels, denied him three times in one night, and accompanied the denial with execrations; yet he was not refused pardon. Those of the Thessalonians who led disorderly lives, are reprehended by the apostle, in order to be invited to repentance. Nor does Peter drive Simon Magus himself to despair; but rather directs him to cherish a favourable hope, when he persuades him to pray for forgiveness.

XXVII. What are we to say of cases in which the most enormous sins have sometimes seized whole Churches? From this situation Paul rather mercifully reclaimed them, than abandoned them to the curse. The defection of the Galatians was no trivial offence. The Corinthians were still less excusable, their crimes being more numerous and equally enormous. Yet neither are excluded from the mercy of the Lord: on the contrary, the very persons who had gone beyond all others in impurity, unchastity, and fornication, are expressly invited to repentance. For the covenant of the Lord will ever remain eternal and inviolable, which he has made with Christ, the antitype of Solomon, and with all his members, in these words: "If his children forsake my law, and walk not in my judgments; if they break my statutes, and keep not my commandments; then will I visit their transgression with the rod, and their iniquity with stripes. Nevertheless my loving-kindness will I not utterly take from him." Finally, the order of the Creed teaches us that pardon of sins ever continues in the Church of Christ, because, after having mentioned the Church, it immediately adds *the forgiveness of sins*.

XXVIII. Some persons, who are a little more judicious, perceiving the notion of Novatus to be so explicitly contradicted by the Scripture, do not represent every sin as unpardonable, but only voluntary transgression, into which a person may have fallen with the full exercise of his knowledge and will. These persons admit of no pardon for any sins, but such as may have been the mere errors of ignorance. But as the Lord, in the law, commanded some sacrifices to be offered to expiate the voluntary sins of believers, and others to atone for sins of ignorance, what extreme presumption is it to deny that there is any pardon for voluntary transgression! I maintain, that there is nothing more evident, than that the one sacrifice of Christ is available for the remission of the voluntary sins of the saints, since the Lord has testified the same by the legal victims, as by so many types. Besides, who can plead ignorance as an excuse for David, who was evidently so well acquainted with the law? Did not David know that adultery and murder were great crimes, which he daily punished in others? Did the patriarchs consider fratricide as lawful? Had the Corinthians learned so little that they could imagine impurity, incontinence, fornication, animosities, and contentions, to be pleasing to God? Could Peter, who had been so carefully warned, be ignorant how great a crime it was to abjure his Master? Let us not, therefore, by our cruelty, shut the gate of mercy which God has so liberally opened.

XXIX. I am fully aware that the old writers have explained those sins, which are daily forgiven to believers, to be the smaller faults, which are inadvertently committed through the infirmity of the flesh; but solemn repentance, which was then required for greater offences, they thought, was no more to be repeated than baptism. This sentiment is not to be understood as indicating their design, either to drive into despair such persons as had relapsed after their first repentance, or to extenuate those errors, as if they were small in the sight of God. For they knew that the saints frequently stagger through unbelief; that they sometimes utter unnecessary oaths; that they occasionally swell into anger, and even break out into open reproaches; and that they are likewise chargeable with other faults, which the Lord holds in the greatest abomination. They expressed themselves in this manner, to distinguish between private offences and those public crimes which were attended with great scandal in the Church. But the difficulty, which they made, of forgiving those who had committed any thing deserving of ecclesiastical censure, did not arise from an opinion that it was difficult for them to obtain pardon from the Lord; they only intended by this severity to deter others from rashly running into crimes, which would justly be followed by their exclusion from the communion of the Church. The word of the Lord, however, which ought to be our only rule in this case, certainly prescribes greater moderation. For it teaches, that the rigour of discipline ought not to be carried to such an extent, as to overwhelm with sorrow the person whose benefit we are required to regard as its principal object; as we have before shown more at large.

14.

The Teachers and Ministers of the Church;
Their Election and Office.

We must now treat of the order which it has been the Lord's will to appoint for the government of his Church. For although he alone ought to rule and reign in the Church, and to have all preëminence in it, and this government ought to be exercised and administered solely by his word,—yet, as he dwells not among us by a visible presence, so as to make an audible declaration of his will to us, we have stated, that for this purpose he uses the ministry of men whom he employs as his delegates, not to transfer his right and honour to them, but only that he may himself do his work by their lips; just as an artificer makes use of an instrument in the performance of his work. Some observations which I have made already, are necessary to be repeated here. It is true that he might do this either by himself, without any means or instruments, or even by angels; but there are many reasons why he prefers making use of men. For, in the first place, by this method he declares his kindness towards us, since he chooses from among men those who are to be his ambassadors to the world, to be the interpreters of his secret will, and even to act as his personal representatives. And thus he affords an actual proof, that when he so frequently calls us his temples, it is not an unmeaning appellation, since he gives answers to men, even from the mouths of men, as from a sanctuary. In the second place, this is a most excellent and beneficial method to train us to humility, since he accustoms us to obey his word, though it is preached to us by men like ourselves, and sometimes even of inferior rank. If he were himself to speak from heaven, there would be no wonder if his sacred oracles were instantly received with reverence, by the ears and hearts of all mankind. For who would not be awed by his present power? who would not fall prostrate at the first view of infinite Majesty? who would not be confounded by that overpowering splendour? But when a contemptible mortal, who had just emerged from the dust, addresses us in the name of God, we give the best evidence of our piety and reverence towards God himself, if we readily submit to be instructed by his minister, who possesses no personal superiority to ourselves. For this reason, also, he has deposited the treasure of his heavenly wisdom in frail and earthen vessels, in order to afford a better proof of the estimation in which we hold it. Besides, nothing was more adapted to promote brotherly love, than a mutual connection of men by this bond, while one is constituted the pastor to teach all the rest, and they who are commanded to be disciples, receive one common doctrine from the same mouth. For if each person were sufficient for himself, and had no need of the assistance of another, such is the pride of human nature, every one would despise others, and would also be despised by them. The Lord, therefore, has connected his Church together, by that which he foresaw would be the strongest bond for the preservation of their union, when he committed the doctrine of eternal life and salvation to men, that by their hands it might be communicated to others. Paul had this in view when he wrote to the Ephesians, "There is one body, and one Spirit, even as ye are called in one hope of your calling; one Lord, one faith, one baptism, one God and Father of all, who is above all, and through all, and in you all. But unto every one of us is given grace according to the measure of the gift of Christ.

Wherefore he saith, When he ascended up on high, he led captivity captive, and gave gifts unto men. (Now that he ascended, what is it but that he also descended first into the lower parts of the earth? He that descended is the same also that ascended up far above all heavens, that he might fill all things.) And he gave some, apostles; and some, prophets; and some, evangelists; and some, pastors and teachers; for the perfecting of the saints, for the work of the ministry, for the edifying of the body of Christ; till we all come in the unity of the faith, and of the knowledge of the Son of God, unto a perfect man, unto the measure of the stature of the fulness of Christ; that we henceforth be no more children, tossed to and fro, and carried about with every wind of doctrine, by the sleight of men, and cunning craftiness, whereby they lie in wait to deceive; but, speaking the truth in love, may grow up into him in all things, which is the head, even Christ; from whom the whole body fitly joined together, and compacted by that which every joint supplieth, according to the effectual working in the measure of every part, maketh increase of the body unto the edifying of itself in love."

II. In this passage he shows that the ministry of men, which God employs in his government of the Church, is the principal bond which holds believers together in one body. He also indicates that the Church cannot be preserved in perfect safety, unless it be supported by these means which God has been pleased to appoint for its preservation. Christ, he says, "ascended up far above all heavens, that he might fill all things." And this is the way in which he does it. By means of his ministers, to whom he has committed this office, and on whom he has bestowed grace to discharge it, he dispenses and distributes his gifts to the Church, and even affords some manifestation of his own presence, by exerting the power of his Spirit in this his institution, that it may not be vain or ineffectual. Thus is the restoration of the saints effected; thus is the body of Christ edified; thus we grow up unto him who is our Head in all things, and are united with each other; thus we are all brought to the unity of Christ; if prophecy flourishes among us, if we receive the apostles, if we despise not the doctrine which is delivered to us. Whoever, therefore, either aims to abolish or undervalue this order, of which we are treating, and this species of government, attempts to disorganize the Church, or rather to subvert and destroy it altogether. For neither the light and heat of the sun, nor any meat and drink, are so necessary to the nourishment and sustenance of the present life, as the apostolical and pastoral office is to the preservation of the Church in the world.

III. Therefore I have already remarked, that God has frequently commended its dignity to us by every possible encomium, in order that we might hold it in the highest estimation and value, as more excellent than every thing else. That he confers a peculiar favour upon men by raising up teachers for them, he fully signifies, when he commands the prophet to exclaim, "How beautiful are the feet of him that publisheth peace;" and when he calls the apostles "the light of the world," and "the salt of the earth." Nor could that office be more splendidly distinguished than when he said to them, "He that heareth you, heareth me." But there is no passage more remarkable than that in Paul's Second Epistle to the Corinthians, where he professedly discusses this question. He contends, that there is nothing more excellent or glorious than the ministry of the gospel in the Church, inasmuch as it is the ministration of the Spirit, and of righteousness, and of eternal life. The tendency of these and similar passages, is to preserve that mode of governing the Church by its ministers, which the Lord appointed to be of perpetual continuance, from sinking into disesteem, and, at length, falling into disuse through mere contempt. And how exceedingly necessary it is, he has not only declared in words, but shown by examples. When he was pleased to illuminate Cornelius more fully with the light of his truth, he despatched an angel from heaven to send Peter to him. When he designs to call Paul to the knowledge of himself, and to introduce him into the Church, he does not address him with his own voice, but sends him to a man to receive the doctrine of salvation, and the sanctification of baptism. If it was not without sufficient reason, that an angel, who is the messenger of God, refrains from announcing the Divine will himself, and directs a man to be sent for in order to declare it,—and that Christ, the sole Teacher of believers, committed Paul to the instruction of a man, the same Paul whom he had determined to elevate into the third heaven, and to favour with a miraculous revelation of things unspeakable,—who can now dare to despise that ministry, or to neglect it as unnecessary, the utility and necessity of which God has been pleased to evince by such examples?

IV. Those who preside over the government of the Church, according to the institution of Christ, are named by Paul, first, "apostles;" secondly, "prophets;" thirdly, "evangelists;" fourthly, "pastors;" lastly, "teachers." Of these, only the two last sustain an ordinary office in the Church: the others were such as the Lord raised up at the commencement of his kingdom, and such as he still raises up on particular occasions, when required by the necessity of the times. The nature of the apostolic office is manifest from this command: "Go preach the gospel to every creature." No certain limits are prescribed, but the whole world is assigned to them, to be reduced to obedience to Christ; that by disseminating the gospel wherever they could, they might erect his kingdom in all nations. Therefore Paul, when he wished to prove his apostleship, declares, not merely that he had gained some one city for Christ, but that he had propagated the gospel far and wide, and that he had not built upon the foundation of others, but had planted Churches where the name of the Lord had never been heard before. The "apostles," therefore, were missionaries, who were to reduce the world from their revolt to true obedience to God, and to establish his kingdom universally by the preaching of the gospel. Or, if you please, they were the first architects of the Church, appointed to lay its foundations all over the world. Paul gives the appellation of "prophets," not to all interpreters of the Divine will, but only to those who were honoured with some special revelation. Of these, either there are none in our day, or they are less conspicuous. By "evangelists," I understand those who were inferior to the apostles in dignity, but next to them in office, and who performed similar functions. Such were Luke, Timothy, Titus, and others of that description; and perhaps also the seventy disciples, whom Christ ordained to occupy the second station from the apostles. According to this interpretation, which appears to me perfectly consistent with the language and meaning of the apostle, those three offices were not instituted to be of perpetual continuance in the Church, but only for that age when Churches were to be raised where none had existed before, or were at least to be conducted from Moses to Christ. Though I do not deny, that, even since that period, God has sometimes raised up apostles or evangelists in their stead, as he has done in our own time. For there was a necessity for such persons to recover the Church from the defection of Antichrist. Nevertheless, I call this an extraordinary office, because it has no place in well-constituted Churches. Next follow "pastors" and "teachers," who are always indispensable to the Church. The difference between them I apprehend to be this—that teachers have no official concern with the discipline, or the administration of the sacraments, or with admonitions and exhortations, but only with the interpretation of the Scripture, that pure and sound doctrine may be retained among believers; whereas the pastoral office includes all these things.

V. We have now ascertained what offices were appointed to continue for a time in the government of the Church, and what were instituted to be of perpetual duration. If we connect the evangelists with the apostles, as sustaining the same office, we shall then have two offices of each description, corresponding to each other. For our pastors bear the same resemblance to the apostles, as our teachers do to the ancient prophets. The office of the prophets was more excellent, on account of the special gift of revelation, by which they were distinguished; but the office of teachers is executed in a similar manner, and has precisely the same end. So those twelve individuals, whom the Lord chose to promulgate the first proclamation of his gospel to the world, preceded all others in order and dignity. For although, according to the meaning and etymology of the word, all the ministers of the Church may be called apostles, because they are all sent by the Lord, and are his messengers, yet, as it was of great importance to have a certain knowledge of the mission of persons who were to announce a thing new and unheard before, it was necessary that those twelve, together with Paul, who was afterwards added to their number, should be distinguished beyond all others by a peculiar title. Paul himself, indeed, gives this name to "Andronicus and Junia, who," he says, "are of note among the apostles;" but when he means to speak with strict propriety, he never applies that name except to those of the first order that we have mentioned. And this is the common usage of the Scripture. But the province of pastors is the same as that of the apostles, except that they preside over particular Churches respectively committed to each of them. Of the nature of their functions let us now proceed to a more distinct statement.

VI. Our Lord, when he sent forth his apostles, commissioned them, as we have just remarked, to preach the gospel, and to baptize all believers for the remission of sins. He had already commanded them to distribute the sacred symbols of his body and blood according to his own example. Behold the sacred, inviolable, and perpetual law imposed upon those who call themselves successors of the apostles; it commands them to preach the gospel, and to administer the sacraments. Hence we conclude, that those who neglect both these duties have no just pretensions to the character of apostles. But what shall we say of pastors? Paul speaks not only of himself, but of all who bear that office, when he says, "Let a man so account of us, as of the ministers of Christ, and stewards of the mysteries of God." Again: "A bishop must hold fast the faithful word as he hath been taught, that he may be able, by sound doctrine, both to exhort and to convince the gainsayers." From these and similar passages, which frequently occur, we may infer that the preaching of the gospel, and the administration of the sacraments, constitute the two principal parts of the pastoral office. Now, the business of teaching is not confined to public discourses, but extends also to private admonitions. Thus Paul calls upon the Ephesians to witness the truth of his declaration, "I have kept back nothing that was profitable unto you, but have showed you, and have taught you publicly, and from house to house, testifying both to the Jews, and also to the Greeks, repentance toward God, and faith toward our Lord Jesus Christ." And a little after: "I ceased not to warn every one, night and day, with tears." But it is no part of my present design, to enumerate all the excellences of a good pastor, but only to show what is implied in the profession of those who call themselves pastors; namely, that they preside over the Church in that station, not that they may enjoy a respectable sinecure, but to instruct the people in true piety by the doctrine of Christ, to administer the holy mysteries, to maintain and exercise proper discipline. For the Lord denounces to all those who have been stationed as watchmen in the Church, that if any one perish in ignorance through their negligence, he will require the blood of such a person at their hands. What Paul says of himself, belongs to them all: "Woe is unto me, if I preach not the gospel," because "a dispensation of the gospel is committed unto me." Lastly, what the apostles did for the whole world, that every individual pastor ought to do for his flock to which he is appointed.

VII. While we assign to them all respectively their distinct Churches, yet we do not deny that a pastor, who is connected with one Church, may assist others, either when any disputes arise, which may require his presence, or when his advice is asked upon any difficult subject. But because, in order to preserve the peace of the Church, there is a necessity for such a regulation as shall clearly define to every one what duty he has to do, lest they should all fall into disorder, run hither and thither in uncertainty without any call, and all resort to one place; and lest those who feel more solicitude for their personal accommodation than for the edification of the Church, should, without any cause but their own caprice, leave the Churches destitute,—this distribution ought as far as possible to be generally observed, that every one may be content with his own limits, and not invade the province of another. Nor is this an invention of men, but an institution of God himself. For we read that Paul and Barnabas "ordained elders in the respective Churches of Lystra, Iconium, and Antioch;" and Paul himself directed Titus to "ordain elders in every city." So in other passages he mentions "the bishops at Philippi," and Archippus, the bishop of the Colossians. And a remarkable speech of his is preserved by Luke, addressed to "the elders of the Church of Ephesus." Whoever, therefore, has undertaken the government and charge of one Church, let him know that he is bound to this law of the Divine call; not that he is fixed to his station so as never to be permitted to leave it in a regular and orderly manner, if the public benefit should require it; but he who has been called to one place, ought never to think either of departing from his situation, or relinquishing the office altogether, from any motive of personal convenience or advantage. But if it be expedient that he should remove to another station, he ought not to attempt this on his own private opinion, but to be guided by public authority.

VIII. In calling those who preside over Churches by the appellations of bishops, elders, pastors, and ministers, without any distinction, I have followed the usage of the Scripture, which applies all these terms to express the same meaning. For to all who discharge the ministry of the word, it gives the title of "bishops." So when Paul enjoins Titus to "ordain elders in every city," he immediately adds, "For a bishop must be blameless." So in another Epistle he salutes more bishops than one in one Church. And in the Acts he is declared to have sent for the elders of the Church of Ephesus, whom, in his address to them, he calls "bishops." Here it must be observed, that we have enumerated only those offices which consist in the ministry of the word; nor does Paul mention any other in the fourth chapter of the Epistle to the Ephesians, which we have quoted. But in the Epistle to the Romans, and the First Epistle to the Corinthians, he enumerates others, as "powers," "gifts of healing," "interpretation of tongues," "governments," "care of the poor." Those functions which were merely temporary, I omit, as foreign to our present subject. But there are two which perpetually remain—"government," and "the care of the poor." "Governors" I apprehend to have been persons of advanced years, selected from the people, to unite with the bishops in giving admonitions and exercising discipline. For no other interpretation can be given of that injunction, "He that ruleth, let him do it with diligence." Therefore, from the beginning, every Church has had its senate or council, composed of pious, grave, and holy men, who were invested with that jurisdiction in the correction of vices, of which we shall soon treat. Now, that this regulation was not of a single age, experience itself demonstrates. This office of government is necessary, therefore, in every age.

IX. The care of the poor was committed to the "deacons." The Epistle to the Romans, however, mentions two functions of this kind. "He that giveth," says the apostle, "let him do it with simplicity: he that showeth mercy, with cheerfulness." Now, as it is certain that he there speaks of the public offices of the Church, it follows that there were two distinct orders of deacons. Unless my judgment deceive me, the former clause refers to the deacons who administered the alms; and the other to those who devoted themselves to the care of poor and sick persons; such as the widows mentioned by Paul to Timothy. For women could execute no other public office, than by devoting themselves to the service of the poor. If we admit this,—and it ought to be fully admitted,—there will be two classes of deacons, of whom one will serve the Church in dispensing the property given to the poor, the other in taking care of the poor themselves.—Though the word itself ($\delta\iota\alpha\kappa o\nu\iota\alpha$) is of more extensive signification, yet the Scripture particularly gives the title of "deacons" to those whom the Church has appointed to dispense the alms and take care of the poor, and constituted stewards, as it were, of the common treasury of the poor; and whose origin, institution, and office, are described in the Acts of the Apostles. For "when there arose a murmuring of the Grecians against the Hebrews because their widows were neglected in the daily ministration," the apostles pleaded their inability to discharge both offices, of the ministry of the word and the service of tables, and said to the multitude, "Wherefore, brethren, look ye out among you seven men of honest report, full of the Holy Ghost and wisdom, whom we may appoint over this business." See what were the characters of the deacons in the apostolic Church, and what ought to be the characters of ours, in conformity to the primitive example.

X. Now, as "all things" in the Church are required to "be done decently and in order," there is nothing in which this ought to be more diligently observed, than the constitution of its government; because there would be more danger from disorder in this case than in any other. Therefore, that restless and turbulent persons may not presumptuously intrude themselves into the office of teaching or of governing, it is expressly provided, that no one shall assume a public office in the Church without a call. In order, therefore, that any one may be accounted a true minister of the Church, it is necessary, in the first place, that he be regularly called to it, and, in the second place, that he answer his call; that is, by undertaking and executing the office assigned to him. This may frequently be observed in Paul; who, when he wishes to prove his apostleship, almost always alleges his call, together with his fidelity in the execution of the office. If so eminent a minister of Christ dare not arrogate to himself an authority to require his being heard in the Church, but in consequence of his appointment to it by a Divine commission, and his faithful discharge of the duty assigned him,—what extreme impudence must it be, if any man, destitute of both these characters, should claim such an honour for himself! But having already spoken of the necessity of discharging the office, let us now confine ourselves to the call.

XI. Now, the discussion of this subject includes four branches: what are the qualifications of ministers; in what manner they are to be chosen; by whom they ought to be appointed; and with what rite or ceremony they are to be introduced into their office. I speak of the external and solemn call, which belongs to the public order of the Church; passing over that secret call, of which every minister is conscious to himself before God, but which is not known to the Church. This secret call, however, is the honest testimony of our heart, that we accept the office offered to us, not from ambition or avarice, or any other unlawful motive, but from a sincere fear of God, and an ardent zeal for the edification of the Church. This, as I have hinted, is indispensable to every one of us, if we would approve our ministry in the sight of God. In the view of the Church, however, he who enters on his office with an evil conscience, is nevertheless duly called, provided his iniquity be not discovered. It is even common to speak of private persons as called to the ministry, who appear to be adapted and qualified for the discharge of its duties; because learning, connected with piety and other endowments of a good pastor, constitutes a kind of preparation for it. For those whom the Lord has destined to so important an office, he first furnishes with those talents which are requisite to its execution, that they may not enter upon it empty and unprepared. Hence Paul, in his Epistle to the Corinthians, when he intended to treat of the offices themselves, first enumerated the gifts which ought to be possessed by the persons who sustain those offices. But as this is the first of the four points which I have proposed, let us now proceed to it.

XII. The qualifications of those who ought to be chosen bishops, are stated at large by Paul in two passages. The sum of all he says is, that none are to be chosen but men of sound doctrine and a holy life, not chargeable with any fault that may destroy their authority, or disgrace their ministry. The same rule is laid down for the deacons and governors. Constant care is required, that they be not unequal to the burden imposed upon them, or, in other words, that they be endowed with those talents which are necessary to the discharge of their duty. So, when Christ was about to send forth his apostles, he furnished them with such means and powers as were indispensable to their success. And Paul, after having delineated the character of a good and genuine bishop, admonishes Timothy not to contaminate himself by the appointment of any one of a different description. The question relating to the *manner* in which they are to be chosen, I refer not to the form of election, but to the religious awe which ought to be observed in it. Hence the fasting and prayer, which Luke states to have been practised by the faithful at the ordination of elders. For knowing themselves to be engaged in a business of the highest importance, they dared not attempt any thing but with the greatest reverence and solicitude. And above all things, they were earnest in prayers and supplications to God for the spirit of wisdom and discretion.

XIII. The third inquiry we proposed was, by whom ministers are to be chosen. Now, for this no certain rule can be gathered from the appointment of the apostles, which was a case somewhat different from the common call of other ministers. For as theirs was an extraordinary office, it was necessary, in order to render it conspicuous by some eminent character, that they who were to sustain it should be called and appointed by the mouth of the Lord himself. The apostles, therefore, entered upon their work, not in consequence of any human election, but empowered by the sole command of God and of Christ. Hence, when they wish to substitute another in the place of Judas, they refrain from a certain appointment of any one, but nominate two, that the Lord may declare by lot which of them he wills to be his successor. In the same sense must be understood the declaration of Paul, that he had been created "an apostle, not of men, neither by man, but by Jesus Christ, and God the Father." The first clause, *not of men*, was applicable to him in common with all pious ministers of the word; for no man can lawfully exercise this ministry without having been called by God. The other clause was special and peculiar to himself. When he glories in this, therefore, he not only claims what belongs to a true and lawful pastor, but likewise brings forward an evidence of his apostleship. For whereas there were, among the Galatians, some who, from an eagerness to diminish his authority, represented him as a common disciple deputed by the primary apostles,—in order to vindicate the dignity of his preaching, against which he knew these artifices were directed, he found it necessary to show that he was not inferior to the other apostles in any respect. Wherefore he affirms, that he had not been elected by the judgment of men, like some ordinary bishop, but by the mouth and clear revelation of the Lord himself.

XIV. But that the election and appointment of bishops by men is necessary to constitute a legitimate call to the office, no sober person will deny, while there are so many testimonies of Scripture to establish it. Nor is it contradicted by that declaration of Paul, that he was "an apostle, not of men, nor by man," since he is not speaking in that passage of the ordinary election of ministers, but claiming to himself what was the special privilege of the apostles. The immediate designation of Paul, by the Lord himself, to this peculiar privilege, was nevertheless accompanied with the form of an ecclesiastical call, for Luke states, that "As they ministered to the Lord, and fasted, the Holy Ghost said, Separate me Barnabas and Saul for the work whereunto I have called them." What end could be answered by this separation and imposition of hands after the Holy Spirit had testified their election, unless it was the preservation of the order of the Church in designating ministers by men? God could not sanction that order, therefore, by a more illustrious example than when, after having declared that he had constituted Paul the apostle of the Gentiles, he nevertheless directed him to be designated by the Church. The same may be observed in the election of Matthias. For the apostolic office being of such high importance that they could not venture to fill up their number by the choice of any one person from their own judgment, they appointed two, one of whom was to be chosen by lot; that so the election might obtain a positive sanction from Heaven, and yet that the order of the Church might not be altogether neglected.

XV. Here it is inquired, whether a minister ought to be chosen by the whole Church, or only by the other ministers and the elders who preside over the discipline, or whether he may be appointed by the authority of an individual. Those who attribute this right to any one man, quote what Paul says to Titus: "For this cause I left thee in Crete, that thou shouldst ordain elders in every city;" and to Timothy: "Lay hands suddenly on no man." But they are exceedingly mistaken, if they suppose that either Timothy at Ephesus, or Titus in Crete, exercised a sovereign power to regulate every thing according to his own pleasure. For they presided over the people, only to lead them by good and salutary counsels, not to act alone to the exclusion of all others. But that this may not be thought to be an invention of mine, I will prove it by a similar example. For Luke relates, that elders were ordained in the Churches by Paul and Barnabas, but at the same time he distinctly marks the manner in which this was done,—namely, by the suffrages or votes of the people; for this is the meaning of the term he there employs—χειροτονησαντες πρεσβυτερους κατ᾽ ἐκκλησιαν. Those two apostles, therefore, ordained them; but the whole multitude, according to the custom observed in elections among the Greeks, declared by the elevation of their hands who was the object of their choice. So the Roman historians frequently speak of the consul, who held the assemblies, as *appointing* the new magistrates, for no other reason but because he received the suffrages and presided at the election. Surely it is not credible that Paul granted to Timothy and Titus more power than he assumed to himself; but we see that he was accustomed to ordain bishops according to the suffrages of the people. The above passages, therefore, ought to be understood in the same manner, to guard against all infringement of the common right and liberty of the Church. It is a good remark, therefore, of Cyprian, when he contends, "that it proceeds from Divine authority, that a priest should be elected publicly in the presence of all the people, and that he should be approved as a worthy and fit person by the public judgment and testimony." In the case of the Levitical priests, we find it was commanded by the Lord, that they should be brought forward in the view of the people before their consecration. Nor was Matthias added to the number of the apostles, nor were the seven deacons appointed, without the presence and approbation of the people.—"These examples," says Cyprian, "show that the ordination of a priest ought not to be performed but with the knowledge and concurrence of the people, in order that the election which shall have been examined by the testimony of all, may be just and legitimate." We find, therefore, that it is a legitimate ministry according to the word of God, when those who appear suitable persons are appointed with the consent and approbation of the people; but that other pastors ought to preside over the election, to guard the multitude from falling into any improprieties, through inconstancy, intrigue, or confusion.

XVI. There remains the Form of ordination, which is the last point that we have mentioned relative to the call of ministers. Now, it appears that when the apostles introduced any one into the ministry, they used no other ceremony than imposition of hands. This rite, I believe, descended from the custom of the Hebrews, who, when they wished to bless and consecrate any thing, presented it to God by imposition of hands. Thus, when Jacob blessed Ephraim and Manasseh, he laid his hands upon their heads. This custom was followed by our Lord, when he prayed over infants. It was with the same design, I apprehend, that the Jews were directed in the law to lay their hands upon their sacrifices. Wherefore the imposition of the hands of the apostles was an indication that they offered to God the person whom they introduced into the ministry. They used the same ceremony over those on whom they conferred the visible gifts of the Spirit. But, be that as it may, this was the solemn rite invariably practised, whenever any one was called to the ministry of the Church. Thus they ordained pastors and teachers, and thus they ordained deacons. Now, though there is no express precept for the imposition of hands, yet since we find it to have been constantly used by the apostles, such a punctual observance of it by them ought to have the force of a precept with us. And certainly this ceremony is highly useful both to recommend to the people the dignity of the ministry, and to admonish the person ordained that he is no longer his own master, but devoted to the service of God and the Church. Besides, it will not be an unmeaning sign, if it be restored to its true origin. For if the Spirit of God institutes nothing in the Church in vain, we shall perceive that this ceremony, which proceeded from him, is not without its use, provided it be not perverted by a superstitious abuse. Finally, it is to be remarked, that the imposition of hands on the ministers was not the act of the whole multitude, but was confined to the pastors. It is not certain whether this ceremony was, in all cases, performed by more pastors than one, or whether it was ever the act of a single pastor. The former appears to have been the fact in the case of the seven deacons, of Paul and Barnabas, and some few others. But Paul speaks of himself as having laid hands upon Timothy, without any mention of many others having united with him. "I put thee in remembrance, that thou stir up the gift of God which is in thee, by the putting on of my hands." His expression, in the other Epistle, of "the laying on of the hands of the presbytery," I apprehend not to signify a company of elders, but to denote the ordination itself; as if he had said, Take care that the grace which thou receivedst by the laying on of hands, when I ordained thee a presbyter, be not in vain.

15.

The Sacraments.

Connected with the preaching of the gospel, another assistance and support for our faith is presented to us in the sacraments; on the subject of which it is highly important to lay down some certain doctrine, that we may learn for what end they were instituted, and how they ought to be used. In the first place, it is necessary to consider what a sacrament is. Now, I think it will be a simple and appropriate definition, if we say that it is an outward sign, by which the Lord seals in our consciences the promises of his good-will towards us, to support the weakness of our faith; and we on our part testify our piety towards him, in his presence and that of angels, as well as before men. It may, however, be more briefly defined, in other words, by calling it a testimony of the grace of God towards us, confirmed by an outward sign, with a reciprocal attestation of our piety towards him. Whichever of these definitions be chosen, it conveys exactly the same meaning as that of Augustine, which states a sacrament to be "a visible sign of a sacred thing," or "a visible form of invisible grace;" but it expresses the thing itself with more clearness and precision; for as his conciseness leaves some obscurity, by which many inexperienced persons may be misled, I have endeavoured to render the subject plainer by more words, that no room might be left for any doubt.

II. The reason why the ancient fathers used this word in such a sense is very evident. For whenever the author of the old common version of the New Testament wanted to render the Greek word μυστηριον, *mystery*, into Latin, especially where it related to Divine things, he used the word *sacramentum*, "sacrament." Thus, in the Epistle to the Ephesians, "Having made known unto us the *mystery* of his will." Again: "If ye have heard of the dispensation of the grace of God which is given me to you-ward; how that by revelation he made known unto me the *mystery*." In the Epistle to the Colossians: "The *mystery* which hath been hid from ages and from generations, but now is made manifest to his saints; to whom God would make known what is the riches of the glory of this *mystery*." Again, to Timothy: "Great is the *mystery* of godliness; God was manifest in the flesh." In all these places, where the word *mystery* is used, the author of that version has rendered it *sacrament*. He would not say *arcanum*, or *secret*, lest he should appear to degrade the majesty of the subject. Therefore he has used the word *sacrament* for a sacred or Divine secret. In this signification it frequently occurs in the writings of the fathers. And it is well known, that baptism and the Lord's supper, which the Latins denominate *sacraments*, are called *mysteries* by the Greeks; a synonymous use of the terms, which removes every doubt. And hence the word *sacrament* came to be applied to those signs which contained a representation of sublime and spiritual things; which is also remarked by Augustine, who says, "It would be tedious to dispute respecting the diversity of signs, which, when they pertain to Divine things, are called *sacraments*."

III. Now, from the definition which we have established, we see that there is never any sacrament without an antecedent promise of God, to which it is subjoined as an appendix, in order to confirm and seal the promise itself, and to certify and ratify it to us; which means God foresees to be necessary, in the first place on account of our ignorance and dulness, and in the next place on account of our weakness; and yet, strictly speaking, not so much for the confirmation of his sacred word, as for our establishment in the faith of it. For the truth of God is sufficiently solid and certain in itself, and can receive no better confirmation from any other quarter than from itself; but our faith being slender and weak, unless it be supported on every side, and sustained by every assistance, immediately shakes, fluctuates, totters, and falls. And as we are corporeal, always creeping on the ground, cleaving to terrestrial and carnal objects, and incapable of understanding or conceiving of any thing of a spiritual nature, our merciful Lord, in his infinite indulgence, accommodates himself to our capacity, condescending to lead us to himself even by these earthly elements, and in the flesh itself to present to us a mirror of spiritual blessings. "For if we were incorporeal," as Chrysostom says, "he would have given us these things pure and incorporeal. Now because we have souls enclosed in bodies, he gives us spiritual things under visible emblems; not because there are such qualities in the nature of the things presented to us in the sacraments, but because they have been designated by God to this signification."

IV. This is what is commonly said, that a sacrament consists of the word and the outward sign. For we ought to understand the *word*, not of a murmur uttered without any meaning or faith, a mere whisper like a magical incantation, supposed to possess the power of consecrating the elements, but of the gospel preached, which instructs us in the signification of the visible sign. That which is commonly practised under the tyranny of the pope, therefore, involves a gross profanation of the mysteries; for they have thought it sufficient for the priest to mutter over the form of consecration, while the people are gazing in ignorance. Indeed, they have taken effectual care that it should be all unintelligible to the people; for they have pronounced the consecration in Latin, before illiterate men; and have at length carried superstition to such a pitch, as to consider it not rightly performed, unless it be done in a hoarse murmur, which few could hear. But Augustine speaks in a very different manner of the sacramental word. "Let the word," says he, "be added to the element, and it will become a sacrament. For whence does the water derive such great virtue, as at once to touch the body and purify the heart, except from the word? not because it is spoken, but because it is believed. For in the word itself the transient sound is one thing, the permanent virtue is another. 'This is the word of faith which we preach,' says the apostle. Whence it is said of the Gentiles, in the Acts of the Apostles, that 'God purifies their hearts by faith.' And the apostle Peter says, 'Baptism doth also now save us, (not the putting away of the filth of the flesh, but the answer of a good conscience towards God.)' 'This is the word of faith which we preach,' by which baptism is consecrated to endue it with a purifying virtue." We see how he makes the preaching of the word necessary to the production of faith. And we need not labour much to prove this, because it is very plain what Christ did, what he commanded us to do, what the apostles followed, and what the purer Church observed. Even from the beginning of the world, whenever God gave the holy fathers any sign, it is well known to have been inseparably connected with some doctrine, without which our senses would only be astonished with the mere view of it. Therefore, when we hear mention made of the sacramental word, let us understand it of the promise, which, being audibly and intelligibly preached by the minister, instructs the people in the meaning and tendency of the sign.

V. Nor ought any attention to be paid to some, who endeavour to oppose this by a dilemma which discovers more subtlety than solidity. They say, Either we know that the word of God which precedes the sacrament is the true will of God, or we do not know it. If we know it, then we learn nothing new from the sacrament which follows. If we do not know it, neither shall we learn it from the sacrament, the virtue of which lies entirely in the word. Let it be concisely replied, that the seals appended to charters, patents, and other public instruments, are nothing, taken by themselves; because they would be appended to no purpose, if the parchment had nothing written upon it; and yet they nevertheless confirm and authenticate what is written on the instruments to which they are annexed. Nor can it be objected that this similitude has been recently invented by us; for it has been used by Paul himself, who calls circumcision a *seal*, σφραγιδα, in a passage where he is professedly contending that circumcision did not constitute the righteousness of Abraham, but was a seal of that covenant, in the faith of which he had already been justified. And what is there that ought to give any man much offence, if we teach that the promise is sealed by the sacraments, while it is evident that among the promises themselves one is confirmed by another? For in proportion to its superior clearness, it is the better calculated for the support of faith. Now, the sacraments bring us the clearest promises, and have this peculiarity beyond the word, that they give us a lively representation of them, as in a picture. Nor ought we to regard the objection, frequently urged, from the distinction between sacraments and seals of civil instruments, that while they both consist of the carnal elements of this world, the former cannot be fit to seal the promises of God, which are spiritual and eternal, as the latter are accustomed to be appended to seal the edicts of princes relative to frail and transitory things. For the believer, when the sacraments are placed before his eyes, does not confine himself to that carnal spectacle; but by those steps of analogy which I have indicated, rises in pious contemplation to the sublime mysteries which are concealed under the sacramental symbols.

VI. And since the Lord calls his promises *covenants*, and the sacraments *seals of covenants*, we may draw a similitude from the covenants of men. The ancients, in confirmation of their engagements, were accustomed to kill a sow. But what would have been the slaughter of a sow, if it had not been accompanied, and even preceded, by some words? For sows were often slaughtered without any latent or sublime mystery. What is the contact of one man's right hand with that of another, since hands are not unfrequently joined in hostility? But when words of friendship and compact have preceded, the obligations of covenants are confirmed by such signs, notwithstanding they have been previously conceived, proposed, and determined in words. Sacraments, therefore, are exercises, which increase and strengthen our faith in the word of God; and because we are corporeal, they are exhibited under corporeal symbols, to instruct us according to our dull capacities, and to lead us by the hand as so many young children. For this reason Augustine calls a sacrament "a visible word;" because it represents the promises of God portrayed as in a picture, and places before our eyes an image of them, in which every lineament is strikingly expressed. Other similitudes may also be adduced for the better elucidation of the nature of sacraments; as if we call them *pillars of our faith*; for as an edifice rests on its foundation, and yet, from the addition of pillars placed under it, receives an increase of stability, so faith rests on the word of God as its foundation; but when the sacraments are added to it as pillars, they bring with them an accession of strength. Or if we call them *mirrors*, in which we may contemplate the riches of grace which God imparts to us; for in the sacraments, as we have already observed, he manifests himself to us as far as our dulness is capable of knowing him, and testifies his benevolence and love towards us more expressly than he does by his word.

VII. Nor is there any force in their reasoning, when they contend that the sacraments are not testimonies of the grace of God, because they are often administered to the wicked, who yet do not, in consequence of this, experience God to be more propitious to them, but rather procure to themselves more grievous condemnation. For, by the same argument, neither would the gospel be a testimony of the grace of God, because it is heard by many who despise it, nor even Christ himself, who was seen and known by multitudes, of whom very few received him. A similar observation may be applied to royal edicts; for great numbers of people despise and deride that seal of authentication, notwithstanding they know that it proceeded from the monarch to confirm his will; some utterly disregard it, as a thing not relating to them; others even hold it in execration; so that a survey of the correspondence of the two cases ought to produce greater approbation of the similitude which I have before used. Therefore it is certain that the Lord offers us his mercy, and a pledge of his grace, both in his holy word and in the sacraments; but it is not apprehended except by those who receive the word and sacraments with a certain faith; as the Father has offered and presented Christ to all for salvation, but he is not known and received by all. Augustine, intending to express this sentiment, somewhere says, that the efficacy of the word is displayed in the sacrament, "not because it is spoken, but because it is believed." Therefore Paul, when he is addressing believers, speaks of the sacraments so as to include in them the communion of Christ; as when he says, "As many of you as have been baptized into Christ, have put on Christ." Again: "By one Spirit are we all baptized into one body." But when he speaks of the improper use of the sacraments, he attributes no more to them than to vain and useless figures; by which he signifies that, however impious persons and hypocrites, by their perversion of the sacraments, may destroy or obscure the effect of Divine grace in them, yet that, notwithstanding this, whenever and wherever God pleases, they afford a true testimony of the communion of Christ, and the Spirit of God himself exhibits and performs the very thing which they promise. We conclude, therefore, that sacraments are truly called testimonies of the grace of God, and are, as it were, seals of the benevolence he bears to us, which, by confirming it to our minds, sustain, cherish, strengthen, and increase our faith. The reasons which some are in the habit of objecting against this sentiment are exceedingly weak and frivolous. They allege, that if our faith be good, it cannot be made better; for that there is no real faith except that which rests on the mercy of God, without any wavering, instability, or distraction. It would have been better for such persons to pray, with the apostles, that the Lord would increase their faith, than confidently to boast of such a perfection of faith, as no one of the sons of men ever yet attained, or ever will attain, in this life. Let them answer what kind of faith they suppose him to have possessed, who said, "Lord, I believe; help thou mine unbelief." For even that, though yet only in its commencement, was a good faith, and capable of being improved by the removal of unbelief. But there is no argument which more fully refutes them than their own conscience; for if they confess themselves sinners, which, whatever they may wish, they cannot deny, they must be obliged to impute it to the imperfection of their faith.

VIII. But they say, Philip answered the eunuch, that he might be baptized "if" he "believed with all" his "heart." And what room, they ask, is there here for the confirmation of baptism, where faith fills the whole heart? On the other hand, I ask them, whether they do not feel a large part of their heart destitute of faith, and whether they do not daily know some fresh increase of it. A heathen gloried that he grew old in learning. We Christians are miserable indeed if we grow old in making no improvement, whose faith ought to be advancing from one stage to another till its attainment of perfect manhood. "To believe with all the heart," therefore, in this passage, is not to believe Christ in a perfect manner, but only signifies embracing him with sincerity of soul and firmness of mind; not to be filled with him, but to hunger, thirst, and sigh after him with ardent affection. It is the custom of the Scriptures to say that any thing is done with the whole heart which is done with sincerity of mind, as in these and other passages: "With my whole heart have I sought thee;" "I will praise the Lord with my whole heart." On the contrary, when it rebukes the fraudulent and deceitful, it reproaches them with "a double heart." Our adversaries further allege, that if faith be increased by the sacraments, the Holy Spirit must have been given in vain, whose work and influence it is to commence, to confirm, and to consummate faith. I confess that faith is the peculiar and entire work of the Holy Spirit, by whose illumination we know God and the treasures of his goodness, and without whose light our mind is too blind to be capable of any sight, and too stupid to be capable of the least relish of spiritual things. But instead of one favour of God, which they mention, we acknowledge three. For, first, the Lord teaches and instructs us by his word; secondly, he confirms us by his sacraments; lastly, he illuminates our minds by the light of his Holy Spirit, and opens an entrance into our hearts for the word and sacraments; which otherwise would only strike the ears and present themselves to the eyes, without producing the least effect upon the mind.

IX. With respect to the confirmation and increase of faith, therefore, I wish the reader to be apprized, and I conceive I have already expressed, in language too plain to be misunderstood, that I assign this office to the sacraments; not from an opinion of their possessing a perpetual inherent virtue, efficacious of itself to the advancement or confirmation of faith; but because they have been instituted by the Lord for the express purpose of promoting its establishment and augmentation. But they only perform their office aright when they are accompanied by the Spirit, that internal Teacher, by whose energy alone our hearts are penetrated, our affections are moved, and an entrance is opened for the sacraments into our souls. If he be absent, the sacraments can produce no more effect upon our minds than the splendour of the sun on blind eyes, or the sound of a voice on deaf ears. I make such a distinction and distribution, therefore, between the Spirit and the sacraments, that I consider all the energy of operation as belonging to the Spirit, and the sacraments as mere instruments, which, without his agency, are vain and useless, but which, when he acts and exerts his power in the heart, are fraught with surprising efficacy. Now, it is evident how, according to this opinion, the faith of a pious mind is confirmed by the sacraments; namely, as the eyes see by the light of the sun, and the ears hear by the sound of a voice: the light would have no effect upon the eyes, unless they had a natural faculty capable of being enlightened; and it would be in vain for the ears to be struck with any sound, if they had not been naturally formed for hearing. But if it be true, as we ought at once to conclude, that what the visive faculty is in our eyes towards our beholding the light, and the faculty of hearing is in our ears towards our perception of sound, such is the work of the Holy Spirit in our hearts for the formation, support, preservation, and establishment of our faith; then these two consequences immediately follow—that the sacraments are attended with no benefit without the influence of the Holy Spirit; and that, in hearts already instructed by that Teacher, they still subserve the confirmation and increase of faith. There is only this difference, that our eyes and ears are naturally endued with the faculties of seeing and hearing, but Christ accomplishes this in our hearts by special and preternatural grace.

X. This reasoning will also serve for a solution of the objections with which some persons are greatly disturbed; that if we attribute to creatures either the increase or confirmation of faith, we derogate from the Spirit of God, whom we ought to acknowledge as its sole Author. For we do not, at the same time, deny him the praise of its confirmation and increase; but we assert that the way in which he increases and confirms our faith is by preparing our minds, by his inward illumination, to receive that confirmation which is proposed in the sacraments. If the way in which this has been expressed be too obscure, it shall be elucidated by the following similitude. If you intend to persuade a person to do a certain act, you will consider all the reasons calculated to draw him over to your opinion, and to constrain him to submit to your advice. But you will make no impression upon him, unless he possess a perspicuous and acute judgment, to be able to determine what force there is in your reasons; unless his mind also be docile, and prepared to listen to instruction; and lastly, unless he have conceived such an opinion of your fidelity and prudence as may prepossess him in favour of your sentiments. For there are many obstinate spirits, never to be moved by any reasons; and where a person's fidelity is suspected, and his authority despised, little effect will be produced, even with those who are disposed to learn. On the contrary, let all these things be present, and they will insure the acquiescence of the person advised, in those counsels which he would otherwise have derided. This work also the Spirit effects within us. Lest the word should assail our ears in vain,—lest the sacraments should in vain strike our eyes,—he shows us that it is God who addresses us in them; he softens the hardness of our hearts, and forms them to that obedience which is due to the word of the Lord; in fine, he conveys those external words and sacraments from the ears into the soul. Our faith is confirmed, therefore, both by the word and by the sacraments, when they place before our eyes the good-will of our heavenly Father towards us, in the knowledge of which all the firmness of our faith consists, and by which its strength is augmented; the Spirit confirms it, when he makes this confirmation effectual by engraving it on our minds. In the mean time, the Father of lights cannot be prohibited from illuminating our minds by means of the lustre of the sacraments, as he enlightens our bodily eyes with the rays of the sun.

XI. That there is this property in the external word, our Lord has shown in a parable, by calling it "seed." For as seed, if it fall on a desert and neglected spot of ground, will die without producing any crop, but if it be cast upon a well manured and cultivated field, it brings forth its fruit with an abundant increase,—so the word of God, if it fall upon some stiff neck, will be as unproductive as seed dropped upon the sea-shore; but if it light upon a soul cultivated by the agency of the heavenly Spirit, it will be abundantly fruitful. Now, if the word be justly compared to seed,—as we say that from seed, corn grows, increases, and comes to maturity,—why may we not say that faith derives its commencement, increase, and perfection, from the word of God? Paul, in different places, excellently expresses both these things. For, with a view to recall to the recollection of the Corinthians with what efficacy God had attended his labours, he glories in having the ministry of the Spirit, as if there were an indissoluble connection between his preaching and the power of the Holy Spirit operating to the illumination of their minds, and the excitement of their hearts. But in another place, with a view to apprize them how far the power of the word of God extends, merely as preached by man, he compares ministers to husbandmen; who, when they have employed their labour and industry in cultivating the ground, have nothing more that they can do. But what would ploughing, and sowing, and watering, avail, unless heavenly goodness caused the seed to vegetate? Therefore he concludes, "Neither is he that planteth any thing, neither he that watereth; but God, that giveth the increase." The apostles, then, in their preaching, exerted the power of the Spirit, as far as God made use of the instruments appointed by himself for the exhibition of his spiritual grace. But we must always keep in view this distinction, that we may remember how far the power of man extends, and what is exclusively the work of God.

XII. Now, it is so true that the sacraments are confirmations of our faith, that sometimes, when the Lord intends to take away the confidence of those things which had been promised in the sacraments, he removes the sacraments themselves. When he deprived Adam of the gift of immortality, he expelled him from the garden of Eden, saying, "Lest he put forth his hand, and take also of the tree of life, and eat, and live for ever." What can be the meaning of this language? Could the fruit restore to Adam the incorruption from which he had now fallen? Certainly not. But it was the same as if the Lord had said, Lest he should cherish a vain confidence, if he retain the symbol of my promise, let him be deprived of that which might give him some hope of immortality. For the same reason, when the apostle exhorts the Ephesians to "remember that" they "were without Christ, being aliens from the commonwealth of Israel, and strangers from the covenant of promise, having no hope, and without God in the world," he states that they were not partakers of circumcision; thereby signifying that not having received the sign of the promise, they were excluded from the promise itself. To the other objection which they make, that the glory of God is transferred to creatures to whom so much power is attributed, and thereby sustains a proportionate diminution, it is easy to answer, that we place no power in creatures; we only maintain that God uses such means and instruments as he sees will be suitable, in order that all things may be subservient to his glory, as he is the Lord and Ruler of all. Therefore, as by bread and other aliments he feeds our bodies, as by the sun he enlightens the world, as by fire he produces warmth,—yet bread, the sun, and fire, are nothing but instruments by which he dispenses his blessings to us,—so he nourishes our faith in a spiritual manner by the sacraments, which are instituted for the purpose of placing his promises before our eyes for our contemplation, and of serving us as pledges of them. And as we ought not to place any confidence in the other creatures, which, by the liberality and beneficence of God, have been destined to our uses, and by whose instrumentality he communicates to us the bounties of his goodness, nor to admire and celebrate them as the causes of our enjoyments,—so neither ought our confidence to rest in the sacraments, or the glory of God to be transferred to them; but, forsaking all other things, both our faith and confession ought to rise to him, the Author of the sacraments and of every other blessing.

XIII. The argument which some persons adduce from the very name of *sacrament* is destitute of any force;—though the word *sacrament* has various significations in authors of the first authority, yet it has but one which has any agreement or connection with *signs* or *standards*, (signa;) that is, when it denotes the solemn oath taken by a soldier to his commander when he enters on a military life. For as by the military oath new soldiers bind themselves to their commander, and assume the military profession, so by our signs we profess Christ to be our Leader, and declare that we fight under his banners. They add similitudes for the further elucidation of their opinion. As the dress of the Romans, who wore gowns, distinguished them from the Greeks, who wore cloaks; as the different orders among the Romans were distinguished from each other by their respective badges, the senatorial order from the equestrian by purple habits and round shoes, and the equestrian from the plebeian by a ring; as French and English ships of war are known by flags of different colours, the French flags being white and the English red; so we have our signs or badges to distinguish us from unbelievers. But from the observations already made, it is evident that the ancient fathers, who gave our signs the name of sacraments, were not at all guided by the previous use of this word in Latin writers; but that they gave it a new sense for their own convenience, simply denoting sacred signs. And if we wish to carry our researches any further, it may be found that they transferred this name to the signification now given, on the same principle of analogy which induced them to transfer the word *faith* to the sense in which it is now used. For as faith properly signifies truth in the fulfilment of promises, yet they have applied it to the assurance or certain persuasion which a person has of the truth itself; so, as a sacrament is an oath by which a soldier binds himself to his leader, they have applied it to the sign by which the leader receives soldiers into his army. For by the sacraments the Lord promises that he will be our God, and that we shall be his people. But we pass over such subtleties, as I think I have proved by sufficient arguments that the ancients had no other view, in their application of the word *sacrament*, than to signify that the ceremonies to which they applied it were signs of holy and spiritual things. We admit the comparison deduced from external badges, but we cannot bear that the last and least use of the sacraments should be represented as their principal and even sole object. The first object of them is, to assist our faith towards God; the second, to testify our confession before men. The similitudes which have been mentioned are applicable to this secondary design, but the primary one ought never to be forgotten; for otherwise, as we have seen, these mysteries would cease to interest us, unless they were aids of our faith, and appendices of doctrine, destined to the same use and end.

XIV. On the other hand, we require to be apprized, that as these persons weaken the force of the sacraments, and entirely subvert their use, so there are others of a contrary party, who attribute to the sacraments I know not what latent virtues, which are nowhere represented as communicated to them by the word of God. By this error the simple and inexperienced are dangerously deceived, being taught to seek the gifts of God where they can never be found, and being gradually drawn away from God to embrace mere vanity instead of his truth. For the sophistical schools have maintained, with one consent, that the sacraments of the new law, or those now used in the Christian Church, justify and confer grace, provided we do not obstruct their operation by any mortal sin. It is impossible to express the pestilent and fatal nature of this opinion, and especially as it has prevailed over a large part of the world, to the great detriment of the Church, for many ages past. Indeed, it is evidently diabolical; for by promising justification without faith, it precipitates souls into destruction: in the next place, by representing the sacraments as the cause of justification, it envelops the minds of men, naturally too much inclined to the earth, in gross superstition, leading them to rest in the exhibition of a corporeal object rather than in God himself. Of these two evils I wish we had not had such ample experience as to supersede the necessity of much proof. What is a sacrament, taken without faith, but the most certain ruin of the Church? For as nothing is to be expected from it, but in consequence of the promise, which denotes God's wrath against unbelievers as much as it offers his grace to believers,—the person who supposes that the sacraments confer any more upon him than that which is offered by the word of God, and which he receives by a true faith, is greatly deceived. Hence also it may be concluded, that confidence of salvation does not depend on the participation of the sacraments, as though that constituted our justification, which we know to be placed in Christ alone, and to be communicated to us no less by the preaching of the gospel than by the sealing of the sacraments, and that it may be completely enjoyed without this participation. So true is the observation, which has also been made by Augustine, that invisible sanctification may exist without the visible sign, and, on the contrary, that the visible sign may be used without real sanctification. For, as he also writes in another place, "Men put on Christ, sometimes by the reception of a sacrament, sometimes by sanctification of life." The first case may be common to the good and the bad; the second is peculiar to believers.

XV. Hence that distinction, if it be well understood, which is frequently stated by Augustine, between a sacrament and the matter of a sacrament. For his meaning is, not only that a sacrament contains a figure, and some truth signified by that figure, but that their connection is not such as to render them inseparable from each other; and even when they are united, the thing signified ought always to be distinguished from the sign, that what belongs to the one may not be transferred to the other. He speaks of their separation, when he observes, that "the sacraments produce the effect which they represent, in the elect alone." Again, when he is speaking of the Jews: "Though the sacraments were common to all, the grace which is the power of the sacrament was not common; so now, also, the washing of regeneration is common to all; but the grace itself, by which the members of Christ are regenerated with their Head, is not common to all." Again, in another place, speaking of the Lord's supper: "We also in the present day receive visible meat; but the sacrament is one thing, and the power of the sacrament is another. How is it that many receive of the altar and die, and die in consequence of receiving? For the morsel of bread given by the Lord to Judas was poison; not because Judas received an evil thing, but because, being a wicked man, he received a good thing in a sinful manner." A little after: "The sacrament of this thing, that is, of the unity of the body and blood of Christ, is prepared on the table of the Lord, in some places daily, in other places on appointed days, at stated intervals of time; and is thence received, by some to life, by others to destruction. But the thing signified by this sacrament is received, not to destruction, but to life, by every one who partakes of it." He had just before said, "He shall not die, who eats; I refer not to the visible sacrament, but to the power of the sacrament; who eats internally, not externally; he who eats in his heart, not he who presses with his teeth." In all these passages we find it maintained, that a sacrament is separated from the truth signified in it, by the unworthiness of a person who receives it amiss, so that there is nothing left in it but a vain and useless figure. In order to enjoy the thing signified together with the sign, and not a mere sign destitute of the truth it was intended to convey, it is necessary to apprehend by faith the word which is contained in it. Thus, in proportion to the communion we have with Christ by means of the sacraments, will be the advantage which we shall derive from them.

XVI. If this be obscure in consequence of its brevity, I will explain it more at large. I affirm that Christ is the matter, or substance, of all the sacraments; since they have all their solidity in him, and promise nothing out of him. So much more intolerable is the error of Peter Lombard, who expressly makes them causes of righteousness and salvation, of which they are parts. Leaving all causes, therefore, of human invention, we ought to adhere to this one cause. As far as we are assisted by their instrumentality, to nourish, confirm, and increase our faith in Christ, to obtain a more perfect possession of him and an enjoyment of his riches, so far they are efficacious to us; and this is the case when we receive by true faith that which is offered in them. Do the impious, then, it will be said, by their ingratitude, frustrate the ordinance of God, and cause it to come to nothing? I reply, that what I have said is not to be understood as implying, that the virtue and truth of a sacrament depends on the condition or choice of him who receives it. For what God has instituted continues unshaken, and retains its nature, however men may vary; but as it is one thing to offer, and another to receive, there is no incongruity in maintaining, that a symbol, consecrated by the word of the Lord, is in reality what it is declared to be, and preserves its virtue, and yet that it confers no benefit on a wicked and impious person. But Augustine happily solves this question in a few words: he says, "If thou receive it carnally, still it ceases not to be spiritual; but it is not so to thee." And, as in the passages already cited, this father shows that the symbol used in a sacrament is of no value, if it be separated from the truth signified by it, so, on the other hand, he states that it is necessary to distinguish them, even where they are united, lest our attention be confined too much to the external sign. "As to follow the letter," says he, "and to take the signs instead of the things signified, betrays servile weakness, so it is the part of unsteadiness and error to interpret the signs in such a manner as to derive no advantage from them." He mentions two faults, against which it is necessary to guard. One is, when we take the signs as if they were given in vain, and disparaging or diminishing their secret significations by our perverse misconstruction, exclude ourselves from the advantage which we ought to derive from them. The other is, when, not elevating our minds beyond the visible sign, we transfer to the sacraments the praise of those benefits, which are only conferred upon us by Christ alone, and that by the agency of the Holy Spirit, who makes us partakers of Christ himself, by the instrumentality of the external signs which invite us to Christ, but which cannot be perverted to any other use, without a shameful subversion of all their utility.

XVII. Wherefore let us abide by this conclusion, that the office of the sacraments is precisely the same as that of the word of God; which is to offer and present Christ to us, and in him the treasures of his heavenly grace; but they confer no advantage or profit without being received by faith; just as wine, or oil, or any other liquor, though it be poured plentifully on a vessel, yet will it overflow and be lost, unless the mouth of the vessel be open; and the vessel itself, though wet on the outside, will remain dry and empty within. It is also necessary to guard against being drawn into an error allied to this, from reading the extravagant language used by the fathers with a view to exalt the dignity of the sacraments; lest we should suppose there is some secret power annexed and attached to the sacraments, so that they communicate the grace of the Holy Spirit, just as wine is given in the cup; whereas the only office assigned to them by God, is to testify and confirm his benevolence towards us; nor do they impart any benefit, unless they are accompanied by the Holy Spirit to open our minds and hearts, and render us capable of receiving this testimony: and here, also, several distinct favours of God are eminently displayed. For the sacraments, as we have before hinted, fulfil to us, on the part of God, the same office as messengers of joyful intelligence, or earnests for the confirmation of covenants on the part of men; they communicate no grace from themselves, but announce and show, and, as earnests and pledges, ratify, the things which are given to us by the goodness of God. The Holy Spirit, whom the sacraments do not promiscuously impart to all, but whom God, by a peculiar privilege, confers upon his servants, is he who brings with him the graces of God, who gives the sacraments admission into our hearts, and causes them to bring forth fruit in us. Now, though we do not deny that God himself accompanies his institution by the very present power of his Spirit, that the administration of the sacraments which he has ordained may not be vain and unfruitful, yet we assert the necessity of a separate consideration and contemplation of the internal grace of the Spirit, as it is distinguished from the external ministry. Whatever God promises and adumbrates in signs, therefore, he really performs; and the signs are not without their effect, to prove the veracity and fidelity of their Author. The only question here is, whether God works by a proper and intrinsic power, as it is expressed, or resigns the office to external symbols. Now, we contend, that whatever instruments he employs, this derogates nothing from his supreme operation. When this doctrine is maintained respecting the sacraments, their dignity is sufficiently announced, their use plainly signified, their utility abundantly declared, and a proper moderation is preserved in all these particulars, so that nothing is attributed, which ought not to be attributed to them, and nothing that belongs to them is denied; while there is no admission of that figment, which places the cause of justification and the power of the Spirit in the sacramental elements, as in so many vehicles; and that peculiar power which has been omitted by others is clearly expressed. Here, also, it must be remarked, that God accomplishes within, that which the minister represents and testifies by the external act; that we may not attribute to a mortal man what God challenges exclusively to himself. Augustine has judiciously suggested the same sentiment. "How," says he, "do Moses and God both sanctify? Not Moses instead of God. Moses does it with visible signs, by his ministry. God does it with invisible grace, by his Holy Spirit. Here also lies all the efficacy of visible sacraments. For what avail those visible sacraments without that sanctification of invisible grace?"

XVIII. The term *sacrament*, as we have hitherto treated of its nature, comprehends generally all the signs which God has ever given to men, to certify and assure them of the truth of his promises. These he has been pleased to place in natural things, and sometimes to exhibit in miracles. Examples of the former kind are such as these: when he gave Adam and Eve the tree of life, as a pledge of immortality, which they might assure themselves of enjoying as long as they should eat of the fruit of that tree; and when he "set" his "bow in the cloud," as a token to Noah and his posterity, that there should "no more be a flood to destroy the earth." These Adam and Noah had as sacraments. Not that the tree would actually communicate immortality to them, which it could not give to itself; or that the rainbow, which is merely a refraction of the rays of the sun on the opposite clouds, would have any efficacy in restraining the waters; but because they had a mark impressed upon them by the word of God, constituting them signs and seals of his covenants. The tree and the rainbow both existed before, but when they were inscribed with the word of God, they were endued with a new form, so that they began to be something that they were not before. And that no one may suppose this to be spoken in vain, the bow itself continues to be a witness to us in the present age, of that covenant which God made with Noah: whenever we behold it, we read this promise of God in it, that he would never more destroy the earth with a flood. Therefore, if any smatterer in philosophy, with a view to ridicule the simplicity of our faith, contend that such a variety of colours is the natural result of the refraction of the solar rays on an opposite cloud, we must immediately acknowledge it, but we may smile at his stupidity in not acknowledging God as the Lord and Governor of nature, who uses all the elements according to his will for the promotion of his own glory. And if he had impressed similar characters on the sun, on the stars, on the earth, and on stones, they would all have been sacraments to us. Why is not silver of as much value before it is coined, as it is after, since the metal is the very same? The reason is, that it has nothing added to its natural state; stamped with a public impression, it becomes money, and receives a new valuation. And shall not God be able to mark his creatures with his word, that they may become sacraments, though before they were mere elements? Examples of the second kind were exhibited, when God showed Abraham "a smoking furnace and a burning lamp;" when he watered the fleece with dew while the earth remained dry, and afterwards bedewed the earth without wetting the fleece, to promise victory to Gideon; when "he brought the shadow ten degrees backward in the dial," to promise recovery to Hezekiah. As these things were done to support and establish the weakness of their faith, they also were sacraments.

XIX. But our present design is to treat particularly of those sacraments which the Lord has appointed to be ordinarily used in his Church, to keep his worshippers and servants in one faith and in the confession of the same. "For," to use the language of Augustine, "men cannot be united in any profession of religion, whether true or false, unless they are connected by some communion of visible signs or sacraments." Our most merciful Father, therefore, foreseeing this necessity, did, from the beginning, institute for his servants certain exercises of piety, which Satan afterwards depraved and corrupted in a variety of ways, transferring them to impious and idolatrous worship. Hence those initiations of the heathen into their mysteries, and the rest of their degenerate rites, which, though fraught with error and superstition, at the same time furnish an evidence that such external signs are indispensable to a profession of religion. But as they were neither founded on the word of God, nor referred to that truth which ought to be the object of all religious emblems, they are unworthy of notice, where mention is made of the sacred symbols which have been instituted by God, and which have never been perverted from their original principle, which constitutes them aids of true piety. Now, they consist not of mere signs, like the rainbow and the tree of life, but in ceremonies; or, rather, the signs which are here given are ceremonies. And, as we have before observed, as they are testimonies of grace and salvation on the part of the Lord, so on our part they are badges of our profession, by which we publicly devote ourselves to God, and swear obedience and fidelity to him. Chrysostom, therefore, somewhere properly calls them *compacts*, by which God covenants with us, and we bind ourselves to purity and sanctity of life; because a mutual stipulation is made in them between God and us. For as the Lord promises to obliterate and efface all the guilt and punishment that we have incurred by sin, and reconciles us to himself in his only begotten Son, so we, on our parts, by this profession, bind ourselves to him, to serve him in piety and innocence of life; so that such sacraments may justly be described as ceremonies by which God is pleased to exercise his people, in the first place, to nourish, excite, and confirm faith in their hearts; and in the next place, to testify their religion before men.

XX. And even the sacraments have been different according to the varieties of different periods, and corresponding to the dispensation by which it has pleased the Lord to manifest himself in different ways to mankind. For to Abraham and his posterity circumcision was commanded; to which the law of Moses afterwards added ablutions, sacrifices, and other rites. These were the sacraments of the Jews till the coming of Christ; which was followed by the abrogation of these, and the institution of two others, which are now used in the Christian Church; namely, baptism and the supper of the Lord. I speak of those which were instituted for the use of the whole Church; for as to the imposition of hands, by which the ministers of the Church are introduced into their office, while I make no objection to its being called a sacrament, I do not class it among the ordinary sacraments. What opinion ought to be entertained respecting those which are commonly reputed the five other sacraments, we shall see in a subsequent chapter. Those ancient sacrifices, however, referred to the same object towards which ours are now directed, their design being to point and lead to Christ, or rather, as images, to represent and make him known. For as we have already shown that they are seals to confirm the promises of God, and it is very certain that no promise of God was ever offered to man except in Christ,—in order to teach us any thing respecting the promises of God, they must of necessity make a discovery of Christ. This was the design of that heavenly pattern of the tabernacle and model of the legal worship, which was exhibited to Moses in the mount. There is only one difference between those sacraments and ours: they prefigured Christ as promised and still expected; ours represent him as already come and manifested.

XXI. All these things will be considerably elucidated by a particular detail. In the first place, circumcision was a sign to the Jews to teach them that whatever is produced from human seed—that is, the whole nature of man—is corrupt, and requires to be pruned: it was likewise a testification and memorial to confirm them in the promise given to Abraham respecting the blessed seed, in whom all the nations of the earth were to be blessed, and from whom their own blessing was also to be expected. Now, that blessed seed, as Paul informs us, was Christ, on whom alone they relied for recovering that which they had lost in Adam. Wherefore circumcision was the same to them as Paul declares it to have been to Abraham, even "a seal of the righteousness of faith;" that is, a seal for the further assurance that their faith, with which they expected that seed, would be imputed by God to them for righteousness. But the comparison between circumcision and baptism we shall have more suitable occasion for pursuing in another place. Ablutions and purifications placed before their eyes their uncleanness and pollution, by which they were naturally contaminated, and promised another ablution, by which they would be purified from all their defilement; and this ablution was Christ, washed in whose blood we bring his purity into the presence of God to cover all our impurities. Their sacrifices accused and convicted them of their iniquity, and, at the same time, taught the necessity of some satisfaction to be made to the Divine justice, and that, therefore, there would come a great High Priest, a Mediator between God and men, who was to satisfy the justice of God by the effusion of blood and the oblation of a sacrifice, which would be sufficient to obtain the remission of sins. This great High Priest was Christ; he shed his own blood, and was himself the victim; was obedient to his Father even unto death, and by his obedience obliterated the disobedience of man, which had provoked the indignation of God.

XXII. Our two sacraments present us with a clearer exhibition of Christ, in proportion to the nearer view of him which men have enjoyed since he was really manifested by the Father in the manner in which he had been promised. For baptism testifies to us our purgation and ablution; the eucharistic supper testifies our redemption. Water is a figure of ablution, and blood of satisfaction. These things are both found in Christ, who, as John says, "came by water and blood;" that is, to purify and redeem. Of this the Spirit of God is a witness; or, rather, "there are three that bear witness, the Spirit, the Water, and the Blood." In the water and the blood we have a testimony of purgation and redemption; and the Spirit, as the principal witness, confirms and secures our reception and belief of this testimony. This sublime mystery was strikingly exhibited on the cross, when blood and water issued from Christ's sacred side; which, on this account, Augustine has justly called "the fountain of our sacraments;" of which we are yet to treat more at large. And there is no doubt, if we compare one time with another, but that the more abundant grace of the Spirit is also here displayed. For that belongs to the glory of the kingdom of Christ; as we gather from various places, and especially from the seventh chapter of John. In this sense we must understand that passage where Paul, speaking of the legal institutions, says, "which are a shadow of things to come, but the body is of Christ." His design in this declaration is, not to deny the efficacy of those testimonies of grace, in which God was formerly pleased to attest his veracity to the fathers, as he does to us now in baptism and the sacred supper, but to represent the comparative superiority of what has been given to us, that no one might wonder at the ceremonies of the law having been abolished at the advent of Christ.

XXIII. I will just observe by the way, that the doctrine of the schools, which asserts such a wide difference between the sacraments of the old and new law, as though the former merely prefigured the grace of God, and the latter actually communicated it, ought to be altogether exploded. For the apostle speaks in a manner equally as honourable of the former as of the latter, when he states that the fathers, in the time of Moses, "did all eat the same spiritual meat" with us, and explains that meat to be Christ. Who will dare to call that an empty sign, which exhibited to the Jews the real communion of Christ? And the state of the case, which the apostle is there discussing, is clearly in favour of our argument. For, that no man might dare to despise the judgment of God, in a reliance on a speculative knowledge of Christ, and the mere name of Christianity, with its external signs, he exhibits the examples of Divine severity displayed among the Jews, to teach us that the same punishments which they suffered await us, if we indulge in the same sins. Now, that the comparison might be pertinent, it was necessary to show that there was no inequality between us and them in those privileges of which he forbids us to indulge unfounded boasts. First, therefore, he shows them to have been equal to us in the sacraments, and leaves not a particle of superiority capable of exciting in our minds the least hope of impunity. Nor is it right to attribute to our baptism any thing more than he attributes to circumcision, when he calls it "a seal of the righteousness of faith." Whatever is presented to us in the present day in our sacraments, was anciently received by the Jews in theirs—even Christ and his spiritual riches. Whatever power our sacraments have, they also experienced the same in theirs: they were seals of the Divine benevolence to them, confirming their hope of eternal salvation. If the advocates of the opinion which we are opposing had been skilful interpreters of the Epistle to the Hebrews, they would not have been so deceived; but when they read there that sins were not expiated by the legal ceremonies, and that the ancient shadows had no power to confer righteousness,—neglecting the comparison intended to be drawn, and confining their attention to this single consideration, that the law in itself was unprofitable to its observers, they have simply concluded that the figures were destitute of any truth. But the design of the apostle was to represent the ceremonial law as of no value till it was referred to Christ, on whom alone depended all its efficacy.

XXIV. But they will allege what Paul says of the "circumcision in the letter," that it is in no estimation with God; that it confers no advantage; that it is in vain; for such a representation they conceive to degrade it far below baptism. But this is not true; for all that he says of circumcision might justly be affirmed of baptism. And it is actually asserted; first by Paul himself, where he shows that God regards not the external ablution by which we enter on the profession of religion, unless the heart be purified within, and persevere in piety to the end; and, secondly, by Peter, when he declares the truth of baptism to consist, not in "the putting away of the filth of the flesh, but the answer of a good conscience." It will be objected, that Paul seems in another place utterly to despise "the circumcision made with hands," when he compares it with "the circumcision of Christ." I reply, that that passage derogates nothing from its dignity. Paul is there disputing against those who required it as still necessary, after it had been abrogated. He therefore admonishes believers to leave the ancient shadows, and adhere to the truth. These teachers, he says, urge you to be circumcised in your bodies. But you have been spiritually circumcised both in body and soul: you have the substance itself, therefore, which is better than the shadow. Some one might object to this, that the figure was not to be despised in consequence of their having the substance; for that the fathers under the Old Testament had experienced the circumcision of the heart, and the putting off of the old man, of which the apostle was speaking, and yet that external circumcision had not been unnecessary or useless to them. He anticipates and supersedes this objection, by immediately adding, that the Colossians had been "buried with Christ in baptism;" by which he signifies that baptism is to Christians what circumcision was to the ancient believers, and consequently that circumcision cannot be imposed upon Christians without injury to baptism.

XXV. But our objectors proceed to allege, that a still stronger argument in their favour arises from what follows, which I have lately quoted,—that all the Jewish ceremonies were "a shadow of things to come, but the body is of Christ;" and that the strongest argument of all is what is contained in the Epistle to the Hebrews, that the blood of beasts did not reach the conscience, that "the law" had "a shadow of good things to come, and not the very image of the things, and that the worshippers could never attain perfection from the Mosaic ceremonies." I repeat what I have already suggested, that Paul called the ceremonies *shadows*, not as if they had nothing solid in them, but because their accomplishment had been deferred till the manifestation of Christ. In the next place, I remark that this is to be understood, not of the efficacy of the ceremonies, but rather of the mode of representation. For till Christ was manifested in the flesh, all the signs prefigured him as absent; however, he displayed his power, and consequently himself, as present in the hearts of believers. But the principal thing to be observed is, that in all these places Paul is not speaking of the subject, considered simply in itself, but with reference to those against whom he is contending. As he was combating the false apostles, who maintained piety to consist in the ceremonies alone, without any regard to Christ,—nothing more was necessary for their confutation, than to discuss what value ceremonies possess of themselves. This also was the object pursued by the author of the Epistle to the Hebrews. Let us remember, therefore, that the question here does not respect ceremonies, taken in their true and natural signification, but as distorted by a false and perverse interpretation; the controversy is not about the legitimate use, but the superstitious abuse of them. What wonder, then, is it, if ceremonies, separated from Christ, are divested of all their virtue? For all signs are reduced to nothing, when the thing signified is taken away. So when Christ was addressing those who supposed the manna to have been mere food for the body, he accommodated his discourse to their gross notion, and said that he would give them better food, to nourish their souls with the hope of immortality. If a clearer solution be required, all that has been said may be comprised in these three observations: first, that all the ceremonies of the law of Moses, unless they were directed to Christ, were vain and useless; secondly, that they had reference to Christ, so that when he was manifested in the flesh, they received their accomplishment; lastly, that it was necessary for them to be abolished at his advent, as a shadow vanishes in the clear light of the sun. But as I defer the more extended discussion of this subject to the chapter in which I intend to compare baptism with circumcision, I touch the more briefly upon it here.

XXVI. It is possible that these miserable sophists have been led into this error by the extravagant encomiums on the sacraments which are found in the writings of the fathers; as when Augustine says, that "the sacraments of the old law only promised the Saviour, but ours give salvation." Not observing that these and other similar forms of expression were hyperbolical, they, also, on their part, have promulgated their hyperbolical dogmas, but in a sense altogether foreign from the writings of the fathers. For the meaning of Augustine in that passage was the same as in another, where he says, "The sacraments of the Mosaic law announced Christ as afterwards to come; ours announce him as already come." Again: "They were promises of things to be fulfilled; these are signs of things accomplished;" as if he had said, that the old sacraments prefigured Christ while he was yet expected, but that ours exhibit him as present, since he has already come. Besides, he speaks of the mode of representation, as he also shows in another place, where he says, "The law and the prophets had sacraments announcing something future; but what they celebrated as about to come, the sacraments of our time announce as already come." His sentiments respecting their truth and efficacy he declares in several places; as when he says, "The sacraments of the Jews were different from ours in the signs; in the thing signified, they were equal; different in visible form, equal in spiritual efficacy." Again: "In different signs, the same faith; in different signs, just as in different words; because words change their sounds in different times, and words are no other than signs. The fathers drank the same spiritual drink as we; though their corporeal drink was different. See, then, the signs have been varied without any change in the faith. To them the Rock was Christ; to us, that which is placed on the altar is Christ. And as a great sacrament, they drank the water flowing from the Rock; what we drink, believers know. If we consider the visible form, there was a difference; if we regard the intelligible signification, they drank the same spiritual drink." In another place: "In the mystery their meat and drink were the same as ours; but the same in signification, not in form; because the very same Christ was prefigured to them in the Rock, and has been manifested to us in the flesh." Yet in this respect, also, we admit that there is some difference between their sacraments and ours. For both testify that the paternal benevolence of God is offered to us in Christ, together with the graces of the Holy Spirit; but ours testify it in a more clear and evident manner. In both there is an exhibition of Christ, but the exhibition of him in ours is richer and fuller, corresponding to the difference between the Old Testament and the New, of which we have already treated. And this is what was intended by Augustine, whom I quote more frequently than any other, as the best and most faithful writer of antiquity, when he states, that after the revelation of Christ, sacraments were instituted, "fewer in number, more noble in signification, and more excellent in efficacy." It is right, also, just to apprize the readers, that all the jargon of the sophists respecting the *work wrought* (*opus operatum*) is not only false, but repugnant to the nature of the sacraments; which God has instituted, in order that believers, being poor and destitute of every good, may come to them simply confessing their wants, and imploring him to supply them. Consequently, in receiving the sacraments, they perform nothing at all meritorious, and the action itself being, as far as they are concerned, merely passive, no *work* can be attributed to them in it.

Enjoyed your Christian reading?

Don't end your introduction to Christian literature here.

Send a blank email to

thegoodchristian10@gmail.com

for access to Christian audiobooks.

Made in the USA
Monee, IL
07 July 2026